ISRAEL IN WORLD RELATIONS

ISRAEL IN WORLD RELATIONS

BY
RICHARD BASS

Information on how to obtain copies of this book is available at:
Web site: www.jedinstitute.com

ISBN 978-0-9918186-0-0.

Every reasonable effort has been made to acquire permission for copyrighted materials used in this book and to acknowl-edge such permissions accurately. Any errors or omissions called to Richard Bass's attention will be corrected in future printings.

Printed in USA.

Table of Contents

Acknowledgements

This project has been made possible through the generous
support of the Friedberg Foundation.

Many people contributed to this book. Special mention goes to the following:

To my wife Ellie, my children Yakira and Yonah, and to my parents, Jack (a"h) and Mimi, for their love and support in whatever demands my work placed on them.

To Rabbi Nissan Applebaum, whose goal of making Judaism "a positive experience" for his students, as well as his years of advice and insight, really opened my mind to exploring a history and tradition I had previously given up on.

To Rabbi Aaron Hoch, whose love of Israel and the Jewish people and whose call to action on their behalf were contagious.

To Rabbis Glenn Black, Steven Burg, and Steven Weil for their vision and support for this initiative and their commitment to educating Jewish youth.

To the following benefactors who made this book possible:

Mr. Dov and Mrs. Nancy Friedberg   Mr. Henry and Mrs. Julia Koschitzky

Mr. Michael and Mrs. Mahra Hart   Mr. David Bronfman

To my longtime friends who supported this project in a variety of ways
from its inception:

Mr. Michael and Mrs. Karen Aron   Mr. Clive Levitt

Mr. Pini and Mrs. Colette Avital   Mr. Steven Sofer and Mrs. Fern Reich

The Bank Family

To Dr. Jacques Gauthier, author of *Sovereignty Over the Old City of Jerusalem: A Study of the Historical, Religious, Political and Legal Aspects of the Question of the Old City*; and to Rabbi Ken Spiro, author of *WorldPerfect*—their writings and scholarship influenced a significant part of this work.

To Benjamin Anthony and Rozita Pnini, for their efforts in promoting this project.

To Jamie Bush, the editor, who made countless suggestions and modifications.

To Tibor Choleva, Melissa McClellan and the BlueApple*Works* Inc. team for the design and layout of the book.

To Esther Fleischer, for proofreading and Shyndee Kestenbaum for the design of the maps and illustrations.

To Ted Temertzoglou, Sarah Davies, Francy Kussner, Melanie Simons, and Amalia Trister Berg for their consulting and advice.

And to all who are not mentioned here but who have offered support in so many different ways. I am deeply grateful for your various contributions to this book.

Preface

This work aims to raise readers' awareness about Israel, so that anyone open to understanding—whether religious Jew, secular Jew, or non-Jew—will be able to arrive at informed and reasonable conclusions about the subject.

What Is "Israel"?

Since 1948, the name *Israel* has meant, for most people, the State of Israel. That definition is understandable, but it is also inadequate; the idea of Israel encompasses more, much more, than a mere political entity. So, from the outset, let's define our terms. In this study, the idea of Israel will include the following:

1. *A People*—both the ancient Israelites and the contemporary Jewish people living inside and outside the state of Israel;
2. *A Place*— both the land or territory referred to in history (as Canaan, Judea, and Palestine) and the modern state currently associated with the name;
3. *A Philosophy*—the ideology (that is, the value system) or world view of Judaism and the political ideology of the State of Israel.

Why Study Israel?

The importance of studying Israel can be shown by way of a parable. The story, an ancient one from India, tells of a group of blind men and an elephant. Each man is asked to determine what an elephant looks like by feeling different parts of its body. One man feels a leg, and says the elephant is like a pillar. The one who feels the tail says the elephant is like a rope. The one who feels the trunk says the elephant is like a tree branch. The one who feels the ear says the elephant is like a hand fan. The one who feels the belly says the elephant is like a wall. The last one, who feels the tusk, says the elephant is like a solid pipe. When they compare notes afterward, they learn they are in complete disagreement.

This parable has been used to illustrate a range of truths and fallacies. For our purposes, it shows the danger of considering only one aspect of a thing. Each blind man has mistaken a part of the elephant for the whole. We need to avoid doing this with Israel. We need to recognize that Israel is composed of many elements, some of them contradictory. To define Israel purely as a political entity (that is, as Israel "the place" or "the state") is to leave out other elements of it—namely, Israel "the people" and Israel "the philosophy." We need to consider Israel in all of its dimensions in order to understand them individually and to appreciate their relationship to each other.

For example, to define Israel as a political entity alone is to define it primarily in terms of conflict. Ironically, doing so makes it virtually impossible to understand what is actually behind the much-publicized dispute between Israel and the Palestinians. To define Israel in terms of conflict is to place it in a historical context that began with the 1948 War of Independence. But the fact is that the roots of the current conflict lie not decades ago, with the founding of the state, but millennia ago. To understand this conflict, you need a broader perspective, one that takes into account Israel's full history and ideology. And there is much at stake in acquiring this broader perspective. Unlike other regional conflicts, those involving Israel affect world relations and even domestic relations well beyond the Middle East. How they do so will become more apparent as you read through this work.

Without a comprehensive understanding of the ideological, religious, historical, and political dimensions of Israel, the issues surrounding the region will always be a puzzle. A failure to grasp these dimensions is one reason for the failure of the numerous peace initiatives to date. No territorial dispute has ever been more deeply rooted in history and ideology.

Why are these factors so often downplayed? One reason may be that the territory under dispute is physically quite small and almost barren of natural resources. For those unaware of Israel's spiritual and religious importance, territorial concessions of this small, unpromising terrain seem insignificant. This view obviously fails to consider that Israel is the site of many of the most momentous events in human history. Anyone aware of Israel's ideological and religious importance understands that this unpromising terrain is profoundly significant to all concerned.

To gain understanding of the roots of Israel's territorial disputes is one reason to study Israel. However, there is a more important reason. Such a study can help us understand our own identity, both as individuals and as a society. We in the West are heirs to the monotheistic tradition, and one of the major premises of this study is that in order to understand ourselves, we need to understand Israel—especially its role in history and ideology.

The Units of Study

This work is divided into two parts.

Part I begins our study of Israel by introducing the concepts of ideology and history. It then continues with monotheism and the religions that grew from it—Judaism, Christianity, and Islam—which underlie the two most significant ideological forces in the current international system: the West, and the Islamic nations. We will demonstrate how the current ideological dynamic came about and in the process will consider the ideologies with which early Judaism had to compete, such as Hellenism. After providing an early history of the Jewish people and showing how Judaism, together with Christianity, created the ideological basis of modern liberal democracy, we will conclude with a review of the origins and aims of Zionistic ideology.

Part II provides a history of the modern state of Israel and looks at the issues currently facing Israel at home and abroad. It follows with the story of Jewish and Arab nationalism from Part I and it examines the competing claims of both Arabs and Jews to the land of Israel/Palestine. It considers the relative legitimacy, with respect to international law, of the following:

■ the key agreements made between the representatives of the Jewish and Arab peoples; and

■ the ensuing decisions, made by the international community, that led to the creation of nation-states in the region.

Part II then proceeds to consider the events since the founding of the state of Israel, including the conflicts involved, and the various efforts to achieve peace. We analyze Israel's prospects for peace, and the factors that must be considered in any final negotiation for peace in the region.

Part II also explores issues such as the challenges of military service, how Israel is portrayed in academia, in the media, and in the international community (for example, the United Nations). We consider that portrayal in the light of Israel's humanitarian efforts and of innovations that have contributed to the well-being of the global community.

Part One

Israel in History and Ideology

Chapter 1

Introduction to Ideology

This work begins its study of Israel with a concept—"ideology." In its most basic, literal sense, ideology means a "system of ideas." But we tend to use it when referring to political ideas and cultures and to the value systems that support them. Our ideas about how our society should operate depend on our ideology. In this work, the word ideology will refer not to the political systems themselves, but to their underlying value systems. To clarify the concept of *ideology* by way of illustration, consider the following scenario:

Imagine that you've won a dream vacation to some tropical island in the south Pacific with over 200 lucky winners. En route to your destination, the plane is forced down. Luckily, all passengers and crew survive. Unfortunately, the plane sinks into a deep sea cavern, so there is no hope that radio signals will be able to broadcast the crash location.

As fortune would have it, the plane has gone down only a very short distance from an isolated tropical island, which everyone manages to reach. The island appears to have the resources necessary for survival, but because it is located in a remote part of the ocean, you are not likely to be rescued for many months.

How would your "society" operate during the months you are stranded? What authority would everyone be under? Who would make the laws or rules? What types of laws or rules, if any, would your new society have? Finally, what was the *source* for the answers you came up with?

These are questions about ideology.

If the island operates under democratic principles, each person on the island would have their say in how things are run and in what major decisions get made. The value which underlies that system is *equality*.

Not all ideologies consider equality as a primary value. For example, in a dictatorship, the person at the top is not concerned whether others have a vote or whether people are treated equally.

All political cultures and societies have an ideological basis. In other words, they have a value system through which most of their members see the world—a system which these members often take for granted and accept as authoritative. It is precisely because our value system is something we take for granted that we sometimes have trouble identifying it. For example, we all know that our society in the West has a democratic political system. But not so many of us can readily identify the ideology or values that underlie this system.

Identifying Ideologies

Let's consider a historical example. In the feudal system of Medieval Europe, there were kings who ruled by divine right. In other words, it was believed that the sovereign's right to rule came directly from God and that these divinely authorized rulers were not accountable to their subjects. Below the kings in the social order were the members of the nobility. These lords made up a very small proportion of the overall population, but they owned most of the land and possessed most of the wealth. At the bottom were the vassals or serfs, who owned no property themselves and had few rights. In return for the protection of the lord whose land they lived on, the serfs did agricultural work and served their lord in time of war. They did not expect to rise in the social order.

To us, this system of fixed social hierarchy seems very unfair, but most people in the society of the time accepted it. What was the ideology or value system that made the feudal system possible? One thing that seems clear is that the people in power in this society did not believe in equality or in equal opportunity for all. They seem to have taken it for granted that people were not equal—that kings and people of high birth deserved better, more comfortable lives than the commoners who made up the majority. That is one aspect of the ideology of feudalism. Another characteristic of this society's ideology was that the kings ruled by divine right. In other words it was a society whose members believed that God was actively involved in how things were organized. To go against the established order was to go against God— that is, to sin. To sum up: you might say that everyone in a feudal society had signed on to a system of divinely sanctioned inequality.

The political culture and ideology of feudalism contrast dramatically with those of the nations of contemporary Western society, which are egalitarian. Citizens of Western countries often take it for granted that all people in their society

- are relatively equal in value
- deserve a chance to improve their living conditions
- have a say in how they are governed.

Western Ideology

In stable Western democratic countries like the United States, the fundamental ideological differences between people, even between fierce opponents, tend to be relatively trivial. In other words, most political parties and most voters accept and participate in a democratic process that is rooted in a single basic ideology: liberal democracy. When we look at the whole international community, with its mosaic of diverse societies, we can see ideological differences that are more significant. We see, for example, that the value system of a Western democracy differs profoundly from that of a theocratic Islamic state, such as Iran, or from that of a dictatorship, such as North Korea.

What are the fundamental values that underlie liberal democracy, the political ideology of most Western societies today? Let's begin by defining the term *liberal democracy*. In a liberal democracy, elected representatives with decision-making power are held in check by a constitution that protects the individual liberties of the society's members. A constitution is a written document that sets out the basic principles by which a society is governed.

The constitutions of most Western democracies are good reflections of their societies' ideologies, because they include references to their citizens' rights in some form, usually a bill of rights. These bills of rights give a strong indication of the values that the society esteems and upholds. A bill of rights is a formal declaration—usually issued by a government—of the individual rights and freedoms considered essential to a people or a society. The individual liberties typically protected in a bill of rights include freedom of speech and assembly, freedom of religion, the right to private property and privacy, equality before the law, and due process under the rule of law.

In the United States, the Bill of Rights is the name given to the first 10 amendments to the US Constitution. These documents guarantee certain political and civil rights to American citizens, and they unify these citizens around a set of principles that embody those rights. Take a look at the excerpts from the US Declaration of Independence and from the Bill of Rights below, and you will see the principles and values these documents emphasize.

US Declaration of Independence and Bill of Rights

The following is from the second paragraph of the US Declaration of Independence, signed on July 4, 1776:

> We hold these truths to be self-evident, that all men are created equal, that they are endowed by their Creator with certain unalienable Rights, that among these are Life, Liberty and the pursuit of Happiness.—That to secure these rights, Governments are instituted among Men, deriving their just powers from the consent of the governed,—That whenever any Form of Government becomes destructive of these ends, it is the Right of the People to alter or to abolish it, and to institute new Government, laying its foundation on such principles and organizing its powers in such form, as to them shall seem most likely to effect their Safety and Happiness. ...

The first and fourth amendments of the United States Bill of Rights (1791) address some other rights that are dear to American society—freedom of religion, freedom of speech, or of the press, and the right of the people to be secure in their persons, houses, papers, and effects, against unreasonable searches and seizures.

Key Influences on Ideology

Why does the American Constitution stress the values it does? Why the emphasis on freedom—freedom of religion, freedom of thought, and freedom of expression? Why the insistence on democratic rights and equality before the law? Where do ideologies come from? Where did our Western value system come from?

Two major influences on a society's ideology (or value system) are its history and its religious foundation. In the next chapter, we will look at the concept of history in more detail. Regarding the influence of religion, if you look at the opening words of the constitutional documents of different Western societies (for example, the US Declaration of Independence), you will see they make allusions to God. The US Declaration asserts as a "self-evident truth" that all men "are endowed by their *Creator* with certain unalienable rights" (emphasis added). The constitutional documents of other societies also refer to God in this way. For example, the Israeli Declaration of Independence closes with the phrase "Placing our trust in the Rock of Israel," which is a metaphorical allusion to God. In Psalm 19:14 of the Old Testament of the Bible, God is referred to as the "Lord, my Rock and my Redeemer."

The inclusion of the term "Rock" in the Israeli Declaration of Independence was the subject of—and solution to—controversy just before the promulgation of this document on 14 May, 1948. The religious members of the Jewish leadership wanted a clear reference to God in the Declaration. However, a large segment of the Jewish leadership had secular and socialist convictions, and they sought a clear separation of church and state. They refused to sign the document if it contained references to "God." In the end, the phrase "Rock of Israel" was chosen as a compromise. Secular Zionists have interpreted the term "Rock" in a non-religious way to mean the cultural and historical heritage of the Jewish people.

Canada's Constitution is more direct than Israel's Declaration in its reference to God. It says Canada is "founded upon principles that recognize the supremacy of *God* and the rule of law" (emphasis added).

The references to God in the constitutions of the United States, Israel, and Canada are evidence of a simple but important fact: monotheistic religions are the wellspring of our ideology. They are the wellspring of other ideologies, too.

The first two articles of the Iranian constitution also make references to God. They describe their political system as "based on belief in… the single God." Does this mean that our religious foundation in the West, and thus our value system, is the same as Iran's?

It is not surprising to find a reference to God in the constitution of Iran. The state of Iran is ruled by (or subject to) the religious authority or Islamic Law, called *Sharia*. Sharia is the foundation for the political institutions and state laws in Iran.

In the US, on the other hand, religious freedom and the separation of church and state are among the basic principles of the society. So what is God doing in the constitution of Western democracies?

This question is one of the focuses of the first unit of this work, which demonstrates that the monotheism of the ancient Israelites had—and continues to have—a profound effect on Western culture and ideology.

Ideology, History, and Critical Thinking

Since religion and history are key components of ideology, critical thinking needs to play an essential role in any study of the history of ideology. Why the need for critical thinking? There are two reasons.

First, history is vulnerable to radical revisions for political ends. Many different interpretations of past events exist, and groups of individuals unified by race or religion have their own interpretations of history, which are frequently at odds with the interpretations of other groups or state governments.

Second, there is an important distinction between belief and truth. To have a belief is simply to accept something as true; it doesn't actually make it so. The degree of truth in a belief is proportional to how much it corresponds to the way things actually are. One justifies the truth of something by showing that there are good reasons for believing it. The process of consciously analyzing whether it is justified to believe something is called *critical thinking*, and it involves two essential components: reason assessment, and a "critical spirit."[1]

Reason Assessment

To be a critical thinker, a person must be able to evaluate whether a claim is justified by the evidence offered for it. Sometimes, people offer reasons that only weakly support their claims and beliefs. Sometimes, their reasons are completely unfounded.

Take, for example, the following proposition: *The Bible is the divine word of God because the Bible says so.* The critical flaw in this statement is that it offers no objective support for its claim. The evidence offered ("because the Bible says so") in support of the claim ("the Bible is the divine word of God") takes for granted what it means to prove. The reasoning is circular; the assertion and the evidence for it are the same. What the statement says, in effect, is the following: The Bible is the divine word of God because the text that is the divine word of God says so. But if the Bible is not the divine word of God, then the Bible's claiming to be so is not evidence that it is. In general, self-declarations of divinity provide no evidence for the divinity of such declarations; if we seek evidence for the assertion that "The Bible is the divine word of God," we must look for evidence outside the Bible itself—for example, to circumstances surrounding the authorship of the Bible that tend to rule out human authorship.

A critical thinker must be able to do the following:

- assess the degree to which a reason supports a claim;
- evaluate the reasons that lead to a conclusion;
- assess how much justification the reasons offered provide in support of a claim or conclusion.

One of the requirements for being a critical thinker is being a competent evaluator of reasons. But how does a person acquire this skill? How does a person know that a particular reason does not support a claim? The short answer is that, to become a critical thinker, a person must master a variety of reason assessment skills and know how to apply them.

Reason assessment skills come in all shapes and sizes. The essence of the skill is the ability to determine a flaw or weakness in reasoning. One common example of bad reasoning is the *ad hominem* attack—that is, when, in the course of a discussion or debate, one of the participants verbally attacks the other person's character rather than his or her intellectual claim. In other words, instead of addressing the truth or justice of your opponent's intellectual position, you attack your opponent personally by insulting their character, calling them names, and so on.

The Critical Spirit

Suppose that someone is able to assess reasons competently. Does that make him or her a critical thinker? No. To be a critical thinker, one must not only be a competent assessor of reasons, one must also possess a *critical spirit*.

There are people who are quite competent at reason assessment, but who won't exercise that competence. For example, a brilliant person can get fooled by a cunning used car salesman. Another example would be politicians who use their skills of reasoning only to favour their own ends or to protect their basic ideological principles from critical assessment. For different reasons, the person buying the car and the politicians have failed to use their critical abilities.

The truly critical thinker has highly developed skills of reason assessment and uses them impartially. Critical thinkers are inclined to analyze reasons and they are disposed to question even their own most fundamental beliefs and attitudes. They have certain habits of mind, and a certain sort of character—namely, a willingness to change their beliefs when it is reasonable to do so.

People who do not have the critical spirit, with its requisite dispositions, habits of mind, and character traits, do not qualify as critical thinkers, however adept at reason assessment they might be. Similarly, a person with the critical spirit, but without the ability to assess reasons, does not qualify as a critical thinker.

In the next chapter, we will see how we need critical thinking in order to assess the reliability and validity of competing historical narratives—for example between the competing narratives of Jewish and Palestinian history.

Endnotes

1   Harvey Seigel, "The Role of Reason in Education," in *Philosophy of Education: Introductory Readings*, 2nd ed., eds. W. Hare et al. (Calgary: Detselig Enterprises, 1996), 107-120.

Chapter 2

What is History?

The subject of Israel, to a far greater extent than many other subjects, requires you to think carefully about how you define history and how you go about establishing historical truth. There's a lot at stake in being historically accurate. Your beliefs about what actually happened in Israel thousands of years ago can influence your perspective on Israel today and on Jewish theology.

What is history? The simple answer is that *history* refers to a continuous, chronological account of human affairs, especially important or public events. But it's more complicated than that. The complication lies in the fact that you cannot know about the past—unless it is something from your own direct experience—except through other people's stories and reports. Events in the recent past may be known through compelling firsthand evidence, such as a visual recording, but the bulk of human history lies beyond the reach of such technology. For the most part, history is mediated by other people. We do not experience the past directly; we learn about the past through the accounts of others.

We tend to think of history as being true, unlike novels and other kinds of creative writing. Therefore, history is—or is expected to be—a kind of writing that describes *what really happened.* The trouble is that history, because it is recorded by someone else, is subject to interpretation.

There are other considerations that must be taken into account in regards to understanding the term *history.* For example, our relationship to the past is connected to how we see the world and to our beliefs about how things should or ought to be, how to value them, which things are good or bad, which actions are right or wrong. In other words, the following is the case: We use some of our stories about the past—our "histories"—to believe or disbelieve a certain worldview, to represent the right way of acting, to assess the character of one nationality as opposed to another, and to justify our conduct. In other words, many histories are value-laden.

The fact that history is value-laden raises certain problems and questions. One major problem is that history is vulnerable to radical revisions for political ends. For example, the current President of Iran, Mahmoud Ahmadinejad, has been challenged for claiming that the Holocaust is a myth. In another instance of revisionist history, some Palestinians claim that the Jews have no historical connection to Jerusalem and that there never was a temple on the Temple Mount. These examples show that groups of people bound by race, religion, or culture are likely to have their own versions of history, and their versions often conflict with those of others.

In the last chapter, we discussed the interplay between history and ideology. A society's ideology is largely a product of its history. Our past, along with our religious foundation, strongly influences our value system. This value system (ideology) often clouds the lens through which history is seen.

The Past as Knowledge

The fact that ideology or tribal hostility can influence a person's understanding of history—his ideas about *what really happened*—is part of a more basic problem when it comes to establishing the truth about the past. That basic problem is the unreliability of human perception itself. Probably we have all been in situations where two people, after witnessing something together, can't agree about what actually happened. What we think we have seen is sometimes different from what actually happened. Sometimes people see what they want to see. Or they see what they think they ought to see. In other words, even firsthand accounts of things can sometimes be inaccurate. For a good demonstration of this phenomenon, consider the following story from entertainer James Randi:[1]

Many years back, I appeared on the NBC-TV *Today Show* doing a "survival" stunt in which I was sealed into a metal coffin in a swimming pool in an admitted and since-regretted attempt to out-do Harry Houdini, who had performed the stunt at the same location back in 1926.

A week following that TV show, I was standing out on Fifth Avenue in a pouring rain, supervising through a window the arrangement of a display of handcuffs and other paraphernalia that I'd loaned to a bank for an eye-catching advertisement. My raincoat collar was up about my ears, and I could thus not be easily recognized.

I was astonished when an NBC director, Paul Cunningham, who had been in charge of my swimming-pool appearance, happened by. We were adjacent to the NBC studios, and he had been on his way to work. Not noticing me, but seeing my name on the bank-window display, he began excitedly describing to his companion how I had been handcuffed, wrapped in a strait-jacket, and sealed into the coffin before being submerged, on his show. "And he was free and at the surface within minutes!" he exclaimed.

With a certain small show of drama, I identified myself. Paul was ecstatic, and invited me to join them for coffee. There, while we warmed ourselves over java, I explained to him that he had unwittingly provided his listener with a description that was not only untrue, but impossible. I told him that no handcuffs nor straitjacket had been involved at all in that event, and that he was mixing up his memories of previous shows with the one he had directed. In addition, I pointed out, it is impossible to place a straitjacket on a person who is handcuffed; this is a topological paradox. In addition, I'd not made an escape from the coffin, nor had that been the stunt: I was merely surviving on a limited amount of air, and I was able to climb from the coffin when it was brought to the surface. Cunningham's version was dramatic, but simply very wrong.

We retired to an NBC studio to view a kinescope of the program in question, since Mr. Cunningham was quite sure that his version was correct, and I admit that I was a bit embarrassed to see his discomfiture as he then saw just how wrong he had been. So it is with many accounts of unusual events, since the viewer tends to incorporate errors and other details from similar events as part of his firm memory of what he believes took place. Magicians, in particular, are very familiar with this phenomenon.

Can History Be Objective?

Is it possible for history to be objective, or is history totally at the mercy of perspective and bias? If two histories disagree, is it possible to figure out which one (if either) is more accurate? Are some histories more *justified* than others? Is it possible for history to meet a basic standard of objectivity?

Given the uncertainty of human perception, can we ever be considered to have actual "knowledge" of the past? If your answer is 'no,' what does this suggest about the procedures used in courts of law? If 'yes,' how direct must this knowledge be? Can information that we receive secondhand—something we have read, for example—be considered knowledge?

It is important for us to answer these questions because, as we have already discussed, the concept of history plays a fundamental role in ideology. Judaism, Christianity, and Islam are all rooted in history. What people believe depends on what they count as history. So before we proceed to address the history of Western ideology, we need to come to some conclusions regarding whether it is possible for history to meet a basic standard of objectivity.

As the Randi example illustrates, some "histories" are clearly more objectively justified and accurate than others. The question is, how are we to determine which are more justified in the absence of a video recording or some other technology?

When it comes to ancient history, of course, videotape is not available. You must rely on other, less conclusive means of uncovering the truth about the past. While the standards for what counts as proof in history are not going to be the same as in mathematics or physics, there is no inherent barrier to our examining different versions of history and developing a fair picture of what probably happened. In other words, there is nothing to stop you from examining the evidence and coming to some objective conclusions.

To arrive at such objective conclusions, you need a willingness to face uncomfortable facts—facts that may not support what you want to believe or have been taught to believe. Good historians are willing to do this. Their conclusions are guided by their interrogation of the evidence rather than by their own ideological presuppositions. That leads us to the next consideration: what qualifies as historical proof? What evidence can we use to legitimize an historical claim?

Historical Evidence: the "Historometer"

Most people can distinguish between good and bad evidence, and they accept good evidence as proof that something has happened. So how do we figure out what constitutes good evidence? We can look to law and philosophy; these are fields of study concerned with defining abstract things like "evidence" and "truth." We can also look to how people actually live and navigate the world. Without thinking about it, we are constantly weighing and evaluating evidence as we go about our day-to-day lives.

People rely on certain types of evidence when trying to determine the truth of something. We can use these categories as we try to determine whether a historical claim is justified. The following are the kinds of evidence that most people accept as trustworthy:

- *Personal Observation*: Most people believe the truth of things that they see or hear themselves. In a court of law, things that people directly see and hear are accepted as testimony. The writings of people in history who experienced things directly and wrote about them provide testimony of this kind.
- *Tangible Documents and Objects:* When the murder weapon is produced in a case and linked to a suspect, the incriminating evidence is strong. Documents, such as written agreements or receipts for a purchase, are also strong evidence of this kind. In terms of evidence relevant to older historical claims, tangible objects and documents include things like buildings, coins, ruins, tombs, records, skeletal remains, and numerous other types of artifacts.
- *Common Knowledge*: Common knowledge is something known by most people and therefore rarely challenged. For example, it is common knowledge nowadays that the earth is round. People will accept that claim even though they've never been up in space and seen it for themselves.
- *Tradition:* A long-established custom or belief that has been passed on for generations or even millennia is also something people will accept as true. For example, people will likely accept the claim that, according to Jewish law, Jews are required to eat matzoh and not leavened bread on Passover, even though they may have never seen the specific law for themselves. The tradition of doing something a certain way for generations becomes an accepted truth.
- *Expert Authority:* A person who has authoritative knowledge and skill in a particular area is accepted as a trustworthy source of information or advice. When a competent doctor says a certain course of action is needed, people generally accept the advice as true.
- *Reasoning:* We also look for sound reasoning—and attempt to practise it ourselves—when trying to determine the believability of a claim. Statements or claims that seem illogical or unreasonable are generally not accepted as

believable. If someone asks you for five dollars with the promise that they can turn it into five hundred dollars in ten minutes, you likely won't believe them—or give them the money—because their promise is inconsistent with your sense of how reality works.

■ *Personal Credibility*: Quite often, people will accept another person's claim about something because that person's ethos or character seems to justify such trust. An ethos or character that we accept as credible will show a combination of competence, trustworthiness, goodwill, and dynamism. If a person lacks these qualities, you are less likely to accept the truth of what he or she says. In day-to-day life, this kind of evidence, based on our faith in someone's personal credibility, may be the most common grounds for accepting a claim. This kind of evidence is not always strong, of course. For example, people will sometimes believe the words of someone they are infatuated with, even if there is evidence that the person's words are untrue.

Taken individually, these various kinds of evidence are each fallible. For example, it was once *common knowledge* that the earth was flat. We know now this is false, even though people at one time accepted it as true. We also know that *personal observations* can be mistaken, as we have all likely experienced and as we saw in the James Randi account.

Nonetheless, these are the criteria that people use when trying to establish the truth. We all act on some evidence when we decide to believe or do something. Taken collectively and systematically applied, these categories of evidence that we all use can serve as a "Historometer"—that is, a tool we can use to measure the merits of competing historical claims.

Defining Truth: Correspondence Theory and Coherence Theory

We have discussed what counts as credible evidence. But what do we mean by *truth*?

In philosophy, two theories have been put forward to define truth: correspondence theory and coherence theory. The *correspondence theory of truth* says that truth equals correspondence to fact or, more broadly, to reality. In other words, you measure the truth of a statement by how accurately it describes (corresponds to) the real world. One of the first philosophers to articulate this theory was Aristotle, who said the following: "To say of what is that it is not, or of what is not that it is, is false, while to say of what is that it is, and of what is not that it is not, is true."[2]

The *coherence theory of truth* holds that you measure the truth or falsity of a statement by its relation to other statements and by whether there is "consistency" as opposed to "contradictions" between the various statements. In other words, you consider a statement true if it is logically consistent with other beliefs that you hold to be true. A belief is false if it disagrees with other beliefs that are considered to be true.

Competing Histories

On an MSNBC interview in September 2006, Mahmoud Ahmadinejad, the current president of Iran, was challenged by anchor Brian Williams to clarify his statements about the Holocaust. Williams said, "It upset a lot of Jews in the United States and around the world, when you called the Holocaust a myth."[3] Ahmadinejad did not admit in the interview to an outright denial of the Holocaust, but he insinuated that the truth about the Holocaust is open to debate.

Is the truth about the Holocaust open to debate? Do you believe the Holocaust to be a historical fact?

It is surprising how many people are unable to marshal a compelling response even if they believe with near certainty that any claims negating the truth about the Holocaust are outrageous. Often, people will get quite upset or insulted that they could even be asked to debate any question about the reality of the Holocaust. They are certain that the event occurred and that millions were murdered, but have difficulty summoning evidence to support their claims.

It becomes even more difficult to support historical claims the further back in history you go. For example, according to Jewish history, there was a temple on the site of the Temple Mount in Jerusalem, and it was destroyed by the Romans in 70 CE. Is that history? What about the historical claim that King Solomon built a Temple on the site circa 950 BCE and that it was destroyed by the Babylonians some 400 years later? Is that history? According to Jewish theology, Abraham's test with regard to the binding of Isaac also took place on the site of the Temple Mount. Is that history?

For some, the answer to these questions is a resounding no. The Jewish claim to having a historical connection to the Temple Mount and to Jerusalem is disputed by the Palestinian Authority. In the summer of 2009, Palestinian Chief Justice Taysir Tamimi stated the following in regards to Judaism's alleged connection with the Temple Mount:[4]

About these so-called two temples, they never existed, certainly not at the [Temple Mount]. ...

Israel started since 1967 making archeological digs to show Jewish signs to prove the relationship between Judaism and the city, and they found nothing. There is no Jewish connection to Israel before the Jews invaded in the 1880s. ...

All this is not real. We don't believe in all your versions. Your Torah was falsified. The text as given to the Muslim prophet Moses never mentions Jerusalem. Maybe Jerusalem was mentioned in the rest of the Torah, which was falsified by the Jews. ...

The Western Wall is the western wall of the Al Aqsa Mosque. It's where Prophet Muhammad tied his animal which took him from Mecca to Jerusalem to receive the revelations of Allah. ...

According to Tamimi, who is considered the second most important Palestinian cleric, the claim that Jews have a historic connection to Jerusalem and that they had temples on the Temple Mount is "baseless and untrue."[5]

What about other evidence concerning the Temple Mount? An aerial photograph of the Temple Mount area would seem to support Tamimi's claims. From above, what you see are two Islamic holy sites: the Dome of the Rock and the Al-Aqsa mosque. And there seems to be other evidence favoring Tamimi. Sir Martin Gilbert's *Historical Atlas of Jerusalem* contains a map entitled "Divided Jerusalem and the Holy Places, 1949-1967," which shows the holy sites in the Temple Mount area.[6] The ones it identifies on the Temple Mount are the Dome of the Rock (the Mosque of Omar) and the Al-Aqsa Mosque. Adjacent to the Temple Mount it identifies the Al Burak and Wailing Wall. The map is based on United Nations Map 229. [7] In other words, the United Nations—the organization that represents the community of nations—has classified the Temple Mount (Haram esh-Sharif) as an Islamic holy place, not a Jewish one.

Tamimi's claims, therefore, seem to be supported by the facts on the ground—the contemporary visual facts—and by the nations of the world.

In other words, we are confronted with competing historical narratives. Is it more reasonable to believe the Jewish claim of an ancient connection to the Temple Mount, or the Palestinian claim that the site is and has always been Muslim and that there is no Jewish historical connection to the site? Both narratives can't be true because they contradict each other. If the Jewish claim is correct, then the Palestinian claim must be false, and vice versa. Is there a way to objectively determine which of the two historical claims corresponds to reality?

The Historometer Applied

What happens when we apply the categories of evidence we used to make up our historometer to the competing claims of the Jews and Palestinians regarding a historical connection to Jerusalem?

As we mentioned above, the writings of people who witnessed firsthand the historical events they describe constitute one form of *personal observation*—the first category of evidence. Flavius Josephus is an ancient Romano-Jewish historian who lived during the first century CE and fought against the Romans. In Books 5-7 of *The Jewish War*, Josephus writes in great detail about the wars between the Romans and the Jews, the siege of Jerusalem, and the destruction of the Temple.[8] His writings strongly support the idea of an ancient Jewish connection to the Temple Mount.

Archaeology is the study of human history through the analysis of artifacts and other physical remains. It is a source for the kind of evidence that we classified as *tangible objects*, often a strong kind of evidence. The Arch of Titus, in Rome, was built in 70 CE to commemorate the victory of the Roman general Titus, after the siege of Jerusalem. On the inside of the Arch is a sculpted scene depicting an artifact being borne away that very closely resembles the Menorah associated with the Temple. It is a detail that explicitly links the siege of Jerusalem to the presence of the Jews on the Temple Mount.

But what grounds do we have for associating the artifact depicted on the inside of Titus's Arch with the Temple Menorah from Jewish history and theology? The Book of Exodus, chapter 25, verses 31-33, contains the following references:

You shall make a Menorah of pure gold.

Six branches shall emerge from its sides, three branches of the Menorah from its one side and three branches of the Menorah from its second side.

The text goes on to refer to "three cups engraved like almonds on the one branch and three cups engraved like almonds on the next branch." These descriptions of the Temple Menorah correspond to the artifact depicted on the Arch of Titus. In short, there is strong archaeological evidence of Titus's victory over the Jews in 70 CE, and strong evidence that the Temple Menorah was involved. This would seem to support the general idea that the Jews have a historical connection to Jerusalem.

Further evidence of a Jewish connection to Jerusalem is provided by a story in the Talmud. The text of the Talmud was compiled in the same historic period (the early centuries of the Common Era) as the events described above. The Talmudic story refers to an act of profanity committed by Titus in the Temple after he conquered Jerusalem.[9] In both Jewish tradition and Roman history, then, we find tangible objects and documents which corroborate accounts of events that took place during the Temple era.

So far, then, we have three kinds of evidence supporting the idea of a Jewish connection to Jerusalem: the *personal observation* of Josephus; the *tangible evidence* provided by the Arch of Titus; and the Talmudic story found in Jewish *tradition*. These three proofs date from the same historical period, and they provide a coherent account of past events. And that is one reason why most historians view these past events—and the Jewish connection to the Temple Mount—as *common knowledge*.

Islamic tradition is also a source of relevant evidence about the Jewish connection to Jerusalem. In 1925, the Supreme Muslim Council in Jerusalem published a work called *A Brief Guide to Al-Haram Al-Sharif*.[10] ("Al-Haram Al-Sharif" is the Arabic name for the Temple Mount.) The Guide describes the site of the Temple Mount as "one of the oldest in the world," and says that "its identity with the site of Solomon's Temple is beyond dispute." In the early 20th century, then, Islamic authorities in Palestine were acknowledging the Temple Mount as the site of Solomon's Temple.

An additional Islamic source supporting Jewish historical claims about Jerusalem is provided by Abdullah Yusuf Ali (1872–1953). He was an Indian Islamic scholar who translated the Qur'an into English. Yusuf Ali knew the entire Qur'an by heart and his translation is one of the most widely known and used in the English-speaking world. In other words, he is an expert authority. Yusuf Ali's commentary on Sura 17 (the Sura that discusses Muhammad's Night Journey) has several references that are relevant to our analysis.[11]

In his footnote number 2174, Yusuf Ali is wondering about the use of the Arabic word for "twice" in the context of the Islamic text. He suggests the possibility that "the two occasions refer to"

(1) the destruction of the Temple by the Babylonian Nebuchadnezzar in 586 B.C. when the Jews were carried off into captivity, and

(2) the destruction of the Jerusalem by Titus in A.D. 70, after which the temple was never rebuilt.

Notice Yusuf Ali's unquestioning assumption that these events in Jewish history occurred. Notice also that, according to Yusuf Ali, the Jews are the Ancient Israelites. In a later footnote, commending the Qur'an's account of the Babylonians, he writes the following:

> A good description of the war-like Nebuchadnezzar and his Babylonians. They were servants of God in the sense that they were instruments through which the wrath of God was poured on the Jews, for they penetrated their lands, their Temple, and their homes, and carried away the Jews, men and women, into captivity.

Yusuf Ali's commentary contains several more passages of this kind. He refers to events from Jewish history and treats them as common knowledge. Some examples follow:

> The return of the Jews from the captivity was about 520 B.C. They started life afresh. They rebuilt their Temple. ...The sceptre of Syria (including Palestine) passed to the Romans in B.C. 65 ... and inevitable doom followed in the complete and final destruction of the Temple under Titus in 70 A.D. (Footnote 2176, on verse 6)

> Titus's destruction of Jerusalem in 70 A.D. was complete. He was a son of the Roman Emperor Vespasian, and at the date of the destruction of Jerusalem, had the title of Caesar as heir to the throne. (Footnote 2179, on verse 7)

The Verdict

You've now been presented with the competing histories concerning the Jewish connection to Jerusalem and the Temple Mount. The history that denies the connection comes from Tamimi and the Palestinian Authority. The history that affirms the connection comes from different sources and is based on various kinds of evidence, including personal observation, tangible objects and documents, tradition, expert authority, and common knowledge. Which version do you find more reasonable? Which one presents the stronger argument?

What about the two theories of truth: the correspondence theory and the coherence theory? How closely does the Jewish version correspond to the available historical evidence? How well do the various pieces of evidence for this narrative cohere? Are they consistent with each other?

Let's apply the Historometer to some questions we haven't considered yet. For example, how does Tamimi himself stack up in terms of *personal credibility*? Does he seem to be a source who is acting out of goodwill and trustworthiness? Do you get the sense that he is objective and dispassionate--willing, like a good historian, to face uncomfortable facts? How open do you think he is to the positive evidence that refutes his claim?

When you apply your own *reasoning* to the evidence for and against a Jewish connection to Jerusalem, where does your common sense take you? To Tamimi's and the PA's side, or to the claims of Jewish history?

Sometimes people will say that, in the end, the two claims are basically equal. That the Palestinians have a story and the Jews have a story. It's just one story against another. Is that really an accurate portrayal of the competing claims? What do Tamimi's claims actually rest on?

Tamimi's claims basically rest on *negation*. To really appreciate what such a claim involves, imagine the following:

You find yourself, heaven forbid, in the middle of a lawsuit. To support your claim, you bring an array of positive evidence, including eyewitness testimony, detailed chronological records, and signed agreements. Your evidence is coherent and corresponds with reality. When the judge asks your adversary to present his arguments, she/he doesn't offer any positive evidence. She/He just says that your eyewitnesses are liars, your records are manufactured, and your signed agreements are forgeries.

How would you feel if his/her claims carried the day over all of your positive evidence? Would it truly be a case of "equal" versions of reality? Do fair-minded courts of law work that way?

The answer is, of course, no. In reality, just courts base their decisions on hard evidence. Tamimi's claims do not meet the standard for historical truth. Measured by the Historometer, his claims fall short; they contradict most of the relevant evidence. On the other hand, the evidence in support of an ancient Jewish connection to the Temple Mount is, unlike Tamimi's, supported by the kinds of evidence that people generally accept as proof: personal observation, tangible documents and objects, common knowledge, tradition, and expert authority.

In the next chapter, we will begin our study of Israel and of the history of Western ideology by recounting the story of Abraham and the appearance of *monotheism* on the world scene. And one of the questions we'll be asking is whether Abraham's story qualifies as history.

Endnotes

1   James Randi, "The Fabulous Automaton Chess Player, Part 1," *Commentary*, January 19, 2000, accessed March 7, 2012, http://www.randi.org/jr/01-19-2000.html.

2   Aristotle, *Metaphysics* 4.7, trans. W. D. Ross, The Internet Classics Archive, accessed May 6, 2012, http://classics.mit.edu/Aristotle/metaphysics.4.iv.html.

3   Iranian President Mahmoud Ahmadinejad, interview by Brian Williams, MSNBC, September 2006, *Iran's Ahmadinejad on Holocaust*, 2006, YouTube, accessed March 7, 2012, http://www.youtube.com/watch?v=ykd-syzZ4ZY.

4   Aaron Klein, "Chief Palestinian Justice: Temples never existed," *WorldNetDaily*, August 27, 2009, accessed March 7, 2012, http://www.wnd.com/2009/08/108142/. For a shorter version see WND Interview, March 15, 2007, accessed February 12, 2012, http://www.wnd.com/2007/03/40628/.

5   Ibid.

6   Martin Gilbert, "Divided Jerusalem and the Holy Places, 1949-1967," *The Routledge Historical Atlas of Jerusalem*, 4th ed. (London: Routledge, 2008), 99.

7   United Nations, *Central Portion of the Jerusalem Area: Principal Holy Places*, Map. New York, November 1949. From U.N. *Map Collection DN-2436*, (received *Jerusalem Holy Places_Map229.jpg* via email from Brenda Brookes, Map Librarian, United Nations Dag Hammarskjöld Library, October 26, 2009).

8   For a detailed analysis of the Roman wars with the Jews and the siege and destruction of Jerusalem, see Josephus, books 5-7, *The Jewish War*, in *The New Complete Works of Josephus*, trans. William Whitson (Grand Rapids: Kregel, 1999).

9   *Babylonian Talmud*, Tractate Gittin, 65B.

10   *A Brief Guide to Al-Haram Al-Sharif* (Jerusalem: Supreme Moslem Council, 1925), 4.

11   *The Holy Quran*, trans. Abdullah Yusuf Ali (New York: Tahrike Tarsile Qu'ran Inc.,1934), 694-5.

Chapter 3

Monotheism and the Ancient Israelites

Introduction

The monotheistic world view introduced by Abraham some 3,700 years ago has been a key element in world relations since antiquity. It is the source of three of the world's most prominent religions: Judaism, Christianity, and Islam. As such, it underlies the two most significant ideological forces in the current international system: the West, and the Islamic nations. To really understand Israel's influence on world relations and ideology today, you need to know the story of Abraham and of his descendants and how their story, with its genealogical components, continues to be relevant to current disputes in the Middle East. One of these disputes concerns whether there is in fact a Jewish people today who are the descendants of Abraham and the Ancient Israelites.

Is There a Jewish People?

The notion that there is a Jewish people with a strong historical connection to Israel is one of the founding principles of the modern State of Israel. Yet it's a principle that some people—not just extremist Muslim clerics but Israeli professors of history, too—have questioned.

In 1922, a document entitled the *Mandate for Palestine* changed the geopolitics of the Middle East and the international community of nations when it incorporated the following principles into international law:

> That the *Jewish people* have a *historical connection* to Palestine and they have *grounds for reconstituting* their national home in that country.[1] [*emphasis added*]

Were these principles justified? Is there in fact a "Jewish people"? If so, do they have a historical connection with the ancient Israelites and with the territory known as Israel (Palestine)? These are obviously important questions, and their answers are central to the longstanding territorial disputes in the region and to Jewish identity.

Yet there are some who think that Jewish claims of peoplehood and of historical connection to the land of Israel are "mythistory."

The Idea of a Jewish People: "Mythistory"?

In 2009, Shlomo Sand, a history professor at the University of Tel Aviv, published a provocative book entitled *The Invention of the Jewish People*. In it, he claimed that the idea of a Jewish people and its connection to Palestine/Israel is "mythistory."[2]

In August 2009, Sand was interviewed on the RT news channel. The following is an excerpt from that interview.

Interviewer: Is there a Jewish people today?

Sand: I don't believe [there is]. There is an Israeli people and there is a Jewish solidarity but there is not a secular Jewish culture that can unify me and a Rabbi in Brooklyn.

Interviewer: If there is no Jewish people, what does this mean for Zionism?

Sand: The raison d'être of Zionism is that there is a Jewish people. If not, what is the legitimization of the colonization that we did here? When you use the word "people" you believe that they have a territory, that they're the owner of a territory. This is the reason we are using the term "Jewish people."

Interviewer: Can you say there is such a thing as an Israeli people?

Sand: I am a denier of the Jewish people, I'm not a denier of the Israeli people. I think that the Israeli people living here today have a right to live here. I don't think that this territory, this land, belongs to a Rabbi in Brooklyn that doesn't want to come.[3]

Sand's book outlines his key objections to what he calls the "disturbing" Jewish narrative according to which the Jews are a people with a claim to the Land of Israel. Sand's objections include the following:

1. Archaeological evidence doesn't support the claim that there ever was an Exodus or that the Kingdoms of David and Solomon (Ancient Israelites) existed.

2. There was no forced exile by the Romans in the first or second century CE that resulted in a longing of a "people" to return to their ancestral homeland.

3. The claim of the Jewish people to genealogical descent from the ancient Hebrews and Israelites, and to a Jewish ethnicity or DNA (a Jewish gene), is far-fetched.

4. The Jews today are primarily the descendants of the converts of the Khazar kingdom that converted to Judaism in the eighth century CE.[4]

Collectively, these objections of Sand's refute the tenets of a modern Zionist narrative, which, as Sand sees it, was created to support the claim of the Jews to the territory of Israel.

Which position is correct, that of Sand or that of the Mandate for Palestine? The Mandate for Palestine asserts that there is a Jewish people with a historical connection to the ancient people and territory of Israel/Palestine, but Sand refutes that assertion. They both can't be correct. So which one is more reasonable to believe? What criteria must a group meet in order to be considered *a people*? Do the Jews meet that criteria? Do they share or need to share a common ancestry? Is there such a thing as a "Jewish people" or is the "Jewish story" a contemporary Zionist narrative created, of necessity, to claim title to a land?

Before we address these questions, let's familiarize ourselves with the story behind the claims of the Jewish people, as recorded in the Bible and Jewish history.

The Bible as History

The Jewish people consider Abraham their patriarch. Most of what we know about Abraham and his descendants, the ancient Israelites, is from the Bible. (All references to the Bible are to the three sections of the Hebrew Bible—The Five Books of Moses, Prophets, and Writings.) But is the Bible a credible source of historical information? Do its narratives count as history, or are they just myths and folklore that have been passed down for thousands of years?

Until about 1800, most people took the Biblical stories to be literally true, a reliable account of ancient Jewish history. Then, in the 19th century, German textual scholars, such as Wellhausen, began to argue that the early Biblical narratives—everything up to the Book of Samuel and the account of Saul and David—were largely myth, no more factual than Greek stories of Hercules. This way of seeing things is still the view of many.

While the Bible is not a history book, it does contain quite a bit of information about ancient history and culture, and this information is sometimes supported by archaeology. As historian Ken Spiro points out:

As far as the early books of the Bible are concerned, there is little direct archaeological evidence for the characters described there. There is, however, a huge amount of indirect or circumstantial evidence--names, places, business contracts, marriage contracts, migratory patterns. That is, as far as the early books of the Bible are concerned.

But once we get to later books—for example, the Book of Kings from 2,800 years ago—there is excellent direct evidence, including the written records of other empires. Unfortunately, the early events exist, more or less, in a historical vacuum and also in an archaeological vacuum.[5]

Quite apart from their truth-value as guides to Jewish history, the early books of the Bible, with their accounts of Abraham and Moses, are important to our understanding of the history of monotheism. Whether or not you believe in the supernatural events described in the Bible, the fact is that the story of Abraham's spiritual journey has altered the course of history, has affected millions of human beings over several millennia, and has played (and continues to play) a critical role in world ideology and relations. So if our aim is to gain some understanding about the origins of Western ideology and the intricacies of world relations, especially those resting on religious and historical beliefs, we need to understand the Biblical narrative.

Abraham and the Promised Land

According to Jewish theology, the story of the Jewish people begins with Abraham. He's the first of the three Jewish Patriarchs, the second and third being Isaac and Jacob. Abraham is revered in Christianity and Islam, as well as in Judaism. For this reason, Abraham's story is crucial to understanding the ideologies of nations that are built on Jewish, Christian, or Muslim theology and law.

According to the Bible, Abraham was 75 years old and living in Haran (modern day Turkey just north of Syria) when he received a divine directive to leave. God gave him the following instructions: "Go from your country and your kindred and your father's house to a land that I will show you, and I will make you a great nation."[6] The Biblical narrative continued in the Canaanite city of Shechem (near the modern-day city of Nablus), where God appeared to Abraham again and made a further promise: "I give this land to your descendants."[7] This promise, or *Covenant*, between God and Abraham was renewed several times, and is described in various Biblical passages.[8] For this reason, the land of Canaan is also called the Promised Land. However, at this point in the narrative Abraham didn't have any descendants. He was 85 years old and Sarah his wife was 75. So Sarah, who assumed she was barren, followed local custom and offered Abraham her handmaiden Hagar, to produce an heir.

Isaac and Ishmael

Hagar, an Egyptian princess, gave birth to a son named Ishmael. But then the story got more complicated, because shortly afterwards, Sarah gave birth to a son. As the boys grew Sarah became concerned about Ishmael's character and about conflicts over the inheritance rights, so she demanded that Abraham send Hagar and Ishmael away.[9]

Following Abraham's requests, God blessed Ishmael, but added that, although he "will be blessed and become a great nation," he will not share in the Covenant.[10] The Covenant will be maintained through Isaac and his offspring.

The casting-out of Hagar and Ishmael is the nexus point where Muslims disagree with the Torah. It is at this point in the story that Muslims allege the Torah becomes falsified and forged to fit a Jewish narrative.

After Hagar and Ishmael are sent away, Abraham is instructed by God to go to the "land of Moriah" and offer up his son for a sacrifice.[11] According to the verses in the Old Testament to which Jews and Christians subscribe, this son is Isaac. Centuries after the Bible was compiled, Islamic theology would dispute this. Muslims believe that the son whom God commands Abraham to offer in a test of faith is Ishmael, not Isaac.

According to Jewish theology, the place where the binding of Isaac took place was Mount Moriah or, in Hebrew, *Har Hamoriya*.[12] Mount Moriah is the location associated with the site of Solomon's Temple (the First Temple) as well as the Second Temple. Hence the name the Temple Mount for the area.

In Islamic theology, the place associated with Abraham's test— the binding of Ishmael—is in or near Mecca. In his annotations to Sura 37:102, Yusuf Ali details the different views of Islamic scholars regarding the location, but all are in the vicinity of Mecca, which is Islam's holiest site.[13]

The Biblical passages are significant because they are at the heart of the issues surrounding the competing claims to the Temple Mount area between Jews and Muslims. The Temple Mount is the holiest site in Judaism and is central to Jewish belief. The Temple Mount (*Haram al-Sharif* in Arabic) is also a holy site in Islam. It is the site of the Dome of the Rock. According to Islamic tradition, the rock is the spot from which Muhammad ascended to heaven in what Muslims refer to as the Night Journey.[14] The rock is called the Foundation Stone in Jewish tradition. According to Judaism, it was from this rock that the world was created. It is where Abraham fulfilled his test with Isaac, and it is where Jacob had his dream. It is the rock that was situated in the Holy of Holies, the most sacred part of the Temple. In other words, it is the holiest spot in Jewish theology and the one all Jews face when praying.

Abraham's Death and Legacy

It is specified in the Bible that, prior to his death, Abraham gave "all he owned to his son Isaac while gifts were given to the sons of his concubines,"—presumably the sons of Hagar (who is also called Keturah in the biblical sources)—whom Abraham sent "eastward".[15]

Abraham's death and burial are described in Genesis 25:7-11. The verses note that "his sons, Isaac and Ishmael buried Abraham in the Cave of Machpelah, with his wife Sarah." The Cave of Machpelah is located in the city of Hebron, southeast of Jerusalem. Abraham's first wife Sarah, Isaac and his wife Rebecca, and Jacob and his first wife Leah, are all considered to be buried there, along with Abraham.[16] Ishmael was not buried there, but the site is still revered by Muslims, as well as by Jews and Christians.

The Bible mentions no special gifts for Ishmael, but it does mention his twelve sons and the places where they lived.[17] In *Antiquities of the Jews*, Flavius Josephus refers to Ishmael's sons, describing them as "an Arabian nation," and he wrote that "the children by Keturah were gone to their own remote habitations."[18]

Abraham's story set up a number of forces in human relations that continue to this day. One involves the opposing worldviews of those who believe in the divinity and truth of ethical monotheism and those who do not. For example between atheistic political ideologies such as communism or national socialism and liberal democratic ideologies built on a monotheistic principles. Another involves the sometimes violent conflicts between the various monotheistic ideologies—for example between Christendom and Islam—that each claim to be the truth. Our journey through the history of Western ideology will show how these forces have played out, and continue to play out, through the various periods of history in both domestic and international relations.

The Covenantal Succession

Continuing with the Biblical story, the Covenantal succession passed from Abraham to his second son, Isaac, and then from him to Isaac's son Jacob. In Jewish theology, the chain of inheritance is determined by merit. It is a divine decision based on who possesses the spiritual characteristics that will allow for the continuation of the process, begun by Abraham, of bringing "ethical monotheism" to the world. The evidence for this is detailed in various verses which describe the personalities and characteristics of Abraham's sons, Isaac and Ishmael, and his grandsons, Jacob and Esau, in the Book of Genesis. In both these cases, the matriarchs intervene to steer the succession first to Isaac and then to Jacob, because their brothers are not worthy of carrying on the "family business."

According to the Biblical narrative, Jacob, the second beneficiary after Isaac, has an encounter with a "divine being." This is relevant to our study because, after this encounter, Jacob is given the name "Israel"[19] and his descendants are called "Israelites" or "Children of Israel" (*B'nei Yisrael*) in the Biblical sources. Earlier Biblical references to Abraham and his descendants use the term *Hebrews*.

Canaan and the Twelve Tribes of Israel

Canaan, the "Promised Land," became the Land of the Children of Israel when Jacob's twelve sons—or rather their descendants, the Twelve Tribes—were led by Moses out of Egypt, as described in the book of Exodus. The Exodus of the Israelites from Egypt is a central event in ancient Jewish history and includes, as well, an important moment in the history of monotheism.

That moment—the revelation at Mount Sinai—is where according to the Torah the entire nation of Israel received instructions from God. These instructions included the Ten Commandments and laid the foundation for the value system that would become, as you'll see in subsequent chapters, the basic ideology of Western civilization. The notion of a single, omnipotent God giving His laws to an entire nation is unprecedented in world religion and a turning point in human history.

It was also at Mount Sinai that the special rights to possess the land promised to Abraham, Isaac, and Jacob, were granted to the Israelites. However, they were conditional on the nation of Israel entering into a Covenant with God, and "obeying" His laws.[20] This is an important concept to understand and relevant to contemporary world relations, because it is the foundation of *replacement theology*.

Replacement Theology

A central concept in Jewish religion and in the history of the ancient Israelites is that of the Covenant. This was a formal agreement between the Israelites and God, first made under Abraham and later renewed under Moses. According to the

Covenant, the Israelites were to worship God alone and to obey his laws; in return, they were to become God's "chosen people" and were promised the land of Canaan.

Among Christians, there are some who claim that the Mosaic Covenant has been superseded. Many Muslims also believe that God rejected the Jews, but for different reasons. There are different versions of *replacement theology*, and they vary in their premises. But the people who subscribe to them, whether Muslim or Christian, always believe that they have replaced the Jews and are therefore the rightful successors to the Covenantal promises.

Christian subscribers to replacement theology believe they are the true inheritors of God's Old Testament promises to Israel. They ignore St. Paul's New Testament assurance that God has not rejected His people, and they believe that the Covenant with Jesus has superseded the Mosaic Covenant, making Christians, not Jews, the chosen people.[21] This school of thought, which many Christians do not accept, is sometimes known as *supersessionism*.

The Muslim notion of replacement theology is more radical and involves the outright appropriation of Old Testament prophets. According to Muslims, Abraham, Moses, and later Hebrew prophets, such as David and Solomon, are prophets of Islam. Jesus too is considered a prophet of Islam. The Muslim concept of replacement is a cornerstone of Islamic claims to the Promised Land and a key to understanding the Middle East conflict.

The Borders of Ancient Israel

Moses himself never reached the Promised Land. He was succeeded as leader by Joshua, who invaded Canaan with the Israelites c. 1230 BCE. When the territory was eventually conquered, the Torah details how it was apportioned between the Twelve Tribes and included land west *and* east of the Jordan River.[22] Judah, Jacob's oldest son, received the greatest portion. From the perspective of contemporary Middle East relations, the distribution of land among the Twelve Tribes of Israel is very significant. This is the area of land to which the Zionist Organization requested title in 1919 and which was afterwards granted the Jewish people in the Mandate for Palestine. (see Chapters 11 and 13.)

The Kingdoms of David and Solomon

The period in Jewish history that comes after Joshua is known as the era of the Judges. During this time, the Israelite tribes appealed to their prophets and God for a king. Saul was anointed and ruled over the Twelve Tribes. After his death, there was a period of civil war, during which the North was loyal to Saul's son, and the South was loyal to David. During his reign, David united the southern kingdom of Judah and the northern kingdom of Israel which had separated after Saul's death.

The story of King David is significant for many reasons. With respect to the geopolitical disputes of the Middle East, it is significant because, according to the Biblical narrative, David moved the capital of the Israelite nation from Hebron to Jerusalem. In the book of Samuel, the verses tell how King David purchased a threshing floor from Aruna the Jebusite.[23] The site David purchased is reputed to be the Temple Mount, which is at the center of the dispute between Jews and Muslims.

In Kings I, it says that King David's son, Solomon, built a Temple (known as the First Temple) to house the Ark of the Covenant, on the site currently associated with the Temple Mount— just above the area known as the City of David.[24] This occurred in approximately 964 BCE.

When the Kingdom of Israel split up (around the 10th century BCE), after the death of King Solomon, ten of the tribes of the Israelites formed a northern kingdom that continued to be called Israel. The remaining tribes, living in the south, were collectively called the Kingdom of Judah. It is from the name "Judah" that the labels *Judaism* and *Jew*, currently used to this day, are derived.

According to Biblical chronology, Solomon's Temple stood for four centuries until Nebuchadnezzar (c. 605-561 BCE), the legendary Babylonian king, marched on Israel, invaded the southern kingdom of Judah, and destroyed Jerusalem and the First Temple.

The Babylonian Exile

Following the destruction of the Temple, Nebuchadnezzar deported thousands of the inhabitants of the southern Jewish Kingdom to Babylon, an event referred to as the "Babylonian Exile." This ended the era of the First Temple and began the dispersion of the Jewish people from their homeland. Psalms 137:1 describes the grief of the dispossessed: "By the rivers of Babylon we sat and wept when we remembered Zion."

The Babylonian Exile is relevant to contemporary politics because it could clearly provide a historical basis for the term "reconstitute" in the Preamble of the Mandate for Palestine. Even though the Mandate document is likely referring to the events in the Roman era centuries later, it is also relevant to the Babylonian era.

According to Jewish history, when the Babylonians were later defeated by the Persians (c. 536 BCE), King Cyrus permitted the Israelite exiles to return to their homeland. The majority, however, chose to remain in Babylon, and early settlements in Mesopotamian cities, such as Nehardea, later became strong Talmudic centers of Jewish learning, thus corroborating historical accounts of the Babylonian Exile. The Jews that did return, including key Biblical figures, Ezra and Nehemia, played an instrumental role in the rebuilding of the walls of Jerusalem and the Second Temple.

Diaspora: The End of the Ancient Jewish "State"

After the rebuilding of the Second Temple, up to two centuries passed (there are differing opinions concerning when the second Temple was completed) before the ancient Greeks under Alexander the Great showed up. The ancient Greeks had presented a strong physical and ideological threat to the Israelites in Judea but the Jews survived the challenges and kept their community relatively intact for roughly the next two hundred years.

The second dispersion of the Jewish people came during the Roman era. The Roman diaspora, which effectively ended Jewish state history in antiquity, came about after two unsuccessful Jewish uprisings against Roman rule.

The first of these was the Great Revolt of 66 CE, which set off an intense four-year struggle between Jewish and Roman forces and ended with the bloody siege and destruction of Jerusalem. The Romans burned the Temple, carried off its sacred contents, massacred many of the people, and sold others into slavery, or kept them for the arenas. This Roman triumph, as we saw in the previous chapter, is memorialized in the Arch of Titus, which has the Temple Menorah carved into its stone.

The final Jewish uprising, organized by the descendants of the survivors from the first campaign, was the Bar Kokhba Revolt of 132-136 CE, the last of the Jewish-Roman Wars. The commander of the revolt, Simon bar Kokhba, was acclaimed by some of his contemporaries as the Messiah who could restore Israel, and he did manage to establish Jewish freedom in a significant part of Judea, but it was short-lived. A Roman army made up of twelve legions finally crushed the rebellion. The Roman vengeance was severe. After laying waste to the land of Judea and killing, according to some reports, almost 600,000 Jews, the Romans plowed the site of the Temple and barred Jews from Jerusalem. The Romans renamed the conquered territory *Syria Palestina*. While it is true that the Romans never "exiled" the Jewish people, their legacy of murder, slavery, and destruction resulted in a diaspora that scattered Jews across the Middle East and into ancient Europe. It is a diaspora that continues to this day, even though a significant number of Jews now live in the Land of Israel.

Jewish History and Jewish Identity

We have just explored the crucial points of Jewish history—from Abraham, through David and Solomon's kingdoms, and up to the middle of the second century of the Common Era. Returning now to the principle—formally enshrined in the Mandate for Palestine—that the Jewish people have a historical connection to Israel, we must ask the following question: Is it myth or history?

To answer this, let's also return to Sand's argument, which is centered on the following question: Is there such a thing as a Jewish people who have a historical connection to the people and territory of ancient Israel?

Let's apply the Historometer, which we introduced in the last chapter, to Sand's claims that the Jewish people are a modern-day Zionist invention and that there is no connection between the contemporary Jew and the ancient Israelites. What evidence would be relevant here? Consider the following:

1. *Genealogical chain of tradition/transmission*: The names of the leaders and sages in each of the approximately 113 generations spanning Jewish history are recorded in Jewish tradition. Judaism has records of the names of its key figures, sages, and teachers from virtually every century since biblical times. Several of these figures are survived by their works, and their teachings and their commentaries on the Written and Oral Law have been studied in Talmudic academies across the globe for millennia. Therefore, there is tangible evidence

of a continued chain of transmission connecting the ancient Israelites to the Jews of today.[25] At what point, then, does the claim by Sand that there is no chain of connection become itself a myth?

2. *Extra-Biblical evidence for Biblical figures:* The main sources for identifying people from the Hebrew Bible are Assyrian and Babylonian inscriptions, as well as seals (bullae) from the kingdoms of Israel and Judah. These date from the 9th century through the late 5th century BCE.[26] There is a body of archaeological evidence from the Biblical and Talmudic era that includes the following:[27]

- scrolls such as the Dead Sea Scrolls that are thousands of years old
- the remains of a burnt house in the Old City of Jerusalem with numerous artifacts[28]
- commemorative arches like the Arch of Titus
- coins such as the "Judea Capta" coin
- bullae (seals)[29]
- tunnels and walls[30]
- inscriptions[31]

3. *Ceremonial chain of tradition:* How many generations of Jews have celebrated Bar Mitzvahs, Passover, and Rosh Hashana (Jewish New Year)? How many, since Biblical times, have fasted on Yom Kippur (Day of Atonement), recited the *Shema* (the central prayer in the Jewish prayer book), or followed Jewish traditions in their marriages and funerals? All of these also incorporate the common language of Biblical Hebrew.

4. *DNA chain of tradition:* Jewish tradition holds that all *Cohanim*—a somewhat distinct status in Judaism— are direct descendents of Aaron the original Cohen (Priest). The line of the Cohanim is patrilineal: according to the tradition, it has been passed, without interruption, from father to son, from Aaron, for over 3,000 years—or approximately 90 generations. In the 1990s, two researchers who specialize in molecular genetics used DNA analysis to test a hypothesis that if all Cohanim are the descendents of one man they should have a common set of genetic markers. Their findings did indicate that a particular marker was found in a much higher percentage of Cohanim than non-Cohanim. They calculated the chances of this happening randomly to be greater than one in 10,000.[32]

5. *City names and famous gravesites in Israel:* Most of the names of the familiar and famous cities in Pre-Mandate and Pre-Islamic Palestine have Hebrew/Biblical origins as well as Greek and Roman ones. This is true of Jerusalem, Hebron, Bethlehem, Jericho, Tiberias, Cesarea, Nablus, and Gaza, to name a few. The tombs of Biblical figures—for example, the Jewish patriarchs Abraham, Isaac, and Jacob, as well as the matriarchs Sarah, Rebecca, Rachel, and Leah—all are located in Israel. So are the graves of great rabbis such as Maimonides (1135-1204) and Johanan ben Zakai (30-90 CE).

The above evidence contradicts Sand's arguments against a Jewish genealogy, against a Jewish connection to the ancient Israelites, and against the plausibility of a Biblical Jewish kingdom. Our evidence does not, however, address his argument that the Jews do not constitute a people because they live in different parts of the world and no longer share a "secular culture." The basis of Sand's argument is that, because Jews throughout the world no longer listen to the same music or eat the same foods or speak the same language, they don't constitute a people.

Sand's claim about what is and isn't a "people" is a *definitional claim.* Claims of definition involve interpretation (explanation), which is often not neutral. The way people define things can be biased. Is Sand's secular definition the only way to define a people—by their food, music, and language? Or are there other criteria to consider, possibly more significant ones—such as common experiences of trials and hardships or common religious practices and values? What about the "voluntary element"—in other words, the way a group *chooses* to identify itself?

An alternative to Sand's definition of peoplehood is that of George Scelle, who takes into consideration the unique history of the Jewish people:

> What characterizes a nation is certainly not a race—for there is no longer a pure race; it is a combination of manifestations of conscious solidarity— some of a historical nature, others of an intellectual, religious, social or even emotional nature—which together result in the creation of a collective desire for common life, an organization of solidarity and permanent relationship. If in truth—as Renan was one of the first to say—it is a psychological element which constitutes the very essence of nationality, there can be no doubt that the whole body of Jewish communities together can be considered one nation or one people. Moreover, the prevalent opinion of jurists concerned with the rights of peoples is that the voluntary element, rather than the ethnic one, is what must be borne in mind in determining whether the solidarity aspirations of a particular group deserve to be satisfied. It is not even essential that the group have common ethnic or traditional roots for it to constitute a nation or a people or for its aspirations to be legitimate. … Undoubtedly, the Jews are exceptional in this respect that, as a result of their dispersion, they lack some of the elements of solidarity encountered in the case of other peoples--in particular the solidarity that derives from the fact of living in close geographical proximity. On the other hand, it can be contended that their traditions, customs, the persecutions they have endured, their religious practices and mystic aspirations are … firmly integrated-- certainly far more so than in the case of other peoples.[33]

Sand's definition of what constitutes a people is a secular definition, which dismisses entirely both the religious element and the other elements discussed by Scelle above. Such dismissal naturally makes for a fallacious and fabricated argument in the case of the Jews, since the concept "Jewish people" naturally includes religious elements and traditions—along with the other factors mentioned in Scelle's definition.

There are some serious consequences to not acknowledging the truth of Jewish peoplehood and Jewish history, both for Jewish identity and for the current situation in the Middle East. The most serious consequences go well beyond the Jewish people and the modern State of Israel. Ignoring what has already been recognized and decided in international law also has consequences for an international system and for a Western ideology that is built on values such as the "rule of law." And that is very significant. In the next chapter, we will explore the source of those Western values.

Endnotes

1   Council of the League of Nations, "The Palestine Mandate," July 14, 1922, Avalon Project, Yale Law School, accessed March 9, 2008, http://avalon.law.yale.edu/20th_century/palmanda.asp.

2   Shlomo Sand, *The Invention of the Jewish People*, trans. Yael Lotan (London: Verso, 2009).

3   "There are no Jewish people, there are Israeli people," Shlomo Sand interview, *RT.com*, August 4, 2009, accessed March 7, 2012, http://rt.com/news/interview/.

4   Sand, *Invention of the Jewish People*.

5   Ken Spiro, *Crash Course in Jewish History* (Brooklyn: Targum Press, 2010), 9.

6   Genesis 12:1.

7   Ibid.

8   For example, Genesis 12:1-3, 12:7, 15:18-21, 17:1-8.

9   Genesis 21: 9-13.

10   Genesis 17:15-21.

11   Genesis 22:1-2.

12   Ibid.

13   *The Holy Qur'an: Text, Translation and Commentary*, trans. Abdullah Yusuf Ali (New York: Tahrike Tarsile Qur'an Inc., 2008), 1204.

14   Ibid, 17:1.

15   Genesis 25:1-6.

16   Genesis 23:19-20, 35:27-29, 49:29-33, 50:12-13.

17   Genesis 25:16.

18   Josephus, chaps. 12:4 and 16:3, book 1, *Jewish Antiquities*, in *The New Complete Works of Josephus*, trans. William Whitson (Grand Rapids, MI: Kregel, 1999).

19   Genesis 32:28.

20   Exodus 23:20-24 .

21   Romans 11:2.

22   Deuteronomy 1:6-8, 2:5,9,19, 31, 3:2,3,12-17, and Josh. 12:1-6, 13:1-3,15:1-63.

23   Samuel II 24:20-25.

24   Kings I 6:1-14.

25   There are numerous sources (online and text) which address the chain of Jewish Transmission, including the following:

(a)   "One Of The Many Chains Of Torah Transmission," *SimpleToRemember.com—Judaism Online*, accessed May 4, 2012, http://www.simpletoremember.com/articles/a/mesora/.

(b)   Rabbi Benyomin and Leah Hoffman, "Part I: Periods of our Mesorah—Chain of Transmission," *Scribd.*, accessed May 4, 2012, http://www.scribd.com/doc/9657286/Chain-of-Transmission-Part-I.

(c)   Irving M. Bunim, chap. 1 in *Ethics from Sinai* (Jerusalem: Feldheim, 1964), 21.

(d)   Rabbi Adin Steinsaltz, "The Generations of the Tannaim and the Amoraim," *The Talmud: The Steinsaltz Edition—A Reference Guide* (New York: Random House, 1989), 31-33.

(e)   Mattis Kantor, *The Jewish Time Line Encyclopedia* (Northvale, NJ : J. Aronson, 1993).

26   For further information, see "Biblical figures identified in extra-biblical sources," Wikipedia, accessed May 13, 2012, http://en.wikipedia.org/wiki/List_of_biblical_figures_identified_in_extra-biblical_sources. Several figures are listed including the following:

(a)   Ahab, king of Israel: Mentioned extensively in Kings and Chronicles, Ahab is identified in the contemporary Kurkh Monolith inscription of Shalmaneser III, which describes the Battle of Qarqar and mentions 2,000 chariots, 10,000 soldiers of Ahab the Israelite defeated by Shalmaneser. Bible Resources: Documenting Bible archaeology and written source material, "Archaeology Series 12: The Kurkh Monolith of Shalmanasser III," Sunday, September 23, 2007, http://bibleresources.blogspot.ca/2007/09/archaeology-series-14the-kurkh-monolith.html.

(b)   Baruch ben Neriah: A scribe in the time of Jeremiah. Imprints of his seal were discovered and read to Berachyahu son of Neriyahu the scribe. (see endnote 27 "Top Ten Archaeological Discoveries of the Twentieth Century Relating to the Biblical World").

27   For a general overview of archaeological discoveries relating to ancient Israel and Jewish history and theology, see the following: The Friends of the Israel Antiquities Authority, http://www.archaeology.org.il/index.php; and Keith N. Schoville, "Top Ten Archaeological Discoveries of the Twentieth Century Relating to the Biblical World," accessed May 4, 2012, http://biblicalstudies.info/top10/schoville.htm.

28   The Company for the Reconstruction and Development of the Jewish Quarter in the Old City of Jerusalem Ltd., "The Burnt House," *The Jewish Quarter in the Old City of Jerusalem*, accessed May 4, 2012, http://www.jewish-quarter.org.il/atar-saruf.asp.

29   Jonathan Kantrowitz, "Seals of Jeremiah's Captors Discovered!" *Archaeology News Report*, a blog by Jonathan Kantrowitz, January 3, 2012, accessed May 6, 2012, http://archaeologynewsreport.blogspot.ca/2012/01/seals-of-jeremiahs-captors-discovered.html .

30   Stephen Flurry, "Did King David Conquer Jerusalem Using This Tunnel?," *The Trumpet.com*, October 30, 2008, accessed May 6, 2012., http://www.thetrumpet.com/?q=5627.3952.0.0.

31   "The Siloam Inscription," *Jewish Encyclopedia.com*, originally published between 1901-1906, accessed May 6, 2012, http://www.jewishencyclopedia.com/articles/13662-siloam-inscription.

32   There are a number of articles online regarding DNA evidence of a Jewish chain of tradition. See, for example, the following:

(a)   Rabbi Yaakov Kleiman, "The DNA Chain of Tradition: The Discovery of the 'Cohen Gene,'" The Tribe, accessed May 4, 2012, http://www.cohen-levi.org/jewish_genes_and_genealogy/the_dna_chain_of_tradition.htm.

(b)   Razib Khan, "The adventure of the Cohen Modal Haplotype," *Discovermagazine.com*, Gene Expression (Blog), September 28, 2009, accessed May 4, 2012, http://blogs.discovermagazine.com/gnxp/2009/09/the-adventure-of-the-cohen-modal-haplotype/.

(c)   Razib Khan, "Ashkenazi Jews are more European in ancestry," *Discovermagazine.com*, Gene Expression (Blog), September 4, 2009, accessed May 4, 2012, http://blogs.discovermagazine.com/gnxp/2009/09/ashkenazi-jews-are-more-european-in-ancestry/.

33 Georges Scelle, "Les Caracteristiques Juridiques Internationales du Foyer National Juif," *Palestine Revue Internationale 2* (1928): 100.

Chapter 4

Judaism and Its Influence

Introduction

To really understand the impact of Judaism's influence on the world, you need to be familiar with two things:

1. The fundamental value system of Western liberal democracies today;
2. The particular values that Judaism brought to civilization.

While developing an idea for a lecture program, historian Ken Spiro, author of *WorldPerfect*, conducted a survey over a period of two years. Over 1,500 people were asked to list the fundamental values that, in their opinion, would need to be upheld to make our world as perfect as humanly possible. Their answers were remarkably similar. Spiro grouped these answers into six categories:

1. *Respect for human life.* All people would be guaranteed certain basic human rights, the foremost being the right to life.
2. *Peace and harmony.* All people and nations would coexist in peace and harmony with one another.
3. *Justice and equality.* All people regardless of race, sex, or social status would be treated equally and fairly before the law.
4. *Education.* All people would receive a basic education that would guarantee functional literacy—that is, literacy sufficient for a person to function in the complex world of today.
5. *Family.* A perfect world needs a strong, stable family structure to serve both as the moral foundation for society and as the socializing/educating influence for children.
6. *Social Responsibility.* In a perfect world, people would take responsibility at every level—individual, community, national, and global—for addressing basic social concerns such as disease, poverty, famine, crime, addiction, and the environment.[1]

Are these six ideals basic to human nature? Have people always felt this way? If not, where did Western values originate? These are the questions that Spiro asked, and the answers formed the foundation of his book *WorldPerfect*, which is the basis of our discussion in this chapter.

Where Do Our Values Come From?

Many of Spiro's respondents, who were mostly residents of Western democratic countries, assumed that their fundamental ethical values originated, like democracy, in ancient Greece and Rome. It is true that many of our ideas about art, beauty, philosophy, government, and modern empirical science have come from classical Greek thought. And the Romans were a powerful influence on Western law, government, administration, and engineering. But our ethical values originated elsewhere.

To prove this, let's take a look at the classical world in relation to the values that we have just equated with Western ideology—respect for life, peace and harmony, justice and equality, education, family, and social responsibility.

Ethical Values in the Classical World

What were the ethics of the classical world in terms of Spiro's six values?

Respect for Life

Virtually every ancient culture practiced infanticide—that is, the killing of newborn children—as a way of population control, of sex selection, and of eliminating potentially burdensome or deformed members from society. There is a famous letter from the first century, written by a Roman citizen named Hilarion to his expecting wife, that illustrates clearly the attitude of the classical world toward infanticide. Hilarion wrote: "If you give birth to multiples, if there is a boy let it [live], but if they are girls, expose [them]."[2]

Virtually every ancient culture practiced human sacrifice, too—the killing of people as part of religious ritual. The Romans of antiquity were one of the few that did not. But they had no reservations about slaughtering people for sport. The famous Coliseum in Rome was only one of the many stadiums throughout their empire where they killed people and animals to entertain the masses. Savage fights to the death between gladiators were the highlight of these spectacles, but sometimes women and children were sent in to fight each other, to keep up the novelty.

Although the great classical societies shared certain ideas of ours, such as the belief that law and order are essential to a society, they did not take it for granted (as we do) that every human being has a basic right to life.

Peace and Harmony

Today, most Western countries are opposed to war. Though armament is viewed as necessary, we see it not as a preparation for war, but as a deterrent. This wasn't the case in the classical world.

The subject of Homer's *Iliad*, one of the greatest works of Hellenic literature, is the siege of Troy. In ancient Greece and Rome, this work was a basic text for teaching values to the young. The primary value it taught was war. The youth got the message that war was the way to glamour, glory, and immortality. War, not peace, was prized in the classical world.

Justice and Equality

Justice and equality are the foundations of democracy, and they are the cornerstones of our constitutional documents. While democracy is not perfect, the average person living in a democratic society today is protected under the law, and is assured a considerable measure of justice, equality, liberty, and happiness in comparison with what a non-democratic system would give him or her. What about the average person of antiquity?

In the classical world, the average person was in most cases a slave, often from a conquered people. These people were permitted to remain as state slaves on the land that had formerly belonged to them. However, they were seen as threats; it was suspected they might revolt at any time, and the laws dealt mildly with those who murdered them.

The ancient Athenians are famous for having invented the idea of government by the people—in other words, the concept of democracy. It is less well known that the only people permitted to vote in this ancient society were "citizens"—that is, male landowners whose parents were Athenian. There were no proper population censuses in ancient Athens, but the educated modern guess puts the total population of fifth-century BCE Athens at around 250,000.[3] This figure included men, women, and children, both free and unfree, enfranchised and disenfranchised. Of these 250,000 people, only a few thousand were eligible to vote. Though they made up the majority of the population, slaves and women were not eligible.

The "democracy" of ancient Greece was relatively short-lived. It began in Athens in 508 BCE and effectively ended once Alexander the Great of Macedon came to power in 336 BCE. From Alexander's time onward, the political ideology of the ancient Greeks was a divinely ordained monarchy or, more accurately, a dictatorship.

Roman democracy, in the form of the Republic, lasted longer than its Greek counterpart. The Roman Republic survived in one form or another for approximately 400 years, from about 500 BCE to 44 BCE, when Julius Caesar declared himself dictator. After Caesar, Roman Emperors set themselves up as gods, to be worshipped and obeyed without question. The Roman Republic, like the Athenian system, was by modern Western standards a very limited kind of democracy. Only male Roman citizens could vote. Women and slaves were not permitted to vote. Nor were former slaves, although their children would potentially be eligible.

Education

The benefits of education are obvious to us, but were they also obvious to people of antiquity? Today, the world literacy rate is around 80 percent. In the Western nations, it is close to 100 percent. The situation in antiquity was very different. Historians estimate that in the most advanced civilizations of the ancient world, about 5 percent of the general population and about 15 percent of the adult male population were able to read and write.[4] In the ancient Greco-Roman world, education was considered necessary and desirable only for the children of the ruling majority. Education is a kind of power, potentially dangerous to a hierarchical society. Therefore, most ancient societies considered leaving the majority in ignorance to be good policy.

Family Values

A solid family structure is now considered one of the bases of a healthy society. In the classical world, marriage was viewed as something a man must endure in order to have heirs. As for the woman, she was not permitted to pick her husband, who generally considered her inferior and regarded her as a necessary evil. The Greco-Roman wife had only one real purpose—to bear legitimate heirs.

Social Responsibility

In the West today, we take it for granted that the government is responsible for providing social welfare programs. The truth is that such programs are recent phenomena; they came about in the last few hundred years, mostly owing to the spread of liberal democracy. In the ancient world, there was no government program to help the very poor.

Foreign aid is likewise a recent phenomenon. Nowadays, when another country is struck by a natural disaster of some kind, the developed countries of the West are quick to respond. This would never have happened in the ancient world.

Pity for the poor and the unfortunate never had much place in classical society. The Romans understood that a large, starving population would be difficult to control, but they did no more than provide them with free or subsidized grain, to appease them.

Ethical Values in Other Ancient Societies

Pretty much every ancient society shared the same attitudes with respect to the six values discussed above. Some of these societies had beautiful philosophies and were highly sophisticated in certain ways. But you need to distinguish between cultural sophistication and the moral reality of a society. The two are not necessarily connected.

We tend to look to these ancient cultures and to the ancient Greco-Roman civilizations when we are trying to account for the values of modern Western nations. Why do we do this? One reason is that we associate these values with democracy, the political system that the ancient Greeks invented. Another reason why we make this mistake is that some historians have given us an idealized picture of these ancient civilizations. They have accentuated the positive contributions of these cultures while downplaying or ignoring the negative aspects. The reality is that the value systems of antiquity were entirely different from those of the Western liberal democracies of today.[5]

The ancient civilizations contributed many positive things to the world: engineering, astronomy, literature, law, art, science, mathematics, philosophy, and politics. But we did not inherit their value system—their ideology. The Western vision of world peace, harmony, justice, and equality is not the product of these empires of the classical world. Where does this vision come from?

The Jewish Contribution

Historian Thomas Cahill had the following to say about the origins of the Western vision:

> The Jews started it all—and by "it" I mean so many of the things we care about, the underlying values that make all of us, Jew and gentile, believer and atheist, tick. Without the Jews, we would see the world through different eyes, hear with different ears, even feel with different feelings. And not only would our sensorium, the screen through which we receive the world, be different: we would think with a different mind, interpret all our experience differently, draw different conclusions from the things that befall us. And we would set a different course for our lives.
>
> By "we" I mean the usual "we" of late-twentieth century writing: the people of the Western world, whose peculiar but vital mentality has come to infect every culture on earth, so that, in a startlingly precise sense, all humanity is now willy-nilly caught up in this "we." For better or worse, the role of the West in humanity's history is singular. Because of this, the role of the Jews, the inventors of Western culture, is also singular: there is simply no one else remotely like them; theirs is a unique vocation. Indeed, as we shall see, the very idea of vocation, of a personal destiny, is a Jewish idea.[6]

Christian historian Paul Johnson has a similar notion of the Jewish contribution to Western civilization:

> Humanity might have eventually stumbled upon all the Jewish insights. But we cannot be sure… To them we owe the idea of equality before the law, both divine and human; of the sanctity of life and the dignity of the human person; of the individual conscience and so a personal redemption; of peace as an abstract ideal and love as the foundation of justice and many other items which constitute the basic moral furniture of the human mind. Without the Jews it might have been a much emptier place.[7]

Jewish Ideology

The ancient Hebrews, later known as the Israelites and then as the Jews, would not have agreed that they invented the values credited to them. They would have credited their world view to God, the source of all their moral authority. Either way, we are left with a question. Are the claims made by Cahill and Johnson—that the world view of the Jews is the source for the foundational values of Western society—justified? Are Cahill and Johnson correct?

The monotheistic religion of the Jews encompassed three core ideas: God, Torah, and the Land of Israel. These three elements are inseparable in Jewish theology. As a religion, Judaism was unique from the outset. What made it special? The following features in particular distinguished it from any previous religion:

- *Monotheism*: The belief that there is only one God, all-powerful, infinite, and invisible, who created everything known to man.
- *Divine Intervention*: The belief that the Israelite people (some 600,000 men and an untold number of women and children) escaped from slavery in Egypt— then the mightiest empire on Earth—through the intervention of their God.
- *Divine Law*: The belief that after the Israelites' escape from Egypt under Moses, they reached a mountain in the wilderness, Mount Sinai, where they had an encounter with God during which they, through Moses, received a code of laws. These laws were compiled in the Torah and later in the Talmud, and they were disseminated through these texts.

The belief in one God—who was the source of morality and for whom people would give their lives—was unprecedented, and seemed irrational to the rest of the ancient world. None of history's ancient empires fought wars for their religion. Only the Jews felt that the spiritual life was more precious than the material world.

Judaism was unique in other ways, too. How did the ancient Jews view the six fundamental values we've been discussing? The answer to this question will give us some idea about where much of modern Western ideology comes from.

Respect for Life in Judaism

One of the fundamental precepts of the Torah is that all human beings are created in the image of God. This means that every human life, regardless of age or disability, has infinite value and must be safeguarded and protected. The sanctity of life is one of the most important concepts in Jewish ideology. The sixth of the Ten Commandments, "Thou shall not murder," clearly expresses this. It goes without saying, then, that infanticide, human sacrifice, and killing for sport are all prohibited by the Torah.

To stress the infinite value of human life, the Torah teaches that no expense or effort be spared to save even a single life. It permits the violation of almost all of its more than 600 commandments if a life is at stake. During the same historical period in which the Romans were watching people slaughtered in the Coliseum, the rabbis wrote the following: "Whoever destroys a single life, it is considered by Scripture as if he destroyed an entire world. And whoever saves a single life, is considered by Scripture as if he saved an entire world."[8]

Peace and Harmony in Judaism

On a wall just outside the New York headquarters of the United Nations—the international organization of countries that was set up in 1945 to promote peace, security, and cooperation—you can find one of the best expressions of Judaism's vision of peace. Inscribed are the words from the prophet Isaiah: "And they shall beat their swords into plowshares and their spears into pruning hooks, nation shall not lift up sword against nation. Neither shall they learn war anymore."[9] That the UN chose those words to put on the wall outside their complex is ironic, in view of the fact that the United Nations has now passed more resolutions condemning Israel—the Jewish state—than it has against every other repressive country on earth combined.

These words from Isaiah reflect the Jewish vision of peace, brotherhood, and harmony. This vision is sometimes known as the Messianic vision, which the Christians call the "Second Coming."

The emphasis on peace was so fundamental in Judaism that "shalom" (peace) became the daily greeting. Judaism's sacred texts are full of sayings from the Jewish sages that stress the importance of peace. For example, Rabban Shimon ben Gamliel said the following (*Pirke Avot*, 1:18): "The world endures on three things—justice, truth, and peace, as it is said: 'You shall adjudicate the verdict of truth and peace at your gates' (*Zechariah* 8:16)."[10] The following words are from Rabbi Shimon ben Chalafta (*Uktzin*, 3:12): "The Holy One, Blessed be He, could find no container which would hold Israel's blessings as well as peace, as it says: 'Hashem will give might to His nation; Hashem will bless his nation with peace.'"[11] Hillel, one of the greatest Talmudic sages, also emphasized peace (*Pirke Avot*, 1:12): "Be among the disciples of Aaron, loving peace and pursuing peace, loving people and bringing them closer to the Torah."[12] And Rav Yosef summarized the importance of peace as follows: "All the laws of the entire Torah were decreed because they are the ways which foster peace."[13]

While peace is a core Jewish value, Judaism does believe that it is sometimes necessary to go to war. However, it permits it only when it is a question of fighting evil, defending one's country, or preserving one's society and values. And even war of this kind should be considered a last resort.

The ancient Israelites only suspended the Jewish policy of peace when it came to settling the Promised Land of Canaan. When King David completed that conquest around 1258 BCE, he made the city of Jerusalem the capital of Israel. "Jerusalem"—*Yerushalayim* in Hebrew—means "City of Peace." Apart from settling Canaan, the Israelites did not engage in conquest, even though, for a time, they had the ability and the power to do so. They understood the real goals of their existence to be peace, harmony, and the unity of mankind.

Another distinguishing feature of Judaism is that its heroes were always scholars and prophets, not the warrior conquerors idealized in other ancient cultures. Glorification of war was alien to the Israelites. Jewish sages taught that real strength did not come from conquering others but from taking control of oneself. "Who is strong? He who subdues his personal inclination, as it is said: 'He who is slow to anger is better than a strong man, and a master of his passion is better than a conqueror of a city'"(*Proverbs* 16:32).[14]

Justice and Equality in Judaism

The word "justice" appears a total of 120 times in the Torah.[15] The Torah devotes considerable space to explaining justice, law, and how to administer them fairly. The idea of justice was not unique to the Jews in the classical world. The ancient Greeks and Romans had it, too. But the Jewish conception of justice was strikingly modern in its even-handedness. Law was just only when it was administered equally to all people, regardless of their status within society.

In Judaism, no one is above the law. It is irrelevant how rich or poor someone is. The Torah admonished, "You shall not commit a perversion of justice; you shall not favor the poor and you shall not honor the mighty; with righteousness you shall judge your neighbor."[16] Even Jewish kings, while vested with privileges and powers, were still accountable to God and to the nation they served. Unlike other monarchs in the ancient world, Jewish kings were burdened with the tremendous responsibility to be role models for their subjects.

Despite the presence of a king, the Jewish government was neither a monarchy nor—as is sometimes thought—a theocracy. It was a sophisticated system of checks and balances that included an executive branch (the king); a religious branch (the High Priest); and a judicial branch (a supreme court, called the Sanhedrin). It was the latter's job to administer justice. The legislative branch found in most modern systems of government was unnecessary, because the Sanhedrin was charged with interpreting and applying Torah law to new situations.

The Sanhedrin was a body of 71 men that made up the Jewish Supreme Court. The criteria for becoming a member of the Sanhedrin had nothing to do with social status or wealth. It was a meritocracy; a person qualified for membership by being wise. Another requirement was paternity. A member of the Sanhedrin must have children. The Torah's rationale for making this requirement was that since every offender is someone's child, only a parent could truly understand and remember the concept of mercy when administering justice. Other requirements for serving on the High Court included an "encyclopedic knowledge of secular and religious subjects (especially Jewish law), fluency in all the languages of the region, and an unquestioned reputation for integrity and honesty. Basically, each judge had to be good and smart."[17]

The Sanhedrin was expected to dispense a justice that was tempered by compassion. While there was provision for capital punishment in Torah law, putting offenders to death was almost unheard of in actual practice. Under Torah law, the conditions required to administer the death penalty made it virtually impossible to carry out.

Sending offenders to prison also did not happen in ancient Israel. The men of the Sanhedrin reasoned that the best way to correct a criminal's mistake was to send him to work for a good family who would take responsibility for seeing that he changed his behavior.

The concept of equality applied to Jews and non-Jews alike. According to Jewish law, any non-Jew who respected Torah law and followed the seven basic Noachide laws was considered equal to a Jew and received the same protection under the law.

The Noachide laws prohibited idolatry, murder, theft, sexual immorality, blasphemy, and eating the flesh of a live animal, and they required the establishment of courts of law. These laws were given, according to the Talmud, as a set of laws for all of humankind—that is, all the "children of Noah." According to Judaism, it is not necessary to be Jewish to get to heaven; people are judged by their actions, not their beliefs.

Interestingly, despite its emphasis on the equality of all people, Judaism makes no provisions for a representational form of democracy in which people vote for their government. Rather, the Torah advocates a political system composed of individuals qualified to lead by their knowledge, integrity, and dedication.

Education in Judaism

In Judaism, one has a religious obligation, according to Torah, to educate oneself and one's children. There is evidence, both from the Talmud and from archaeological artifacts, that the literacy rate among Jews in the ancient world rivaled that of contemporary Western civilization. In other words, the rate of literacy was virtually 100 percent.

Called the "people of the book," the universality of Jewish education impressed non-Jewish intellectuals of the past. Peter Abelard, a French monk and scholar of the Medieval period, wrote the following in the twelfth century: "A Jew, however poor, even if he had ten sons, would put them all to letters, not for gain … but for understanding of God's law. And not only his sons, but his daughters."[18] Universal education was standard among Jews many centuries before it became an ideal in the rest of the world.

Family and Marriage in Judaism

Judaism's attitude toward women, marriage, and the family was completely at odds with the norms of the ancient world and was millennia ahead of its time. There are many Torah laws intended to preserve the sanctity of marriage and family, the most obvious of which is the prohibition of adultery. Within Judaism, not only is a husband prohibited from causing his wife pain, he is also required to respect her in all ways. This attitude is exemplified in numerous Biblical stories, including those that discuss the lives and relationships of the Jewish patriarchs and matriarchs in the book of Genesis. The sages wrote in the Talmud that a man should love his wife as he loves himself and honor her more.[19]

While it is true that parts of the Talmud seem to convey a negative view of women, these parts are offset by numerous expressions of high regard. In the Jewish world, women were not seen as second-class citizens, as they were in other ancient societies. The Torah view of women is, of course, quite different from the liberal/feminist view of women that has become characteristic of today's Western democratic countries. The principle that best describes Judaism's attitude toward men and women is "different but equal."[20]

Social Responsibility in Judaism

In Jewish law, giving to those who need help was not a matter of voluntary charity; it was a legal obligation. In Hebrew, "charity" is called *tzedakah*; it is based on the Hebrew word *tzedek*, meaning "fairness" or "justice."

The concept of the tithe—the donation of one-tenth of a person's earnings—originated in the Torah. Every Jew, no matter what their financial situation, was obligated to contribute to the welfare of the poor, the sick, the widows, the orphans, and whoever else was in need of assistance. This obligatory charity was not only extended to the Jewish community. According to Jewish law, Jews were socially responsible for non-Jews as well. And they were responsible not only for people, but for animals and for the environment, too. It's no exaggeration to say that the foundation of all the liberal and democratic principles we cherish may be found in the Torah.

Jewish Principles of Ethical Behaviour

Chapter 19 of the book of Leviticus provides a concise enumeration of Judaism's major principles of ethical behavior and social responsibility. These include the following prescriptions:

- You shall not deal deceitfully with one another.
- You shall not swear falsely.
- You shall not lie to one another.
- You shall not cheat your fellow.
- You shall not steal.
- You shall not rob.
- You shall not withhold a worker's wages.
- You shall not insult the deaf (meaning also that you should not inflict damage verbally).
- You shall not place a stumbling block before the blind (meaning also that you are prohibited from deceiving or tricking others, and from intentionally giving bad advice).
- You shall not take revenge.
- You shall not bear a grudge.
- You shall rise before the aged and show deference to the old.
- You shall love the stranger.

And that is by no means a complete list. For example, among the directives of social responsibility, we also find the injunction not to stand by while your neighbor is in trouble. In other words, when you see a human being in distress—physical or otherwise—you have a duty to help him or her. This principle seems commonplace enough today; part of a basic standard of decency. But it was unheard of in the ancient world.

There is ample evidence that, throughout history, Jews took social responsibility very seriously. Even during times of dire poverty and anti-Semitic segregation in

19th century Europe, Jewish charitable activities flourished. And the Jews brought this pattern of principled generosity with them when they began to emigrate to America in large numbers at the end of the 19th century.

The Impact of Judaism

Judaism's worldwide influence has been two-fold. The first source of influence is monotheism itself. The notion of a single, all-powerful God—a concept that originated with the ancient Israelites—was adopted by Christianity and Islam when they emerged as religions, millennia after Judaism. Christians and Muslims both owe their theological foundations to Judaism.

As well as giving monotheism to the world, Judaism contributed its ideology to Western civilization. The value system we now see as fundamental to a civilized society and to ethical social behavior originated in the Torah. In no ancient society other than the Jewish one were the following values seen as all-important: respect for human life; peace and harmony; justice and equality; education; the family; and social responsibility. What are the implications of all of this for world ideology today? Consider the following:

- Over one third of the world's population follows a religion that has its origins in Jewish theology.
- The political and legal systems of the entire Western world are built on the concept of *rule of law*. Judaism brought this principle into the world when it introduced the notion of a law-giver to whom all must subordinate themselves. One of the cornerstones of democratic ideology is that no-one is above the law.
- The legal concept of restitution—the belief that one human being must compensate another for damages caused, and that we are responsible for one another—had its origins in Jewish law and in Talmudic sources, which predate Western legal systems by millennia.

How is it that a belief system followed by less than 0.01 percent of the world's population has had such a huge influence on world relations and politics? For over two millennia—arguably, since the Babylonian exile—the history of the Jewish people has been far from insular. Owing to the diaspora, Jewish culture and ideas have been diffused through many of the world's societies over many centuries. That is part of the answer, but only a small part. How did the Jewish value system become the value system that most Western societies uphold today? The remaining chapters in this unit will address this question. First of all, however, we are going to look at Judaism's first major ideological challenge—the Hellenism of the ancient Greeks.

Endnotes

1   Ken Spiro, *WorldPerfect: The Jewish Impact on Civilization* (Florida: Simcha Press, 2002). This chapter is essentially a summary of the ideas presented by Rabbi Spiro in Parts 1 and 2 of *WorldPerfect*. Rabbi Spiro's ideas regarding how Jewish values made their way into Western democratic society are also the basis of my account in subsequent chapters.

2   Chrys C. Caragounis, "Hilarion's Letter to his Wife Alis (P Oxy 744): A New Suggestion to Solve Its Problem," accessed May 6, 2012, http://www.chrys-caragounis.com/Inscriptions.and.Papyri/Hilarion%20Letter.pdf.

3   Professor Paul Cartledge, "The Democratic Experiment," *BBC History*, http://www.bbc.co.uk/history/ancient/greeks/greekdemocracy_01.shtml (Last updated, February 17, 2011).

4   Spiro, *WorldPerfect*, 37.

5   Ibid, 67-68.

6   Thomas Cahill, *The Gifts of the Jews* (New York: Talese/Anchor, 1998), 3.

7   Paul Johnson, *A History of the Jews* (New York: Harper, 1988), 585.

8   *The Schottenstein Daf Yomi Edition, Talmud Bavli, Sanhedrin* 37a3. Chapter 4, Elucidated by Rabbi Abba Tzvi Naiman (Brooklyn: Mesorah Publications, 2005).

9   Isaiah 2:4.

10   Shimon Ben Gamliel, quoted in chap. 1, Mishna 12, of *The Pirkes Avos (Ethics of the Fathers) Treasury*, commentary by Rabbi Moshe Lieber (Brooklyn: Mesorah Publications, 1997), 54-55.

11   Rabbi Simon ben Chalafta, *Uktzin*, 3:12, quoted in *The Artscroll Tanach Series: Tehillim (Psalms)*, trans. and commentary Rabbi Avrohom Chaim Feuer, eds. Rabbis Nosson Sherman and Meir Zlotowitz (Brooklyn: Mesorah Publications, 1995), 355.

12   Hillel, quoted in chap. 1, Mishna 12 of *The Pirkes Avos (Ethics of the Fathers) Treasury*, commentary by Rabbi Moshe Lieber (Brooklyn: Mesorah Publications, 1997), 39.

13   Rav Yosef in chap. 5 of *The Schottenstein Daf Yomi Edition, Talmud Bavli, Gittin* 59b2, elucidated by Rabbi Yitzchok Isbee (Brooklyn: Mesorah Publications, 2005).

14   Ben Zoma, quoted in chap. 4, Mishna 1 of *The Pirkes Avos (Ethics of the Fathers) Treasury*, commentary by Rabbi Moshe Lieber (Brooklyn: Mesorah Publications, 1997), 211-212.

15   Spiro, *WorldPerfect*, 85.

16   Leviticus 19:15.

17   Spiro, *WorldPerfect*, 86.

18   Peter Abelard, *Commentary to Paul's Epistle to the Ephesians*, quoted in Spiro, WorldPerfect, 93.

19   *The Schottenstein Daf Yomi Edition, Talmud Bavli, Yevamot* 62b5, elucidated by Rabbi Avrohom Neuberger (Brooklyn: Mesorah Publications, 2005), chapter 6.

20   Spiro, *WorldPerfect*, 100.

Chapter 5
The Challenge of Hellenism

Introduction

This chapter focuses on the civilization whose ideology posed the most significant challenge to that of Judaism in the ancient world: classical Greece. The ancient Greeks were a sophisticated and powerful society that had a far-reaching influence on Western civilization, especially in the areas of culture and politics. With the rise of Alexander in the 4th century BCE, they came into contact with the ancient Israelites. The conflict that ensued had its basis in fundamental ideological differences: between Hellenism and Judaism; between Greek humanism and Jewish monotheism.

The Greek Empire

The origins of the Greeks as a people are uncertain. There is a general recognition, however, that the ancient inhabitants of mainland Greece developed an extraordinarily advanced culture. The history of ancient Greece in the 5th and 4th centuries BCE is one of constantly warring city-states, but there is an abundance of evidence that it was also a golden age in culture, politics, and philosophy. Democracy was practiced in Athens during this period, and it was the time of the great trio of philosophers: Socrates, Plato, and Aristotle. It was also the period of Alexander the Great (356–323 BCE).

The son of a Macedonian king, Alexander was educated by the great philosopher Aristotle. He came to power at the age of 20 and, after unifying Greece by force, set out to conquer the rest of the known world. The campaign he then embarked upon is still seen as one of the greatest feats in military history. He was undefeated in battle, and before his death at the age of 33, Alexander had conquered most of Asia, the Middle East, and parts of North Africa. He disassembled the entire Persian Empire and introduced Hellenism—the Greek world view and culture—to the regions he conquered.

The ancient Greeks of Alexander's era were history's first practitioners of cultural imperialism. In other words, they systematically imposed Greek civilization—Hellenism—on the peoples they conquered, which included the Egyptians, Assyrians, and Persians, as well as the Israelites.

Hellenism Meets Monotheism

During his military campaign against Persia in 312 BCE, Alexander's army went south to the region that is modern-day Israel, which was part of the Persian empire at that point. According to Jewish history, Alexander was planning to destroy the Temple, but—uncharacteristically—did not. His choice to absorb Israel and Jerusalem peacefully into the Greek empire was also unprecedented. Both the Talmud and the historian Flavius Josephus tell a legendary story of Alexander's first interaction with the Jews.[1]

According to both accounts, the Temple High Priest (in the Talmudic narrative, he is identified as Simon the Righteous, the last surviving member of the Men of the Great Assembly), fearing that Alexander would destroy the city of Jerusalem, went out to meet him before he arrived at the city gates. Upon seeing the High Priest, Alexander dismounted and bowed to him (the Josephus translation uses the term "adored"). This was very uncharacteristic; Alexander never bowed to anyone. Josephus tells us that when Alexander's general, Parmenio, asked him to explain his actions, he answered as follows:

> I did not adore him, but that God who has honored him with his High Priesthood, for I saw this very person in a dream, in this very [apparel]… [and he] exhorted me to make no delay, but to boldly pass over the sea there, for that he would conduct my army and would give me the dominion over the Persians.[2]

The story is that, because of his dream, Alexander spared Jerusalem and the Temple.

In the early stages of Greek colonization, the Greek authorities preserved the rights of the local Jewish population and didn't attempt to interfere with Jewish religious practice. The Jews continued to flourish as a separate and distinct entity within the Greek empire for approximately 165 years—a rare phenomenon in the Hellenistic world.[3] Over time, however, Judaism and its uncompromising principles of ethical monotheism began to stand out, which presented a challenge to Greek imperialism and the Hellenistic world view.

After Alexander's sudden death, there were rivalries and conflicts between his generals, which led to his empire's subdivision into four centers of power: the Ptolemaic Kingdom of Egypt in North Africa, the Seleucid Empire in the east, the Kingdom of Pergamon in Asia Minor, and Macedon on the Greek peninsula. The Seleucid Empire was named after Seleucis Nicator, the Greek general who ruled Babylonia and the large eastern part of Alexander's empire after Alexander's death. Israel was part of this domain.

In 169 BCE, the Seleucid emperor, Antiochus Epiphanes, decided that the weak link in his defenses against the Ptolemaic and Roman empires was Israel, because it was bordered by Egypt and the Mediterranean Sea. He was anxious to speed up the Hellenization of his territories and was less tolerant of Jewish religious and cultural independence than previous Seleucid rulers had been. He had allies in the reformist, Hellenized Jews of the region. These people saw Judaism in its traditional form as backward and provincial, and wanted to establish a more moderate, less exclusive form of the religion—one that incorporated Hellenistic principles. This attitude towards Judaism can be seen today in many Jewish communities in the Western world; even in Israel.

Forced Hellenization

Between 169 BCE and 167 BCE, Antiochus Epiphanes took steps to Hellenize the ancient Israelites and to destroy Judaism. The Books of Maccabees detail the persecutions the Jews faced during his reign.[4] In the midst of a quarrel over succession to the High Priesthood, one of the would-be successors—a Hellenized Jew named Menelaus—asked Antiochus for permission to build a Greek gymnasium in Jerusalem.[5] The gymnasium, a fixture in every Hellenized city in the Greek empire, was a facility where male athletes trained in the nude, and where people socialized and engaged in intellectual pursuits. Having a gymnasium so close to the Temple Mount was an outrage to traditional Jews.

Antiochus's measures for undermining Judaism became increasingly aggressive. They are recorded in Maccabees I and in Josephus's *Jewish Antiquities* and included the following:

1. He forbade the observance of the Sabbath, the New Moon, and the observance of the high holidays and festivals (for example, Passover).
2. He forbade keeping kosher. As is mentioned in 1 Maccabees 1:41-64, he forced the High Priest both to perform swine sacrifices in the Holy Temple in Jerusalem, and to permit the worship of Greek gods.
3. He forbade Torah study, even going so far as to have Torah scrolls publicly burned.
4. He forbade circumcision. To the Jews, circumcision is the physical, tangible sign of their Covenant with God. The Greeks, who worshipped the perfection of the human body, found it an abhorrent practice; they regarded it as mutilation.[6]

Things came to a head when a citizen of Jerusalem named Mattathias (whom Josephus referred to as "a person of great character") was commanded to offer a sacrifice on the orders of Antiochus. He refused. Mattathias had told his five sons (who would become known as the Maccabees) that it was better to die for their laws than to submit to a Hellenistic world view.

Religious persecution and martyrdom were virtually non-existent in the polytheistic ancient world, where people were not inclined to die for their religious beliefs. Polytheistic worshippers tended to be easygoing about the gods of other societies. They were happy to accept new gods into their pantheon or to practice *syncretism*—in other words, the practice of fusing overlapping gods into a single deity. The Jewish refusal to see things in this light seemed unreasonable to the ancient Greeks, and it provoked them.

The Jews maintained that certain things, such as ethical monotheism, were more meaningful than life itself and they were willing to die for this belief and to give up their lives for Judaism. They were willing to do this not because God needs people to die for Him, but because, according to Jewish ideology, humanity is doomed without monotheism and its guidebook, the Torah. The Jews—who, according to Torah, are supposed to be "the light unto the nations"—could not abandon their mission, not even when their lives were threatened.[7]

The Jewish Revolt Against the Seleucid Empire

When the Seleucids attacked Judaism, they were actively supported by a segment of Jewish society—namely, the Hellenized Jews. These Jews were attracted to Greek culture and embraced Hellenistic ideology. (You can see this pattern throughout Jewish history. Some Jewish people become attracted to the culture and ideology of the nations and societies in which they live, and they often do so at the expense of their Judaism.)

The corruption of the Temple and the forced Hellenization and persecution finally became too much for the Jews to bear. They revolted against Antiochus and against his Jewish collaborators. The conflict was as much a civil war within Jewish society as it was a war between Seleucids and Jews. Jews who were loyal to Judaism fought Jews who had become Hellenized and who now sided with the Seleucids.

The successful Jewish revolt against the Seleucid Empire was led by Judas Maccabeus (Judah the Maccabee).[8] The Jews drove the Seleucids out of Jerusalem and the surrounding areas, and they purged the Temple of the impure elements that Antiochus had introduced—a victory that Jews celebrate today during the Festival of Chanukah. The struggle between the Hellenists and the ancient Israelites continued for two more decades.

In 142 BCE, the wars between the Jews and Hellenists came to an end when Simon, the last survivor of the five sons of Mattathias, restored Jewish sovereignty over the Land of Israel and gave the people their freedom after 170 years of Seleucid dominion.[9]

The Jewish rebellion set a precedent in human history. It was not a war for national liberation, nor was it a struggle for physical freedom. It was a struggle of ideas, Hellenism versus Judaism: the world's first ideological/religious war. No one in the ancient world—before the Jews—thought their religion was worth dying for.

Hellenism and Judaism: An Ideological Struggle

What was it about Hellenism—the culture and civilization of ancient Greece—that clashed so strongly with the world view of the ancient Israelites? At the root of Hellenism was an idea that has been one of the most influential in human history: *humanism*. The humanism of the ancient Greeks asserts that the human being is the center of all things and that human reason is the ultimate source of truth, knowledge, and wisdom. Another significant feature of Hellenism was its universalist aims. Alexander's goal was to fuse together the diverse races of his empire using Hellenistic ideology. The idea was that being "Greek" would be a matter of culture and education rather than of ethnic background. The Hellenistic Jews, who sided with the Seleucids against the Maccabees, approved of Alexander's vision.

Judaism's vision of the world, while radically different from that of the Hellenists, also has a universalist element. In monotheistic ideology, there is only one God and other gods and their paths are false. That doesn't mean that, according to Jewish theology, everyone has to be Jewish. Judaism believes that one does not have to convert to Judaism to achieve spiritual heights. However, according to Judaism, only one God can be worshipped, end of story. The Jewish vision was of a world united by the belief in one God and in one absolute moral standard—including the values of respect for life, peace, justice, and social responsibility.

Jews and Hellenists differed ideologically in a number of fundamental respects. To the Jews, human beings were created in the image of God. To the Hellenists, gods were made in the image of human beings. To the Jews, the physical world was something to be perfected and elevated spiritually. To the Hellenists, the physical world was perfect. Such disparate views were bound to clash.

The ideological conflict between the ancient Hellenists and the ancient Israelites came down to their different approaches to morality. But how is that relevant to us today?

Hellenism and Judaism in the West Today

The ideologies of Hellenism and Judaism are still at odds today in Western society. To illustrate how, let's look at the following story from *Maclean's* magazine and at an excerpt from the book of a decorated professor of ethics. Both the story and the excerpt deal with euthanasia. We'll begin with the former.

In September of 2005, the cover of *Maclean's* magazine bore a picture of a newborn baby with the headline "Should this baby die?" The subheading read as follows: "In Holland, doctors routinely euthanize severely ill infants. The pros and cons of a wrenching debate that's headed our way."[10] In the article, health-care practitioners acknowledge that euthanasia is routinely practiced in North American facilities in the case of terminally ill and suffering infants. One of these practitioners said the following: "Of course it's not passive, because we are giving narcotic analgesics—so in fact we are killing. But it is professionally and ethically appropriate under these rare circumstances."[11]

Peter Singer, the Ira W. DeCamp Professor of Bioethics at the University Center for Human Values at Princeton University, writes about euthanasia in his book *Practical Ethics*. He presents the case of a hemophiliac infant whose parents are daunted by the challenge of raising a child with that condition:

> When the death of a disabled infant will lead to the birth of another infant with better prospects of a happy life, the total amount of happiness will be greater if the disabled infant is killed. The loss of happy life for the first

infant is outweighed by the gain of a happier life for the second. Therefore, if killing the hemophiliac infant has no adverse effect on others, it would, according to the total view, be right to kill him. ...[12]

It may still be objected that to replace either a fetus or a newborn infant is wrong because it suggests to disabled people living today that their lives are less worth living than the lives of people who are not disabled. Yet, it is surely flying in the face of reality to deny that, on average, this is so.[13]

Most people who have grown up with a Western sensibility take issue with Singer's view and also are quite shocked and disturbed by the findings presented in the *Maclean's* article. But why? The ideas expressed in the *Maclean's* article are distasteful to most Westerners today, but they are not irrational. Most of us acknowledge the value our society places on each individual's right to "quality of life" and his or her "right to choose." And we understand the rationale behind taking a human life when suffering and illness will compromise that life's "quality."

Singer's conclusions about the ethics of euthanizing a newborn infant would be a tough sell to many members of a modern democracy. Nonetheless, if we leave our emotions out of it, most of us would have to acknowledge the rationality both of Singer's arguments and of the decisions of the health-care practitioners discussed in the *Maclean's* article on euthanasia. In other words, we can probably understand both sides of the debate.

This unresolved conflict in Western societies today over the ethics of euthanasia reflects—is, indeed, a modern manifestation of—the ancient struggle between Hellenistic relativism and Jewish ethical monotheism. It is what one author has called the struggle between the ideologies of "Jerusalem and Athens."[14]

Jerusalem and Athens in Contemporary Western Ideology

Leo Strauss, author of *Jewish Philosophy and the Crisis of Modernity,* says that, to really understand Western ideology, we must recognize the presence of both ancient Greek and Jewish thought in our civilization:

Western civilization consists of two elements, has two roots, which are in radical disagreement with each other. We may call these elements, as I have done elsewhere, Jerusalem and Athens, or, to speak in non-metaphorical language, the Bible and Greek philosophy. ...[15]

Western man became what he is and is what he is through the coming together of biblical faith and Greek thought. In order to understand ourselves and to illuminate our trackless way into the future, we must understand Jerusalem and Athens.[16]

To understand the bases of Western ideology, we must try to understand the difference between Biblical wisdom and Greek wisdom. According to Strauss, their point of divergence centers on "that which completes morality." He calls the Biblical completion "piety." The Greek philosophers, on the other hand, transcend the whole dimension of piety and of pious obedience to a pregiven code. Instead they embark on a free quest for the beginnings, for the first things, for the principles. And they assume that on the basis of the knowledge of first principles, of the beginnings, it will be possible to determine what is by nature good.[17]

In other words, the Hellenistic quest for "beginnings" or "first principles" proceeds through reasoning and intellect. And the radical difference between the ancient Greek ideology of Hellenism and the Jewish ideology of ethical monotheism is that, in the latter case, there is no beginning made by an individual; ultimately, man does not begin.

According to the Bible, it's God who begins. Human wisdom begins with what God reveals. According to the ancient Greek philosophers, the beginning of human wisdom is reason. In the Jewish view, revelation—not reasoning—is the root of wisdom. Each of these two positions claims to be true wisdom and denies the other its claim to be wisdom in the highest sense. Regarding this conflict, Strauss says the following: "We are thus compelled from the beginning to make a choice, to take a stand. We are confronted with the incompatible claims of Jerusalem and Athens. Where then do we stand?"[18]

Jewish and Secular (Hellenistic) Ethics

When Strauss asks where we stand, he is asking which wisdom we are going to give authority to in the moral dimension of our lives. Each day, we make ethical decisions based on our sense of right and wrong. How we go about making such decisions depends on whether our allegiances are primarily to Jewish ethics or to secular philosophical ethics. The source of Jewish ethics is God and Torah, while the basis of secular ethics is primarily humanism and rational intellect.

Not that Judaism is opposed to rational thinking and logic. These hold a very high place in Jewish ethics and are an integral part of both the written and the oral law (the Bible and the Talmud). According to Jewish theology, God gave both the written and the oral law to Moses on Mount Sinai. They weren't, however, given as rote commandments that people were to follow blindly. Judaism does not believe in blind faith. There are numerous principles in Judaism that human beings are supposed to apply when confronted with an ethical dilemma. You apply them by using reason to arrive at the "right" answer, according to the situation that has arisen.

The commandments are categories rather than specific rules meant to cover every situation. They are a crib sheet, so to speak (or lecture notes). The real wisdom is supposed to come from studying the oral law and learning to apply it to specific situations. In Judaism, there is a sophisticated body of rabbinic literature to provide a training ground for the difficult ethical dilemmas and questions that come up in the course of a human life. This training has been practiced in Talmudic academies for millennia. Judaism recognizes that not everyone has the same capacity or time to study. This is where rabbis and scholars come in. They are supposed to be learned and righteous individuals who have the ability to adjudicate on matters too difficult for the general population to work out for themselves.

The basic differences between Jewish and secular (Hellenistic) ethics are well-illustrated in the area of medicine, where serious moral dilemmas frequently occur. In Judaism, the value of human life is supreme and nearly all Biblical laws can be waived in order to save a human life. In secular ethics, human life is just one of many values, and often quality of life is given greater weight. Even in Judaism, the value of human life is not absolute, and in certain rare and well-defined circumstances, other values can supersede it. But in Judaism, one must examine each situation according to its individual circumstances and respond according to the specific details and characteristics of that situation, taking into consideration the many rules and principles in the written and oral law. By contrast, Western secular ethics uses a limited number of ethical principles and applies them to all situations.

The true story below is a good illustration of how the many rules and principles of Jewish law can be applied with sophisticated reasoning to a difficult issue of life and death.

The Twins Case

The following account of the twins case has been adapted from an article by Donald C. Drake that appeared in the *Philadelphia Inquirer*.[19]

On September 15th, 1977, newborn twins were flown by helicopter to a community hospital in New Jersey. They were joined at the chest. Their vital signs were comparatively good. But when the cardiologist summoned from home late that night saw the twins' electrocardiogram (EKG) and listened to their chest with a stethoscope, he knew something was desperately wrong.

> One heartbeat. He could only hear one heartbeat and the EKG tracing suggested that there was only one heart. Special X-rays done the next day revealed that one of the twins, designated Baby Girl B, had an essentially normal four-chambered heart that was fused to the stunted two-chambered heart of her sister, Baby Girl A.[20]

The wall of heart tissue which connected the two twins was only one tenth of an inch thick—too thin to be divided so that each girl could get what belonged to her. And even if it was possible to divide them, Baby Girl A's stunted heart would not be able to support the child for long.

The doctors knew that they could not leave the babies as they were for long. They knew that if they didn't do something, both babies would die. Dr. C. Everett Koop, the hospital's Chief of Surgery and future Surgeon General of the United States, was brought in to examine the twins and determine the viability of surgically separating them. It would be a rare operation, one that few pediatric surgeons do even once. Dr. Koop had separated conjoined twins twice before, but neither case had involved a shared heart.

Dr. Koop, a deeply religious Christian, had spoken out nationally about the sanctity of human life. In a speech to the American Academy of Pediatrics entitled "The Slide to Auschwitz,"[21] Dr. Koop said the following: "Perhaps more than the law, I fear the attitude of our profession in sanctioning infanticide and in moving inexorably down the road from abortion to infanticide, to the destruction of a child who is socially embarrassing, to you-name-it."[22] It was hard for a man with Dr. Koop's world view to be faced with an operation that would certainly leave one child dead. But as soon as he had examined the twins, he knew what he had to do. He placed a call to the twins' father to arrange a meeting.

The twins had been born to an Orthodox Jewish family of rabbinical scholars, and their father was himself a rabbinical student. The young father decided he was unable to answer the question of what should be done on his own. So he consulted the rabbis in his community and the rabbis in his and his wife's families. Ultimately, Rabbi Moshe Feinstein, who for many years had served as the final arbiter in questions of Jewish law and ethics, was called to provide his opinion. Scholars throughout the world had sought his counsel in ethical dilemmas.

While the team of twenty or so professionals were awaiting Rabbi Feinstein's decision, and were expressing impatience at the lapse of time, Dr. Koop quieted the group with the following statement:

> The ethics and morals involved in this decision are too complex for me. I believe they are too complex for you as well. Therefore I referred it to an old rabbi on the Lower East Side of New York. He is a great scholar, a saintly individual. He knows how to answer such questions. When he tells me, I too will know.[23]

The unique characteristics of this specific case made it possible to choose one life over the other and to separate the babies. But the decision was preceded by a rigorous debate. Rabbi Feinstein and other scholarly rabbis, some of whom were also doctors, met into all hours of the night for several days discussing the various principles in Jewish law and how they should be applied to the twins' unique case. Their decision applied human reason to the existing body of laws, religious principles, and rabbinical discourse that were relevant to the matter at hand. This was why it took so long. Dr. Koop showed that he knew something about the intricacies of Jewish law when he observed that Rabbi Feinstein, through his lifelong study of Jewish law and through the development of his character, was best equipped to deal with a complicated ethical matter.

Contrast the twins' case with the cases we discussed earlier: the case of euthanasia featured in the *Maclean's* article, and the hemophilia case described in Singer's book. Professor Singer came to the conclusion that it is acceptable to euthanize a hemophiliac infant if the total happiness of the people involved would thereby be greater. This type of ethical reasoning in philosophy is called *utilitarianism*. This doctrine proposes that an action is right insofar as it promotes happiness or utility, and that the greatest happiness of the greatest number should be the guiding principle of conduct.

As we mentioned earlier, one major difference between Jewish and secular ethics is that Western secular ethics uses a limited number of ethical principles and applies them to all situations. This is what happened in the Singer example, where the ethical principle was utilitarianism. In the *Maclean's* example, the overriding principle was quality of life. Both are Hellenistic/humanistic in their approach: they are based on human reason and/or use one overarching principle to reach their conclusions.

In Judaism, by contrast, narrow applications like these are not the rule. For example, while Jewish law considers quality of life important, it generally does not accept euthanasia. According to Judaism, we do not own our lives. We are given free will to make decisions, but life itself belongs to God. Therefore, according to Judaism, only laws that come from the source of life itself—that is, God—can be used to make ethical decisions that involve life and death.

So, unlike the Hellenistic world view, Judaism does not believe that ethics begin with human reason. In Judaism, as we've seen, reason does have an important place, but it is not the starting point. Judaism believes that problems arise when human beings make human reason the "god." When we appeal only to human reason, ethical decisions become based solely on self- or political interest.

Which ought to be our authority, a system of ethics based on human reason or one based on revelation? That is the central question separating Hellenism from Judaism, and it is a question that challenges Western society today.

The Question of God

Whether monotheism or Hellenism/humanism ought to be the supreme guide is still a part of our public dialogue in the West. Best-selling books like *The God Delusion* continue to ignite debate concerning whether God exists. And in political campaigns, issues such as whether to legalize same-sex marriage or abortion still divide voters along monotheistic or humanistic lines. These are topics which candidates are expected to address during their campaigns.

Dr. Armand Nicholi Jr., a professor at Harvard University and author of *The Question of God*, explains why questions based on the monotheism–Hellenism opposition are still debated after all these years:

Whether we realize it or not, all of us possess a world view. A few years after birth, we all gradually formulate our philosophy of life. Most of us make one of two basic assumptions: we view the universe as a result of random events and life on this planet a matter of chance; or we assume an Intelligence beyond the universe who gives the universe order, and life meaning. Our world view informs our personal, social and political lives. It influences how we perceive ourselves, how we relate to others, how we adjust to adversity, and what we understand to be our purpose. Our world view helps determine our values, our ethics, and our capacity for happiness. It helps us to understand where we come from, our heritage, where we are, our identity; why we exist on this planet, our purpose; what drives us, our motivation; and where we are going, our destiny.[24]

Nicholi adds that both views have existed since the beginning of recorded history—that is, "the spiritual worldview, rooted primarily in ancient Israel, with its emphasis on moral truth and right conduct and its motto of 'Thus saith the Lord'; and the materialist or 'scientific' worldview, rooted in ancient Greece, with its emphasis on reason and acquisition of knowledge and its motto 'What Says Nature.'"[25] Nicholi goes on to say that all of us embrace some form of the two world views. If we accept materialism we may call ourselves atheists, agnostics or skeptics. There are likewise different expressions of the spiritual world view. Nicholi continues as follows.

> Are these world views merely philosophical speculations with no right or wrong answer? No. One of them begins with the basic premise that God does not exist, the other with the premise that He does. They are therefore mutually exclusive—if one is right the other must be wrong. Does it really make any difference to know which one is which?[26]

The famous author C.S. Lewis thought so. He writes the following of belief in God: "Here is a door behind which, according to some people, the secret of the universe is waiting for you. Either that's true or it isn't. ..."[27] If it is not true, as Lewis says, it is the "greatest fraud" ever perpetrated on the human race. "But if the spiritual worldview is true," as Nicholi says, "then all other truth fades in significance. Nothing has more profound and far reaching effects for our lives."[28]

The answer to the question whether God exists is both a personal and a societal one, and it affects many dimensions of our lives, including our politics.

Hellenism and Judaism in our Politics

In 2001, a professional football player named Pat Tillman walked away from a three-year $3.6 million contract to take an $18,000 per year position in the United States Armed Forces. From the minute he decided to enlist in the Army, Tillman refused interview requests and book and movie deals. What he did wasn't a publicity stunt. It wasn't a career move. Tillman ended up serving in a Special Forces unit in Afghanistan and was part of Operation Mountain Storm, a U.S. initiative against Taliban and al-Qaeda fighters who were regrouping along the border with Pakistan. In April 2004, Tillman's patrol was attacked and he was killed. He was 27 years old.[29] Pat Tillman risked his material and worldly possessions to fight for democracy, or rather for the rights and values it stands for.

Democracy is usually traced to the ancient Greeks and to Solon (c. 638–558 BCE), an Athenian statesman, lawmaker, and poet. Solon is often the person credited with laying the foundations for ancient Athenian democracy. But is the democracy that Tillman went to war for the same as ancient Athenian democracy—that is, the ancient democracy in which human rights depended on gender and "citizenship"?

Not according to Lord Rabbi Jonathan Sacks. According to Sacks,

We tend to associate democracy with human rights and vice versa. As if one inevitably led to the other. But there is no necessary connection between them at all. The fact that for us they grew together has to do with the specific history of the West and the way it combined these two different traditions.[30]

In the next chapter, we will look at how the two different traditions, ancient Greek democracy and Jewish ethical monotheism, evolved and—with the help of Christianity—became fused in Western liberal democracy.

Endnotes

1   The Talmudic story about Alexander the Great and the High Priest Simon the Righteous is found in Yoma 69a. See chap. 7 in *The Schottenstein Daf Yomi Edition, Talmud Bavli, Yoma*, 69a3-69a4, elucidated by Rabbi David Kamenetsky (Brooklyn: Mesorah Publications, 2005).

2   Josephus, book 11, *Jewish Antiquities*, in *The New Complete Works of Josephus*, trans. William Whitson (Grand Rapids, MI: Kregel, 1999), 384.

3   The time frame of 165 years was calculated from the beginning of Alexander's campaign in 334 BCE up to Antiochus's campaign against the Jews in 169 BCE. See Josephus, chap. 5:3, book 12, *Jewish Antiquities*, and endnote 2 in *New Complete Works*, 403, 405.

4   The Books of the Maccabees are held as canonical scripture by some Christian churches (including Catholic, Orthodox, and Coptic churches), but not by most Protestant groups. Such Protestants consider it to be an apocryphal book. In modern-day Judaism, the book is often of great historical interest, but has no official religious status.

5   For the full story of Menelaus's petition to build a gymnasium in Jerusalem, see Josephus, chap. 5:1, book 12, *Jewish Antiquities*, in *The New Complete Works*.

6   The measures imposed by Antiochus are recorded in 1 Maccabees 13:34-51.

7   Ken Spiro, *Crash Course in Jewish History* (Brooklyn, NY: Targum, 2010).

8   The story of Mattathias' refusal to submit to the wishes of Antiochus's generals is detailed in Josephus, chap. 6:2, book 12, *Jewish Antiquities*, in *New Complete Works*.

9   Simon's victories are recorded in chap. 6, book 12, *Jewish Antiquities*, in *New Complete Works*.

10   Danylo Hawaleshka, "We Are Killing," *Maclean's*, September 5, 2005, accessed March 16, 2012, http://www.macleans.ca/canada/national/article.jsp?content=20050905_111653_111653.

11   Ibid.

12   Peter Singer, "Taking Life: Humans" in *Practical Ethics,* 2nd ed. (New York: Cambridge, 1999), 186.

13   Ibid, 188.

14   Leo Strauss, *Jewish Philosophy and the Crisis of Modernity* (Albany: SUNY, 1997), 377.

15   Ibid, 104.

16   Ibid, 377.

17   Ibid, 118-119.

18   Ibid, 379-380.

19   Donald C. Drake, "The twins decision: One must die so one can live," *Philadelphia Inquirer,* Sunday, October 16, 1977, accessed March 16, 2012, http://profiles.nlm.nih.gov/ps/access/QQBBXZ.pdf.

20   Ibid.

21   Ibid.

22   Ibid.

23   Rav Moshe Feinstein zt"l, "'So One May Live'—Siamese Twins," trans. and annotated by Rabbi Moshe Dovid Tendler, *Jewish Law Articles*, accessed May 7, 2012, http://www.jlaw.com/Articles/rav-moshe.html.

24   Dr. Armand Nicholi, Jr., *The Question of God* (Chicago, Free Press, 2002), 7.

25   Ibid.

26   Ibid, 8.

27   C.S. Lewis, "Man or Rabbit," quoted in Nicholi, *The Question of God*, 9.

28   Ibid.

29   Sean Gregory et al., "Death of a Volunteer: One for the Team," *Time*, May 3, 2004, 26-28. Also http://www.time.com/time/magazine/article/0,9171,994061-1,00.html, accessed March 16, 2012.

30   Chief Rabbi Lord Jonathan Sacks, *Democracy or Rights*, YouTube, 2011, accessed March 6, 2012, http://www.youtube.com/watch?v=cldHAt0zXE0.

Chapter 6

Christianity and the Spread of Monotheism

Introduction

By the middle of the 2nd century BCE, Rome had conquered Greece militarily. But Rome didn't conquer the Greeks culturally. To the contrary, Rome itself was Hellenized. The Romans readily adopted the ancient Greeks' human-centered view of the world—their humanist ideology.

The collapse of the Roman Empire left a vacuum, and the Roman Church stepped into it. With its well-organized bureaucracy, modeled on that of the now-defunct Empire, the Church of Rome occupied a position of paramount importance in European feudal society.

Beginning in the late 5th century, in the Medieval period sometimes known as the "Dark Ages," the Roman Church became a great worldly power with much land and wealth. In the process, however, it compromised its basic Biblical principles of compassion, brotherhood, and the equality of mankind. The challenge to the Roman Church eventually came from within its own ranks, roughly one thousand years later, when the defiance of a monk named Martin Luther became a catalyst to the Christian Reformation.

This chapter traces the rise to power of the Church of Rome, from its beginnings in the Roman Empire through to its eventual reformation at the hands of Martin Luther and European leaders such as Henry VIII. It also explains how the value system of the Hebrew Bible entered Western ideology through the Christian Reformation, and it answers the question of how the Hellenized Romans, with their ideological hostility to Judaism, ultimately came to accept the Jewish idea of ethical monotheism.

The Roman Empire and the Jews

The Romans, like the Greeks, originally left the Jews to themselves. This didn't last, however. A series of Roman provocations which included oppressive taxation, confiscation of property, and stealing from the Temple treasury led to a major Jewish rebellion in 66 CE, known as the Great Revolt. Like the Hasmonean revolt against the Seleucids centuries earlier (see Chapter 5), it was rooted in the longstanding ideological tension between Judaism and Hellenism. In response to Roman provocations, the Jewish masses rioted and wiped out the small Roman garrison stationed in Jerusalem. But the early successes of the Jews did not last.

Rome sent its best general, Vespasian, and his son, Titus, to put down the revolt. The Jewish historian Flavius Josephus, a general in the Jewish army during this period, provides several accounts of the revolt and the subsequent war with the Romans in his *Wars of the Jews*.[1] He describes the massive campaign the Romans led against the Jews, which began in the north, in Galilee, and ended with the siege of Jerusalem. The final results were the deaths of several hundred thousand Jews and the destruction of Jerusalem and the Temple.

Modern archaeological excavations have enabled historians to uncover clues to the events surrounding the destruction and burning of Jerusalem. For example, the "Burnt House" is an excavated house from the Second Temple period. It is situated six metres below current street level in the Jewish Quarter of the Old City of Jerusalem, only steps away from the Western Wall—the site of the ancient Temple. The house was found under a layer of ashes and destruction, and is believed to have been set on fire during the Roman destruction of Jerusalem in 70 CE. This archaeological finding is significant because it corroborates events from Jewish history that Josephus describes. He writes the following, for example: "And now the Romans set fire to the extreme parts of the city, and burned them down, and entirely demolished its walls."[2]

Coins issued by the Roman governors of Judea, together with those issued by the Jewish rebels in 67–69 CE, were found in the house. No later currency was found there. This indicates that the house was burned down at the end of this time. Also found in the house was a round stone weight, 10 cm in diameter, bearing, in square Aramaic script, the Hebrew inscription "Bar Kathros" (son of Kathros). This indicates that the house belonged to the Kathros family.[3] According to the Talmud, the Kathros family was a priestly family. The Talmud describes them in Pesahim 57A, in a poem that lists the priestly families that abused their positions in the Temple.

As we've mentioned in previous chapters, the Roman triumph is memorialized on the triumphal Arch of Titus that still stands in Rome. Inscribed in stone on the inside of the arch are images of spoils being taken by the Romans. The spoils include a menorah, one of the sacred artifacts located inside the Temple before its destruction. After Titus destroyed the city and demolished the Temple, Rome introduced new laws forbidding Jews from entering the Holy City.

The Final Revolt

Only sixty years after the destruction of Jerusalem and the Temple, Judea was in a process of recovery, but it would not last long. The Roman emperor at the time was Hadrian, whose reign (117–138 CE) was marked by strained relations with the Parthian kingdom to the east. Like Antiochus Epiphanes, Hadrian believed that all the inhabitants of his empire, especially those in Rome's eastern territories, should adopt a single culture and form of worship—Roman Hellenism. Only such uniformity of thought, he felt, would guarantee protection from the expansion of the Parthian kingdom into Roman territories. Historian Meir Ben-Dov writes the following about Hadrian's concerns: "Hadrian feared that the existence of different ideologies and nations, each aspiring to its own, distinctive, national identity, would arouse Parthian hopes that the conquered people would rise against Rome."[4]

Like his predecessor Antiochus, Hadrian attempted to impose Roman culture on the Jews. His harsh decrees included a ban on Jewish education, on the ordination of rabbis, and on circumcision. Like their ancestors the Hasmoneans, the Judeans of the 2nd century resisted Rome's attempts to forcibly convert them. A powerful conflict was thus ignited, which culminated in an open revolt.

The immediate stimulus for the revolt was Hadrian's order that a temple to Jupiter be built on the ruins of the destroyed Jewish Temple. This time, it was Simeon Bar Kochba who hoisted the banner of rebellion (132–135 CE). Bar Kochba was supported by the famous Talmudic sage, Rabbi Akiva. Like the previous revolt, the Bar Kochba revolt was initially successful because Rome was dealing with various other trouble spots throughout their empire. After their initial victories over the Romans, the Judean rebels established an independent state and even minted coins.

Hadrian then proceeded to send one of his greatest generals, Julius Severus, to put down the rebellion. A fierce two-year struggle followed. The Romans' superior numbers and systematic methods wiped out one Jewish stronghold after another in Judea and the Galilee. The Roman vengeance that followed was severe. Many Jews that survived the massacres were sold into slavery.

Hadrian also sought to obliterate all traces of Jerusalem as a Jewish city. All the structures and ruins remaining from the Great Revolt of the previous century were razed to the ground. Hadrian then built a new pagan city on the site of Jerusalem, named it Aelia Capitolina, and forbade Jews to live there. The name was a combination of "Aelius," which was the name of Hadrian's family, and "Capitolinus," the name of his favorite deity. Hadrian also renamed the whole region—formerly Judea—Syria Palestina, a name that was later adopted by the British when they called the region Palestine. The name Palestine was chosen by Hadrian because it was associated with the Philistines, the ancient enemies of the Jews.[5] Hadrian's goal was to eradicate the name and memory of any Jewish heritage from the region, and what better way to do so than to rename the territory after the Jews' former enemies?

In the years following the revolt, Hadrian made anti-religious decrees forbidding Torah study, Sabbath observance, circumcision, Jewish courts, meeting in synagogues, and other ritual practices. This period of persecution lasted throughout the remainder of Hadrian's reign, until 138 C.E. The Talmud records the martyrdom of the famous sage Rabbi Akiva, executed for ignoring Hadrian's decrees and teaching Torah.[6]

The ancient Jews' relations with the Romans were as tense and unstable as their relations with the ancient Greeks had been. The basis of the tension was the same in both cases: Roman/Hellenistic ideology and Judaism were incompatible.

So, how is it that, within two centuries, the Romans came to adopt the very monotheism they had previously rejected and sought to stamp out? The answer lies in the story of how Christianity grew from a relatively insignificant and persecuted ideology to become the major religion of the West. This story is also the key to understanding the development of Western democratic ideology.

The Origins of Christianity

It is generally believed that Jesus was born around the year 4 BCE, during the reign of the Roman Emperor Augustus (Octavius). He is thought to have been born near Jerusalem, in Bethlehem (*Beit Lechem* in Hebrew). The name "Jesus" is the English translation of the Greek name *Iêsous* (*Yeshu* in Hebrew), derived from the Hebrew word *Yeshu'a,* meaning "salvation." In Christian theology, Jesus delivers Christians from sin and brings them salvation.

The facts about Jesus' early life are uncertain, but there is general agreement that he was a Jew who was familiar with the Torah, observed the Law of Moses, and taught many of its precepts, though he departed from others. The New Testament, particularly the Gospels, recounts the events of Jesus' life. These events—the Last Supper, his arrest, trial, Crucifixion, burial, and resurrection—took place in Israel and, in particular, in the Old City of Jerusalem, according to Christian theology.[7]

It was Paul, formerly Saul of Tarsus (a city in Asia Minor, now in Turkey), who transformed and popularized Christianity. He did so by retaining the basic value system of Judaism and the connection to the Bible, while getting rid of the elements that non-Jews had always found most objectionable, such as circumcision and the obligations of the Mosaic Law. Paul, who was a Jew, never physically met Jesus, but he is responsible for having carried the message of Christianity to Rome and to various parts of the Empire (circa 47–60 CE). Largely through his efforts, Christianity underwent tremendous growth through the 1st and 2nd centuries CE.

Paul gained converts to Christianity when he offered them a New Covenant and claimed that it had replaced the original Jewish Covenant as the means of achieving grace and salvation. According to this New Covenant, being Jewish wasn't necessary and ethnic categories were irrelevant; a person became eligible for salvation solely through their belief in Jesus. With the new Christian message, Paul made Judaism more appealing to the masses, and by doing so he promoted its spread.[8]

By the year 64 CE, some two years after the death of Paul, Christianity had become so widespread in Rome that it was seen as a threat and was outlawed by the Roman emperors Nero (54–68) and Domitian (81–96).[9] Christianity could have ended there. Instead, something remarkable happened in 312 CE that led to the establishment of Christianity as the official state religion of the Roman Empire.

Constantine I and the Christianization of the Roman Empire

Many historians associate the Roman Empire's conversion to Christianity and the transformation of the Roman province of Palestine into a Christian Holy Land with a single individual—Constantine I, who was the Emperor from 306 to 337 CE. It's unclear whether Constantine's conversion arose from a true shift of beliefs or from a desire for power and stability in a time of crisis, or from both. The first direct references to his conversion come from the surviving writings of Lactantius and Eusebius, both early Christian writers who lived during Constantine's time.[10] Their accounts vary slightly, but both agree that Constantine's conversion was owing to a dream in which he was visited by the Christian God.

Regarding Constantine's motivations for converting to Christianity, one historian has written as follows:

> Adept at regarding the political map of the world, Constantine understood that the principal danger to Rome's existence lay in the east. Like his predecessors, he realized that a uniform culture, based on religion, would be a unifying force and ensure continuity of Roman rule... Realizing that he could not eradicate Christianity, he pursued his goal of making religion and culture uniform in the empire by first permitting the practice of the new faith and subsequently proclaiming it the empire's principal religion... the Roman Empire, at that point in time in a state of decline, was granted another three hundred years of rule in the east—the period known in the history of the Middle East as the Byzantine period.[11]

Following his conversion in 313, Constantine, together with joint Emperor Licinius, ended all persecution against the Christians by issuing the Edict of Milan, also known as the Edict of Toleration. In this letter, the two Emperors declared Christianity entirely legal throughout the Empire, and also ordered all confiscated possessions of persecuted Christians to be returned.

Nearly a decade after legalizing Christianity, Constantine moved the capital of the Roman empire from Rome to Byzantium and changed the city's name to Constantinople—the "City of Constantine." This shift marked the beginning of a new culture, which was a blend of three elements:

- Roman culture
- Eastern civilization
- the new religion of Christianity.

The Roman Empire's conversion to Christianity under Constantine changed the entire region ideologically. The Council of Nicea in 325 resulted in the first uniform Christian doctrine and significantly more unity in the Roman Church. Constantine likely had political reasons for wanting a unified church. Whatever his motives, this unification contributed greatly to the spread of the faith.

What Constantine's reign did to establish Christianity is indisputable. And his conversion had a significant impact on Palestine. In 326, his mother Empress Helena, a fervent Christian, visited Jerusalem. During her visit, she tried to locate Christianity's sacred sites—for example, the sites of Jesus' crucifixion and burial. As a result of her visit, several new structures were built in Jerusalem with Constantine's support, the most important being the Church of the Holy Sepulcher. According to Christian theology, this is where Jesus was crucified, where he was buried, and where he will be resurrected. The name of the Holy City was also changed from Aelia Capitolina back to Jerusalem.

By the late 4th century, under Constantine's successors, Christianity had become the state religion, according to the principle of *cujus regio ejus religio* (in other words, the religion of the ruler is the religion of the state).[12] Christianity was well on its way to becoming a mass religion.

The Ideology of the Christianized Roman Empire

Rome might have been able to switch from a polytheistic worldview to Christianity, but changing its value system was not so simple. Constantine, the man who did more than anyone—including Jesus and Paul—to promote the growth of Christianity, was a ruthless ruler. Paul Johnson writes that he had no respect for human life, as evidenced by the way he treated prisoners of war; by the massacres he carried out in North Africa; and by the executions of, among many others, his eldest son, his second wife, and his favorite sister's husband. Though he was originally tolerant of non-Christian faiths such as paganism, he eventually turned against them.[13]

By the late 4th century CE, official government efforts had largely succeeded in imposing Christianity on most of the Empire. And once paganism had been eradicated, Judaism became a target. Why? Judaism did not accept that Jesus was the Messiah and did not recognize Christianity's New Covenant.

Christianity became the state religion of the Roman Empire, but the Biblical ideas that had originated in Judaism and formed the foundation of the new religion—the ideas of love thy neighbor, peace and harmony, and justice for all—went missing in the process. Monotheism had prevailed, but the values of ethical monotheism had not. They were lost amid the internal power struggles of the Roman Empire.

Medieval Society and the Church

In the 5th century CE, the Western Roman Empire collapsed, overrun by the Goths and the Franks. As the ancient infrastructure of Roman society—economic, administrative, and legal—gave way to chaos, the Church of Rome became the only remaining source of order in the West.

The Goths came first, sacking Rome in 410 and conquering most of Rome's western territories. The Franks came in the next century, conquering Rome's northern territories and eventually overwhelming the Goths as well.

The Franks had been converted to Christianity in the 5th century, and they were not hostile to the Roman Church. So when Pope Stephen II (715–757) found Rome threatened by another Germanic tribe, the Lombards, he made an alliance with the Frankish king, Pepin the Younger. This alliance benefitted both sides. In return for land and security, the Pope gave the Franks legitimacy and special authority within Christian Europe.

Pepin's successor as king of the Franks was Charles the Great, better known as Charlemagne (742–814), whose successful military conquest of the Saxons, Italians, Bavarians, and Slavs did much to spread Christianity across Medieval Europe.

Charlemagne's aggressive evangelism pleased the Medieval Church authorities, and in 800 CE, the Pope crowned him "Emperor of Europe."

Charlemagne's military success also helped feudalism to become Medieval Europe's main political system. How? The Frankish war effort came to depend heavily on its cavalry. To maintain the large numbers of horses needed for this, the kings took to giving their soldiers generous estates of land, which peasant laborers would farm for them in return for bare subsistence. This system wasn't entirely new. Other imperial civilizations, such as the Greeks and the Romans, had pensioned off their soldiers by similar means. But the system was refined into its medieval form under the Franks.

Medieval feudalism worked in the following way. All the land belonged to the king. The king bestowed portions of it (fiefs) on his most significant subordinates— the lords—in return for their loyalty and military service. The lords conferred land, in turn, on those who protected them and supported them militarily: the knights and vassals. The lords were also responsible for bestowing titles on church administrators and for apportioning land to the Church. At the very bottom of the social scale were the peasants and serfs, who, in return for a bare subsistence, worked the land on behalf of the land-holder. They were virtually slaves.

It was an unjust system, far from the egalitarian ideal of ethical monotheism and modern liberal democracy. But the Medieval Church had no interest in changing things. It was now the largest landowner in Europe and a thoroughly worldly institution, and its main concern was to maintain its wealth and power. It taxed the peasants and had no motivation to improve their lot. To justify the unjust society, the Medieval Church came up with certain principles.

One of these principles was the divine right of kings—that is, the idea that the king was ordained by God and therefore unquestionable in his authority.[14] A corollary of this principle was that the whole social order was divinely ordained and beyond question. Another principle was that social inequality was God's punishment for the sinful nature of man. The vast majority of people were poor peasants and the Medieval Church taught them that God wanted things the way they were and that the people on the bottom should simply accept their state.

The Medieval Church and the Suppression of Learning

The Medieval Church supported a social and economic structure that was completely at odds with the Biblical principles of brotherhood and equality. Had it returned to the moral precepts of its Jewish and Christian origins, the Church would have had to give up much of its worldly power. It was in the institution's best interest to keep the masses in the dark about the value system of ethical monotheism—especially the idea that all human beings are created in the image of God and are equal. Ironically enough, widespread knowledge of the Bible would have hurt the Medieval Church. For this reason, the Church authorities preferred that most people not be literate and that knowledge of the Bible be severely restricted. Even priests had limited access to the Bible.

The Medieval Church forbade translating the Bible from Latin into modern languages, because this would have made it too accessible. Those who disobeyed this law were burned at the stake. By keeping people ignorant about the true ideology of ethical monotheism, the Medieval Church was able to continue enlarging its power and wealth. As it did so, it strayed further and further from its original ideals. In Rome, the center of the Medieval Church's empire, the situation grew ever more scandalous, with fortunes spent on armies and lavish buildings, and Church leaders plotting against each other.[15]

The Medieval Church and the Jews

At the beginning of the Dark Ages, Jews living in Christian countries were subject to oppressive measures, barred from state office, military service, and most professions, and forbidden on pain of death from intermarrying with non-Jews.[16]

Early in the 11th century, with the launching of the first Christian Crusades to the Holy Land, things got considerably worse for Jews living in Western Europe. Throughout Medieval Europe, violent attacks erupted against the Jewish population. In a strange twist of history, however, the esteem for Judaism and for the Biblical values it preached was about to increase dramatically in parts of the Christian world.

The Reformation and the Influx of Jewish Ethical Ideas

The Medieval Church was a powerful institution, wealthier than any state government. In achieving this wealth and preeminence, however, it had compromised the founding precepts of its faith. These precepts, derived from Judaism, were essentially anti-hierarchical and democratic; they taught the equality of all human beings and the value of every life, however humble. The feudal order the Medieval Church upheld was built on opposite principles. It was an oppressive system based on inequality. The Church authorities did what they could to maintain this system, which served them very well, and for centuries they were successful. The challenge, when it came, arose not from outside the Roman Church, but from within it.

The Reformation of the Medieval Church came about in various stages, and the Bible was central to this process. Keeping Scripture and its egalitarian teachings out of the hands of common people was one way the Medieval Church had always maintained control. For this reason, translations of the Bible were strictly forbidden. In the 14th century, this prohibition began to be challenged, and "illegal" translations began to appear. In England, an Oxford scholar named John Wycliffe translated the Bible into English. He was persecuted for this and dismissed from his position, but his defiance reflected a growing trend. The preface to Wycliffe's Bible read as follows: "The Bible is for the government of the people, by the people and for the people."[17]

Martin Luther and the Reformation

The most important single actor in the Protestant Reformation was a man named Martin Luther. Born in Germany to a wealthy family, he defied his father's wish that he study law. Instead, he chose a career in the Roman Church and became an Augustinian friar. As a young man, travelling to Rome to consult with ecclesiastical authorities, he became extremely disillusioned by the clerical abuses he witnessed and returned to Germany in a state of spiritual crisis.

Luther took exception to certain practices of the Roman Church, such as the sale of indulgences. This was essentially a fundraising strategy whereby the Church authorities offered to forgive people on God's behalf for their sins—in return for money or services. Luther instead preached that forgiveness comes to sinners through God's grace, not through their purchasing pardons from the Church. Given the climate of the time, this was a revolutionary and dangerous idea. Luther's next step, on October 31, 1517, was to post his "Ninety-Five Theses" on the door of the Castle Church of Wittenberg.[18] This was his protest against various clerical abuses of the time, especially the sale of indulgences. The Church authorities asked him to recant and he refused. Four years later, he was excommunicated. This was the catalyst for the Protestant Reformation.

Luther's successful defiance and the whole Protestant Reformation succeeded largely because of the printing press, invented some seventy-five years earlier (around 1440) by Johann Gutenberg. Before its invention, no written document could be reproduced except by hand, slowly and laboriously. With a printing press, multiple copies of a document could be printed in minutes. Luther's written protest spread far and wide, and soon became a public controversy. The Roman Church could not contain it.

Luther defied the Church authorities and furthered the Reformation in another way, again assisted by the printing press. Despite the Roman Church's ban on translating the Bible, Luther translated the Old Testament from the original Hebrew into German, and the New Testament from Greek into German. Thus, the Bible came at last into the hands of the general public, who were able to see for themselves what it said and to measure Medieval Church policies against Biblical moral principles.

Luther and the Jews

The Jews of Europe initially welcomed the Reformation, which brought a revival of interest in Hebrew studies in general, and in the Old Testament in particular. Reformers like Luther were, to begin with, well-disposed to the Jewish people. These good relations did not last, however. Luther's expectation that the Jews, if treated better, would voluntarily convert to Christianity was mistaken. Instead, the Jews invited him to convert to Judaism. In his disappointment, Luther wrote a viciously hostile pamphlet, "On the Jews and Their Lies," that Christian historian Paul Johnson has described as the first work of modern anti-Semitism and a giant step forward on the road to the Holocaust:

> 'First,' he [Luther] urged, 'their synagogues should be set on fire and whatever is left should be buried in dirt so that no one may ever be able to see a stone or cinder of it.' Jewish prayer books should be destroyed and rabbis forbidden to preach. Then the Jewish people should be dealt with, their homes 'smashed and destroyed' and their inmates 'put under one roof or in a stable like gypsies, to teach them they are not master in our land.' Jews should be banned from public places, their property seized, drafted into forced labor and finally kicked out 'for all time.'[19]

Though Luther turned violently against the Jews, his association with Jewish ideology was—with respect to the evolution of Western ideology—fruitful. His brave stand against the Roman Church and his translation of the Bible were crucial to the Protestant Reformation and to the deeper process the Reformation eventually brought about—namely, bringing Biblical values into the mind of Europe. Before the Reformation was complete, however, one more step was necessary.

The Reformation in England

The next important event in the Protestant Reformation occurred in England. It involved the English king, Henry VIII. Throughout Medieval Europe, there was tension between the Roman Church and the ruling monarchs of various states. It was a struggle for power and wealth. The monarchs often felt undermined by the Church Establishment, which, in addition to its great influence over the people, competed for their wealth. Many Medieval rulers, Henry VIII among them, longed to be rid of the Roman Church. Eventually he found a pretext. Henry wanted to annul his marriage to his first wife, Catherine of Aragon, so that he could marry Anne Boleyn, but the Church leadership would not allow it. So Henry took matters into his own hands; he had himself declared head of the Church of England and moved on to his new wife. The English people supported him, and so did the English nobles—in return for gifts of Church land.

Henry's next measure was crucial to the Reformation and crucial, in the long run, to the evolution of Western ideology. A few years before, when the Roman Church still held sway in England, the Bible had been translated into English by a man named William Tyndale, who was burned at the stake for his efforts. Now Henry issued a proclamation requiring that a Bible be placed in every church. Within a few decades, the Bible was read aloud, in English, as a part of public worship, and many people had their own copies, which they read in their homes. As a result, the English people became familiar with the Bible's value system.

Henry VIII had thrown off the yoke of the Roman Church, and other European monarchs soon followed suit, as the Reformation spread through the West.

The Renaissance and the Philosophy of Renaissance Humanism

Two other factors contributed to the diffusion of ethical monotheism through Western ideology: the Renaissance and the new type of humanism that accompanied it—Renaissance humanism. The Renaissance was, broadly speaking, a period of history that spanned roughly the 15th to the 17th centuries. During this time, Europe emerged from the social and intellectual oppressions of the Middle Ages. We also use the term Renaissance in reference to the cultural movement of this period that encompassed a revival of classical learning, new directions in art, and a fresh premium on intellectual curiosity. Renaissance humanism involved a new confidence in the intellect of man to discover truths about the world, and a corresponding mistrust of the old authorities, among them the Medieval Church. This change in the intellectual climate, in combination with the Reformation, terminally weakened the old Church's hold over the European mind.

European society changed in other ways during the Renaissance. The growth of cities in this period eroded the old feudal system, which depended on a rural population to work the land. A system of city-centered leadership and bureaucracy developed, challenging the rural-based bureaucracies of the Medieval Church. A new middle class emerged, literate, primarily Protestant, and mistrustful of the old authorities, both cultural and religious. These middle class people, steeped in the values and concepts of Scripture, would shape the world to come.[20]

The Road to Democracy

The most important thing about the Renaissance, for our purposes, is that it was the period in which Protestant reformers convinced many people in Europe—in England's case, the majority of people—that the Bible, not the Medieval Church, reflected Christianity's true values. These reformers promoted Bible reading and Bible study. Barbara Tuchman describes the significance of this in *The Bible and the Sword*:

> With the translation of the Bible into English and its adaptation as the highest authority for an autonomous English Church, the history, traditions and moral code of the Hebrew nation became part of the English culture; became for a period of three centuries the most powerful single influence on that culture.[21]

The goal of these reformers was to return Christianity to its pure roots, which they located not in Rome, but in Israel. So it came about that one of the primary tasks of Reformation Bible study was understanding the Jewish roots of Christianity. Study of the Hebrew Bible became a fundamental component of Protestantism.

As the Renaissance progressed and gave way to the Modern era, the Bible became immensely influential, not only in England, but in all of Europe—especially in those countries touched by the Reformation. The impact was felt in all areas of life, political, social, and religious. Ken Spiro has described this impact as follows:

> The idea, adopted by the Protestants, of using the Bible not only as a religious guidebook, but also as the blueprint for society and government, played a very significant role in the political and social evolution of Western society.[22]

Thus the popularization of the Bible created another major step forward in the transmission of Old Testament ideas into Western consciousness. These ideas would take hold in the modern democracies soon to take shape.

Endnotes

1   For a detailed history of the relationship between the Romans and the Jews, including the major revolts of the first and second century of the CE and the destruction of the Second Temple, see Josephus, *The Jewish War*, in *The New Complete Works of Josephus*, trans. William Whitson (Grand Rapids, MI: Kregel, 1999). Josephus also writes about the early relationship between the Jews and the Romans in books 14-20, *Jewish Antiquities*, in *New Complete Works*. Vespasian's campaign against the Jews, which was concluded by his son Titus, is detailed in Josephus, books 3-7, *The Jewish War*, in *New Complete Works*.

2   Josephus, chap. 9:4, book 6, *The Jewish War*, in *New Complete Works*, 906.

3   Regarding the The Burnt House and the Bar Kathros family, the Babylonian Talmud, Pesachim 57a says the following: "Woe is me because of the House of Kathros, woe is me because of their pens. ... For they are the High Priests, and their sons are treasurers, and their sons-in law are trustees, and their servants beat the people with staves." Images of the Burnt House and the artifacts in the museum can be seen at "Burnt House," *BibleWalks.com*, http://www.biblewalks.com/Sites/BurntHouse.html (accessed May 7, 2012).

4   Meir Ben-Dov, *Historical Atlas of Jerusalem* (New York: Continuum, 2002),143.

5   Regarding the origins and meaning of the term "Palestine" and its association with the ancient Philistines, see Sir Harry Luke and Edward Keith-Roach, eds., *The Handbook for Palestine* (London: MacMillan and Co., 1922), 5; and Howard Grief, *The Legal Foundation and Borders of Israel under International Law* (Jerusalem: Mazo, 2008), 484.

6   The Babylonian Talmud *Berachos 61b* records Rabbi Akiva's torture and death at the hands of the Romans.

7   The four Gospels of the New Testament—Matthew, Mark, Luke, and John—give an account of the life, teaching, and death of Jesus.

8   For a history of the life of Jesus, see Paul Johnson, *A History of Christianity: The Rise and Rescue of the Jesus Sect (50 BC to 250 AD)* (Riverside: Simon and Schuster, 1976).

9   "The Basics of Christian History," BBC online, last modified June 8, 2008, http://www.bbc.co.uk/religion/religions/christianity/history/history_1.shtml.

10   Eusebius (c. 264–340), bishop and church historian. His Ecclesiastical History is the principal source for the history of Christianity (esp. in the Eastern Church) from the age of the Apostles to 324 CE. Lucius Caecilius Firmianus Lactantius (c. 240–320) was an early Christian author who became an advisor to the first Christian Roman emperor, Constantine I, guiding his religious policy and tutoring his son. For more on Constantine's "conversion" and excerpts from the writings of Lactantius and Eusebius, see Jack Percival, "On the question of Constantine's conversion to Christianity," *Clio: The Journal of the ACT HTA*, 2008, http://cliojournal.wikispaces.com/On+the+Question+of+Constantine%27s+Conversion+to+Christianity.

11   Ben-Dov, *Historical Atlas*,148-149.

12   Jacques Paul Gauthier, *Sovereignty Over the Old City of Jerusalem: A Study of the Historical, Religious, Political and Legal Aspects of the Question of the Old City*, Thèse No. 725 (Geneva: Université de Genève, 2007), 186.

13   For further reading on Constantine, the early rise of Christianity, and the decline in toleration for other faiths under his rule, see Johnson, *History of Christianity*, 67-76.

14   Regarding the Christian origins of the divine right of kings, the Emperor Constantine was represented as God's vicar and representative on earth, as is shown by a seal that shows him being crowned by the hand of God. His empire was thus a reflection of the kingdom of God, and he the interpreter of God's word and charged with the mission of preparing his subjects for God's kingdom by proclaiming God's laws to all men. See John McManners, ed., *The Oxford Illustrated History of Christianity*

(Oxford: Oxford UP, 1990), 71.

15   For a good synopsis of the Church in Medieval society, the allegations of corruption, and the connection to the rise of feudalism, see Ken Spiro, *WorldPerfect: The Jewish Impact on Civilization* (Deerfield Beach: Simcha Press, 2002), 206-209.

16   For more on the conditions of the Jews under the early Church, see Paul Johnson, *A History of the Jews* (New York: Harper, 1987), 165.

17   Spiro, *WorldPerfect*, 214-215.

18   The full text and background of Luther's *Ninety-Five Theses* can be found at a number of online sites, including "Luther's 95 Theses in Latin and English," *ConradAskland.com*, accessed March 3, 2012, http://www.conradaskland.com/blog/2008/11/martin-luthers-95-theses-in-latin-and-english/.

19   Regarding Martin Luther's relationship with the Jews, see Paul Johnson, *History of the Jews*, 241-242.

20   For an excellent and detailed synopsis of the role that the Reformation and the Renaissance played in the evolution of Western democratic ideology and in the introduction of biblical values into the mainstream, see Spiro, *WorldPerfect*, 221-228.

21   Barbara Tuchman, *The Bible and the Sword* (New York: Ballantine, 1984), 80. On the same page are details of King Henry VIII's proclamation ordering that a Bible be placed in every church where parishioners could read it.

22   Spiro, *WorldPerfect*, 228.

Chapter 7

Democracy and the Rise of Biblical Values in the West

Introduction

In the last chapter, we saw how the Protestant Reformation, sparked by Luther in Germany, eventually brought familiarity with the Bible to the common people in Europe. This development had significant ideological consequences. The values and ideals enshrined in the Bible began to diffuse through the ideologies of Western countries, which led in turn to historic social change. The system of feudalism, founded on a theory of divinely sanctioned inequality that had gone unchallenged for a thousand years, became vulnerable. New ways of thinking moved to the fore. The people driving this process, especially in England, were the Puritans. This chapter looks at the process by which the English Puritans absorbed Old Testament values through their devotion to the Bible, and at the momentous events that followed from this—the Civil War in England, and the export of those values and democratic principles to the New World.

The Puritans and the English Revolution

When King Henry VIII died in 1547, his son Edward VI ascended to the throne. During his brief reign, Edward did much to further the Reformation initiated by his father. Unfortunately for the Protestant cause, he was succeeded by Henry's daughter Mary, who tried to return England to the authority of the Roman Church. Religious persecution marked her reign (1553–1558) during which Protestants were burned at the stake.

Mary's sister and successor Elizabeth I reinstated the Church of England. Some Protestants, however, found this new church too much like the old Roman one and wanted a more radical departure. These were the Puritans.

That the ethical values of the Bible became, in time, the values of the Western world is due, in no small part, to Puritan influence. The Puritans took the Bible—especially the Old Testament—as their main authority in matters that went beyond religion and into politics. The Puritans were at the forefront of a post-Reformation process that has been described as follows:

> In the wake of the reformation, independent thinkers turned their attention to the legislative and social organization of ancient Israel and also came to appreciate the Biblical concept of justice and morality as expounded by the Rabbis after the time of Jesus. The "Old" Testament thus became the model for the concepts and ideals of a world feeling its way toward democratic government.[1]

Religiously and politically, the Puritans refused to accept the intervention of any worldly power between themselves and God. They believed the Bible's authority superseded that of any earthly or temporal authority, and they were committed to the ideal of a just society under God, organized in conformity with God's commandments as established in the Bible. This ideal soon brought them into conflict with the established government of England.

The 17th-century English Revolution (1642–1651)—also known as the Puritan Revolution—centered on whether England was to be governed by a parliament or by a king whose authority was based on the old claim of divine right. It was a conflict between the old feudal order, represented by Charles I, and a new, proto-democratic order, represented by the Puritans. The civil war lasted eight years, with the Puritans prevailing in the end. Charles I was tried and beheaded in 1648, and for the next decade (1649–1659) the Puritans ruled England under Oliver Cromwell, who was named Lord Protector of the Commonwealth.

The Puritans and the Jews

The Puritans clearly identified with the ancient Israelites. Embattled with both the monarchy and traditional Church authorities, they linked their situation in England to that of the ancient Hebrews and their sufferings. The Hebrew Bible influenced them at least as much as did the New Testament, and they adopted religious customs that were more Jewish than Christian, such as strict Sabbath observance. They also gave their children Old Testament names. Ken Spiro has suggested that some of them saw England as the new Zion, and hoped to transform England into a theocracy based on Mosaic law.[2] The Puritan zeal for ancient Israel is demonstrated in the writings of the great Puritan poet John Milton, who served as a civil servant under Cromwell. He wrote the following: "There are no songs comparable to the song of Zion; no oration equal to those of the Prophets; and no politics like those which the Scriptures teach."[3]

While the Puritans' identification with the Old Testament Israelites did not necessarily translate into an abiding love for the Jews of 17th-century England, the condition of the Jews did improve under their rule. Having been persecuted by the official Church themselves, the Puritans valued religious tolerance, and they extended such tolerance to the Jews. In 1653, they allowed the Jews—who had been expelled from England nearly 400 years earlier by Edward I—to return to England. Their expectations in doing so were similar to those of Martin Luther a century before. They believed that, because the Puritan religious practice was so closely modeled on the ideals and principles of Judaism, the Jews would gladly convert to the Puritan form of Christianity. This expectation proved mistaken. Nonetheless, to their credit, the English Puritans still honored their precept of religious tolerance and allowed the Jewish people to remain in England and to practice their faith.

The Legacy of the Puritans

Religious tolerance as a principle of government was part of the Puritan legacy in England, but their influence was lasting in other ways. The Puritan Revolution ended in 1660, with the restoration of Charles II to the English throne. But the Restoration did not represent a return to the old feudal order. Democratic ideas—such as parliamentary government—had taken hold in England and, despite challenges in the period immediately ahead, would grow steadily stronger over the coming centuries.

Regarding the impact of the Puritans on contemporary democracy, Barbara Tuchman writes that they "gave permanent underpinning to two principles that are the basis of democratic society: for one thing, the security of parliamentary government; for another, the right of nonconformity or freedom of worship, as we call it today."[4]

Not just England but all of Europe was changed by the Puritan Revolution. The removal and execution of a king sent a strong signal throughout the continent and was the inspiration for revolutions to come—in America, France, and, eventually, Russia.

The Puritans in America

The founding of American democracy represents the next important phase in the dissemination of Old Testament values through Western civilization. In 1620, two decades before the start of the civil war in England, the Mayflower landed at Plymouth Rock with the first of what would ultimately be thousands of English Puritans determined to make a new society founded on God's laws as set out in the Old Testament.

Describing this unique pioneer society, Gabriel Sivan, in *The Bible and Civilization*, writes as follows:

No Christian community in history identified more with the People of the Book than did the early settlers of the Massachusetts Bay Colony, who believed their own lives to be a literal reenactment of the Biblical drama of the Hebrew nation. They themselves were the Children of Israel; America was their Promised Land. ... [They] saw themselves as instruments of Divine Providence, a people chosen to build their new commonwealth on the Covenant entered into at Mount Sinai. The Cornerstone of the 'New Jerusalem' which the Puritans yearned to establish in the American wilderness was, of course, the Bible.[5]

With the signing of the Mayflower Compact, the first American democracy was established on the foundation of Biblical ethical monotheism. Unlike most of the world's democracies, the United States was a democracy from the outset, and the Bible—especially the Old Testament—was crucial to this process. Ken Spiro notes that the earliest legislation of New England colonies was determined by Scripture. He adds that at the first assembly of New Haven in 1639, John Davenport—an English Puritan clergyman and co-founder of the American colony there—"clearly stated the primacy of the Bible as the legal and moral foundation of the colony."[6]

Why did the Puritans in America (and in England, too) focus so much on the Old Testament, and why did they identify so closely with the ancient Israelites? Why not the New Testament? The New Testament, after all, is the definitively Christian part of the Bible, and the Puritans were Christians. The fact is that the Old Testament suited the politics of the Puritan reformers better than the New Testament did. Paul wrote the following in Romans (13:1): "Every person must submit to the authorities in power, for all authority comes from God, and the existing authorities are instituted by him." This message of submission did not appeal to the Puritans, opposed as they were to both the Roman Church and the old feudal order it upheld. The Hebrew Bible, with its emphasis on personal responsibility and obedience to God alone, and its narratives concerning Jewish struggles against tyranny, fit with the Puritans' sense of their place in the world. They made the Old Testament their main source of authority both spiritually and politically.

At the time of the Exodus—the period in Jewish history with which the Puritans identified—the ancient Israelites had had no monarchy or centralized government, only prophets whom the people followed voluntarily. The American Puritans likewise rejected a centralized government. Their communities were directed by councils of elected elders. These communities were stable and prosperous. Even the legislation in the Puritan communities was based on Scripture. For example, half of the 79 statutes in the New Haven Code of 1655 contained Biblical references—mostly from the Hebrew Bible.[7]

Education in Puritan America

Many colleges and universities—Harvard and Yale, for example—were established under the auspices of various Puritan sects, and the Bible played a central role in the curriculums of these institutions of higher learning. A significant number of the founding fathers of America were products of these American universities.

The influence of the Bible in shaping the democratic political ideology of America cannot be overstated. As we noted in Chapter 1, the opening sentence of the Declaration of Independence—"We hold these truths to be self-evident, that all men are created equal, that they are endowed by their Creator with certain inalienable rights, that among them are life, liberty and the pursuit of happiness"—is one of the most obvious illustrations of this influence. The reference to "inalienable rights" reflects John Locke and the Enlightenment, but the notion that these rights come from God is from the Old Testament. With the birth of American democracy the ideas of ethical monotheism were "legally enshrined into the laws of a non-Jewish nation."[8]

Possibly the best tribute to the centrality of the Bible in American life came from President Franklin D. Roosevelt, who said the following in a 1935 Fireside Chat:

> We cannot read the history of our rise and development as a nation, without reckoning with the place the Bible has occupied in shaping the advances of the Republic... The ancient Greeks evolved their concept of *demokratia*, popular or majority government, through the conclusions of their philosophers; the Hebrews were imbued with the idea that the common people were party to a social and political contract deriving from God's Covenant with the Patriarchs and with Moses and the congregation of Israel... Democracy in its modern sense thus owes its origin both to the Greeks and to the Hebrews.[9]

Roosevelt here expresses ideas we have touched on previously in this text—that the ideology of Western society is a product of the ideologies of ancient Greece and ancient Israel.

Revolution and Democracy

The infusion of democratic ideals into Western culture and global politics was furthered by the American Revolution, but it didn't end there. It continued with the revolutions that followed in Europe. While these revolutions—especially in France—derived their inspiration from what had happened in England and America, there were significant ideological differences between them.

It is a well-known fact that the American Revolution inspired the French Revolution. But the Bible did not play the significant role in the French uprising that it did in the American one. The American society that rose up against the English Crown was, as we have seen, steeped in the Bible, especially in the Old Testament, and this society was therefore thoroughly imbued with the value system of Judaic ethical monotheism. For a country involved in revolution, such a moral code has a steadying effect, imposing limits on the extent to which revolutionary violence will be taken.

The French Revolution lacked such a steadying influence. The men who brought it about were products of the Enlightenment, and their revolutionary impulse came from non-religious sources. It was thinkers such as Voltaire and Rousseau of the Enlightenment—also known as the Age of Reason—who ultimately brought secular-humanistic values to the fore in France. The Enlightenment, as mentioned above, put its faith not in any particular religious creed but in the power of human reason to understand the laws of nature and existence and to bring about social improvement. Though some of them were deists, the Enlightenment thinkers generally did not subscribe to ethical monotheism.

With their faith in the power of human reason, the French revolutionaries dispensed with anything that smacked of the old order and set about creating their perfect society. But things didn't go as planned. When morality is divorced from ethical monotheism, it is more vulnerable to human manipulation. The French

Revolutionaries' rejection of scriptural authority left a vacuum that terror and tyranny crowded into. The justly named Reign of Terror ensued, in the course of which over 40,000 people died in mass executions throughout France.

It is a pattern that has repeated itself in human history since. Civil rights—or what most people in liberal democracies of the West regard as such—seem to suffer when a society cuts itself off from the influence of ethical monotheism. This is the case even when, as with the French Revolution, the betterment of mankind is the goal.

We have now traced the evolution of democratic ideology through 4,000 years of history. We began with the monotheism introduced by Abraham and traced its progress to the point where it became the basis of the dominant political ideology of the contemporary West—liberal democracy. But what is liberal democracy, and how has it managed to thrive while non-democratic ideologies, such as communism, have failed?

The Growth of Democracy

Human civilization has seen many political ideologies, including monarchies, fascism, communism, and dictatorships, to name some of the more recent ones. The only political ideology that seems to have thrived in the last two centuries is liberal democracy. By the end of the 19th century, there were 13 democratic countries in the world, all of them products of Christian Europe.[10] By the end of the 20th century, there were over 100, with democracy the fastest growing political ideology in the world. Between 1975 and 1995, the proportion of authoritarian countries in the world dropped from 68 percent to 26 percent.[11]

Freedom in the World is the annual survey of Freedom House, an independent watchdog organization concerned with the expansion of freedom around the world. Since 1972, this survey has rated and reported on the political rights and civil liberties of the 195 countries and 14 territories in the world. The survey is used by policymakers, the media, international corporations, civic activists, and human rights defenders to monitor trends in democracy and track freedom worldwide. *Freedom in the World* measures freedom according to two broad categories: political rights and civil liberties. Political rights ratings are based on an evaluation of three subcategories: electoral process, political pluralism and participation, and functioning of government. Civil liberties ratings are based on an evaluation of four subcategories: freedom of expression and belief, associational and organizational rights, rule of law, and personal autonomy and individual rights.

Freedom in the World applies one of three broad category designations to each of the countries and territories included in the index: Free, Partly Free, and Not Free.[12] The survey also identifies whether a country is an electoral democracy.

A *Free* country is one where there is open political competition, a climate of respect for civil liberties, significant independent civic life, and independent media. A *Partly Free* country is one in which there is limited respect for political rights and civil liberties. Finally, a *Not Free* country is one where basic political rights are absent, and basic civil liberties are widely and systematically denied.

According to Freedom House, there were 117 electoral democracies in 2011—up from 69 in 1989. Of those electoral democracies, 87 received a rating of Free and the rest received a rating of Partly Free.[13] None of the electoral democracies were rated as Not Free. By contrast, all the countries that had a status of Not Free, meaning an absence of political rights and civil liberties, were not electoral democracies. In the Middle East and North Africa, only Israel was rated Free.[14]

Clearly, there is a direct relationship between the growth of democracies in the world and the growth of countries that respect civil liberties and human rights. However, it is also important to note that there is no absolute guarantee that democracy and civil rights are synonymous.

We have spent much time looking at the history of contemporary democracy and at the role Israel—that is, Judaic ideology—has played in its evolution, but we haven't yet addressed what contemporary democracy actually is.

What Is Democracy?

One of the best ways to understand what democracy is, is to look at what it isn't. As a political ideology, democracy basically sits in the center of a continuum. On the extreme right are ideologies like fascism or Islamic fundamentalism. On the extreme left is Marxist communism.

Communism

It may seem odd to call communism a "left wing" ideology. We usually associate "left" with individual freedom and minimal government intervention, and we generally think of communism as the opposite. We associate communism with a rigidly controlled state ideology, where individuals have little freedom and where there is overbearing governmental control.

The goal of Marxist communism, however, has always been to create a stateless, classless, completely egalitarian society. In the 19th century, Marx saw the European working class (the proletariat) being completely exploited by the bourgeoisie—the rich landowners, the factory owners, and the ruling aristocracy. He theorized that all elements of the social order—the economic system, the state, and the religious institutions—were in reality ways for the rich and powerful to stay rich and powerful. Marx decided that a revolution was needed so that true equality could be restored in the form of a classless society.

Since religion was a tool of control, according to Marx, it needed to be purged from society. That is why communist states are atheistic. Since the state (that is, the government) and nationalism were likewise tools of the ruling bourgeoisie, they too needed to be purged.

To believe that a society can operate without the control of a state, a religion, or a class system requires complete faith in people to govern themselves. The Marxist faith is, in this regard, akin to the Enlightenment faith that human beings can perfect their society by means of human reason alone, without the support of the ethical monotheism basic to Judaic ideology. Viewed in this light, Marxist theory represents an extension of the Enlightenment and the kind of secular humanistic thought that produced the French Revolution.

Communism has never succeeded very well as a political system, in large part because it overestimates the power of people to govern themselves in a civilized way without the influence of religion. Communist states have always been vulnerable to dictatorship and to the tyranny that attends totalitarian systems. Stalin in Russia, Mao in China, and Pol Pot in Cambodia conducted their own reigns of terror, murdering millions in the name of a communist utopia that did not arrive. At the same time, communism seems to underestimate the importance of individual enterprise and ambition in creating a healthy society. Generally speaking, communist states have never borne much resemblance to the society Marx envisioned. Indeed, according to Marxist theory, the phrase "communist state" is an oxymoron; communist society is supposed to be stateless. In the real world, so-called communist states have been very state-focused or *nationalistic*.

Nationalism and Fascism

Nationalism proved to be one of the strongest motivating forces of the 19th and 20th centuries, uniting millions of people under national banners. Nations defined themselves in terms of a common language, common history, common customs, and a loyalty to a common homeland. Cultural nationalism became transformed into a political ideology that asserted the importance of common culture and identity. This belief spread rapidly.

In its extreme form, nationalism manifested itself in ideologies like fascism. For example, the ideology of Nazi Germany (also known as National Socialism) combined fascism and nationalism. Unlike Marxist Communism (but much like the communism of Russia and China) fascism is extremely right wing. According to fascist ideology, all individuals exist to enhance the power of the state and the nation it represents. Fascism is strongly anti-democratic and—partly for deep ideological reasons, which should now be clear to you—anti-Semitic. Fascist states are characterized by an absence of individual rights, natural rights, or a social contract between individuals and the government, all of which are fundamentals of liberal democracy.

Nationalism is not inherently evil, but in Nazi Germany it became terribly destructive—an expression of irrational obsession. Those who did not follow the official prescriptions of super-patriotism were treated as "aliens," and racism became a strong element of Nazi society. Racism is always a useful tool for fascist regimes, enabling them to unite people on nationalistic lines. Such regimes have a further motive for racism, in the case of anti-Semitism; Judaism is always an ideological threat to a far right, anti-democratic world view. In a fascist regime, the state is the God.

When we compare the various forms of government of the past 400 years, we are likely to conclude that liberal democratic ideologies, influenced by a Biblical standard and rooted in ethical monotheism, are, if not perfect, fundamentally different from and more civilized than other ideologies.

Now that we have looked at what democracy is not, let's look more closely at what it is.

Characteristics of Democratic Ideologies

The term democracy means "rule of the people" (*demos*, "the people" + *kratia*, "power, rule"). As we mentioned earlier in our study, it is a system of government that is usually traced back to the ancient Greeks. During the 5th century BCE, the Athenians, in particular, used the term *democracy* to refer to government by the many, as contrasted to government by the few (oligarchy), or government by one person (monarchy). The earliest Greek democracies emphasized the equality of all who qualified as citizens, but the term *citizen* usually excluded a significant segment of the population, including women and slaves. Many of the fundamental principles we now identify with democratic thought took many more centuries to develop.

At the heart of a democracy is constitutionalism. A constitution is a nation's formal expression (usually written) of its political ideology. However, as some have noted, a constitution is no guarantee of a democracy. In some countries, these documents are a kind of window-dressing, allowing them to appear democratic to the rest of the world.

True Democracy and Constitutionalism

Constitutionalism is to a genuine democracy what character is to an individual. It provides principles and prescriptions that orient the society's members and check the government's power. The essence of constitutionalism is a belief that a government's power must be limited and must take a back seat to the individual's "inalienable rights."

All democratic constitutions actually *restrict* government power and aim to emphasize the features and principles of democracy, which include the following:

- *Rule of Law:* The notion that the law is supreme, and that all individuals are equal in the eyes of the law and no-one is above the law.
- *Responsible government:* The principle that all public officials are accountable to the people, who can be ruled only with their consent.
- *Civil liberties:* The fundamental rights and freedoms guaranteed every person— for example, the right to life, liberty, and security, and the freedom of thought, expression, association, religion, and of the press.
- *Constitutionalism:* The notion that there should be a written document that sets out the powers the people are prepared to give to their government, and that outlines, defines, and limits the exercise of that power.
- *Individualism:* The principle that the government's chief function is to foster the well-being of each individual, and that each individual is entitled to seek his or her own self-fulfillment.
- *Majority rule:* The principle that public decisions are weighted in favor of the greater number of citizens, who are represented by their elected officials.

■ *Pluralism*: The principle that there should be widespread acceptance of different cultures, religions, values, and lifestyles, and that all law-abiding people should have equal opportunity to play a constructive role.[15]

In order to evaluate the democratic character of a nation, we must take into account how well it scores in the above categories. A constitution that does not place limitations on its government or spell out individual rights is not really consistent with the spirit of a Western liberal democracy. In addition, a government that does not act in accordance with those principles may call itself democratic, but it is not actually grounded in the democratic ideals and value system—an ideology whose roots we have traced to the marriage of humanism and Biblical monotheism.

Pseudo-Democracy: The Case of Iran

The current Iranian government is an example of a country that has a constitution but is not a full democracy. It is a fundamentally theocratic country, with an overlay of democracy. At the top of Iran's current political and religious pecking order is the supreme leader, the Ayatollah Ali Khamenei. The current Iranian president, Mahmoud Ahmadinejad, is, in practice, second to the supreme leader, but the power of the president is closely tied to the political whims of the supreme leader.

The Majlis, or parliament, in Iran is a 290-member body representing all 30 of Iran's provinces. Its job is to introduce and pass legislation. Members are elected to four-year terms. Governing alongside the Majlis is a 12-member body called the Council of Guardians—six theologians appointed by the supreme leader, and six jurists approved by the Majlis—who review not only legislation, but also candidates seeking election, to ensure consistency with Islamic law.

The Iranian Supreme Court is chosen by the head of the judiciary, who is appointed by the supreme leader. There is also a Special Clerical Court, overseen by the supreme leader, which has effectively silenced many of the regime's clerical critics.

This top-down autocratic system in Iran is a complex mix of elected and non-elected institutions and is less democratic than it appears. Secular nationalists, liberal democrats, and other opponents of the Islamic Republic have little voice in public debate. Challenges to the Ayatollah's regime, which operates according to strict Sharia (Islamic) law, are not tolerated.

Hence a number of human rights that are recognized as fundamental in the West, such as the freedom to choose a same-sex relationship, are not tolerated in Iran and are tried as capital offences, punishable by death.

Iran provides a good example of how a nation's having a written constitution is no guarantee of genuine democracy. In its written dimension, a constitution encompasses the documents, statutes, and charters that outline the structure and goals of a government. But these documents are less significant, in the end, than the actual *modus operandi* of a nation, which may, as in Iran, involve practices not spelled out in the written constitution.

Can an Islamic state be democratic? And what about a *Jewish* state? Can such a state be democratic without endangering its fundamental identity?

Is Israel a "Pseudo" Democracy?

In contrast to Iran, Israel is a country that has no formal constitution. It is, however, a parliamentary democracy, and like most democracies has three branches—executive, legislative and judicial. It was stated in Israel's Declaration of Independence (1948) that the governing body, which turned into the First Knesset (Israel's parliament), would draft a constitution for Israel. But this was not done, owing to differences of opinion between the secular and the religious parties. It was decided to set out a series of Basic Laws that would eventually form the basis of a constitution. Yet even now, more than 60 years after the country's establishment, no Israeli constitution exists.

It does have the Basic Laws of Israel, however. There are eleven of these Basic Laws, and they serve many of the functions of a formal constitution. They prescribe, for example, the order of government, the rights of citizens, and the holding of elections, and they are based on the following principles:

- majority rule;
- minority rights;
- separation between the legislative, executive and judiciary branches of government; and
- freedom of the press.

There is no religious leader at the head of the Knesset, which is the legislative branch of the Israeli parliament. The Knesset is seated in Jerusalem. Its 120 members are elected to four-year terms through party-list proportional representation as mandated by the Basic Laws. The prime minister is the chief of the executive branch and the most powerful political figure in the country. Elected by the Knesset, he or she appoints Cabinet ministers, who vote on foreign and domestic policy. The Cabinet is composed of ministers who are usually the heads of government departments. The Cabinet's composition must also be approved by the Knesset.

Even though Israel is known as the Jewish state, Jewish law is not the final authority in most matters. The legal authority in Israel—the judicial branch of the government—includes both secular and religious courts. Israel's mixed legal system is composed of English common law, British Mandate regulations, and Jewish, Christian, and Muslim religious laws.

There is often spirited debate about whether Israel can be both a Jewish state and a full democracy, given that it must maintain a Jewish majority in order to remain a Jewish state. One argument is that a state could be Jewish—or Islamic, for that matter—and still be democratic as long as the civil rights that are characteristic of liberal democracies are present. It is true that there would need to be some limitations on voting rights in order to keep a democratic Jewish state "Jewish" in character. This may seem regrettable. But few democracies have ever offered universal suffrage. There have always been restrictions on voting, some rational (for example, withholding the vote from children or federal criminals) and some irrational (for example, withholding the vote from racial minorities or women).

Does it seem rational or irrational for a definitively Jewish state to impose voting restrictions that would safeguard its Jewish identity?

We should keep in mind, too, that democracy involves more than just majority rule. It is possible to have policies for maintaining a Jewish majority and yet still have civil rights for a non-Jewish minority citizenry. The real question in assessing whether a state is or isn't democratic is whether democratic benefits such as rule of law, minority rights, freedom of the press, and freedom of religion, to name just a few, are protected. If these elements are present, then that state can be considered democratic.

Different Types of Democracy

As we mentioned earlier, there are now, according to Freedom House, 117 electoral democracies in a world of 195 countries. As an ideology, democracy sits in the center of the political continuum we spoke about earlier. On the extreme right is fascism; on the extreme left, Marxist communism. While democracy sits in the middle of the ideological spectrum, not all democracies operate in an identical fashion.

Differences of opinion between democratic nations and between parties, candidates, and individuals in democracies often revolve around whether their world view is rooted in humanism or monotheism. Between humanism and ethical monotheism there is a fundamental ideological disagreement that we can trace back to the tensions between Hellenism and Judaism, discussed in Chapter 5. As you may recall, the humanism of the ancient Greeks holds that the human being is the center of all things and that human reason is the ultimate source of truth, knowledge, wisdom, and morality. Judaism, by contrast, while not discounting the importance of human reason, holds that God is the ultimate authority in the areas of truth, knowledge, wisdom, and morality.

Within a democratic framework, these two ideological camps—one camp subscribing to the Jewish or Christian world view, which is rooted in the Bible and the ethical monotheism of the ancient Israelites; the other camp subscribing to the humanistic perspective of the ancient Greeks and French Enlightenment philosophers—may clash. They do so, for example, in the pro-life versus pro-choice debate. Despite that, in a democracy they have found a way to co-exist. It's not a perfect system, but, generally speaking, disagreements within a democratic context tend to be much more civilized and peaceful than those in other political contexts. Citizens of liberal democracies, whether holding to a humanist perspective or to one shaped by ethical monotheism, seem able, more often than not, to find common ground on human rights. It is an interesting fact of history that, so far, no democracy has gone to war with another democracy.

How then do we explain the fact that Islamic ideology—which is rooted in monotheism, a Biblical principle—has so much difficulty with Western democratic thinking? This is the topic of our next chapter.

Endnotes

1   Gabriel Sivan, *The Bible and Civilization* (Jerusalem: Keter Publishing House, 1973), 57.

2   For a detailed discussion of the Puritan identification with the ancient Israelites, see Ken Spiro, *WorldPerfect: The Jewish Impact on Civilization* (Deerfield Beach: Simcha Press, 2002), 233-243.

3   "John Milton," *Bartleby.com*, accessed February 27, 2012, http://www.bartleby.com/349/authors/141. html.

4   Barbara Tuchman, *The Bible and the Sword* (New York: Ballantine Books, 1984), 126.

5   Sivan, *The Bible and Civilization*, 236.

6   Spiro, *WorldPerfect*, 247.

7   For a detailed analysis of the political ideology of the early Puritans in America, see Spiro, *WorldPerfect*, 245-250. The reference to the statutes in the Code of 1655 containing Biblical references can be found in Spiro, *WorldPerfect*, 248.

8   Ibid, 254.

9   Quoted in Spiro, *WorldPerfect*, 255.

10   Spiro, *WorldPerfect*, 261.

11   David Potter, David Goldblatt, Margaret Kiloh, and Paul Lewis, eds., *Democratization* (Cambrige, Mass.: Open University Press, 1997), 1.

12   "Freedom in the World 2012," Freedom House, accessed April 18, 2012, http://www.freedomhouse. org/report/freedom-world/freedom-world-2012.

13   Ibid, 3, 29.

14   Ibid, 14-18.

15   James John Guy, People, *Politics and Government* 5th ed. (Toronto: Prentice Hall, 2001), 148.

Chapter 8

Islam and Islamism

Introduction and Background

The religion of Islam has existed for more than 14 centuries, and has over 1.3 billion adherents. There are 56 sovereign Islamic states in the world, with growing Muslim minorities in Asia, Africa, Europe, and the Americas. Islam's contributions to world culture have been profound. The period between the 8th and 15th centuries was a golden age in this respect. During this time, Islamic scholars significantly advanced astronomy, chemistry, engineering, mathematics, medicine, and philosophy. Musa al-Khwarizmi (780-850), a Persian, developed algebra in 9th century Baghdad, drawing on work by mathematicians in India. Abū Alī ibn Sīnā, better known as Avicenna (980–1037), wrote *The Kitab al-shifa* (*The Book of Healing*), which was a standard work in Europe's universities until the 1600s. And Ibn Rushd, also known as Averroes (1126–1198), is known for his Commentaries on Aristotle. After the 17th century, however, Islam hit a period of stagnation which has contributed to the rise of extremism in its ranks. This chapter aims to provide some background on Muslim ideology and to develop some understanding of its current relationship with the West and with Israel, and some understanding of the groups within Islam.

The Origins of Islam

The founder and prophet of Islam was Muhammad, who was born, according to Islamic tradition, in about 571 CE, in the small oasis town of Mecca in the Hijāz region—western Arabia. Muhammad's family was from the Arab tribe of Quraysh and the clan of Hashim.[1] Descendents of the Hashim clan include the royal family of Jordan who claim direct descendancy from Muhammad.

Muhammad was a merchant by trade, familiar with the local Jewish people and their monotheistic religion. According to Islamic tradition, in the year 610, when Muhammad was 40 years old, he received his first revelation, with the angel Gabriel calling on him to become a prophet.

During the early years of his mission, as his following and influence increased, Muhammad began to encounter opposition from the leading families of Mecca, who saw him and his teaching as a threat. In the year 622 CE, Muhammad entered into an agreement with emissaries from the small town of Yathrib (later known as Medina), who offered to give him and his converts refuge in return for his becoming an arbitrator in their disputes. The migration of Muhammad and his followers from Mecca to Yathrib is known in Arabic as the *hijra*, and is regarded by Muslims as the decisive moment in Muhammad's evolution as a prophet. It also marks the first year of the Islamic calendar.

The population of Yathrib, in the early part of the 7th century, included a large Jewish community, as did much of the Arabian Peninsula and Mesopotamia. The content and structure of Islam clearly indicate that Muhammad was both familiar with and strongly influenced by Judaism.

Muhammad and Judaism

Muhammad accepted Judaism's concept of monotheism, its prophets, and its idea of a fixed law embodied in scripture and an oral law. There are a number of additional similarities between Islam and Judaism. Paul Johnson describes them as follows:

> Like the Jews, the Moslems were originally reluctant to commit [their] Oral Law to writing. Like the Jews, they eventually did so. Like the Jews, they developed the practice of submitting points of law to their rabbis or muftis, soliciting a responsum, and the earliest responsa seem to have consciously adopted a Judaic formula. Like the Jews, the Arabs accepted strict and elaborate codes covering diet, ritual purity, and cleanliness.[2]

It is likely that Muhammad wanted the Jewish community to adopt his teachings. He made the first *qibla* (the direction Muslims face during prayer) towards Jerusalem, probably in the hope of attracting Jews to his teachings. It has also been suggested that Muhammad turned against the Jews of the region only after they refused to convert to his version of their religion. As Paul Johnson has said,

> Mohammed was rebuffed, and he thereafter gave a deliberate new thrust to Islamic monotheism. He altered the nature of the Sabbath and changed it to Friday. He changed the orientation of prayers from Jerusalem to Mecca. He redated the principal feast. Most important of all, he declared that most of the Jewish dietary laws were simply a punishment for their past misdeeds, and so abolished them, though he retained the prohibitions on pork, blood and carcasses, and some of the slaughtering rules. All these changes made it quite impossible to bring about a merging of Jewish and Muslim communities, however much they might agree on ethical or dogmatic fundamentals.[3]

In short, the Jewish community rejected Muhammad and his teachings, and thereafter his relationship towards the Jews changed dramatically. Muhammad's ambivalent attitude toward Jewish monotheism and the Jews—indebtedness to the former, and resentment of the latter—may also explain the Qur'an's contradictory portrayals of Jews.

Yathrib, Muhammad's new home, became the center of the Muslim faith and *umma* (the Islamic community). In time, the city came to be known as Medina— now the second holiest city in Islam. The movement from Mecca to Medina marked a dramatic change in Muhammad's status. He went from being a person with no real political authority, viewed with indifference and then with mistrust by the people in power, to being himself a ruler who wielded political, military, and religious authority.

Muhammad had by this point acquired a dual role: he was at once a source of religious revelation and a powerful political leader. As the head of the Muslim *umma*, Muhammad promulgated laws, dispensed justice, collected taxes, conducted diplomacy, made war, and made peace. The *umma* began as a community, but in a relatively short time, it became an empire.

When Muhammad died in 632 CE, his spiritual mission was complete. His purpose had been to abolish idolatry and polytheism, to bring God's final revelation, and to restore the true monotheism that earlier prophets (such as Abraham and Moses) had taught and that had, in his view, been abandoned or distorted. According to Muslim belief, he was the last of the prophets and he completed what the earlier prophets had begun.

But if Muhammad's own spiritual mission was complete, the proselytizing by others on behalf of Islam had only just begun. There remained to his successors the task of maintaining and defending the Divine Law and of bringing it to the rest of the world. Fulfilling this task required the ongoing use of political and military power.

The Caliphate and the Divisions of Sunni and Shi'a Muslims

After Muhammad's death, his followers confronted a difficult problem. Who would succeed him as leader of the religious community and political order he had created? In his spiritual function as the Prophet, there could be no successor. For his political role, however, a successor was urgently needed.

Muhammad left no son, but his daughter was married to his cousin, Ali. Some thought the best choice to succeed Muhammad was Ali, the prophet's nearest male relative and the father of his grandchildren. The inner circle of Muhammad's followers thought otherwise; they chose Abū Bakr, one of Muhammad's earliest disciples and most respected converts. Abū Bakr was given the title of *khalifa*, an Arabic word that means both "successor" and "deputy." This word came, in time, to be applied to the institution of the caliphate—the supreme sovereign office of the Islamic world for centuries.

Sunni Muslims regard the first caliphs, who came to the office in non-hereditary succession, as having been legitimate heads of the Muslim state and community, and they revere their reign as a period surpassed only by the period in which Muhammad himself lived. *Shi'a Muslims*, on the other hand, regard these caliphs as usurpers, who took the place that rightfully belonged, after the Prophet's death, to his cousin Ali and, after him, to the descendants of the Prophet.

The Muslim world has always been divided between the Sunnis and the Shi'a—by far the most important of the various divisions that have arisen among Muslims worldwide.

At the beginning of the 16th century, a new development brought a radical change in the relationship between Sunni and Shi'a across the Middle East. The Safavids, who were followers of the Twelver (or Imami) Shi'a faith, seized control in Iran and proclaimed Twelver Shiism to be the state religion. This gave an ideological base and identity to the newly-recovered Iranian unity and separated Iranian Muslims from Sunni Muslims in the Ottoman lands, in India, and in Central Asia.

A long conflict ensued between the shahs of Iran and the Ottoman sultans. The two sides struggled for control of the border province of Iraq—part of a larger competition for supremacy, both in the Middle East and in the broader world of Islam. The conflict between Sunni and Shi'a Muslims is still unresolved and is reflected in the ongoing discord between the Islamic Republic of Iran, which is Shi'a, and the Sunni Arab states, such as Saudi Arabia, Egypt, Iraq, and Jordan.

At present, the Sunnis constitute the great majority in the Muslim world. Only Iran and Iraq have Shi'a majorities.

The decline of the caliphate's religious authority within the Muslim world has led to the emergence of a new kind of authority—namely, the Islamic clergy, both Sunni and Shi'a, who control much of what the political entities do in Iran and in the Arab states of the Middle East. While Sunni and Shiite Muslims have their differences, one thing most of them agree on is their vigorous resistance to Jewish sovereignty in Jerusalem.

Jerusalem and Islam

The Arabian Peninsula has always been viewed as the birthplace of Islam, with Mecca and Medina seen as, respectively, the first and second holiest sites in the Muslim world. Where does Jerusalem factor into this? Although Jerusalem is never mentioned by name in the Qur'an, most Muslims believe that, one night, Muhammad was taken from Mecca to heaven via the Temple Mount in Jerusalem. Islamic beliefs pertaining to the Night Journey are based on the verses of Sura 17:1 in the Qur'an. They contain the following lines:

> *Glory to (God)*
>
> *who did take His Servant*
>
> *for a journey by night*
>
> *From the Sacred Mosque*
>
> *to the Farthest Mosque ...* (Sura 17:1)

While not all Islamic scholars agree, contemporary Islam generally holds that the "Farthest Mosque" is the Temple Mount in Jerusalem and that the "Sacred Mosque" is Mecca. This makes the Temple Mount the third holiest site for Sunnis and the fourth holiest for Shiites. The site of the Tomb of Ali, the cousin and son-in-law of the prophet Muhammad and First Shiite Imam, is the third holiest site to Shiites (the tomb is in Najaf, an Iraqi city about 160 km south of Baghdad).

Jerusalem's association with Islam dates back to the early days of the caliphate. Within a few years of Muhammad's death in 632, the Caliph Omar, in his conquest of the Middle East, reached Jerusalem and named the city *Madinat Bayt al-Maqdis*— "City of the Temple," referring to the First and Second Jewish Temples.

The city's importance to Islam began around 690 CE, when the first Umayyad Caliph, Muawiyah I, who was well aware of the Christian and Jewish attachment to Jerusalem, saw a need to give the city sacred status to Muslims. He constructed the structure now known as the Dome of the Rock, which dominates the Old City and the Temple Mount. The other Islamic structure on the Temple Mount, the al-Aqsa Mosque, was constructed later (around 715) by the Umayyad Caliph al-Walid.

The Muslim constructions in Jerusalem had a clear polemical and strategic purpose. They were intended to combat Christian identification with the city and to challenge and, in some sense, defy Christianity and Judaism—thus demonstrating that Islam was not merely a successor religion, but a universal system, superseding the older faiths. The Muslim colonization of Jerusalem was meant, above all, to show that a new religion had arrived to replace the older ones.

The Temple Mount was a likely choice because it already possessed sanctity, was a large vacant area, and was, after all, the original *qibla*, or "direction of prayer," established by Muhammad. The *qibla* was subsequently changed to Mecca, the site of the Ka'ba, which Muslims believe is the House of God built by Abraham—one of the main reasons that it is the holiest city in Muslim tradition.[4]

While Islamic theologians often present versions of history and of Old and New Testament narratives (for example, the stories of Abraham and Jesus) that are different from those of Judaism and Christianity, there are Islamic clerics who maintain that the Qur'an is in agreement with Biblical and Jewish history regarding the Temple. Sheikh Professor Abdul Hadi Palazzi, a leading figure in the Muslim community of Italy, in an interview with Pastor Kenneth Rawson, claimed that there are references in the Qur'an and Islamic sources that acknowledge Judaism's connection and history with the Temple Mount and the Land of Israel.[5] Sheikh Palazzi's views, however, are not shared by many Muslim clerics, who instead choose to focus on the ideological differences between Islam and the West (Christendom).

Islam and the West

The early history of Islam was marked by continual wars against Christendom and Christianity. Conflict between the vast, zealous communities attached to these two religions continued for many centuries. During the first millennium of Islam's existence, dominance passed back and forth between Muslim and Christian forces. The Middle East was subjected to a long interchange of conquest and reconquest, jihad and crusade.

A decisive change came in 1683. The Muslim Turks—who controlled much of Europe at this point—were defeated while trying to capture Vienna. In a forceful wave of reaction, Christian Europe subsequently recovered its lost lands and pushed far into the Islamic heartland. The Muslims saw themselves threatened not just with the loss of their remote provinces, but with the centers of their faith and power.

By the end of the 18th century, over a thousand years after the birth of their religion, Muslims were becoming painfully aware that they were losing the long struggle against their Western adversary. By the beginning of the 20th century, European empires controlled, directly or indirectly, virtually the entire Muslim world. By this point, only three Islamic powers retained their independence: Afghanistan, Persia, and the Ottoman Empire. By the end of World War I, the Ottoman Empire, which was the last of the great Sunni empires, had been defeated, its capital occupied, its ruler deposed, and its territories partitioned between the victorious Allied Powers.

For Muslims, this was the lowest point in their history. They began to concern themselves with how Islam was going to defeat its ancient rival. The proposed solutions and their advocates fell into two broad categories, the "Westernizers" and the "anti-Westernizers."

The Westernizers felt that the only way to defeat the West was to adopt its ways (for example, democracy) and become part of the modern world. The Islamic rulers who adopted this goal had limited success in achieving it. The one outstanding example of success was the Turkish Republic, which emerged in 1923 from the ruins of the Ottoman Empire.

The second group, the anti-Westernizers, were Muslims who saw Westernization not as the remedy but as the source of the disease. They believed that by adopting the destructive ways of the Western unbelievers, Muslims brought defeat and humiliation on themselves and on the entire Islamic world. The clear remedy, in their view, was a return to what they saw as authentic Islam. This movement first appeared in Arabia in the 18th century. Since then, it has developed along different lines and has spread to much of the Islamic world.

In light of the foregoing discussion, we might ask the following question: What is it about Islamic ideology (theology and law) that is so at odds with the West, given that the two share a common patriarch (Abraham) and a common ideological basis (ethical monotheism)?

Principles of Islam

The word *Islam* belongs to a group of Arabic words that are derived from the root s-l-m. This group includes words meaning both "peace" (*salam* in Arabic) and "surrender." It is the latter meaning, "surrender" or "submission," that is uppermost in the term *Islam*. Islam, then, is the act or state of submission, and a Muslim is one who submits.[6] What does a Muslim submit to? A Muslim submits to the word of Allah (Arabic for God), as it was transmitted by Muhammad. There are, however, differing interpretations within Islam regarding its laws—Shari'a.

Shari'a—Islamic Law

Shari'a is the moral code and religious law of Islam. Shari'a deals with many topics addressed by secular law as well as personal matters such as diet, prayer, and fasting. While interpretations of Shari'a vary between cultures, there are two primary sources of Islamic law: the Qur'an and the Sunnah/Hadith. Where it has official status, Shari'a is interpreted and administered by Islamic judges and religious leaders (imams). The application of Shari'a is a goal for Islamist movements, but in non-Muslim countries there are clerics, such as Sheikh Palazzi of Italy, who hold that the law of the land takes precedence over Shari'a.[7]

In Shari'a, there are concepts that clash with Western democratic ideology. These concepts include the following: dār al-Islam, jihad, and dhimmi.

Dār al Islam and Dār al Harb

In *Islam and the Modern Law of Nations*, Professor Majid Khadduri provides an account of the fundamental Islamic concepts of dār al-Islam and the dār al-harb, explaining that

> the world was sharply divided, under the law of Islam, into the dār al-Islam (abode or territory of Islam) and the dār al-harb (abode of war or enemy territory). The first corresponded to the territory under Islamic sovereignty. Its inhabitants were Muslims, by birth or conversion, and the people of the tolerated religions (Jews, Christians, and Zoroastrians) who preferred to remain non-Muslims at the sacrifice of paying a poll tax [jizya]. The dār al harb consisted of all the states and communities outside of the territory of Islam. Its inhabitants were harbis or people of the territory of war. In theory the dār al-Islam was always at war with the dār al harb. The Muslims were under legal obligation to reduce the latter to Muslims in order to achieve Islam's ultimate objective, namely the enforcement of God's law (the Shari'a) over the entire world. The instrument by which the Islamic state was to carry out that objective was called the jihad (popularly known as holy war), which was always just if waged against the infidels and the enemies of the faith.[8]

Jihad

According to the traditional law of Islam, war or *jihād* is recognized as a legitimate "instrument for both the universalization" of the Muslim religion and "the establishment of an imperial world state." Professor Khadduri describes this interpretation of the law of war in Islam as follows:

> The Islamic state, whose principal function was to put God's law into practice, sought to establish Islam as the dominant reigning ideology over the entire world. It refused to recognize the coexistence of non-Muslim communities, except perhaps as subordinate entities, because by its very nature a universal state tolerates the existence of no other state than itself.

Although it was not a consciously formulated policy, Muhammad's early successors, after Islam became supreme in Arabia, were determined to embark on a ceaseless war of conquest in the name of Islam. The jihād was therefore employed as an instrument for both the universalization of religion and the establishment of an imperial world state.[9]

When a territory does come under Muslim rule, there are laws under which non-Muslims, called *dhimmi*, must live.

Dhimmi

Islam identifies two major categories of non-Muslims. The first category includes pagans or idol worshippers (polytheists). The second category includes people called *dhimmi*. Dhimmi are non-Muslim monotheists—mainly Jews and Christians. [10]

Under traditional Islamic law, a pagan must choose between converting to Islam, becoming a slave to a Muslim, or dying. Islam has prohibited the practice of paganism since the beginning of Muhammad's ministry, and Muslims originally identified the eradication of polytheistic paganism and idol-worship as basic to their mission. Jews, Christians, and other dhimmi have three choices: conversion, the poll tax, or jihad. If they convert to Islam, they are granted the full rights of Muslim citizens. If they accept their subordinate position—recognizing the supremacy of Islam and the dominance of the Muslim state—but choose not to convert, they are treated as second-class citizens and required to pay the poll tax (jizya) in return for security of life and property, freedom of worship (usually with limits), and a degree of autonomy in their affairs. If they choose to resist, they are treated no differently from polytheists and are subjected to jihad.

What is actually involved in *dhimmitude*? The standard notion, which is somewhat euphemistic, is that dhimmitude is the condition of "protected people" within Muslim society. Practically speaking, it is based on certain policies that Muhammad established during his lifetime with respect to non-Muslims (primarily Jews) living under Muslim rule. While dhimmi are allowed to practice their religion and live amongst Muslims, there is a whole system of punitive legislation concerning dhimmitude. Collectively, these laws create a second-class status, a segregated status, and an apartheid status that separates the Muslim from the non-Muslim monotheist. Dhimmi laws are in place today in a number of countries including Egypt, Lebanon, Sudan, and Saudi Arabia to name a few. Among the conditions these laws impose on dhimmi are the following:

■ They must pay discriminatory taxes (jizya);
■ Their testimony in court is not accepted;
■ Their places of worship, when permitted to be built, have to be constructed in a manner that shows their inferiority to Islam.

During the first centuries of Islam, many of the Muslim dynasties were not very strict on dhimmi laws. Jews and Christians enjoyed a large measure of autonomy and sometimes rose to positions of prominence, power, and economic achievement in Muslim society. However, they were never actually on a par with Muslims. Dhimmi laws were always in place, enforceable whenever it became convenient for Muslim authorities to persecute Jews, Christians, and other minority groups.

Anyone trying to understand Islam's relationship to the world needs to understand the concepts discussed above, for the following reason: How a particular Islamic nation, organization, or cleric views each concept will ultimately define their relationship with the West and with Israel.

Shari'a and Israel

If, according to Shari'a, a territory (for example, Israel) that has once been dār al Islam cannot be allowed to go back to being dār al harb, and dhimmis (for example, Jews) are never allowed to rule over Muslims, what prospects are there for peace between Muslim states and the State of Israel?

For 1300 years, Israel was dār al Islam, ruled by Muslims. Now, dhimmis rule in that country. For many Muslims, that poses a serious theological problem. In Chapter 3, we discussed "replacement theologies"—in other words, Christian or Muslim beliefs that their own covenant has replaced the original Jewish Covenant with God. According to the standard Muslim replacement theology, the Jews were rejected by God and replaced by the Christians, who were then rejected in turn and replaced by the Muslims. The existence of a Jewish state, therefore, is a theological impossibility for most Muslim clerics.

As mentioned, not all Islamic clerics (for example, Palazzi of Italy) or Muslims hold to the concepts of Shari'a law described above. Therefore, not all Muslims find the existence of a Jewish state to be incompatible with Islam. How Shari'a is practiced depends on its interpretation. Unfortunately, one of these interpretations has led to extremism.

Islamist Extremism

British Pakistani Maajid Nawaz, born in 1978, was recruited when he was a teenager to the global Islamist party Hizb ut-Tahrir. The goal of this organization, broadly speaking, was to unite all Muslim countries into one caliphate ruled by Islamic law. Nawaz spent over a decade in the organization, rising to become part of its leadership, until he was sentenced to four years in an Egyptian prison for his affiliation with this party. After serving his sentence, Nawaz decided that Hizb ut-Tahrir was hijacking Islam for political purposes, and he gave up being an Islamist while still remaining a Muslim.[11]

Nawaz says his goal now is to help Muslims in the West engage in their current political frameworks, while encouraging non-Western Muslims to work for a democratic culture that values peace and women's rights. To that end, in 2009, he founded Khudi, a counter-extremism social movement working to promote a democratic culture in Pakistan. Nawaz says: "I can now say that the more I learnt about Islam, the more tolerant I became."[12]

In his TED talk, which has had hundreds of thousands of hits, Nawaz begins by asking, "Have you ever wondered why extremism seems to have been on the rise in Muslim-majority countries over the course of the last decade?"[13] He continues as follows:

> Well my personal story, my personal journey, what brings me to the TED stage here today, is a demonstration of exactly what's been happening in Muslim-majority countries over the course of the last decades, at least, and beyond. I want to share some of that story with you, but also some of my ideas around change and the role of social movements in creating change in Muslim-majority societies. If we look at Islamists…one thing they've been very good at, one thing that they've actually been exceeding in, is communicating across borders, using technologies to organize themselves, to propagate their message and to create truly global phenomena. Now I should know, because for 13 years of my life, I was involved in an extreme Islamist organization. And I was actually a potent force in spreading ideas across borders, and I witnessed the rise of Islamist extremism as distinct from Islam the faith, and the way in which it influenced my co-religionists across the world.[14]

Nawaz says that in his organization they were laughing at democratic activists because they felt they were out-of-date. Nawaz learned how to use technology to his advantage because he was part of an extremist organization that was forced to think beyond the confines of the nation-state.

Nawaz calls our time "the age of behavior" because he believes ideas and narratives are increasingly defining behavior, identity, and allegiances. Nawaz explains that it's not just Islamist extremists that have learned to use technology and social media. Anti-Islamist rhetoric is also on the rise and affecting the political climate across Europe.

Where does that leave advocates for democracy? Nawaz believes they're getting left far behind. He asks, "Why is it that Islamists—*Islamism* meaning those who wish to impose one version of Islam over the rest of society—are succeeding in organizing in a globalized way, whereas those who aspire to democratic culture are falling behind?"[15] Nawaz gives four reasons for this trend:

1. *Complacency.* Since those who aspire to democratic culture are generally already in globalized powerful societies, they don't feel the need to advocate for that culture.

2. *Political correctness.* We hesitate to espouse the universality of democratic culture and values because we associate that kind of ideological advocacy with extremists. Even though we say that human rights are universal, the process of actively promoting the ideology that supports those rights is associated with extremism. To go around saying that democratic culture is the best that humanity has arrived at is therefore politically incorrect.

3. *Political Choice.* Democracy in Muslim-majority societies has been relegated to a political choice. Rather than an all-embracing system, it is merely one political choice among many others in those societies.

4. *Resistance Ideology.* This term refers to an ideology whose guiding principle is to resist the predominant power under any circumstances--in other words, an "underdog" ideology, reflexively opposed to those in power. If the world super-ideology today were communism, advocates of democracy would have a much easier time promoting their cause; resistance ideology would be on their side. As it stands, however, the world's greatest superpower—America—is also the world's main representative of democracy. So resistance ideology focuses on defying America and its allies, such as Israel, while perceiving Islam as their victim.

Regarding resistance ideology, Nawaz points out that many citizens of democratic societies have the misconception that Islamist extremism is a product of grievances and a lack of education. The truth, he says, is that, statistically, the majority of those who join and/or lead extremist organizations are highly educated.

But education is not the main reason Islamists and far-right organizations have succeeded. Their success, according to Nawaz, is owing to the fact that, for decades, these organizations have been cultivating demand for their ideology at the grassroots level; patiently and diligently, they have fostered a preference for Islamism. Nawaz cites Pakistan as an example of a state where this vigorous ideological promotion has gone on. As a result, Pakistan is now controlled by organizations who favor theocracy over democracy.

Nawaz suggests that advocates for democracy can learn from Islamist extremists; they ought to develop transnational youth-led movements that promote democracy in the same way that Muslim groups promote Islamist extremism. This needs to involve more than just campaigning for democratic elections. What is needed are organizations that cultivate democratic culture at the grassroots level.

Ideally, this process will lead to societies in which people are voting not for a democracy but *within a democratic system*—in other words, societies that are thoroughly democratic, not just societies in which democracy is one of the choices at the ballot box. A dynamic, youth-focused movement is required for this.

Islamism and Judaism

Another Muslim trying to combat Islamism, especially in regards to its attitude towards Jews, is Tarek Fatah. In *The Jew is not My Enemy*, Fatah has written that Jews and Muslims pray to the same God and honor many of the same prophets, and he cites verses from the Qur'an to support his claims of kinship between the three great monotheistic religions.

While he does not directly address the verses of the Qur'an that are ambivalent or even anti-Semitic towards Jews, Fatah holds that anti-Semitism first entered the Islamic world after the Muslim conquest of Europe, via Christians who converted to Islam during the first millennium of the religion's existence.[16]

Fatah argues that the most important figure in the history of Muslim anti-Semitism is a man named Sayid Qutb (1906-1966), celebrated in the Arab world for his thirty-volume commentary on the Qur'an, but most influential on other grounds. Nearly half a century after Qutb's execution by the Egyptian dictator Gamal Abdel Nasser, the world is still feeling his impact.

Qutb's 1951 essay "Ma'rakatuna ma'a al Yahud" ("Our Fight against the Jews") clearly set out his hostile view of the Jewish world. It was later included in a collection, published in Saudi Arabia in 1970, that bore the same title as Qutb's essay. The Wahhabi Saudis distributed this book widely in the Arab world and it became the definitive expression of the Islamist view of the Jews.

In this influential essay, Qutb defines what he calls the "nature of the Jew" and alleges that destroying Islam is a Jewish goal. Qutb's view is that Arab setbacks at Jewish hands are a matter of divine dispensation. Such defeats signify that Arabs are not following Shari'a closely enough. If they were, then Israel would simply disappear.

Fatah says that Sayyid Qutb's essay misrepresents Islamic history as a long battle against a Jewish monolith bent on destroying Islam. According to Fatah, any Muslim reader taking this essay as a serious guide to Muslim-Jewish relations—and there are many Muslims who do so—would be likely to conclude that Muslims concerned with self-preservation ought to be striving for the total annihilation of the Jewish people. Sayyid Qutb's essay has had a lasting effect on the Muslim psyche. And it isn't just the Jewish people and Jewish ideology that have been the target of Islamism.

Islamism and the West

Since the late 19th century, factions within Islam have increasingly seen Western secular influence as a mortal threat, both practically and morally. To protect Islam from this threat, religious teachers and leaders in certain regions of the Islamic world have initiated "revivalist" movements, some of which have become very active and powerful. These movements have become the driving force in what is becoming a global struggle. Their aim is not to reform or modernize Islam, but to restore it to its original purity.

Extremist movements within a society tend to grow stronger under certain conditions—for example, during periods of

- military or political defeat;
- economic distress;
- social strain;
- national/communal humiliation.

Such conditions have prevailed in much of the Muslim world since the end of the 19th century. This has made it easier for the leaders of Islamist movements to persuade Muslims that their religion has taken a wrong turn and that the solution is a return to an "authentic" Islamic way of life.

In modern times, the first major movement of this kind was Wahhabism. Developed in 18th-century Arabia by a Muslim theologian named Muhammad ibn Abd al-Wahhab (1703–1792), Wahhabism had little or no impact on the rest of the Muslim world for many years. This changed in the 1920s, when the creation of the Saudi monarchy catapulted Wahhabism to official status in Arabia. The house of Saud gained control of the Hijaz region in Arabia, which contains the holy cities of Mecca and Medina. These holy cities thus became part of the new entity of Saudi Arabia. Before long, this kingdom discovered oil, and immense funds were placed at its disposal.

Wahhabism is not opposed to the West so much as to the Westernizers—that is, to those Muslims whose solution to the threat of the West is to adopt Western ways. The Wahhabis consider such adoption a betrayal of Islam, and they believe that the only way to combat Western influence is to revive "authentic" Muslim practices.

Wahhabi anger is focused not only on the Westernizing Muslim factions, but on Muslims who do not share their particular Wahhabi beliefs—most notably, the members of the Shi'a movement. In particular, they oppose the regime which arose after the Iranian Revolution of 1979. The Shi'a are the Sunni-Wahhabi's main rivals for the leadership of the Islamic world. The Wahhabis consider Muslims who do not share their views not as Muslims but as apostates.

Saudi wealth has spread Wahhabism all over the Muslim world, not only to Muslim countries, but also to Muslim communities in non-Islamic European countries and in North America. Wahhabism has sprouted variant movements and organizations, all concerned with the struggle against Western imperialists and against Muslim factions whom the extremists regard as dangerously soft on Western values. One of these Wahhabi offshoots is the *Muslim Brotherhood*, a fundamentalist sect seeking a return to the "authentic" faith of the first Muslims.

The most recent movement—in some ways, a product of all the previous movements—is made up of extremist (and often violent) Sunni factions that arose in the early 1990s. These factions include Al-Qaida. The Shi'a have their own extremist terrorist groups, notably Hizballah (literally, "the Party of God"), which is centered in Iran and currently most active in Syria and Lebanon. The Iranian extremists, despite being Shi'a, are reported to have links with the strongly Sunni Hamas organization in Gaza—although allegiances in the region are prone to fickleness.

In the West, we have sometimes wondered what to call these extremist movements within Islam. While they are, for the most part, fundamentalist movements, we need to keep two important facts in mind: first, that most Muslims are not fundamentalists; and second, that most fundamentalists are not terrorists.

Whether extremist or not, Islam, with its 1.3 billion adherents, is a formidable presence in world society. Though some of the concepts in Shari'a, as we have seen, run contrary to a democratic mindset, is it possible that the vast Muslim population could be infused with democratic ideals? Maajid Nawaz, no stranger to Islamist extremism, seems to think so; he believes that Islam and democracy are compatible. He is attempting to promote a democratic culture among Muslims with the social movement (Khudi) he founded in 2009. Nawaz offers himself as evidence that Islam and democracy are compatible; as he has said, the more he learned about Islam, the more tolerant (that is democratic) he became, and the less extreme. Tarek Fatah and Sheikh Palazzi have also seen ways to reconcile Islam with democratic ideology.

Perhaps, then, Nawaz and others like him can effect significant social change through reconciling Islam and democracy at a grassroots level. Democracy, as we have discussed, is not perfect, but history has shown it to be the political ideology that is most respectful of human rights and therefore an ideology worth advocating for.

In the meantime, we in the West face the considerable challenge of combatting the extremist ideas of Sayyid Qutb, ideas that now pervade Arab societies across the Middle East and Africa. Such a task is particularly pressing for anyone trying to find a peaceful resolution to the ongoing disputes between the state of Israel and the modern Arab states—both of which are outcomes of the 19th-century Arab and Jewish nationalist movements, discussed in the next chapter.

Endnotes

1   Bernard Lewis, *The Middle East* (London: Phoenix, 2000), 52.

2   Paul Johnson, *History of the Jews* (New York: Harper, 1987), 167.

3   Ibid.

4   Several verses, including Sura 2:142, 143, 144, and 149 in the Quran, refer to the importance of the new *qibla* in Mecca. Mecca's status as the holiest city in Islam is also based on the following Muslim beliefs: God tested Abraham when Ishmael (not Isaac, as in the Jewish version of this narrative) was required as a sacrifice in or near Mecca; the well of Zam Zam, which God gave to Hagar after she was expelled by Abraham, was located in or near Mecca; Abraham built the House of God (Ka'ba) in Mecca; the Ka'ba in Mecca is the "Centre of Universal Worship and the Symbol of Islamic Unity." See Jacques Paul Gauthier, *Sovereignty Over the Old City of Jerusalem: A Study of the Historical, Religious, Political and Legal Aspects of the Question of the Old City*, Thèse No. 725 (Geneva: Université de Genève, 2007), 195-196.

5   Sheikh Abdul Hadi Palazzi, *Rights to Jerusalem according to Qu'ran - Sheikh Abdul Hadi Palazzi*, 2011, YouTube, accessed April 24, 2012, http://www.youtube.com/watch?v=wzIU9D6qbCo.

6   Regarding the definitions for "Islam" and "Muslim," see Bernard Lewis and Buntzie Ellis Churchill, *Islam: The Religion and the People* (New Jersey: Wharton School Publishing, 2009), 7-8.

7   Sheikh Abdul Hadi Palazzi, *Rights to Jerusalem according to Qu'ran - Sheikh Abdul Hadi Palazzi*, 2011, YouTube, accessed April 24, 2012, http://www.youtube.com/watch?v=wzIU9D6qbCo.

8   Majid Khadduri, *War and Peace in the Law of Islam* (Baltimore: The Johns Hopkins Press, 1955), 52-53.

9   Ibid, 51-52.

10   Regarding dhimmi, see Bat Ye'or, *Islam and Dhimmitude: Where Civilizations Collide*, trans. Miriam Kochan and David Littman (Madison: Fairleigh Dickinson University Press, 2002); and Ken Spiro, *Worlds in Collision (Today's Islam Factor)*, aishaudio, accessed May 15, 2009, https://aishaudio.com/.

11   Maajid Nawaz, "A global culture to fight extremism," TED, July 2011, accessed April 24, 2012, http://www.ted.com/talks/maajid_nawaz_a_global_culture_to_fight_extremism.html?quote=1001.

12   Ibid.

13   Ibid.

14   Ibid.

15   Ibid.

16   Tarek Fatah, *The Jew Is Not My Enemy* (Toronto: McClelland and Stewart, 2010), 23.

Chapter **9**

Religious and Political Zionism

Introduction

The Arab world has been critical of Zionism, labeling it "imperialistic," "colonial," "aggressive," and identifying it as the cause of the Arab-Israeli conflict in the Middle East. Criticism of Zionism has come from Jews as well. A Jewish history professor has recently said that Zionism is not a religious concept and is, in fact, "a contradiction to the Jewish religion."[1] In this chapter, we'll examine the validity of these claims, while defining both religious and political Zionism, and considering the aspirations and ideologies to which they refer. We'll put political Zionism in its historical context, looking at the background of the movement and at its founders and key leaders. We will also look at the Arab equivalent of the Zionist movement—the Arab National Movement.

What Is Zionism?

In its broadest sense, the term *Zionism* simply signifies a strong spiritual longing for Jerusalem. But it is commonly used to refer to a more specific aspiration, which we will call *political Zionism*—that is, the movement and ideology dedicated to creating a Jewish state in Palestine, or *Eretz Israel* ("the Land of Israel"). For our purposes, religious and political Zionism are not synonymous and we will distinguish between the two, while acknowledging that they have a good deal in common.

The term *Zionism* is derived from the word *Zion*, a frequent synonym in the Bible for "Jerusalem." There are numerous Biblical verses which refer to "Zion" or "Mount Zion" and directly associate it with Jerusalem. Isaiah 2:3, for example, states the following: "For out of Zion shall go forth the law, and the word of the Lord from Jerusalem."

With respect to usage, the term *Zionism* is relatively recent, and most probably coined by Nathan Birnbaum in the late 19th century, in his periodical, *Self-Emancipation!*. But the concept of Zionism is ancient. As Paul Johnson has said,

Of course Zionism was not new. It was as old as the Babylonian exile. Had not the psalmists sung: 'By the rivers of Babylon, there we sat down, yea, we wept, when we remembered Zion'? For more than a millennium and a half, every Jewish generation, in every Jewish community, had contained one or two who dreamed of Zion. Some had fulfilled the dream personally by going there: to Tiberias, to Safed, to Zion itself. Others had thought to found little congregations or colonies. All of these, however, had been religious Zionists.[2]

As Johnson suggests, Zionism—or, more specifically, *religious Zionism*—has long existed among the Jewish people, some of whom have always felt a strong spiritual connection to Jerusalem and, by extension, to Israel. (And one might argue that Zionism of this kind is not exclusive to Jews, but is also felt by Muslims and Christians.) Zion, or Jerusalem, has been central to Judaism for millennia. It is mentioned in the Bible over 600 times and, as we have discussed in previous chapters, its connection to Judaism is undeniable and well documented in Biblical verses and stories.

Dr. Jacques Gauthier has noted that Chaim Weizmann, one of the key leaders of the Zionist Organization, "believed that in order to understand Zionism it was necessary to comprehend the deep connection between the 'people of Israel, the God of Israel, and the Land of Israel'."[3]

In an essay on Zionism published in August, 1916, Dr. Weizmann wrote the following:

The persistence of the Jewish people through 2000 years of dispersion is due to its capacity for organizing a group life of its own, under whatever external conditions, on the basis of a spiritual idea—the idea of the eternity of Israel as bound up with the universality of the God of Israel. This idea, carrying with it as a corollary the belief in a future restoration of the people to its homeland had been at the root of the Jewish attitude to life, and has supplied in the Jewish struggle for existence the place of the more concrete expressions of nationality. The people of Israel, the God of Israel, the land of Israel—these are the indestructible kernel around which has grown an outer shell of belief tradition, religious observance, and social custom.[4]

Weizmann combined politics with religion in his vision of the Zionist enterprise, but religiosity is not always integrated into Zionism. Herzl, for example, who presided over the inception of political Zionism, was not motivated by religious concerns. Nor are a great many Zionists today. As we discussed earlier, Shlomo Sand, a Jewish history professor at Tel Aviv University, said that Zionism is not a religious concept and is in fact antithetical to Judaism.[5]

What Sand likely means is that the secular elements of political Zionism contradict the tenets of the Jewish religion. And it is true that religious Zionists have, from the beginning of political Zionism, taken issue with its secular dimension. (We touched on this conflict in Chapter 1, when discussing the controversy over the mention of God in Israel's Declaration of Independence.) Religious Zionists generally hold that the Land of Israel was meant for a spiritual purpose and that creating a political entity with secular aims in the "Holy Land" is antithetical to Judaism.

This conflict between religious and political Zionism is a relatively new phenomenon in Jewish history, but the conflict between secular and religious Jews in Israel is ancient. The dynamic was in place in the 4th century BCE, when Hellenistic and traditional Jews battled over whose ideology would dominate in ancient Israel.

But how did the political and religious Zionist ideas merge in the 19th and 20th centuries to create the circumstances that would result in the creation of the State of Israel? To answer this question, we need to consider the ideas and personalities that arose in the Jewish communities of Eastern and Western Europe during that period.

The Modern Zionist Idea

Before the Russian pogroms of the 19th century, the great majority of Jews believed that their future would be assimilation in one form or another. This idea of assimilation was most firmly rooted in France, home to the revolutions that inspired the spread of liberal democracy in Europe. These revolutions had been helpful to France's Jews, who were emancipated in 1791. But the social progress of French Jews was hardly due to their popularity in that country. France had deep historic ties to the Roman Catholic Church, in which anti-Semitism was deeply entrenched. When the Emperor Napoleon came to power and, surprisingly, ordered the revival of the ancient Jewish superior court (Sanhedrin), he expected certain commitments in return.

Howard Sachar has said the following of Napoleon:

> He demanded specific assurances that rabbinical jurisdiction in Jewish civil and judicial affairs was a thing of the past, that the Jews turned their backs forever on their separate nationhood, on their corporative status, and not the least of all, their traditional hope for redemption in Palestine.[6]

The members of the revived Sanhedrin declared that their rabbinical laws would be applied exclusively to matters of religious tradition and practice, and that France would have sole claim on their political allegiance. The French Jews would, from this point on, "renounce forever their dream of a collective exodus to the ancestral Land of Israel."[7]

These commitments, made by the French Jews to Napoleon in the late 18th century, exerted a significant influence even beyond the borders of France. Throughout Western Europe, Jews began to reject their traditional identification with Zion and their historic civilization in the hope of acquiring or protecting new civic freedoms. The 19th-century German reform movement within Judaism, for example, was rooted in the increasing secularization and nationalism of Western Europe's Jews—a period that came to be known as the *Haskalah* (Jewish "Enlightenment").

Eastern European Jews during this period, the majority of whom were in Russia, continued to cherish their Jewish cultural heritage and to lament the loss of their ancestral homeland. But despite being Zionistic in the religious sense, the Russian Jews, like the Jews of Western Europe, resisted the notion of a mass Jewish return to the Land of Israel. A factor in this resistance was Alexander II's ascension to the throne of Russia in 1855. His humanistic philosophy opened up new opportunities for Russian Jews and gave them no incentive to return to Zion.

Things began to change when the next tsar, Alexander III, succeeded to the throne in 1881. Intolerant and anti-Semitic, he shattered Russian Jewry's hopes for equality and achievement under the tsarist regime.

The anti-Jewish policies of Tsarist Russia, always severe compared with the rest of Europe, grew even more oppressive under Alexander III. Russian Jews were banned or severely restricted from entering government service, from attending state schools, serving on juries, and voting. With these intolerably harsh policies, the Russian government's aim was simple—to radically reduce the country's Jewish population by driving the Jews elsewhere.

When official persecution failed, the Russian government resorted to mob violence. The first modern Russian pogrom took place in Odessa in 1871. In 1881, there were pogroms all over Russia, condoned—and in some cases organized—by the government. Events of this kind occurred continually in Russia through the next decades and into the 20th century. In the face of these cruel hardships, the Jews of Russia began to emigrate in large numbers.

The flight of Jews from Russia was a significant factor in the rise of Zionism. In the other countries of Europe, there was a groundswell of popular resentment against the Jewish newcomers from the East, who were both destitute and highly visible. Anti-Semitism took on a virulent new edge in countries such as France and Germany. It changed the way European Jews thought about themselves. For a long time, established Jewish communities in France, Austria, England, and elsewhere had assumed that assimilation would be their destiny. After 1881, these dreams began to dissipate, and a new dream arose.

The seeds of contemporary Zionism can be found in the works of key 19th-century Jewish thinkers in both Western and Eastern Europe. Two of these thinkers--Moses Hess in the West, and Leo Pinsker in the East—underwent radical shifts in their attitudes about Zionism during the period of the Jewish exodus from Russia. Both had once shared in the prevailing optimism of the Haskalah movements, believing that things were looking up for the Jews. But their optimism did not last.

Pinsker became the leader of a network of hundreds of Zionist study circles in Russia, which came to be known as *Chovevei Zion*—"Lovers of Zion." Their common credo was that "there is no salvation for the People of Israel unless they establish a government of their own in the Land of Israel."[8] By the 1890s, the Chovevei Zion had a strong presence throughout parts of Europe, setting the stage for the man who would propel Zionism to the international political level: Theodor Herzl.

France, the Dreyfus affair, and Herzl

France had been a relatively hospitable home to Jews for almost a century. The 1789 Revolution's legacy of civil liberties had benefited the Jewish population, and French Jews tended to be intensely nationalistic, seeing France as a haven for Jews and Judaism.

But French anti-Semitism was, in fact, deeply entrenched, and The Dreyfus Affair would bring it to the surface in a way that caught most of the Jews of Western Europe by surprise. Captain Alfred Dreyfus (1859–1935) was a Jewish officer in the French army. In 1894, he was falsely accused of selling military secrets to the Germans and was subsequently sentenced to life imprisonment on Devil's Island. He was eventually exonerated and released, but the army didn't officially acknowledge any wrongdoing until years later. The case polarized French society for a decade and revealed the strength of the country's anti-Semitism.

Among the journalists covering the case was Theodor Herzl (1860–1904), an Austrian Jew and the Paris correspondent for a Viennese newspaper. Herzl had grown up, like many European Jews, aspiring to total assimilation. But the scandalous injustice of the Dreyfus case and the anti-Semitic mob behavior it inspired in France—a country that many Jews imagined to be a bastion of tolerance—convinced Herzl of something he had suspected for years, namely, the great vulnerability of the Jews of Europe. Herzl felt that an autonomous Jewish state was the only chance the Jews had to survive.

Within months of Dreyfus's conviction, Herzl had written a draft of *Der Judenstaat* ("The Jewish State"), which heralded the coming of age of Zionism. "We are a people—one people," Herzl wrote in this seminal work. "We have honestly endeavored everywhere to merge ourselves in the social life of surrounding communities and to preserve the faith of our fathers. We are not permitted to do so."[9] As Herzl saw it, the only solution was to emigrate and build a Jewish nation. With this aim in mind and with the power of his personality, Herzl managed to organize a Zionist congress in 1897.

The Growth of Political Zionism

The First Zionist World Congress was held in Basel, Switzerland, from August 29 to August 31, 1897. It was attended by delegates from many nations and marked the birth of Zionism as a political movement. It was during the Basel Congress that political Zionism gained significant momentum.

At the conclusion of the Congress, the following resolution relating to the "aim" of Zionism was adopted:

The aim is to create for the Jewish people a legally assured home in Palestine. In order to attain this object, the Congress adopts the following means:

1. To promote [Jewish] settlement in Palestine...

2. To centralize the entire Jewish people...

3. To strengthen Jewish sentiment and national self-conscience...

4.   To obtain the sanctions of governments...[10]

How did Zionism go from the ideas at Basel to a movement whose aims would receive international recognition and support?

Weizmann and Balfour

After Herzl's early death, at the age of 44, in 1904, it was Dr. Chaim Weizmann (1874–1952) who led the cause of political Zionism. Weizmann grew up under the repressive anti-Jewish policies of the Tsarist government in Russia. He received his doctorate in chemistry from Freiburg University in Switzerland and then went to England, where he taught biochemistry and conducted scientific research at Manchester University. His chemical discoveries were critical to the Allied war effort in World War I.

It was in England on January 9, 1906, that Weizmann was introduced to Lord Arthur Balfour, the leader of the opposition and former British prime minister. The relationship that Weizmann developed with Balfour was key in furthering the aims established at the Basel conference seven years before—specifically, the aims of obtaining the "sanctions of governments" for the new Jewish state and of promoting "Jewish settlement in Palestine." Weizmann's meetings with Balfour fostered a decade-long political process in England that ultimately resulted in the Balfour Declaration of 1917. The Balfour Declaration, which will be discussed in the next chapter, was Britain's formal approval for the establishing of a Jewish national home in Palestine.

Building the Jewish National Home

Herzl put Zionism on the map, and Weizmann furthered the Zionist agenda by gaining the sanction of the British government, among others. But the actual building of the Jewish National home was being fought on the ground by the early settlers of the *Yishuv*—the Jewish community living in Palestine from the late 19th century until the formation of the state of Israel in 1948.

The leaders of the Yishuv had strong—and often conflicting—ideas about the ideology on which to found the Jewish national home, and in general did not believe (or refused to believe) that political Zionism was a Jewish nationalistic endeavor on a collision course with Arab nationalism in Palestine. The inevitability of the clash between Arabs and Zionists became clear to David Ben Gurion, one of the key early leaders of the Yishuv, during his 1936 meetings with George Antonius, a leading Arab figure.

After his talks with Antonius in May 1936, Ben Gurion stated publicly for the first time that there was a conflict between Arab and Jewish nationalism in Palestine. "We and they want the same thing: We both want Palestine. And that is the fundamental conflict."[11]

Nationalism

We briefly discussed *nationalism* in Chapter 7, but the subject warrants more attention now. As a political ideology, nationalism involves a group of people strongly identifying with a political entity—for example, a nation-state. Precisely where nationalism emerged is difficult to determine—it is an ancient phenomenon—but its modern development is closely tied to the American and French Revolutions of the late 18th century. As a political ideology, it continued in 19th century Europe, with various ethnic/national revolutions, such as the Greek war of independence. Like Europe, Palestine became embroiled in nationalist aims. There are a number of forms that nationalism can take, but the two that are most relevant to the ideological differences between Jews and Arabs (and between Jews themselves), at least with regard to Palestine, are civic and ethnic nationalism.

According to the principles of *civic nationalism*, a nation is not based on a common ethnic ancestry. Civic nationalism defines a nation as an alliance between people who have equal and shared political rights, and who are devoted to similar political procedures. The civic concept of nationalism was described in Ernest Renan's 1882 lecture "What is a Nation?" in which he defines the concept of "the nation" in terms of a people's willingness to live together. This is civic nationalism, and it is compatible with such values as freedom, tolerance, equality, and individual rights, which are characteristic of liberal democracies.

Other forms of nationalism are less accommodating than civic nationalism. Some nationalist ideologies define their national community in ethnic, linguistic, cultural, historic, or religious terms (or any combination of these), and these forms of nationalism tend to exclude certain minorities from the "national community" as they define it. One of these exclusory forms of nationalism is *ethnic nationalism*. A defining assumption of ethnic nationalism is that all legitimate members of a given nation are descended from the same ethnic stock and that ethnicity remains unchanged over time. Ethnic nationalists believe that nations are defined by a shared heritage, which usually includes a common language, a common faith, and a common ethnic ancestry.

Nationalism, then, can be a belief that a nation state should be limited to one ethnic, cultural, or religious group. It can also manifest itself as a movement to establish or protect a "homeland" for an ethnic group. Jewish nationalism remained primarily a religious and cultural experience until the 19th century, when the idea of creating a Jewish state in Palestine assumed the character of a political/ nationalistic ideology.

Jewish Nationalism and Political Zionism

David Ben-Gurion (1886–1973) was arguably the most influential figure in developing the Zionist ideology that came to dominate the Yishuv. In a series of articles included in the volume *From Class to Nation* (1933), Ben-Gurion wrote that Zionism was concerned with taking masses of uprooted, impoverished, sterile Jewish masses, living parasitically off the body of an alien economic body and dependent on others—and introducing them to productive and creative life, implanting them on the land, integrating them into primary production in agriculture, in industry and handicraft—and making them economically independent and self-sufficient. ...

Zionism in its essence is a revolutionary movement. One could hardly find a revolution that goes deeper than what Zionism wants to do to the life of the Hebrew people. This is not merely a revolution of the political and economic structure—but a revolution of the very foundation of the personal lives of the members of the people. The very essence of Zionist thinking about the life of the Jewish people and on Hebrew history is basically revolutionary—it is a revolt against a tradition of many centuries, helplessly longing for redemption. Instead of these sterile and bloodless longings, we substitute a will for realization, an attempt at reconstruction and creativity on the soil of the homeland. Instead of a people dependent on others, instead of a minority living at the mercy of the majority, we call for a self-sufficient people, master of its own fate. Instead of a corrupt existence of middlemen, hung-up in mid-air, we call for an independent existence of a working people, at home on the soil and in a creative economy.[12]

Ben-Gurion believed that Zionism's aim was not merely the geographical relocation of Jews to the Land of Israel but a total restructuring of the Jewish socioeconomic fabric. He believed that, for Jewish independence to be successful in Palestine, it had to be established on a foundation of economic independence—in other words, a self-sufficient Jewish community that was not dependent on the labor of others. In Ben Gurion's view, there was no political power without economic power. He felt it essential that the Zionist enterprise be built with Jewish labor.

Ben Gurion was aware that changing the mindset of the Jewish people once they arrived in Israel would be more difficult than enticing them to immigrate. Their successful adaptation to the new life would require a shift from an urban lifestyle to an agricultural one based on physical labor. Many of the Jews of Eastern Europe were not accustomed to such a lifestyle.

Ben Gurion's views, though socialist, were not the views of the European socialist parties of the Zionist labor movement. In 1935, in an article called "Our Action and Our Direction," Ben Gurion took issue with fellow Zionists who did not share his belief in the importance of agricultural settlements. In making his case, Ben Gurion provided a historical example, which he said should be a lesson:

Once there was a great Canaanite military leader [Hannibal], from a stock close to the ancient Hebrews. ... Yet ultimately all his heroism and all his military and political genius did not sustain him—and he was not only a strategic genius, but also a statesman of genius. Eventually he was defeated, despite the fact that his adversaries were rather mediocre generals with no talent. Roman mediocrity defeated Canaanite genius. For Carthage was a *city-state*, whereas Rome was a village-state, and in the desperate conflict between a city-people and a village-people, the village-people proved victorious, and all the commercial wealth of Carthage and the ingenuity of its military leaders were to no avail. Hannibal's heroism was broken by the obstinate warfare of the Roman peasants. These peasants were not taken aback by the successive defeats inflicted on them—because they were integrated into their soil and tied to their land. And they overcame Carthage and wiped it off the face of the earth without leaving a trace.[13]

Though he did not see eye to eye with other Zionist socialists, Ben Gurion believed that Zionism and *socialism* were two sides of the same coin. In his opening speech at the 1950 convention of the Labor Party (Mapai), he said the following:

The terms Zionism and socialism are but two different expressions and manifestations of the same praxis: the creative praxis of the working Jewish person and his vision, aiming at molding national and general human life according to his own image; for only an image of a creative society of workers, free and enjoying equal rights, can guarantee independence, liberty and equality to all members of the Jewish people and all nations of the world.[14]

Ben Gurion's philosophy was a form of democratic socialism that incorporated Western principles, such as equal rights. He saw socialism not only as the end, but as the means through which Zionism would be realized. In his view, the only secure foundation for the Jewish state was a strong national labor force, spread throughout the country in the form of agricultural settlements. But what were the grounds of Ben-Gurion's beliefs in this regard? Why did he believe that the Zionist enterprise, to be effective politically and militarily, needed to be based on a socialist mindset with a "village-state" mentality. Perhaps he saw that a strong national labor force, with unions, would make an effective communication network within Israel—an important factor in homeland security. As for his insistence on agricultural settlements, perhaps Ben-Gurion understood that the Jewish farmers—like the Roman peasant farmers who overcame the Carthaginians—would fight harder and more desperately for land they felt to be their own.

Whatever the basis of his thinking, Ben Gurion turned out to be correct. His wisdom was verified in 1948. This was the year that, under his leadership, the *Haganah* (the National Military Organization) was able to repel the Arab armies. The Haganah's success came from their social infrastructure—hundreds of Jewish settlements (the Yishuv) across the country, sustained by the collective partnership of the *Histadrut* (the federation of labor unions established in 1920, with Ben-Gurion at their helm).

One of Ben-Gurion's strongest ideological opponents was a Russian Jew named Ze'ev Jabotinsky (1880-1940). Jabotinsky, like Herzl, regarded the escape from anti-Semitism and the relief of Jewish suffering to be the ultimate aims of the

Zionist enterprise. For this reason, he demanded a radical revision of the Zionist organization's gradualist approach to building the Jewish national home. Jabotinsky called instead for mass immigration to the Jewish state. He said the following:

> The first aim of Zionism is the creation of a Jewish majority on both sides of the Jordan River. This is not the ultimate goal of the Zionist movement, which aspires to more far-reaching ideals, such as the solution of the question of Jewish suffering throughout the entire world and the creation of a new Jewish culture. The precondition for the attainment of these noble aims, however, is a country in which the Jews constitute a majority. It is only after this majority is attained that Palestine can undergo a normal political development on the basis of democratic, parliamentary principles without thereby endangering the Jewish national character of the country.[15]

For all their differences, both Jabotinsky and Ben-Gurion shared a democratic vision for the future Jewish national home. However, Jabotinsky did not underestimate the Arab resistance to the Zionist aim of a Jewish majority. He made the following prediction about the future relations between Jews and Arabs in Israel:

> It is a dangerous falsehood, however, to present such a reconciliation as an already existing fact. Arab public opinion in Palestine is against the creation of a Jewish majority there. The Arabs will continue to fight for a long time—sometimes energetically and sometimes apathetically, sometimes with political means and sometimes with other means—against all that which leads to the creation of this majority until the moment that the overwhelming might of the Jews in the country, i.e., the Jewish majority, becomes a fact. Only then will true reconciliation commence. To close our eyes to this state of affairs is unwise and irresponsible. We Revisionists are keeping our eyes open and want to be prepared for every eventuality. With all the sincere goodwill [we feel] toward the Arab people, we nevertheless firmly believe that the transformation of Palestine into a Jewish state is a postulate of the highest justice and that of all opposition to it is unjust. One may either come to terms with injustice or make any concessions to it. In this case especially, namely, the question of the formation of a majority, there is from our side no possibility to concede anything. One can only struggle against injustice, with peaceful means as long as it is not expressed in acts of violence, and with other means when it assumes the form of violence.[16]

As one can see from the views of both Jabotinsky and Ben-Gurion, the ideology of political Zionism in the first half of the 20th century was a strange mixture of ideas and concepts. As Anita Shapira has noted,

> The accumulated impact of diverse sources (e.g. ancient Jewish tradition, nineteenth-century humanistic and liberal enlightenment thought, and twentieth century nationalism and socialist-revolutionary ideology) gave

rise to a complex and varied collective personality, in which the desire for justice and sovereignty, moral elevation and physical power, the fraternity of man and national greatness were all mixed.[17]

These ideological divides are still evident in Israeli politics and in Israel's relationship with the Palestinian Arabs. It is not difficult to see from the above how Jewish and Arab nationalism came to a head in Palestine.

Zionism and the Arab-Israeli Conflict

Many people have identified Zionism (by which they mean "political" Zionism) as the primary cause of the Arab-Israeli conflict. The Palestinian National Charter, adopted by the National Congress of the Palestine Liberation Organization in July, 1968, certainly defines Zionism in this way. Article 22 of this document says the following:

> Zionism is a national political movement organically associated with international imperialism and antagonistic to all action for liberation and to progressive movements in the world. It is racist and fanatic in its nature, aggressive, expansionistic, and colonial in its aims, and fascist in its methods. Israel is the instrument of the Zionist movement, and a geographical base for world imperialism placed strategically in the midst of the Arab homeland to combat the hopes of the Arab nation for liberation, unity, and progress.[18]

Is this the case? Is Israel really the "instrument" of the Zionist movement, and is the latter, as the Palestinian document implies, really the source of the Arab-Israeli conflict? Not so, according to King Abdul Aziz Al-Saud (1876–1953), also known as Ibn Saud, the first monarch of Saudi Arabia. According to him, the enmity between Jews and Muslims has a much deeper source and is enshrined in the Qur'an. In March, 1946, Ibn Saud said the following:

> I am greatly interested in the question of Palestine because I am [an] Arab and a Muslim. The enmity between Jews and Muslims is not new. It is an old one, which goes back thousands of years, and Allah mentioned it in the Holy Qur'an, 'Strongest among men in enmity to the Believers wilt thou find the Jews and pagans…' The content of this Holy Aya [from Sura Al-Maidah, Verse 82] is the pillar of my policy and Muslim religious policy in general.[19]

The words of this Arab leader seem to contradict the idea that political Zionism is the sole source of the Arab-Israeli conflict. As Ibn Saud suggests (and as we noted when we discussed Islam in Chapter 8), the animosity between Jews and Arab Muslims is mentioned in the Qur'an; the hostility that Arabs feel toward Jews is ancient, dating from the inception of Islam, which means that it has theological roots.

There is a solid basis for Ibn Saud's claims that the tensions between the Jews and the Arabs are rooted in theology—though these claims are routinely dismissed in certain quarters. But it is also true that the modern conflict between the Palestinian Arabs and Israel is a product of another recent historical development—namely, the rise of Arab nationalism, which was becoming an ideological and political force around the same time as political Zionism.

The Origins of the Arab National Movement

Many people believe that the Arabs had no political organization themselves, no equivalent of the Jewish Zionist movement.

History reveals a different picture. While Weizmann was meeting with Balfour and the British Government on behalf of the Zionist Organization, the Arabs were developing their own political movement. A gathering of Arabs met in June 1913, at a meeting referred to as the First Arab Congress. The delegates of the First Arab Congress sought greater autonomy for the Arabs within the Ottoman Empire, which was declining in power even as Arab nationalism was beginning to emerge. The Congress proposed a decentralized Ottoman State, with Arab representation on all legislative and executive levels.

According to Dr. Jacques Gauthier, this meeting was significant because it tells us that, prior to World War I, the Arabs, like the Zionists, had begun to organize a political movement with sovereignty aims. What this also tells us is that, at this time, the Arabs had no autonomy in the Ottoman territories, including the territory of Palestine/Eretz Yisrael. Autonomy in the region rested with the Ottoman Empire, as it had for approximately five centuries. In the early 20th century, in other words, the Arabs had no sovereignty over any area in the Middle East.[20]

But that was about to change. The decision of the Ottoman (Turkish) Empire to join Germany and Austria-Hungary (collectively, the Central Powers) against the British Empire, France, Russia, and their allies (collectively, the Allied Powers) in World War I contributed significantly to the evolution of Arab Nationalism and to the dispute that is ongoing today between the Arabs and the State of Israel. How that is so, and the events which led to the creation of the modern state of Israel are the focus of Part II of this work.

Endnotes

1   "Shlomo Sand: Challenging notions of a Jewish People " video clip accessed March 4, 2012, Youtube, http://www.youtube.com/watch?v=1EmvANgw9Mk.

2   Paul Johnson, *History of the Jews* (New York: Harper Perennial, 1987), 374. See also Psalms 137:1.

3   Jacques Paul Gauthier, *Sovereignty Over the Old City of Jerusalem: A Study of the Historical, Religious, Political and Legal Aspects of the Question of the Old City*, Thèse No. 725 (Geneva: Université de Genève, 2007), 249.

4   *The Letters and Papers of Chaim Weizman*, vol. 2. Series B, December 1931-April 1952, Ed. Barnet Litvinoff (Jerusalem: Israel University Press, 1983), Paper 28, 135, 139.

5   "Shlomo Sand: Challenging notions of a Jewish People " Youtube.

6   Howard Sachar, *A History of Israel from the Rise of Zionism to Our Time*, 3rd ed. (New York: Alfred A. Knopf, 2010), 3.

7   Ibid, 4.

8   Ibid, 16.

9   Theodor Herzl, "Introduction," *The Jewish State* (1896), trans. Sylvie D'Avigdor (1946), *Jewish Virtual Library*, accessed May 8, 2012, http://www.jewishvirtuallibrary.org/jsource/Zionism/herzl2a.html (accessed May 8, 2012).

10   Gauthier, *Sovereignty Over the Old City*, 244.

11   David Ben Gurion, JAG—Protocols of the Jewish Agency Directorate in the Central Zionist Archives (Jerusalem, May 19, 1936), quoted in Shabtai Teveth, *Ben-Gurion and the Palestinian Arabs: From Peace to War* (New York: Oxford University Press, 1985), 166.

12   David Ben Gurion, *Mi-maamad le-am* [From Class to Nation], rev. ed. (Tel Aviv, 1974), 196-197. Quoted in Shlomo Avineri, *The Making of Modern Zionism* (New York: Basic Books, 1981), 200.

13   Yaacov Becker, ed., Mishnato shel David Ben Gurion [The Teaching of David Ben Gurion], (Tel Aviv: 1958), vol. 2, 525-26, quoted in Avineri, Making of Modern Zionism, 202.

14   Yaacov Becker, *Mishnato shel David Ben Gurion*, 1: 190-191, quoted in Avineri, *Making of Modern Zionism*, 204.

15   Vladimir Jabotinsky, "What the Zionist-Revisionists Want," in *The Jew in the Modern World*, eds. Paul R. Mendes-Flohr and Jehuda Reinharz (New York: Oxford University Press, 1995), 594.

16   Ibid.

17   Anita Shapira, *Land and Power: The Zionist Resort to Force, 1881-1948*, trans. William Templer (Stanford: Stanford University Press, 1999), 354.

18   *Palestinian National Charter*, (as amended in 1968), Avalon Project, Yale Law School, accessed March 25, 2012, http://avalon.law.yale.edu/20th_century/plocov.asp.

19   *The Holy Qu'ran & the Sword: Selected Addresses, Speeches, Memoranda and Interviews by HM Late King Abdul Aziz Al-Saud*, ed. Mohyiddin al-Qabesi (Riyadh: Saudi Desert House for Publishing 1998), 166-169.

20   Gauthier, *Sovereignty Over the Old City*, 263.

Part Two

Israel Among the Nations

Chapter 10

WWI Pledges and Agreements

World War I and the Ottoman Empire

By the first decade of the 20th century, the Arab and Jewish nationalist movements were in full bloom. Both needed territory to fulfill their aims. The Jews sought Palestine; the Arabs sought an area that included the Arabian Peninsula, Mesopotamia, and Syria. These lands, however, had been in the hands of the Ottoman Empire for approximately five centuries and were not available. It took World War I to loosen the Turkish grip. On October 31st, 1914, the Ottoman Empire joined Germany and the Austro-Hungarian Empire (the Central Powers) against the British Empire, France, Russia, and their allies (the Allied Powers). And thus began a new phase in the history of the Middle East.

The Turkish government's decision to join the Central Powers in the Great War increased the significance of the Arab people to the Allies and stimulated Arab nationalism. Why? The Allied Powers feared the general antagonism of the Muslim world. Their specific concern was that Turkey, the premier Islamic state, would rouse the Arab Muslim world against them. They foresaw how this could happen. If the Ottoman Sultan declared that Turkey was at war with the Christian Powers and that the Holy Places were in danger, all true Muslim believers would feel obliged to rally around the banner of the Faith.

It was in the Allied Powers' interest, then, to forge an alliance with the Arabs against the Turks. This was especially the case for Great Britain, which had a further consideration in the region. Turkey's hold on Syria and Iraq was a threat to two vital British interests: the Suez Canal, and the head of the Persian Gulf, where the valuable oil-fields of the Anglo-Persian Company were located. The Arabs, for their part, saw that forging an alliance with the Allied Powers could help them further their nationalist aims and throw off the Turkish yoke.

The Arab Revolt Against the Turks

Arab nationalist leaders prepared to approach the British with a proposal. First they sent a message to Husain bin Ali, the Sharif of Mecca. Husain was the last of the Hashemite rulers over the Hejaz and, because he claimed direct descent from the Prophet Muhammad, he was regarded by many as the leading figure in the Arab–Islamic world. This message informed Husain that

> the nationalist leaders in Syria and Iraq, including senior Arab officers in the Turkish army, favor a revolt for the attainment of Arab independence; would the Sharif consent to lead it, and if so, would he receive a deputation in Mecca or delegate persons of trust to Damascus to concert measures?[1]

There followed a series of covert meetings in Damascus, beginning in March and April of 1915, between the Sharif's youngest son, Faisal, and six principal Arab leaders. During the second of these meetings, the Arab nationalists presented Faisal with a concerted plan of action—a protocol defining the conditions under which they would be prepared to cooperate with Great Britain against Turkey. Their plan was to have Faisal ask his father to approach the British, with a view to finding out whether the Arab leaders' proposal, later known as the Damascus Protocol, would be acceptable to the British government as a basis for a united Arab action against Turkey.

Arab Unity

After the meeting in Damascus, Faisal returned to Mecca to submit the protocol for his father's approval. In his absence the Arab leaders took an oath of allegiance, pledging to recognize the Sharif as the spokesman of the Arab race. They vowed that if Husain secured an agreement with Great Britain on the basis of the Damascus Protocol, they would rally the Arabs in Syria in support.[2]

That Husain became, through the Damascus negotiations, the spokesman of the Arab people is very significant, from the perspective of later territorial disputes between Israel and the Arabs. It bears keeping in mind that the leaders of a broad Arab population had promised to support the agreements later made by Faisal on behalf of his father.

Following the meeting in Damascus, crucial pledges and agreements relating to the Turkish (Ottoman) territories were struck. These included the McMahon–Husain Correspondence, the Sykes–Picot Agreement, and the Balfour Declaration. In the whole context of Arab and Jewish statehood in the Middle East, these documents constituted *promises* of future statehood, not binding agreements under international law. It is worth emphasizing that, at the time these promises were made, World War I was still ongoing, and the territories in question still belonged to the Ottoman Empire. The Allied Powers pledged these territories in the expectation—correct, as it turned out—that they would win the war and take control of the region.

The McMahon–Husain Correspondence

The McMahon–Husain correspondence was an exchange of letters (July 1915 to January 1916) between Husain bin Ali, Sharif of Mecca, and Sir Henry McMahon, British High Commissioner in Egypt. Their correspondence concerned the future political status of the lands under the Ottoman Empire. Husain's first letter to McMahon stated the terms on which the Sharif was prepared, on behalf of the Arab people, to enter an alliance with Great Britain against Turkey. The terms he set out were the ones listed in the Damascus Protocol.

Arab Territorial Demands

The first clause related to the boundaries of the future independent Arab territory. Great Britain was to recognize the independence of the Arab countries lying within the following frontiers:

- North: The line Mersin-Adana to parallel 37° N. to the Persian frontier;
- East: The Persian frontier down to the Persian Gulf;
- South: The Indian Ocean (with the exclusion of Aden);
- West: The Red Sea and the Mediterranean Sea back to Mersin.[3]

These frontiers included all the territory from the Persian frontier (today's Iran) in the East to the Mediterranean Sea in the West; and from today's northern borders of Syria and Lebanon to the southern tip of the Arabian Peninsula. In other words, Husain's request included the current countries of Israel, Lebanon, Syria, Jordan, Iraq, and Saudi Arabia. All of these were to become one unified Arab State.

Husain's demands were very clear. McMahon sent an evasive reply that the Sharif found distasteful. Husain complained that McMahon's reply to his territorial request and proposed frontiers was unclear and vague and showed signs of "lukewarmth and hesitancy."[4]

In his second note, dated September 9 1915, Husain wrote that his proposed frontiers had to be treated as fundamental and that they represented much more than the suggestions of one individual. They represented the demands of all the Arab people living in those territories, "who believe that those frontiers form the minimum necessary to the establishment of the new order for which they are striving."[5]

In that second letter, Husain also noted the following:

I may state that the people of all those countries … are awaiting the result of the present negotiations, which depend solely upon whether you reject or admit the proposed frontiers, and upon whether or not you will help us to secure their spiritual and other rights against evil and danger. Please communicate to us the decision of the British Government on this point.[6]

McMahon's Response

McMahon was now left with only one choice: to answer yes or no. It's been said that his ensuing note to Husain was the most important in the correspondence and arguably the most important international document in the history of the Arab national movement; it contained the pledges that brought the Arabs into the war on the side of the Allies.[7] The note is a bone of contention to the present day. The Arabs still cite it as evidence of subsequent British faithlessness. The paragraphs in McMahon's note setting out the British pledge and its accompanying reservations—paragraphs that would later become a focus of Arab resentment—ran as follows:

I regret to find that you inferred from my last note that my attitude towards the question of frontiers and boundaries was one of hesitancy and lukewarmth. Such was in no wise the intention of my note. All I meant was that I considered that the time had not yet come in which that question could be discussed in a conclusive manner.

But, having realized from your last note that you considered the question important, vital and urgent, I hastened to communicate to the Government of Great Britain the purport of your note. It gives me the greatest pleasure to convey to you, on their behalf, the following declarations which, I have no doubt, you will receive with satisfaction and acceptance.

The districts of Mersin and Alexandretta, and portions of Syria lying to the west of the districts of Damascus, Homs, Hama and Aleppo, cannot be said to be purely Arab, and must on that account be excepted from the proposed delimitation.

Subject to that modification, and without prejudice to the treaties concluded between us and certain Arab Chiefs, we accept that delimitation.

As for the regions lying within the proposed frontiers, in which Great Britain is free to act without detriment to the interests of her ally France, I am authorised to give you the following pledges on behalf of the Government of Great Britain, and to reply as follows to your note:

That, subject to the modifications stated above, Great Britain is prepared to recognize and uphold the independence of the Arabs in all the regions lying within the frontiers proposed by the Sharif of Mecca.[8](emphasis added)

The upshot of the McMahon–Husain correspondence was the following: the Sharif pledged to publicly declare an Arab revolt against the Turks and denounce them as enemies of Islam, in return for Great Britain's promising to recognize and uphold Arab independence "in all the regions lying within the frontiers proposed by the Sharif of Mecca."

The British pledge was unequivocal, but the territories it covered were not clearly defined. This later resulted in much controversy. The controversy became particularly intense with regard to the mandated territory of Palestine. The Arabs concluded from the correspondence that all of Palestine, including Jerusalem and its Old City, would be part of the independent Arab State or confederation of Arab States to be recognized by Great Britain. Britain, however, has never accepted this interpretation of the McMahon–Husain correspondence. To this day there is disagreement. So let's examine each side's claims and assertions in light of the evidence.

Controversy Over the British Pledge

In March of 1939, twenty-five years after the McMahon–Husain correspondence, the British government published a report on it. The report consisted of the proceedings of a committee set up to consider the matter. The committee functioned in the following way: Arab representatives submitted a memorandum explaining the Arab interpretation, and then the United Kingdom did the same, from the British perspective.

The key arguments of the Arab memorandum were as follows:

> There is no room for doubt that Palestine was in fact and in intention included by both parties to the McMahon–Husain Correspondence in the area of Arab independence.
>
> Such geographical description as he [McMahon] and the Sharif give of the portions to be *reserved* points unmistakably to the coastal regions of *northern* Syria. (emphasis added)
>
> It cannot be (and it has never been) disputed that Palestine was included in the area demanded by the Sharif Husain as the area of future Arab independence. That area was accepted by Sir Henry McMahon *in toto*, save for certain reservations. Palestine was not mentioned in those reservations. The fact that he does not mention Palestine, either specifically or by paraphrase, makes it impossible for anyone to contend that Palestine was excluded from the area which Sir Henry McMahon had accepted as the area of future Arab independence.[9]

The contentions of the United Kingdom representatives were set forth at the second meeting and the key ones were as follows:

> Palestine was in a very special position at the time of the correspondence, having in view its position as the Holy Land of three great religions, the interest which it held for Christians, as well as for Moslems and Jews, all over the world, the large number of religious and other buildings and institutions belonging to non-Arab persons, and the obvious practical interests of Great Britain in a territory so close to Egypt and the Suez Canal. The United Kingdom representatives also contend that Palestine was not a purely Arab country. ...
>
> The exclusion in Sir Henry McMahon's letter of the 24th October, 1915, of "portions of Syria lying to the west of the districts of Damascus, Homs, Hama and Aleppo" from the area of Arab independence claimed by the Sharif of Mecca in his letter of the 14th July, 1915, excluded, and

should reasonably have been understood to exclude, the part of southern Syria, consisting of portions of the former Vilayet of Beirut and the former independent Sanjaq of Jerusalem, now known as Palestine. ...

Sir Henry McMahon and the late Sir Gilbert Clayton, who were both concerned in the drafting of the letters sent from Cairo, have both placed it on record that it was intended in the correspondence to exclude Palestine from the area of Arab independence. Sir Henry McMahon said in 1937: "I feel it my duty to state, and I do so definitely and emphatically, that it was not intended by me in giving the pledge to King Husain to include Palestine in the area in which Arab independence was promised." While Sir Gilbert Clayton, who was on Sir Henry McMahon's staff in 1915 and 1916, said in 1923: "I was in daily touch with Sir Henry McMahon throughout the negotiations with King Husain, and made the preliminary drafts of all the letters. I can bear out the statement that it was never the intention that Palestine should be included in the general pledge given to the Sharif; the introductory words of Sir Henry's letter were thought at that time—perhaps erroneously—clearly to cover that point. It was, I think, obvious that the peculiar interests involved in Palestine precluded any definite pledges in regard to its future at so early a stage."[10]

The McMahon–Husain Correspondence in International Law

It is likely that the controversy regarding Sir Henry McMahon's pledge to the Sharif of Mecca will never be resolved. The pledge's standing in international law is a separate matter, and numerous jurists have considered this question. One authority in this area, international lawyer Jacques Gauthier, has concluded that the correspondence between Sir Henry McMahon and Sharif Husain could not result in binding legal obligations on the nations or parties concerned unless its pledges were officially adopted and incorporated into some international instrument. According to Gauthier, there is no evidence that such a process ever took place.[11]

The Sykes–Picot Agreement

Even as McMahon and the Sharif of Mecca were exchanging letters, the British government was holding secret meetings with the other Allied powers—Britain, France, Russia, and Italy—about the future partition of the Ottoman Empire. These meetings produced the Sykes–Picot agreement, named after the two chief negotiators, Sir Mark Sykes on the British side and Francois George-Picot for the French.

According to this agreement, Britain and France were to divide Syria and Iraq into two zones. Each nation would subdivide its particular zone into two areas: an area of direct control and an area of indirect control. France's portion was divided into "Blue" and "A" areas (corresponding to modern-day Lebanon and Syria, respectively), Great Britain's into "Red" and "B" areas (corresponding to modern-day Jordan and Iraq, respectively). In the Blue and Red areas, the French and

British would have direct administrative control. The A and B areas would be semi-independent Arab states. A special provision was made for Palestine (the Brown area), which would be placed under international administration.[12]

Other areas of the former Ottoman Empire were to be under the control of Italy (the Green zone) and of Russia (the Yellow zone), respectively. The Green zone would consist of territories in Southern Turkey; the Yellow zone would consist of Northern Anatolia.

The Sykes–Picot Agreement was significant, according to Gauthier, because later, in San Remo in 1920, it influenced the Allied Powers' choice of which nations should be mandatories in Palestine. The Agreement is also significant in that it may have conflicted with the pledges Great Britain previously made to the Arabs.

The Balfour Declaration

A third document from this period was the Balfour Declaration. It dealt with the allocation of the Ottoman region known as Palestine. The pledges that the British government made in this document were for the Jewish people worldwide, and they changed the course of history in the Middle East.

In June of 1917, over a decade after Weizmann and Lord Arthur Balfour's initial meeting, Balfour urged Weizmann to formulate a declaration regarding Zionist goals in Palestine. Balfour agreed to submit this document to the British War Cabinet and to endorse it on the Zionists' behalf.

Preparing the Text

With his closest associates, Sacher and Sokolow, Weizmann began to prepare a suitable text. Sacher wanted Palestine to be identified in the document as a "*Jewish State* and *the* National Home of the Jewish People [emphasis added]." Sokolow, more cautious, preferred that Palestine be identified only as the "National Home of the Jewish People." The version given to Balfour reflected Sokolow's more cautious approach, but it was still candid. Submitted on July 18th, 1917, it stated the following: "His Majesty's Government accepts the principle that Palestine should be reconstituted as the National Home of the Jewish People. His Majesty's Government will use its best endeavors to secure achievement of this object and will discuss the necessary methods and means with the Zionist Organization."[13]

The letter was formally discussed in a Cabinet conference of September 3rd, and it met with the approval of Lloyd George, the prime minister. The only major opposition came, ironically, from Edwin Montagu, the lone Jew in the Lloyd George government. He feared that the prospect of creating a "Jewish National Home" might undermine the position of Jews who held rank and status in Britain. Owing to Montagu's opposition, the Cabinet left the matter of the declaration unresolved at that time.

Lloyd George would not be deterred, however; he put the matter of the declaration on the agenda for the next Cabinet session on October 4th. This time Montagu opposed the draft even more vigorously than before, and he was joined now by conservative statesman Lord Curzon. Their opposition did not change the minds of

Balfour, Lloyd George, and the other Cabinet members, but the British supporters of Zionism now saw that a *milder* text was needed to move the declaration forward.

As the new declaration was drafted, certain wordings from the earlier version were dropped, such as the suggestion that Palestine "should be *reconstituted* [emphasis added] as the National Home"[14] of the Jews. The Zionists were very distressed by this alteration but did not risk tampering with it.

The Final Version

This time, with Lloyd George determined to force the issue, the War Cabinet voted in favor of the declaration on October 31st, over Montagu's and Curzon's closing objections. The final version of the declaration was incorporated in a letter that Balfour sent on November 2nd, 1917, to Lord Rothschild, the president of the British Zionist Federation. This famous letter, which preceded the British entry into Jerusalem by a few weeks, set out the British government's support for the primary aim of the Zionist movement. It said the following:

Dear Lord Rothschild,

I have much pleasure in conveying to you, on behalf of His Majesty's Government, the following declaration of sympathy with Jewish Zionist aspirations which has been submitted to, and approved by, the Cabinet. 'His Majesty's Government view with favor the establishment in Palestine of a national home for the Jewish people, and will use their best endeavors to facilitate the achievement of this object, it being clearly understood that nothing shall be done which may prejudice the civil and religious rights of existing non-Jewish communities in Palestine, or the rights and political status enjoyed by Jews in any other country.' I should be grateful if you would bring this declaration to the knowledge of the Zionist Federation.

Yours Sincerely,

Arthur James Balfour

The particular wording of the Balfour Declaration was significant and, in the long run, problematic. The final version, as noted above, reflected Sokolow's desire to avoid the phrase "Jewish State." Unfortunately, the phrase "national home," unlike the word "state," was unknown in international usage and had no established legitimacy. The Zionists had coined this expression at the 1897 Congress, specifically to avoid using the term "Jewish State." They believed the Turks, who controlled the region at that time, would find that phrase provocative. The Zionist leadership's choice to follow a similar cautious approach with the British in 1917 opened the door for much of the controversy that still surrounds Arab–Israeli relations today.

Nor did the final version of the Balfour Declaration contain the reference to the "*reconstitution* of Palestine *as* the National Home of the Jewish people [emphasis added]." The British Cabinet had found that concept too strong and definitive. Instead, the final version spoke of "the *establishment in* Palestine of a national home for the Jewish people [emphasis added]." The difference in meaning between the two phrasings is considerable. The original signifies that *all of Palestine* would be reconstituted as the Jewish national home. The revised version signifies something comparatively modest, and much less definite—that is, the establishment of a Jewish national home *in* Palestine.

The indefinite turns of phrase in the Balfour Declaration stemmed from practical diplomatic necessity. But they left it open to later disputes. Future readers of the document would interpret it according to their particular political interests, and they could do so without violating the letter of the Declaration. For example, with the "reconstitution" phrase removed, the document did not commit the British Government to making *all* of Palestine the Jewish National home. Five years later, they took advantage of this loophole. To appease the Arabs, the British government took 70 percent of Mandate Palestine and formed modern-day Jordan. Further partitions of Palestine were to follow—and are still being proposed today. And this is all because the phrase "national home for the Jewish people" did not identify any boundaries or statehood necessities.

Later interpretations of—and attacks on—the Balfour Declaration were not consistent with the hopes and original intentions either of its authors or of the British politicians of the time. "My personal hope," Balfour told a friend in 1918, "is that the Jews will make good in Palestine and eventually found a Jewish State."[15] That same year, Lord Robert Cecil declared the following: "Our wish is that Arabian countries shall be for the Arabs, Armenia for the Armenians, and Judea for the Jews."[16] In 1920, Churchill, who was a member of the War Cabinet when the Balfour Declaration was issued, spoke of "a Jewish State by the banks of the Jordan … which might comprise three or four million Jews."[17] Lloyd George was also quite explicit in his account of the British view at the time of the proposal:

> It was contemplated that when the time arrived for according representative institutions in Palestine, if the Jews had meanwhile responded to the opportunity afforded them by the idea of a National Home and had become a definite majority of the inhabitants, then Palestine would thus become a Jewish Commonwealth.[18]

The above statements indicate that, in 1917, the British foresaw Palestine becoming a Jewish State.

International Reaction

On November 9, 1917, the Balfour Declaration appeared in the British press. France and Italy both announced their support for it and sent their formal confirmation a few months later. Japan, too, issued an official declaration of support.[19]

With these official endorsements from France, Italy, and Japan, the Zionists believed that the Balfour Declaration and its pledges now constituted an "international commitment." Lloyd George stated the following: "I am persuaded that the Allied nations, with the fullest concurrence of our Government and our people, are agreed that in Palestine shall be laid the foundations of a Jewish Commonwealth [that is, Jewish State]."[20]

Arab Reaction

Lloyd George recalled, in *The Truth About the Peace Treaties* (1938), that the Arab leaders "did not offer any objections to the declaration, so long as the rights of the Arabs in Palestine were respected."[21] A few months after the Balfour Declaration was made public, seven Arab leaders submitted a memorandum to the British Foreign Office through representatives in Cairo, requesting that Great Britain clarify its aims with respect to Palestine.

The British government replied on June 16th, 1918, in a document now called the "Declaration of the Seven." This document provided certain assurances to the Arabs. The British government recognized the "complete and sovereign independence of the Arabs" inhabiting certain territories—namely, territories that "were free and independent before the outbreak of the war," and territories "liberated from Turkish rule by the action of the Arabs themselves."[22] These territories consisted of most of the Hejaz (a coastal region in western Saudi Arabia that borders the Red Sea) and of other areas in the Arabian Peninsula.

These territories did not include Palestine.

The timing of the Declaration of the Seven in relation to the Balfour Declaration is important. The Balfour Declaration was announced in November of 1917 and endorsed by all the key allies of Great Britain shortly thereafter. The Declaration of the Seven was announced the following year. According to Gauthier, this means that the Balfour Declaration's pro-Zionist policies had priority over British assurances to the seven Arab leaders. In any case, the Arab leaders who received the Declaration of the Seven did not object to its lack of assurances about Palestine. This is probably because Palestine constituted a very small portion of the territories liberated by the British and their allies.

The leaders of the Arab National Movement had little objection to the Balfour Declaration. But some of the Arabs in and near Palestine, who were not integrated with the larger Arab movement, took exception to it. The British Foreign office received a number of petitions from them setting out their grievances and objections. The following is typical of these grievances: "The country is ours. … Our historical and religious relations with it, Muslims and Christians, far exceed those of the Jews."[23]

There is little evidence, however, that there was, in 1917, large-scale opposition to the Balfour Declaration from Arabs in Palestine. As we will see in Chapter 13, Zionist initiatives and Jewish immigration to Palestine were creating job opportunities for Arabs, who were now flocking to Palestine in hope of a better life and economic future.

Long-Term Controversy

In the near-century since its release, the Balfour Declaration and its ambiguous wording have been the focus of much criticism and controversy. Lord Grey, the British foreign secretary from 1905 to 1916, had the following to say about it:

It [the Balfour Declaration] promised a Zionist home without prejudice to the civil and religious rights of the population of Palestine. A Zionist home, my Lords, undoubtedly means or implies a Zionist Government over the district in which the home is placed, and if 93 per cent of the population of Palestine are Arabs, I do not see how you can establish other than an Arab Government, without prejudice to their civil rights. That one sentence alone of the Balfour Declaration seems to me to involve, without overstating the case, very great difficulty of fulfillment.

It is not from any prejudice with regard to that matter that I speak, but I do see that the situation is an exceedingly difficult one, when it is compared with the pledges which undoubtedly were given to the Arabs. It would be very desirable, from the point of view of honor, that all these various pledges should be set out side by side, and then, I think, the most honorable thing would be to look at them fairly, see what inconsistencies there are between them, and, having regard to the nature of each pledge and the date at which it was given, with all the facts before us, consider what is the fair thing to be done.[24]

More than twenty years after the Balfour Declaration was published, in a letter dated November 23rd, 1938, King Abdul Aziz Al–Saud, founder of the Kingdom of Saudi Arabia, listed his objections to the declaration:

Regarding the Jewish leaning on the Balfour statement, we argue that the statement was in itself an act of gross injustice committed against a peaceful country, that the government who issued the statement did not have any authority at the time, for imposing the Promise in Palestine, and that the people of Palestine were not given the chance to say what they thought of it or of the dictated mandate … despite the many pledges by the Allies–including America–that they would be given the right to self-determination… [and] that the Balfour Promise, which the Jews are holding up as good grounds, *runs contrary to right and justice and contrary to the Palestinians' right to self-determination.*[25] (emphasis added)

Saud's objections reflected the view of most leaders in the Arab world in 1938.

The Balfour Declaration in International Law

The position of many Arab jurists is that the British had no legal standing to make the Balfour Declaration. One such jurist, Henri Cattan, has argued that the Balfour Declaration was "legally null and void," for two reasons:

First, on the date the Balfour Declaration was made, Palestine formed part of Turkey. … The Declaration was void on the principle that a donor cannot give away what does not belong to him. Secondly, the Balfour Declaration is void on the ground that it violated the natural and legitimate rights of the people of Palestine.[26]

Cattan's point, in other words, is that, in 1917, Palestine was not Britain's to pledge to the Jewish people; the region still belonged to Turkey. Therefore, the Balfour Declaration has no legal standing according to the principles of common law.

Gauthier has addressed this argument of Cattan's. He notes an inconsistency in the Arab position: "It's interesting to note that Arab jurists argue that Britain had no legal authority to promise land to the Jewish people as they did in the Balfour Declaration but they affirm Britain's powers to dispose in the McMahon–Husain correspondence."[27] In other words, if the British had no authority to pledge Palestine to the Jews, then they likewise lacked the authority to pledge what became Syria, Lebanon, Jordan, and Iraq to the Arabs. If one pledge is null and void, so is the other.

Gauthier compares the international legal standing of the McMahon–Husain correspondence with that of the Balfour Declaration, and he notes the following difference:

> It should be stressed that although the pledges of the British Government contained in the McMahon correspondence created some expectations for the Arab people, the McMahon pledges never received the formal endorsement and approval of the Principal Powers and the Allies. The same is not true for the Balfour Declaration whose principles and commitments were endorsed, signed and recognized internationally at the San Remo conference in 1920 and by the Council of the League of Nations on July 24, 1922 when it approved the Mandate for Palestine.[28]

In other words, the provisions of the Balfour Declaration ultimately took on legal authority when the San Remo Resolution and the Palestine Mandate— internationally sanctioned vehicles—enshrined them. (This will be explained in more detail in the upcoming chapters.)

The same cannot be said of the provisions in the McMahon–Husain correspondence. No international treaties or agreements ever enshrined the pledges concerning Palestine that the Arabs inferred from that correspondence. Therefore, the McMahon–Husain correspondence carries no weight in international law.

Objections to the Declaration: A Summary

The main objections to the Balfour Declaration, according to the particular criticisms of Lord Grey, King Abdul Aziz Al-Saud, and Arab jurists, are that it was

- made without the consent and knowledge of the Arab population;
- contrary to the principles of national self-determination and democracy;
- inconsistent with the pledges given to the Arabs before and after the date it was made.

There is no doubt that the Balfour Declaration proposed a different set of rights for the Jewish and non-Jewish populations in Palestine. The civil and religious rights that the document pledged to the region's non-Jewish populations did not include political rights. Those rights were reserved for the Jewish people. Since the Jews were a minority in Palestine, many jurists and proponents of the Arab position have argued that this ran contrary to the principles of self-determination and were unjust.

What response can be made to these charges? Consider, first of all, that the Arab leaders at the time of the declaration—namely, Faisal and Sharif Husain, as well as the other Arab leaders who supported them—knew very well that the British intended to create a National Home for the Jewish people in Palestine. It was not a secret; they were informed about it. Second, according to Gauthier, "there is no doubt that Lord Balfour understood and accepted the fact that one of the consequences of the Declaration of November 2, 1917 was to take away from the Arab inhabitants of Palestine the right to self-determination."[29]

In a letter to Prime Minister Lloyd George, dated February 19th, 1919, Balfour wrote the following:

> The weak point of our position of course [Great Britain's position concerning a Jewish national home in Palestine] is that in the case of Palestine we deliberately and rightly decline to accept the principle of self-determination. If the present inhabitants were consulted they would unquestionably give an anti-Jewish verdict. Our justification is that we regard Palestine as being absolutely exceptional; that we consider the question of the Jews outside Palestine as one of world importance and that we conceive the Jews to have an historic claim to a home in their ancient land; provided that a home can be given them without either dispossessing or oppressing the present inhabitants.[30]

Balfour further defined his vision of Palestine, and his sense of its uniqueness, in a memorandum forwarded to the French prime minister, George Clemenceau, at the Paris Peace conference in June 1919: "Palestine presented a unique situation. We are dealing not with the wishes of an existing community but are consciously seeking to re-constitute a new community and definitely building for a numerical majority in the future."[31] Balfour's intentions—his vision of Palestine—are highly relevant to our perspective on territorial claims in the Middle East, according to Gauthier. As he notes, "It is to the intention that all law applies. Law always regards the intention."[32]

It is clear that the parties to the Balfour Declaration intended a Jewish State in Palestine. And clearly they understood that, in order to achieve that end, they would need to vest political rights in the Jewish population both inside and outside the territory.

The Balfour Declaration granted Jewish people worldwide the rights to self-determination in Palestine. The same rights were granted to the Arabs in the regions that became Syria, Lebanon, Jordan, Iraq, and the Arabian Peninsula (an area that now contains a total of 11 Arab states).

End of the War

On, September 18th, 1918, the British defeated the Turks, thus dissolving the Ottoman Empire and gaining complete control over Palestine. Shortly thereafter, on November 11th, 1918, Germany signed an armistice agreement, ending the First World War. The conclusion of the war led to profound territorial changes worldwide. Many plans for dismembering the Ottoman territories were under consideration by the British government and were the subject of intense debates among the Allies. How to allocate the Ottoman territories under international law would be a matter for the Allied Supreme Council to determine. They did so in the proceedings that followed in Paris, France, in 1919, and in San Remo, Italy, in 1920.

Endnotes

1   George Antonius, *The Arab Awakening* (Safety Harbor, Fl: Simon Publications, 2001), 149.

2   Ibid, 158.

3   Ibid, 157.

4   Ibid, 416.

5   Ibid.

6   Ibid, 418.

7   Ibid, 169.

8   Ibid, 419.

9   Secretary of State for the Colonies, Report of a Committee Set up to Consider Certain Correspondence Between Sir Henry McMahon (His Majesty's High Commissioner in Egypt) and The Sharif of Mecca in 1915 and 1916 (London: March 16, 1939), accessed March 18, 2012, http://unispal.un.org/UNISPAL.NSF/0/4C4F7515DC39195185256CF7006F878C. Note: George Antonius was among the representatives of the Arab Delegation at these meetings.

10   Ibid.

11   Jacques Paul Gauthier, *Sovereignty Over the Old City of Jerusalem: A Study of the Historical, Religious, Political and Legal Aspects of the Question of the Old City*, Thèse No. 725 (Geneva: Université de Genève, 2007), 221.

12   Ibid, 227.

13   Howard Sachar, *A History of Israel: From the Rise of Zionism to Our Time*, 3rd ed. (New York: Alfred A. Knopf, 2010), 107.

14   Ibid, 108.

15   Ibid, 110.

16   Ibid.

17   Ibid.

18   Ibid.

19   Gauthier, *Sovereignty Over the Old City*, 299-302.

20   Ibid, 299-300.

21   Ibid, 302-303.

22   Ibid, 308-309.

23   Ibid, 310-311.

24   Lord Grey, "Enclosure in Annex A," in Report of a Committee Set up to Consider Certain Correspondence Between Sir Henry McMahon (His Majesty's High Commissioner in Egypt) and The Sharif of Mecca in 1915 and 1916 (London: March 16, 1939), accessed March 18, 2012, http://unispal.un.org/UNISPAL.NSF/0/4C4F7515DC39195185256CF7006F878C.

25   Gauthier, *Sovereignty Over the Old City*, 312.

26   Ibid, 281.

27   Ibid, 277.

28   Ibid, 221.

29   Ibid, 313.

30   Ibid.

31   Ibid.

32   Ibid, 314.

Chapter 11

The Paris Peace Conference

The End of World War I: Nations In Flux

Introduction

On the morning of November 11, 1918, the last shots of World War I were fired. The scope of the Great War, with 60 million wounded and nearly 10 million dead, was unprecedented in human history. In January 1919, the nations of the world came to Paris in the hope of preventing such a war from ever happening again. The hope was for permanent peace.

The Paris Peace Conference changed the world. Margaret MacMillan has summed up its importance memorably:

> For six months in 1919, Paris was the capital of the world. The Peace conference was the world's most important business, the peacemakers, its most powerful people. They met day after day. They argued, debated, quarreled and made it up again. They created new countries and new organizations.[1]

Most people assume that the story of Israel's modern statehood began in 1947, with the UN Partition Resolution, and continued with the War of Independence, in 1948. But this story began decades earlier. The Paris Peace Conference of 1919 was a pivotal moment in the national narrative. It was the second stage in the process that would culminate in Jewish statehood in the Middle East. Other Middle Eastern nations, too, were conceived at this time. The Paris Peace Conference laid the ground for the states of Syria, Lebanon, Jordan, and Iraq. To summarize: the McMahon–Husain Correspondence, the Sykes–Picot Agreement, and the Balfour Declaration marked the point where promises were made to the Jews and Arabs. The Paris Peace Conference marked the point where the Jewish and Arab nationalists formally *petitioned* the Allied Powers to honor those earlier pledges. The formalization of those pledges came later, at the San Remo Conference, and their fulfillment, binding under international law, came with the Mandate for Palestine.

The Paris Peace Conference and the ideals and systems to which it gave birth—the League of Nations, Wilson's principle of self-determination, the mandate system—are crucial to our account of Israel in world relations. So are certain meetings and agreements tangential to the conference, in particular those of Faisal and Weizmann. This chapter will focus on these matters.

Faisal and Weizmann: First Meeting

Prior to the Peace Conference, meetings and agreements took place regarding the former Ottoman territories. There were several meetings between Dr. Chaim Weizmann, head of the Zionists, and the Emir Faisal, the son of the Sharif of Mecca, concerning the territory of Palestine/Israel. The two men met for the first time in Akaba, in June 1918.

Weizmann's autobiography includes the following account of the meeting with Faisal:

> With the help of an interpreter, we carried on a fairly lengthy and detailed conversation. After the usual exchange of politenesses, I explained to him the mission on which I had come to Palestine, our desire to do everything in our position to allay Arab fears and susceptibilities, and our hope that he would lend us his powerful moral support. He asked me a great many questions about the Zionist program, and I found him by no means uninformed. At this time, it must be remembered, Palestine and TransJordan were one and the same thing, and I stressed the fact that there was a great deal of room in the country if intensive development were applied, and that the lot of the Arabs would be greatly improved through our work here. With all this I found the Emir in full agreement, as Lawrence later confirmed to me by letter. … The Emir promised to communicate the gist of our talk to his father, the Sharif Husain, who was, he said, the ultimate judge of all his actions, and carried responsibility for Arab policy. From subsequent events, it was clear that his father raised no objections to the views expressed by me to his son. The first meeting in the desert laid the foundations of a lifelong friendship. I met the Emir several times afterward in Europe, and our negotiations crystallized into an agreement, drawn up by Colonel Lawrence and signed by the Emir and myself, which has been published several times, both in British and French diplomatic papers.[2]

The Faisal–Weizmann Agreement

The agreement entered into in London on January 3rd, 1919, just a few days prior to the Paris Peace Conference, is known as the Faisal–Weizmann Agreement. Its language regarding Arab and Jewish relations is remarkably cordial compared with the equivalent language today.

The Preamble to the Agreement states that the parties are

mindful of the racial kinship and ancient bonds existing between the Arabs and the Jewish people, and realiz[e] that the surest means of working out the consummation of their national aspirations, is through the closest possible collaboration in the development of the Arab State and Palestine.[3]

The key points of the Agreement are as follows:

■ Article I stipulated that "the Arab State and Palestine in all their relations and undertakings shall be controlled by the most cordial goodwill and understanding."[4]

■ Article II contained the following provisions: "Immediately following the completion of the deliberations of the Peace Conference, the definite boundaries between the Arab State and Palestine shall be determined by a Commission agreed upon by the parties hereto."[5]

■ Article III referred to the future condition of Palestine, which "shall afford the fullest guarantees for carrying into effect the British Government's Declaration of the 2nd of November 1917."[6]

■ In Article IV, recognition was given to the right of "large scale" Jewish immigration into Palestine.

■ Articles IV and V contained provisions protecting the rights of the Arab tenant farmers and keeping Muslim Holy Places under the custody of Muslims.

Arab State Distinct from Palestine?

International lawyer Jacques Gauthier, author of *Sovereignty Over the Old City of Jerusalem: A Study of the Historical, Religious, Political and Legal Aspects of the Question of the Old City*, has noted the importance of the Preamble's distinction between the "Arab State" and "Palestine"—a distinction repeated in Articles I and II of the Agreement.[7]

Gauthier also notes that the Faisal–Weizmann agreement referred to the Balfour Declaration. This suggests that Faisal acknowledged the earlier document and accepted its terms. That acknowledgment, along with the distinction between the Arab State and Palestine, signified to the Zionist movement that the Arabs accepted the basic Jewish claims regarding a national home in Palestine. Having agreed to the terms of the agreement, Faisal sought to explain the aims of Zionism to various Arab officials. Gilbert Clayton, a British general who was party to the meetings, reported the following to the British Foreign Office: "Feisal has ... informed an Arab delegation in Damascus that he did not consider Arab and Zionist aims to be incompatible and the delegation seemed favorably impressed."[8]

The Faisal–Weizmann Agreement, according to Gauthier, produced the following determinations:

1. A new independent Arab State was contemplated by the parties;
2. Palestine was not included in the proposed Arab state; and

3. The policies of the Balfour Declaration—including immigration of the Jews to Palestine "on a large scale"—were to be implemented with the support of Faisal.[9]

The Arabs, through Faisal, had--on paper at least—conceded what the Zionists were striving for. In return for a Zionist promise to help the Arabs pursue their nationalist goal of an independent state, the Arabs had agreed to do the same for the Zionists in Palestine. Faisal included an escape clause, however, in the Arab version of the document. He added a proviso, in Arabic, that contained the following qualifications:

> Provided the Arabs obtain their independence as demanded in my Memorandum dated the 4th of January, 1919, to the Foreign Office of the Government of Great Britain, I shall concur in the above articles. But if the slightest modification or departure were to be made [that is to say, in relation to the demands in the Memorandum] I shall not then be bound by a single word of the present Agreement which shall be deemed void and of no account or validity, and I shall not be answerable in any way whatsoever.[10]

Paris Peace Conference: Reshaping the Maps

Shortly after Faisal and Weizmann's meeting, the Paris Peace Conference began on January 18th, 1919, in the French Foreign Ministry, the Quai D'Orsay. For a few months in 1919, Paris was the world's government, and the Supreme Council of the Principal Allied Powers—consisting of Great Britain, the United States, France, and Italy—was both its court of appeal and its parliament. Decisions made at the Peace Conference regarding the creation of new countries are still being felt today.

It is important to understand the vast scope of the Supreme Council's powers during the Peace Conference. It had a *power of disposition* over ex-German and ex-Turkish territories. In other words, the Supreme Council was authorized to establish new borders for the territories of the world, borders that were subsequently recognized as law. The Council's decisions changed the maps of Europe and the Middle East forever, creating a new international order.

The key figures on the Supreme Council were the following: Woodrow Wilson, the US president; David Lloyd George, the British prime minister; George Clemenceau, the French prime minister; and Vittorio Orlando, the Italian prime minister.

President Wilson and the League of Nations

When President Wilson set sail for Europe in December of 1918, Europe had just finished four years of the most devastating war the world had ever seen. People everywhere wanted reassurance that such a war would never happen again. Wilson brought with him ideas for a new international order, a League of Nations that, he hoped, would prevent future world wars.

Wilson's ideas became the foundation of many of the policies adopted by the Supreme Council at the Paris Peace Conference. These ideas, expressed in Wilson's addresses to the American Congress in the early months of 1918, included the following all-important one:

> Peoples are not to be handed about from one sovereignty to another by an international conference or an understanding between rivals and antagonists. National aspirations must be respected; peoples may now be dominated and governed only by their own consent. "Self-determination" is not a mere phrase.[11]

Self-Determination and the Case of Palestine

Regarding the self-determination of peoples, Wilson also said that "every territorial settlement involved in this war must be made in the interest and for the benefit of the populations concerned" and that "the final settlement must be based upon the essential justice of that particular case."[12] These concepts affected the Supreme Council's decisions regarding "national minorities" in the former Ottoman Territories.

Many have argued that Wilson's principle of self-determination should have applied to the Arabs in 1919 Palestine. According to this argument, the Arabs were the majority population in the region at the time and therefore should not have been disposed of—"dominated and governed"—except by their own consent. It's significant that Wilson himself never made this argument; he viewed Palestine as the British did—that is, as a prospective Jewish state. Evidence for this comes from David Lloyd George, the British prime minister, who found Wilson "fully committed to the Balfour Declaration."[13] Further evidence comes from a report prepared by the Enquiry Commission, a special commission formed by Wilson. Its task was to develop proposals for reshaping the world map in accordance with his peace plans. The Enquiry Commission's report included the following conclusion:

> It is right that Palestine should become a Jewish State, if the Jews, being given full opportunity, make it such. It was the cradle and home of their vital race, which has made large spiritual contributions to mankind, and is the only land in which they can hope to find a home of their own, they being in this last respect, unique among significant peoples.[14]

Article 22 and the Mandate System

The newly-created League of Nations drew up a charter, a treaty made up of 26 articles that entered into force on 10 January, 1920. Entitled the Covenant of the League of Nations, it incorporated Wilson's principles and applied them to the separate treaties that the Allied Powers signed with Germany, Austria, Bulgaria, and Hungary at Versailles. Treaties are the strongest source of international law. In other words, those of Wilson's principles that were incorporated into a treaty subsequently became law.

Article 22 of the Covenant of the League of Nations contained principles that were important to later decisions in San Remo regarding the former Ottoman territories. It stated the following:

> To those colonies and territories which as a consequence of the late war have ceased to be under the sovereignty of the States which formerly governed them and which are inhabited by peoples not yet able to stand by themselves under the strenuous conditions of the modern world, there should be applied the principle that *the well-being and development of such peoples form a sacred trust of civilization* and that securities for the performance of this trust should be embodied in this Covenant.
>
> The best method of giving practical effect to this principle is that *the tutelage of such peoples should be entrusted to advanced nations* who by reason of their resources, their experience or their geographical position can best undertake this responsibility, and who are willing to accept it, *and that this tutelage should be exercised by them as Mandatories on behalf of the League.*
>
> The character of *the mandate must differ according to the stage of the development of the people, the geographical situation of the territory, its economic conditions and other similar circumstances.*[15] (emphasis added)

Article 22's key principle was that the well-being and development of specific peoples "not yet able to stand by themselves" ought to become "a sacred trust of civilization." Article 22 is the basis of the Mandate system.

Supporters of Arab claims to Palestine contend that only the main *inhabitants* of the mandated territories—and the Arabs outnumbered the Jews in Palestine in 1919, and had done so since the 13th century CE—were meant to be the beneficiaries of the "sacred trust" referred to in Article 22. Gauthier does not credit this argument. His view is that, where Palestine was concerned, the intended beneficiaries of the "sacred trust" were the *prospective* Jewish inhabitants of the Jewish national home provided for by the Balfour Declaration.[16] Why Does Gauthier believe this? One reason, and a compelling one, is that the creators of the mandate system—the Principal Allied Powers of Great Britain, the United States, France, and Italy—had endorsed the Balfour Declaration only a couple of years before, in 1917.

We will discuss the mandate system in more detail in upcoming chapters. For now, keep in mind that it was essentially a trusteeship. In other words, world powers such as Britain and France were to act as trustees in certain territories and assist the populations in those territories to become autonomous.

British Trusteeship in Palestine

How did Britain come to be the Mandatory in Palestine? A few weeks prior to the Paris Peace Conference, Chaim Weizmann asked Lord Balfour to support the proposal of a British trusteeship for Palestine. He told Balfour that the Jewish people would declare themselves united behind such an idea. Balfour was agreeable.

Zionist Choice of the Mandate System

Not all Zionists shared Weizmann's faith in the trustee route to Jewish statehood. The mandatory system seemed too gradual and uncertain to some, who felt strongly that a Jewish state in Palestine needed to be established from the outset.

In *A Jewish Palestine: The Case for a British Trusteeship* (1919), Harry Sachar, a key assistant and supporter of Weizmann, described the possible routes to achieving Jewish statehood in Palestine. In the following passage, Sachar considers the merits of establishing a Jewish state directly, without the transitional mandatory phase:

> The idea of the establishment forthwith of a Jewish republic has certain obvious attractions, and in the rather loose language of some Zionists, both writers and speakers, has found acceptance. *The merit of such a solution is that it puts beyond all question that the future of Palestine is given forthwith into the government and control of Jews [and] all questions as to the Jewish right to and claim on Palestine now and in the future are disposed of.* It may also be urged that in favor of such a solution that *it releases a Jewish Palestine at its birth from the political complications involved in the other solutions*, complications which will be developed later in this essay. An independent Jewish state in Palestine would be, so it can be argued, *free from the interference of a suzerain or mandatory whose duties as trustee might conflict with its other interests or ambitions.* It would be free from the dangers of that multiple control inherent in international control, and would not be a pawn or plaything in the political purposes of any power. In short, it can be argued for this solution that it would remove from the Jewish Palestine the shadow of imperialism and enable the Jewish people to concentrate all their energies and their minds upon the single important purpose of developing their Jewish national home.[17] (emphasis added)

This account was prophetic. The path to Jewish statehood chosen by the Zionist Organization—that is, the mandate system, with a British trusteeship--did eventually lead to significant problems. As we will see in upcoming chapters, these problems took the form of questions and challenges regarding Jewish claims to a significant portion of Palestine. Much controversy, none of it helpful to the Jewish cause, arose after 1919 owing to the conflicting interests and ambitions of the trustee power— Great Britain.

So why did the Zionist Organization pursue the trusteeship route? Why did they decide, on the eve of the Paris Conference, that Jewish independence in Palestine should be carried out in stages? Why did they opt for a period of incubation and preparation, entrusting their dream of a Jewish state to an international power?

The Challenge of Independence

The Zionist Organization chose the path it did because, in the first decades of the 20th century, the Jewish pursuit of independent statehood in Palestine faced daunting challenges of a practical nature. One major challenge, according to Sachar, had to do with the fact that the Jewish people actually living in Palestine were a minority population there:

> The root of these troubles is the fact that, whereas the bulk of the Jewish people, whose title to Palestine is recognised, reside outside Palestine, within Palestine here and now the Jewish people constitute a minority. There are in Palestine today some 100,000 Jews, or less than one fifth of the total population. The country as a whole is at present too small in human strength and in material wealth to bear the full weight of administration. An independent state must guard its own borders by its own military strength, and maintain by its own strength internal order. An independent state must find from its own resources and its own credit the expenses of government, the cost of development, the cost of education, the cost of opening up all the waste places of a new land.[18]

In the light of later events, we might doubt the wisdom of Weizmann and the Zionist leadership in choosing the mandate route. Hindsight is 20-20, as many have remarked. And yet, looking back at the circumstances of the Zionist leadership in 1919 and at the real conditions they faced in Palestine, we can appreciate their choice. It is natural that they opted for the support of Great Britain—a country that seemed quite committed to their cause—to assist them in their task of nation-building.

Paris: Arab and Jewish Submissions

During the Paris Peace Conference, delegates representing peoples from around the world—for example, Greece, Yugoslavia, Vietnam—petitioned the Supreme Council for territory and for their rights to "self-determination." There were numerous such delegations, all jockeying for position. This was their great opportunity to acquire territory before borders were frozen. The major powers themselves were privately hoping to secure new ports or new colonies for their own benefit. It was only Wilson's principled vision of ending colonization that prevented Britain, France, and Italy from using the Conference to increase their own colonial holdings. Among those who presented to the Supreme Council were Faisal, petitioning for an Arab State, and Weizmann, who, along with representatives of the Zionist Organization, was asking for a Jewish state in Palestine.

Faisal appeared before the Supreme Council on February 6th, 1919, as leader of the Hedjaz delegation, with T.E. Lawrence at his side. In petitioning for Arab independence, he specifically excluded Palestine from the territory he asked for.[19]

On February 27th, 1919, at the 46th Session of the Peace Conference, representatives of the Zionist Organization (including Nachum Sokolow, Chaim

Weizmann, Manahem Ussishkin, Andre Spire, and Sylvain Levi) addressed the Supreme Allied Council.

Defining the Proposed Jewish State

The plan presented by the Zionist Organization set out boundaries for the proposed Jewish State. It was to comprise all of the territory of Palestine, which included territory west *and* east of the Jordan River. The plan was based on the notion that the territory of the ancient Israelites was the historic home of the Jews, and should constitute the modern-day Jewish State.

Nahum Sokolow made the following submissions on behalf of the Zionist organization:

I have the honour to place before the Peace Conference the statement of claims of the Jewish People... [who] have been waiting eighteen centuries for this day. We claim our historic right to Palestine, to the Land of Israel, to the country where we created a civilization that has had so great an influence upon humanity. ... This then is the project that the Zionist Organization has the honour to submit to the Peace Conference for examination:

1) The contracting parties shall recognize the historic title of the Jewish people to Palestine and the right of the Jews to reconstitute their National Home in Palestine.

2) The Frontiers of Palestine shall be indicated in the exposé annexed hereto [a map was attached showing the frontiers of Palestine to include territory on the west and east side of the Jordan River]

3) The sovereignty of Palestine shall be vested in the League of Nations, and Government will be entrusted to Great Britain acting as Mandatory of the League....

4) The Mandate shall be subject to these special conditions: Palestine must be given the political, administrative and economic conditions that will ensure the establishment of the Jewish National Home and ultimately render possible the creation of an autonomous 'Commonwealth'. It is clearly understood that nothing must be done that might prejudice the civil and religious rights of the non-Jewish communities at present established in Palestine, nor the rights and political status enjoyed by Jews in all other countries.[20]

It goes almost without saying that the Zionist Organization's petition in Paris was for territory they should be allowed to own rather than for territory they did own. In other words, the argument was based not on established law but on considerations seen as superior to the law.[21] There was nothing unusual in this. These kinds of claims are most common at peace conferences, where new settlements—and legal boundaries—are being established.

The Arab claims were also "non-legal" insofar as the Arabs, like the Jewish people, did not own the territories they were claiming in Paris. Both parties, the Arabs and the Jews, sensed that they needed each other in order to realize their parallel aims of a sovereign state. In his negotiations with Weizmann and with other prominent Zionists, Faisal had acknowledged this need for cooperation.

Faisal's Ambivalence

There were indications, however, that Faisal's views regarding the Zionists and Palestine were unsettled. In an interview with a French newspaper on March 1—less than a month after explicitly excluding Palestine from his petition for Arab territory before the Supreme Council—Faisal seemed to object to the demands made by the Jewish representatives at the Peace Conference. These published statements were completely inconsistent with his previous declarations of support for the Zionist cause. After the interview was published, a meeting took place between Faisal, Felix Frankfurter, who was a key member of the American Zionist delegation, and T.E. Lawrence, who acted as interpreter. After the meeting, Faisal wrote the following letter to Frankfurter to clarify his position:

> I wanted to take this opportunity ... to tell you what I have often been able to say to Dr. Weizmann in Akaba and in Europe. We feel that the Arabs and Jews are cousins in race, suffering similar oppressions ... and by a happy coincidence have been able to take the first steps toward the attainment of their national ideals together. We Arabs, especially the educated among us, look with deepest sympathy on the Zionist movement. Our deputation here in Paris is fully acquainted with the proposals submitted by the Zionist Organization to the Peace Conference, and we regard them as moderate and proper. We will do our best, in so far as we are concerned, to help them through; we will wish the Jews a most hearty welcome home.
>
> We are working together for a reformed and revived Near East, and our two movements complete one another. The Jewish movement is national and not imperialistic. Our movement is national and not imperialistic and there is room in [Greater] Syria for us both.
>
> I think that neither can be a real success without the other. People less informed and less responsible than our leaders, ignoring the need for co-operation of the Arabs and the Zionists, have been trying to exploit the local differences that must necessarily arise in Palestine in the early stages of our movements. Some of them have, I am afraid, misrepresented your aims to the Arab peasantry, with the result that interested parties have been able to make capital out of what they call differences. I wish to give you my firm conviction that these differences are not on question of principle, but on matters of detail, such as must inevitably occur in every contact with neighbouring peoples, and as are easily dissipated by mutual good will. ...
> I look forward, and my people with me look forward, to a future in which we will help you and you will help us, so that countries in which we are mutually interested may once again take their place in the community of civilized peoples of the world.[22]

The Arab and Jewish nationalist claims were interdependent, as Faisal concedes in this letter. This point was also strongly expressed by Lord Robert Cecil, who was assistant foreign secretary and member of the British delegation at the Paris Peace Conference in 1919. He remarked that the Arabs had no ground of complaint regarding the Zionist policy, for the following reason: "The recognition of a Jewish national home was part of the terms on which the Arab State was brought into existence."[23]

End of the Faisal–Weizmann Accord

The relationship between Faisal and Weizmann seemed to offer significant possibility for cooperation. Unfortunately, their accord did not bear fruit and it did not last. The end came through a diplomatic disagreement over Mandate Syria, which the Supreme Council had allocated to the French. Faisal's advisers approached the Zionist leaders and suggested that the two peoples—Jews and Arabs—join forces to oppose the French claims in Syria. Weizmann, unwilling to act independently of his British supporters, could not offer Faisal the support he asked for. As a result, by mid-1919, Faisal had terminated his public support for the Zionists.[24]

Faisal turned against the Zionists, perhaps inevitably, but not before making certain crucial concessions to their enterprise. The formal agreement he made with Weizmann, on January 3, 1919, defined the prospective "Arab State" and Palestine as separate entities. So did his letter to Professor Frankfurter, published in the *New York Times* on March 5, 1919. At the Paris Peace Conference, appearing before the Supreme Council and making territorial demands, Faisal was the authorized representative of the Arab nationalist movement. And—the point is worth emphasizing—his territorial claim on behalf of this movement specifically excluded Palestine.[25] All Arab grievances over Palestine since 1919 should be considered in the light of Faisal's exclusion.

Decisions made at the Paris Peace Conference reshaped the map of the world. Changes to the European borders were incorporated into the treaties of Versailles, Trianon, Neuilly, and St. Germain. Drafting these treaties took more time than the world leaders had expected, and they took a recess before turning their attention to the Middle East—to the questions about Palestine, Syria, and Mesopotamia, and the new borders for the Ottoman Territories. The Supreme Council reconvened in April of 1920, in San Remo, Italy, to address these questions.

Endnotes

1   Margaret MacMillan, *Paris 1919—Six Months that Changed the World* (New York: Random House, 2003), xxv.

2   Chaim Weizmann, *Trial and Error* (Westport: Greenwood Press, 1972), 234-235.

3   George Antonius, *The Arab Awakening* (Florida: Simon Publications, 2001), 437-438.

4   Ibid, 438.

5   Ibid.

6   Ibid.

7   Jacques Paul Gauthier, *Sovereignty Over the Old City of Jerusalem: A Study of the Historical, Religious, Political and Legal Aspects of the Question of the Old City,* Thèse No. 725 (Geneva: Université de Genève, 2007), 333.

8   General Clayton, "Report to the British Foreign Office, May 1919," FO 371/4181, in Abdul-Wahhhab Kayyali, Palestine: A Modern History (London: Croom Helm, 1979), 65.

9   Gauthier, *Sovereignty Over the Old City of Jerusalem,* 333.

10   Antonius, *Arab Awakening,* 439.

11   Gauthier, *Sovereignty Over the Old City of Jerusalem,* 328.

12   Ibid, 328.

13   David Lloyd George, *The Truth About the Peace Treaties* (London: Gollancz, 1938), 2: 759.

14   David Hunter Miller, "Document 246: Outline of Tentative Report and Recommendation Prepared by the Intelligence Section, In Accordance with Instructions for the President and the Plenipotentiaries, January 21, 1919," in My Diary at the Conference of Paris: With Documents (New York, 1924), 4: 264. Note: David Hunter Miller was a member of the U.S. delegation at the Peace Conference and compiled a diary with documents consisting of 21 volumes.

15   Covenant of the League of Nations, Avalon Project, Yale Law School, accessed March 25, 2012, http://avalon.law.yale.edu/20th_century/leagcov.asp.

16   Gauthier, *Sovereignty Over the Old City of Jerusalem,* 364.

17   Harry Sacher, *A Jewish Palestine: The Jewish Case for a British Trusteeship* (London: Zionist Organization, 1919), 2.

18   Ibid, 4.

19   Benny Morris, *Righteous Victims: A History of the Zionist-Arab Conflict* (New York: Vintage Books, 200), 81.

20   Gauthier, *Sovereignty Over the Old City of Jerusalem,* 350.

21   Norman Hill, *Claims to Territory in International Law* (London: Oxford University Press, 1945), 26-27.

22   Weizmann, *Trial and Error,* 245-246. Also *The Letters and Papers of Chaim Weizmann,* vol. 1. Series B, August 1898–July 1931. Ed. Barnet Litvinoff (Jerusalem: Israel University Press, 1983), Paper 52, 237.

23   J. de V. Loder, *The Truth about Mesopotamia, Palestine, and Syria* (London: G. Allen & Unwin, 1923). Cited in Howard Grief, *The Legal Foundation and Borders of Israel under International Law* (Jerusalem, Mazo, 2008), 217.

24   Howard Sachar, *A History of Israel: From the Rise of Zionism to Our Time,* 3rd ed. (New York: Alfred A. Knopf, 2010), 121-122.

25   Gauthier, *Sovereignty Over the Old City,* 355.

Chapter 12

The San Remo Conference

Introduction

The Peace Conference in Paris in 1919 produced peace treaties between the Allied Powers and Germany, Hungary, Austria, and Belgium. It also introduced the Wilsonian concept of self-determination—the notion that a people has a right to determine its own future. The Allied Powers accepted Wilson's concept of self-determination, but with a condition; they stipulated that the advanced nations ought to nurture the less developed ones till the latter were ready to be autonomous. This stipulation was the basis of the mandate system. Article 22 of the Covenant of the League of Nations enshrines these ideas.

Though it accomplished many things, the Paris Peace Conference did not produce a peace treaty with Turkey. Nor did it resolve the question of what to do with the former Turkish territories. Which of the Allied Powers would become Mandatories for these territories—namely, Palestine, Syria, and Iraq (Mesopotamia)? And what would the borders of these territories be? The most significant meetings concerning these territories took place in the Italian resort city of San Remo, from April 18th to April 26th, 1920.

The San Remo Conference had various aims, including the following:

- to prepare for the signing of a treaty with Turkey regarding their former territories;
- to draft mandate proposals for these territories and to determine in the process whether the Balfour Declaration of 1917, with its promise of a Jewish national home in Palestine, would be substantially incorporated into the new Palestine Mandate and be thereby enshrined as law; and
- to appoint the Mandatory Powers for Palestine, Iraq (Mesopotamia), and Syria, and to determine the borders of these territories.

Jurists and legal scholars increasingly recognize an important fact about the San Remo Conference—namely, that it marks the historical point where the Jewish people finally received, under international law, prospective title to a national home in Palestine. The Balfour Declaration, though it was Britain's formal pledge of support for the Zionist enterprise and was endorsed by other nations, had no real standing under international law. It expressed an intention, merely. Cast in the form of a letter to Lord Rothschild, it was not an official document. But when the San Remo Resolution incorporated the Balfour document in 1920, that earlier pledge became a substantive and binding commitment. This was a critical juncture on the Zionist journey to Jewish statehood. With the Balfour Declaration, promises were made. At the Paris Peace Conference, the Zionists petitioned for the fulfillment of those promises. At San Remo, the Allied Powers formally committed themselves to honoring those earlier pledges.

This chapter has various aims. One is to give the reader a vivid sense of the actual diplomatic process by which the world powers convening at San Remo reached some of their resolutions concerning Palestine. Using the actual minutes of the 1920 meetings, we reconstruct the words and viewpoints of the statesman involved and present them to the reader in the form of transcribed speech. Another aim of this chapter is to clarify the importance of the San Remo Resolution where Jewish—as well as Arab—statehood is concerned. Though it has been called the "Magna Carta of the Zionist Movement," people often overlook this document's importance with respect to the Jewish people's title to Palestine. The Arab world in 1920 understood its significance in this regard, and their backlash against it will be another focus of this chapter.

The Allied Powers on Palestine: An Inside View

For nine days in 1920, from April 18th to 26th, the Allied Powers met in San Remo to decide how to allocate the League of Nations mandates for the former Ottoman territories of the Middle East. From the San Remo meetings emerged Mandates for Syria, Lebanon, Mesopotamia (Iraq), and Palestine.

On April 24th and 25th, the discussion focused on Palestine. Britain and France had drafted separate proposals for the Palestine Mandate. The French thought the Balfour Declaration should not be included in the mandate document. Their stated view was that the Declaration was not an official document and therefore should not be incorporated into the formal treaty with Turkey. Inclusion of the Balfour Declaration would give the document's pledges official status and make them binding under international law. The British, represented by Lord Curzon, disagreed with the French position. They were prepared to stand by the Balfour pledges.

It is rare to get an inside account of what world leaders say at a historic conference such as San Remo. From the original minutes prepared by the British Secretary at these meetings, we have put together an edited recreation of the key exchanges between the chief delegates.[1]

Saturday, April 24th, 1920

The participants were as follows:

■ *Italy*: Signor Nitti, Prime Minister (in the Chair)

- *The British Empire*: The Right Hon. David Lloyd George, Prime Minister; The Right Hon. The Earl (Lord) Curzon of Kedleston, Secretary of State for Foreign Affairs
- *France*: M. Millerand, President of the French Council; M. Berthelot; M. Kammerer
- *United States of America*: Mr. Robert Underwood Johnson, American Ambassador in Rome; Mr. Leland Harrison
- *Japan*: Mr. Matsui
- *Interpreter*: Mr. Gustave Henri Camerlynck

NITTI. The next matter before the Supreme Council is the question of Mandates for the territories formerly under Turkish domination and the proposal that they should be administered by the Principal Allied Powers.

CURZON. Regarding Palestine, two years ago, [the British] government promulgated a formal declaration which was accepted by the Allied Powers, that *Palestine was in future to be the National Home of the Jews throughout the world* [emphasis added]. The Supreme Council now has to consider what exact form the repetition of this pledge should take. I think the only safe plan is to repeat the pledge in the precise form in which it was originally given. I sincerely hope that the French delegation will not refuse to adhere to the terms as originally drafted. I understand that the French delegation has an alternative draft which they propose to submit to the council, but I sincerely trust they will not press its acceptance.

BERTHELOT. I think that the whole world is sympathetic to the aspiration of the Jews to establish a national home in Palestine, and we would be prepared to do our utmost to satisfy their legitimate desires. The French government does not desire to stand in the way of Great Britain's wish to give the Jews due opportunity to achieve those passionate aspirations. So far as these are concerned, the French delegation has no objection to offer and we are prepared to recognize the responsibilities of the country accepting the mandate.

Regarding Mr. Balfour's declaration on behalf of the Zionists, has it been accepted by the Allied Powers? I don't have the text in front of me, but to my recollection, it is framed in general terms. I cannot recall that [any] general acceptance has ever been given to Mr. Balfour's declaration by the Allied Powers. I have no desire to embarrass the British Government, but I must state that, so far as my recollection goes, there has never been any official acceptance of Mr. Balfour's declaration by the Allies of the British Government.

CURZON. I think that Monsieur Berthelot is possibly not fully acquainted with the history of the question. In November, 1917, Mr. Balfour made a declaration on behalf of the Zionists. The terms of this declaration were communicated by Mr. Sokolov, in February, 1918, to Monsieur Pichon, who at that time was head of the French Foreign Office. I have before me a copy of the letter from Monsieur Pichon which was published in the French press, and which I presently ask the interpreter to read out to the Supreme Council. The Italian government has also expressed its approval of the terms of the declaration, and it has been accepted by the President of the United States and by Greece, China, Serbia and Siam as well.

I think, therefore, I am quite justified in saying that Mr. Balfour's declaration has been accepted by a large number of the Allied Powers. I think it is impossible for the Supreme Council to determine, today, exactly what form the future administration of Palestine will take. All we can do is to repeat the declaration which was made in November, 1917.

That declaration contemplated first, *the creation of a national home for the Jews whose privileges and rights were to be safeguarded under a military Power* [emphasis added]. Second, it was of the highest importance to safeguard the rights of minorities; first, the rights of the Arabs, then of the Christian communities; and provision was made for this in the second part of the declaration. In view of the explanation which I have submitted to the Supreme Council, I sincerely hope the French government will not press their objections.

NITTI. *It appears to me that in principle the Powers are generally in agreement as to the desirability of instituting a national home for the Jews* [emphasis added].

MILLERAND. As regards Palestine, [the questions are] *First, [whether] there should be a national home for the Jews. Upon that, we are all agreed* [emphasis added]. Second, [how to] safeguard the rights of the non-Jewish communities. That again, I think, offers no insuperable difficulties. I also have no objection to the mandate which I understand Great Britain desires to exercise in Palestine. I am quite sure that England will faithfully discharge their duty. My understanding is that in undertaking a mandate for Palestine, Great Britain is undertaking, first, to establish a national home for the Jews in that country and also, not to neglect the traditional rights of the inhabitants generally.

NITTI. What future business is still to come before the Supreme Council?

BERTHELOT. There are a number of essential questions which still remain for discussion and decision. We have yet to fix the limits of certain States. For instance, Mesopotamia, Syria, and so on, and also to name the Powers which would have the mandates for those states.

NITTI. It will be necessary then for the Supreme Council to hold two sittings tomorrow if we are to conclude our business.

Day 2: Sunday, April 25th, 1920

On the next day, April 25, 1920, the Supreme Council discussed the selection of the Mandatory Powers for Palestine, Mesopotamia, and Syria, and the proposed boundaries of those Mandated territories.

NITTI. The first item on the agenda is the resumption of the discussion held yesterday in regard to mandates.

BERTHELOT. There are two very important things which have to be settled. The first is the appointment of the mandatory Powers, and the second is the fixation of the boundaries of the mandate countries. Regarding the question of boundaries, as far as Syria is concerned, her northern frontiers are already indicated in the terms of the Treaty of Peace with Turkey. The southern frontier would follow the Sykes–Picot line with the exception of a slight modification of *the frontier of Palestine, which would conform to the definition advocated by Mr. Lloyd George, who had been in favor of the ancient boundaries of Dan and Beersheba* [emphasis added]. These frontiers were included in the draft I submitted to the British delegation in London. They raised no difficulties at all. Complete agreement was reached between the British and French delegations.

LORD CURZON. The nomination of the Powers is a matter that can be taken up any time this afternoon, if necessary. M. Berthelot referred to Syria, which he hoped would be, with Palestine, included in the treaty. The council, I think, is in agreement as to the boundary of Palestine to the north, but we have not yet settled what the eastern frontier will be. The Emir Feisal will almost certainly be coming to Europe very shortly, and I urge that it would be better to await his arrival before we commit ourselves. To fix the boundaries now is unnecessary and unwise.

BERTHELOT. The last thing we want is to indefinitely prolong the discussion regarding these frontiers. Mr. Lloyd George has indicated a formula, and has stated that if the French accept this, the British delegation will not press their points in other directions. *There is no difficulty in regard to the eastern frontiers of Palestine. The 'B' zone of the Sykes-Picot Agreement fixed the limit of the British influence* [emphasis added]. I suggest that the simplest thing to do is to have it stated that the two Powers adhere to the line that was fixed in the Sykes-Picot Agreement, and I trust that the British delegation will agree to this. Otherwise the French Government will be bound to seek something further later on.

LLOYD GEORGE. I fully agree with M. Berthelot that a complete and comprehensive understanding between the British and French is most desirable. Serious difficulties have arisen between the two Governments previously, but fortunately, these have now vanished. To take the northern limit of Palestine. The Zionists had claimed the whole of the country up to the [Litani] river including Tyre and Sidon. These, however, had never been included in the history of the boundaries of Palestine. When in London, I had informed M. Berthelot that M. Clemenceau had agreed to *my suggestion that the limits [of Palestine] should be fixed by the old historic towns of Dan and Beersheba* [emphasis added]. The French had not favored this suggestion, but they did agree to it, and now you are loyally standing by it. The British Government also perceived many objections to it, but we are equally prepared to stand by it. But it is not [the best] arrangement because the head waters of the Jordan [River] will be outside the control of the men who have been inhabiting Palestine. [That being said,] these waters have never been under their control at any time in history. To the east, difficulties might arise but those difficulties would not be with the Arabs, but with the Druses. I agree with Lord Curzon that the council surely cannot dispose of the countries now under discussion without giving the Emir Feisal a chance of stating his case.

MILLERAND. I thank M. Lloyd George very much for what he's said and I will rejoice with him that no real difficulties remain between the French and the British. Regarding the question of mandates, I am anxious that the decision should be reached today if possible, and *I enquire whether we could decide now that the British be given a mandate over Mesopotamia and Palestine, and the French over Syria* [emphasis added].

NITTI. I think that a formal decision could be taken this morning. The question of mandates is now closed.

The San Remo Resolution

At the conclusion of the San Remo meetings, several decisions were made. These decisions were recorded in the minutes. The following is sometimes known as the San Remo Resolution (though the name is not used in political, diplomatic, and legal reports):

The high contracting parties agree that Syria and Mesopotamia shall, in accordance with the fourth paragraph of article 22, Part I (Covenant of the League of Nations), *be provisionally recognized as independent States* [emphasis added], subject to the rendering of administrative advice and assistance by a mandatory until such time as they are able to stand alone. The boundaries of the said States will be determined, and the selection of the mandatories made, by the Principal Allied Powers.

The high contracting parties agree to entrust, by application of the provisions of article 22, the administration of Palestine, within such boundaries as may be determined by the Principal Allied Powers, to a mandatory, to be selected by the said Powers. The mandatory will be responsible for putting into effect the declaration originally made on November 2nd, 1917, by the British Government, and adopted by the other Allied Powers, in favor of the establishment in Palestine of a national home for the Jewish people, it being clearly understood that nothing shall be done which may prejudice the civil and religious rights of existing non-Jewish communities in Palestine, or the rights and political status enjoyed by Jews in any other country [emphasis added].

The terms of the mandates in respect of the above territories will be formulated by the Principal Allied Powers and submitted to the Council of the League of Nations for approval.

Turkey hereby undertakes, in accordance with the provisions, to accept any decisions which may be taken in this connection.

That mandatories chosen by the Principal Allied Powers are: France for Syria and Great Britain for Mesopotamia and Palestine [emphasis added].

The Significance of the San Remo Conference

Why did Lord Curzon refer to the San Remo Resolution as the "Magna Carta of the Zionists"?[2] Why did Weizmann see it as the most important development in the history of the Zionist movement?

We mentioned above that San Remo marks the moment where the Jewish people finally received, under international law, prospective title to a national home in Palestine; it was the point where the earlier pledge of the Balfour Declaration became a substantive and binding commitment. Why did it become binding at this moment? The significance of San Remo consists in the fact that it fused the particular pledge of the earlier Balfour Declaration with the principles of Article 22 of the Covenant of the League of Nations. It is important to keep in mind that, at the time of the Balfour Declaration, the Covenant of the League of Nations and Article 22 did not exist.

Article 22, as noted in Chapter 11, established two things:

1. It obliged the developed nations of the world to promote the well-being and development of nations "not yet able to stand by themselves" after World War I. This obligation was defined as a "sacred trust."

2. It recognized that "certain communities formerly belonging to the Turkish Empire" were ready to have their existence as independent nations "provisionally recognized subject to the rendering of administrative advice and assistance by a Mandatory until such time as they are able to stand alone." In other words, Article 22, adhering to the Wilsonian principle of self-determination, recognized the prospective statehood of "certain communities formerly belonging to the Turkish Empire."

But what were these "certain communities"? Were the Jewish people one of them? Did the Jews worldwide constitute a community "formerly belonging to the Turkish Empire"? The answer, obviously, is no. This is where the San Remo Resolution's incorporation of the Balfour Declaration becomes crucial.

The San Remo Conference established that the Balfour Declaration would be closely incorporated into the prospective Mandate for Palestine. The British insisted on this over the resistance of the French, as we saw in the transcribed exchanges above. Once this incorporation was decided upon, the prospective Palestine Mandate became a special case; it would differ from the mandates concerning Syria/Lebanon and Mesopotamia (Iraq). The latter mandates were to be focused on the actual communities existing in these regions—the current inhabitants. In other words, the Mandatories of Syria/Lebanon and Mesopotamia (Iraq) were bound to consider—to accept as a "sacred trust"—the rights, interests, and wishes of the native populations and authorities. The Mandate for Palestine would not do this. In Palestine, the Mandatory would be responsible not for assisting the existing population (that is, the Arabs) to achieve self-determination, but for following through on the pledges of the Balfour Declaration regarding the national home for the Jewish people.

By fusing the Balfour Declaration with Article 22 of the Covenant of the League of Nations, the San Remo Resolution accomplished several things. First, it officially identified Palestine as the place where a Jewish national home would be established. Second, it reserved this Jewish national home not just for the 60,000 Jews living in Palestine at the end of World War I but for the Jewish people as a whole—that is, for the Jewish people worldwide. Hence Lord Curzon's saying, in the meetings on April 24th, "that Palestine was in the future to be the National Home of the Jews throughout the world." Lastly, it made the Jewish people worldwide the beneficiary of Wilson's principle of self-determination; one of the premises of Article 22 is that the undeveloped communities being helped to their feet are entitled to future self-government and independence.

By virtue of San Remo, the Jewish people worldwide received prospective sovereignty rights in Palestine. The Arabs living in Palestine did not. At the same time, the Arabs received prospective sovereignty rights in Syria and Mesopotamia—that is, in most of the Middle East.

The San Remo agreements officially established Syria, Mesopotamia, and Palestine as new mandated states in the Middle East—as "sacred trusts" to their respective Mandatories. These agreements, though they weren't officially ratified until 1922, proved binding.[3]

The importance of the San Remo conference to the prospect of a Jewish state in Palestine is evident from Weizmann's response to it. Hearing what the Supreme Council had decided, Weizmann said the following:

> The San Remo decision has come. That recognition of our rights in Palestine is embodied in the Treaty with Turkey, and has become part of international Law, *this is the most momentous political event in the whole history of our movement, and, it is, perhaps, no exaggeration to say in the whole history of our people since the Exile.*[4] (emphasis added)

Weizmann's joy over the San Remo decision was owing to one development above all. At San Remo, the allied powers decided that the principles and provisions of the Balfour Declaration were to be invested with legal attributes and to become part of the Law of Nations.

Why Is San Remo Ignored?

Most people don't understand San Remo's importance. Though largely forgotten in political, diplomatic, and legal circles today, it is the single strongest proof that in 1920, under international law, all of Palestine west of the Jordan River and (arguably) some of the territory east of the Jordan River were to be given exclusively to the Jewish people.[5]

What does this proof consist in? First, the San Remo participants designated an area for the Jewish national home that included the historical frontiers of ancient Israel and ancient Judea (Judah). The basis of David Lloyd George's "Dan to Beersheba" formula—several times discussed by the British and French representatives, both before and during the San Remo sessions (see the transcribed exchanges above)— was a map titled "Palestine under David and Solomon," in George Adam Smith's *Atlas of the Historical Geography of the Holy Land*.[6] The first use of the "Dan to Beersheba" phrase in international discussion was likely in 1918, two years before San Remo. British Prime Minister David Lloyd George met with the French Premier Georges Clemenceau in London on December 1, 1918, to revise the terms of the previous 1916 Anglo-French Sykes-Picot Agreement. The two leaders decided that Palestine "from Dan to Beersheba" would be placed under British control in exchange for other British concessions to France.[7] On Smith's map, "Dan to Beersheba" included the territory west of the Jordan River to the Mediterranean. Within this territory lie Judea and Samaria, the area known today as the West Bank.

There is a second proof that Palestine, as originally conceived, included territory on the east and west sides of the Jordan River. We find this proof in Article 25 of the Mandate for Palestine, ratified in 1923. Article 25 was a special provision giving Britain the right to allocate the territory "lying between the Jordan [River] and the *eastern* boundary of Palestine"[8] to something other than a Jewish national home (emphasis added). The phrasing indicates that this territory—that is, the territory east of the Jordan River—was part of Britain's Palestine Mandate. Britain proceeded to exercise this right when it partitioned the mandated territory a year later (see below), creating Trans-Jordan east of the Jordan River. Britain had no such right in the territory west of the Jordan River. There were no special provisions concerning this area. Why not? Everybody understood that this entire area was to be the Jewish national home.

How could such an important agreement have been virtually absent from the Middle East dialogue over the past decades? One reason may be that the Treaty of Sèvres, which incorporated it, was aborted.

The Treaty of Sèvres

With the San Remo resolutions, the Allied Powers were laying the ground for a treaty with Turkey concerning that country's former territories. This prospective agreement turned out to be the Treaty of Sèvres. By this treaty, Turkey was to relinquish all of its rights and title to the territories covered by the mandates—that is, Syria and Lebanon, Palestine, and Iraq (Mesopotamia). According to international law, until Turkey officially renounced its rights to those territories, they still belonged to Turkey in law (*de jure*) if not in fact (*de facto*).

After San Remo, in anticipation of the Turks' relinquishing their title, France and Great Britain entered into an agreement that clarified their respective rights as Mandatories to the "former" Ottoman Territories. This was the Franco-British Boundary Agreement of 1920, signed in Paris on December 23. The agreement defined in broad terms the boundaries between the Mandate territories of Palestine and Mesopotamia, which had been assigned to Great Britain, and the Mandate of Syria and the Lebanon, which had been assigned to France. This agreement also established a joint commission to settle the precise details of the border. The particulars of this agreement were to be incorporated into the formal treaty with Turkey.

Sultan Muhammad VI, the last sultan of the Ottoman Empire, accepted the Treaty of Sèvres. It was signed by the Allied and Associated Powers and by the Sultan's four representatives at Sèvres on August 10, 1920. The treaty incorporated the provisions of the San Remo Resolution concerning Great Britain's obligations in the mandated territory of Palestine.

There was a hitch, however. In Turkey, the rival government of Kemal Ataturk Pasha succeeded in overthrowing Sultan Muhammad's regime, and the new government rejected the Treaty of Sèvres and its terms.

Nonetheless, from the perspective of international law, the Treaty of Sèvres is still relevant to the Jewish claims of sovereignty in Palestine. How so? This treaty is relevant because, even though it was aborted, its provisions (in Articles 94-97) concerning the creation of Syria, Lebanon, Jordan, and Iraq were enacted. In these territories, in accordance with the treaty, Britain and France assumed their mandate responsibilities with the approval of the League of Nations.[9] In other words, the nations of the world proceeded as if the Treaty of Sèvres were legally legitimate; its non-ratification had no practical effect on the creation of Syria, Lebanon, Jordan, and Iraq.

Of the states recognized at San Remo and in the Treaty of Sèvres, only the Jewish state is still having to fight to legitimize its legal status and sovereignty over the territory allocated to it. The sovereignty of the Arab states created at the same time—and by the same processes—has never been questioned.

Arab Response to the San Remo Decisions

Even before the San Remo Conference, there had been disturbances in Jerusalem between the Arabs and the Jews. The Arabs in Palestine recognized the Supreme Council's aims with respect to a Jewish homeland; they saw which way things were tending. The year 1920 brought the first armed Arab uprisings against the post-War settlement imposed by the Allies in Palestine. There were outbreaks of serious violence.[10]

The Nebi Musa riots started just prior to the San Remo sessions. Nebi Musa is a seven-day-long religious festival that is celebrated annually by Palestinian Muslims around the time of Easter and Passover. The festival involves a collective pilgrimage from Jerusalem to what Palestinian Muslims believe to be the Tomb of Moses, near Jericho. This pilgrimage was underway, in April of 1920, when Haj Amin al-Husseini, a prominent Palestinian Arab, incited a large Muslim crowd. There followed three days of violence that saw dozens of Arabs and Jews killed.

The San Remo decisions, by supporting the objectives of the Balfour Declaration, further aroused the Arab ire. The Arabs now saw their two cherished goals—

of independence on the one hand, and unity, or a pan-Arab nation, on the other—being denied them. The San Remo decisions seemed to them a betrayal of the pledges and commitments made to them previously by the Western powers, especially Britain.[11]

As a result of the Supreme Council's decisions at San Remo, Arabs refer to the year 1920 as the "Year of Catastrophe" ("Am al-Nakba"). In the wake of San Remo, a group of leading Palestinians, al-Husseini among them, formed the Palestinian Arab Society. In May of 1920, this group released a statement protesting the decision to grant Britain a mandate over Palestine.[12] Al-Husseini was for many years a key figure in stirring up Arab opposition and hostility to the British and Zionist efforts in Palestine.

The League of Nations did not formally ratify the Mandate for Palestine till 1922. In the meantime, however, with the mandate confirmed by the San Remo decisions, the British began their civil administration in Palestine. Trying to reconcile the Arabs in Palestine to a pro-Zionist agenda was no easy task for the British. British policies designed to placate the Palestinian Arabs were rejected, and Arab dissatisfaction grew throughout 1921.

One British attempt at appeasement was particularly unfortunate in its effects. The first High Commissioner of Palestine, Herbert Samuel, sought to soothe the Arabs by pardoning the leaders of the 1920 riots and appointing the most implacably hostile of them, Haj Amin al-Husseini, as Grand Mufti of Jerusalem. Al-Husseini, far from being softened by this measure, used his new position to promote his strong and inflammatory anti-Zionist agenda. Owing largely to his efforts, Arab violence started up again in May of 1921, resulting in the deaths of 47 Jews and 48 Arabs, with several hundred others wounded.

The British appointed a commission of inquiry to investigate the cause of the violence. The commission's final report contained a detailed account of the Arabs' grievances, including their loathing for Zionist social ideals and their resentment of Jewish immigration and land purchases. Unabashedly sympathetic to the Arabs, this report foreshadowed Britain's eventual shift away from the pro-Zionist policies of the Balfour Declaration.

The Partition of Palestine: 1921

Palestine under the British mandate, as set out at San Remo, was to include territory on both the east and west sides of the Jordan River. The San Remo meetings neither finalized the precise borders of the mandated territories nor formally ratified the mandates themselves. The League of Nations did that in 1923, with the Mandate for Palestine. In the interval between 1920 and 1923, Britain and France administered the regions according to the approximate territorial arrangements they worked out under the previous Sykes-Picot agreement of 1916. According to this agreement, Britain's Palestine mandate applied to the following territories:

1. the territory east of the Jordan River, which covered an area exceeding 92,000 square kilometers (35,000 square miles);

2. the area west of the Jordan, which covered approximately 26,158 square
kilometers (10,100 square miles).

In March 1921, Colonial Secretary Winston Churchill convened meetings in Cairo
to consider, among other things, how to resolve the rising Arab–Zionist tensions
in Palestine. As a result of that Cairo conference and the recommendations that
emerged from it in the Churchill White Paper, Great Britain decided to partition
the mandated territory. Article 5 of the Mandate provided that "no Palestine
territory shall be ceded or leased to, or in any way placed under the control of
the Government of any foreign Power." But Article 25 authorized the British
government to introduce amendments with respect to territory east of the Jordan
River. Great Britain proceeded to exercise this authority by establishing Trans-
Jordan in this territory. (It was evidently decided that partition did not contravene
the rights of the small Jewish community living there.) The Churchill White Paper
also advocated limiting Jewish immigration. With these measures, the British
government sought to placate the Palestinian Arabs after the San Remo decisions.

And yet many people in England were unmoved by the Arab grievances. They
agreed with Arthur Balfour, who said the following:

> So far as the Arabs are concerned … I hope they will remember that it
> is we who established an independent Arab sovereignty of the Hedjaz
> [modern day Saudi Arabia]. I hope they will remember it is we who desire
> in Mesopotamia [Iraq] to prepare the way for the future of a self-governing,
> autonomous Arab State, and I hope that, remembering all that, they will not
> grudge that small notch … in what are now Arab territories being given to
> [the Jewish] people who for all these hundreds of years have been separated
> from it.[13]

Balfour's statement remains perfectly valid today. The 11 sovereign Arab States in
the Middle East, including Saudi Arabia, Syria, Lebanon, Iraq, and Jordan, all owe
their full independence to the Allied efforts in WWI and to the League of Nations
mandate system. They collectively encompass a territory of millions of square miles.
The area of the State of Israel, by comparison, is only 10,000 square miles (8,000
without the disputed territories).

So why is Palestine the only territory in the Middle East whose status is still
disputed? We will address this question in the coming chapters.

Endnotes

1   Jacques Gauthier, "Minutes of Palestine Meeting of the Supreme Council of the Allied Powers Held in San Remo at the Villa DeVachan, April 24, 1920," appendix 14 in *Sovereignty Over the Old City of Jerusalem: A Study of the Historical, Religious, Political and Legal Aspects of the Question of the Old City*, Thèse No. 725 (Geneva: Université de Genève, 2007), 917-928.

2   Curzon referred to the San Remo Resolution as the "Magna Carta" of the Jewish people in a letter to Lloyd George: "The important thing is that we got the Balfour Declaration—you will remember how hard a fight I had made for it—into the Treaty [of Peace with Turkey] at San Remo, and that is the Magna Carta of the Zionists." Documents on British Foreign Policy 1919-1939, First Series, vol. 13, p.375 in Howard Grief, *The Legal Foundation and Borders of Israel under International Law* (Mazo Publishers: Jerusalem, 2008), 40.

3   Howard Grief, *The Legal Foundation and Borders of Israel under International Law* (Jerusalem: Mazo, 2008), 33-37.

4   Chaim Weizmann, "Building the Jewish National Home: Opening Address to Zionist Annual Conference," London, 7 July, 1920, in *The Letters and Papers of Chaim Weizmann*, Series B Papers, vol. 1, August 1898–July 1931, ed. Barnet Litvinoff, (Jerusalem: Israel University Press, 1983), Paper 58, 290.

5   Gauthier, *Sovereignty Over the Old City*, 374.

6   Grief, *Legal Foundation and Borders of Israel*, 50. For the map see George Adam Smith, "Palestine Under David and Solomon," *Atlas of the Historical Geography of the Holy Land* (Hodder and Stoughton: London, 1915), Plate No. 34.

7   Grief, *Legal Foundation and Borders of Israel*, 25.

8   Mandate for Palestine, Article 25, The Avalon Project, Yale Law School, http://avalon.law.yale.edu/20th_century/palmanda.asp.

9   See Gauthier, *Sovereignty Over the Old City*, 374: "Treaty of Sèvres, signed by the dying Turkish regime 10 Aug., incorporated a statement that the Mandatory Power in Palestine would be responsible for putting the Balfour Declaration into effect. Though the Treaty was abrogated by the insurgent leader Mustapha Kemal (Ataturk) and was re-negotiated as the Treaty of Lausanne, July 1923, the portion relating to Palestine [See section VII of the Treaty of Sèvres, Articles 94-97] was unaffected. But the Articles of the Mandate sustained various revisions detrimental to Zionism on their way to the Council of the League of Nations. References to a 'Jewish Commonwealth' were excised, while the policy of a Jewish National Home was, by request of [Great] Britain, excluded from Transjordan. Mandate passed by the League 24 July, and amended relative to Transjordan 23 Sept. 1922." Chaim Weizmann, *The Letters and Papers of Chaim Weizmann*, ed. Barnet Litvinoff, Paper 58, Footnote 1, 290.

10   Ibid, 312.

11   George Antonius, *The Arab Awakening* (Safety Harbor, Fl: Simon Publications, 2001), 305.

12   Gauthier, *Sovereignty Over the Old City*, 379.

13   Martin Gilbert, *The Routledge Atlas of the Arab–Israeli Conflict*, 9th ed. (London: Routledge, 2008), 7.

13

The Mandate for Palestine

Introduction

The San Remo Resolution on Palestine was never actually incorporated into a ratified treaty. It was incorporated into the Treaty of Sèvres on August 10th, 1920. But Turkey refused to honor that treaty. Turkey did sign a subsequent agreement, the Treaty of Lausanne, on July 24th, 1923. But that treaty did not incorporate the San Remo Resolution. The Resolution was instead incorporated into a formal document in international law called the Mandate for Palestine, which was approved by the Council of the League of Nations on July 24th, 1922.

The focus of this chapter is the Mandate for Palestine. This is the document that set out the rights and beneficiaries to Palestine according to international law and that detailed Britain's obligations as Mandatory. This chapter also discusses the significant events of the period that preceded the founding of the State of Israel, a period known as the Mandate era (1920–1948).

The Mandate Document

Fifty-one nations were members of the League of Nations when it accepted the Palestine Mandate, and it became law on September 29th, 1923. From the perspective of international law, the Mandate was considered binding, and it remains the basis of Jewish legal title to Palestine.[1] It was a legal charter of 28 articles, prefaced by a preamble, drawn up to serve as a legal guide for the Mandatory, Great Britain, which was administering Palestine on behalf of the League of Nations.

Key Provisions

The preamble to the Mandate document contained certain key provisions, including the following:

> Whereas the Principal Allied Powers have agreed, for the purpose of giving effect to the provisions of Article 22 of the Covenant of the League of

Nations, to entrust to a Mandatory selected by the said Powers the administration of the territory of Palestine, which formerly belonged to the Turkish Empire, within such boundaries as may be fixed by them; and

Whereas the Principal Allied Powers have also agreed that the Mandatory should be responsible for putting into effect the declaration [the Balfour Declaration] originally made on November 2nd, 1917, by the Government of His Britannic Majesty, and adopted by the said Powers, in favor of the establishment in Palestine of a national home for the Jewish people, it being clearly understood that nothing should be done which might prejudice the civil and religious rights of existing non-Jewish communities in Palestine, or the rights and political status enjoyed by Jews in any other country; and

Whereas recognition has thereby been given to the *historical connection of the Jewish people with Palestine and to the grounds for reconstituting their national home in that country*; and [emphasis added]

Whereas the Principal Allied Powers have selected His Britannic Majesty as the Mandatory for Palestine …

Whereas His Britannic Majesty has accepted the mandate in respect of Palestine and undertaken to exercise it on behalf of the League of Nations in conformity with the following provisions … .

Among the most crucial of the Palestine Mandate's 28 articles were the following:

Article 2

The Mandatory shall be responsible for placing the country under such political, administrative and economic conditions as *will secure the establishment of the Jewish national home*, as laid down in the preamble, and the development of self-governing institutions, and also for safeguarding the civil and religious rights of all the inhabitants of Palestine, irrespective of race and religion. … [emphasis added]

Article 4

An appropriate Jewish agency shall be recognised as a public body for the purpose of advising and co-operating with the Administration of Palestine in such economic, social and other matters as may affect the establishment of the Jewish national home and the interests of the Jewish population in Palestine, and, subject always to the control of the Administration to assist and take part in the development of the country. [emphasis added]

Article 5

The Mandatory shall be responsible for seeing that *no Palestine territory shall be ceded or leased* to, or in any way placed under the control of the Government of any foreign Power. [emphasis added]

Article 6

The Administration of Palestine, while ensuring that the rights and position of other sections of the population are not prejudiced, *shall facilitate Jewish immigration* under suitable conditions and shall encourage, in co-operation with the Jewish agency referred to in Article 4, *close settlement by Jews on the land, including State lands and waste lands* not required for public purposes. [emphasis added]

Article 7

The Administration of Palestine shall be responsible for enacting a nationality law. There shall be included in this law provisions framed so as to *facilitate the acquisition of Palestinian citizenship by Jews* who take up their permanent residence in Palestine. [emphasis added]

Unique Features of the Palestine Mandate

The Palestine Mandate, while similar in some respects to other mandates—for example, those of Syria and Mesopotamia (Iraq)—was designed to be unique. It has been described as *sui generis*, one of a kind.[2] Following are some of its singular features:

- It recognized "historical connection" and "reconstitution" as a basis for the Jewish people's claim to Palestine, and it acknowledged this in law.
- It provided that Jewish people living *outside* the mandated territory constituted the majority in Palestine and had legal claim to it (as implied in the phrase "Jewish people" in the Preamble).
- It provided that the majority of the inhabitants living *within* the territory of the Palestine Mandate (that is, the Arab population) did not receive the right to self-determination.

The rights to mandated territories normally went to the people living in them. The case was different with the Mandate for Palestine. It extended those rights not to the Arab residents of the region but to the prospective or potential Jewish residents worldwide. Summing up this novel principle, Norman Bentwich, attorney general of Palestine from 1918 to 1931, explained that Britain was to administer the country "not simply on behalf of the population which is there, but with a view to help the people which desires to come there."[3]

The drafters of the Palestine Mandate recognized the Jewish people's *historical connection* with Palestine and their grounds for *reconstituting* their national home in that country. In doing so, they expanded the policy of the Balfour Declaration, which had merely committed the British government to helping establish a national home for the Jewish people in Palestine.

What did the term "reconstitute" mean, in this context? It meant not the creation of something new but the re-creation of a previously existing political situation— that of the first and second Temple periods, when the land in question had been settled and governed by Jews.[4] It meant the reconstitution of Jewish statehood in Palestine. In other words, the League of Nations was acknowledging that Jewish rights to the land go back to the Biblical era.

It is important to emphasize that the rights set out for Jews in Palestine by the Balfour Declaration and the Mandate for Palestine were different from the rights set out for non-Jews. Where Jews were granted the right to establish a national home—that is, sovereignty rights—non-Jews were granted only civil and religious rights. Those who drafted these documents expected non-Jews to live as a protected minority within a sovereign Jewish state.[5]

Objections to the Mandate for Palestine

The Palestine Mandate's unique features were problematic for the peoples involved. The indigenous Arab population and the Jewish people both claimed to be the beneficiaries of the "sacred trust" described in Article 22 of the Covenant of the League of Nations. As discussed in Chapter 11, this was the obligation of advanced nations to nurture the well-being and development of the indigenous populations in the former Turkish territories. In other words, the advanced nations made themselves responsible for communities in the region that, owing to World War I and the demise of Turkish control, were "not yet able to stand by themselves under the strenuous conditions of the modern world."

Opponents of the Palestine Mandate—and of Jewish claims to the Land of Israel/ Palestine--argue that it, along with the Balfour Declaration, was inconsistent with the objectives of Article 22. Palestinian Arabs claim to be one of the indigenous populations whose well-being and development was, or should have been, a sacred trust of civilization and the responsibility of the Mandatory power. Arab supporters argue that Palestinian Arabs, not the Jewish people worldwide, were the indigenous people in Palestine. Arab jurist Khaled El Shalakany, for example, has asserted that "the Jewish people, even assuming that they are the descendants of the Biblical Jews, had not been in Palestine (prior to Zionist immigration) for centuries, while the Palestinians have been living there continuously since time immemorial."[6]

Another objection to the Palestine Mandate was that it was illegal. Its alleged illegality is based on the idea that it breached the rights of self-determination— the principle in international law that peoples have the right to freely choose their sovereignty and international political status with no external compulsion or interference. As noted in Chapter 11, the concept of the right of self-determination was one of the foundational principles defined by Woodrow Wilson at the Paris

Peace Conference. There, he stated that national aspirations "must be respected; peoples may now be dominated and governed only by their own consent. 'Self-determination' is not a mere phrase." El Shalakany invokes this principle in arguing that "the imposition of the British mandate over Palestine was illegal as it was imposed without the consent of the peoples of Palestine."[7]

Another argument against the Mandate was that a people's having a historical connection to a place does not entitle them to reconstitute there; such an idea has no basis in law. Palestinian jurist and author of *Palestine and International Law—The Legal Aspects of the Arab-Israeli Conflict*, Henry Cattan, for example, has taken the following position:

> [T]he Zionist claim of an historic title to Palestine has no basis in law, or in fact. The modes of acquiring territory are well defined under international law and the claim of an historic title is not one of them. ... It is evident that an ancient historical connection gives no title, no rights, no claim to territory. Much less does it displace the title or justify the dispossession of the original inhabitants of the country.[8]

As the above suggests, Arab supporters' objections to the Mandate generally rest on at least one of the following arguments:

1. Giving title in Palestine to the Jewish people worldwide was in violation of the spirit and intent of Article 22, since they are not the indigenous population in the region; the Arabs are.
2. The Mandate breaches the Wilsonian principle concerning a people's right to self-determination—the principle in international law that nations have the right to freely choose their sovereignty and international political status with no external compulsion or interference.
3. Claiming that a people's historical connection to a place gives them the right to reconstitute there has no basis in law.

Responses to Arab Objections

The Palestinian Arabs' claim to being the indigenous population of Palestine—their claim to having lived in the mandated territory "continuously since time immemorial"—lacks the ample evidence supporting Jewish claims to ancient statehood. We detailed the Jewish claims in the opening chapters of this work (see, in particular, Chapters 2 and 3). In the process, we showed that contemporary Arab denials of an ancient Jewish presence in Palestine are contradicted by compelling evidence of every kind. As for the Arab presence in Palestine, it is true that they have been associated with the region since the early centuries of the Common Era. However, prior to the 7th century, the Arabs, along with a variety of other ancient societies, were a minority in the region.

The demography of Palestine changed after the 7th century, when Islam and its Arab adherents spread through the Middle East. Even then, however, the Arabs did not settle in large numbers in Palestine. Ottoman censuses from the 19th century indicate a Muslim population in Palestine of only about 300,000. Of the millions of Arabs that live in the mandated area of Palestine today, most are descendants of those who came to the region since the 19th century—attracted, in many cases, by the economic opportunities created by Jewish immigration and development.

But what about the Palestinian Arab peoples' right to self-determination? Did the Wilsonian self-determination principle not apply to them? One response is that the Palestinians did in fact receive those rights when, in 1921, the British government partitioned the territory covered by the Palestine Mandate and allocated 77 percent of that territory to the Arabs, in the form of the state of Jordan. As one Jewish jurist put it,

> the Palestinian Arabs have long enjoyed self-determination in their own state–the Palestinian Arab state of Jordan. ... More than two thirds of Jordan's citizens are Palestinian Arabs, and similarly, the vast majority of Palestinian Arabs are Jordanian citizens. ... It is patently false, therefore, to maintain that the Palestinian Arabs do not have a state of their own.[9]

It is worth emphasizing that the mandates awarded at San Remo ultimately created Arab rights to self-determination in Syria, Lebanon, Iraq, and, later, Jordan. The Supreme Council's decisions, approved by the League of Nations, created Arab rights to self-determination in over a million square miles of the Middle East. Today, Arab states in the region enjoy sovereignty as a result of the efforts of the Allied Powers and the decisions of the Supreme Council and League of Nations. Jewish rights to self-determination were limited to the 10,000 square miles west of the Jordan River that were left after the 1921 partition of Palestine. It is likely for these reasons that no member state of the League of Nations ever charged the Palestine Mandate with contravening the provisions of Article 22.

Another response to the self-determination argument hinges on the definition of a "people." It is often overlooked that, in 1919, the Palestinian Arabs were not regarded as a distinct "people" in the same way the Jewish people were. The Palestine Mandate reflects this perception; it addresses the rights and entitlements of the Jewish people but does not define Palestine's Arab inhabitants as a "people."[10] The Palestinian Arabs were considered to be part of the larger Arab nation. For this reason, the League of Nations' granting of rights over Palestine to the Jewish people cannot be taken as violating the principles of self-determination.[11]

The actual language of the Mandate is telling in this regard. It never refers to the Arabs by name, while the words "Jews" or "Jewish" appear fifteen times. Palestinian Arabs are referred to indirectly, as "existing non-Jewish communities" or as "inhabitants of Palestine." This indicates that the interest, welfare, and rights of the Jewish people constituted the fundamental aspect of the Mandate.[12]

The Balfour Declaration and the Mandate for Palestine, as we noted above, extended one set of rights to Jews in Palestine, and another to non-Jews. Jews were given the right to establish a national home in Israel; Arabs, subsumed under the more general term "non-Jews," were given only civil and religious rights. In other words, there was a general assumption that all non-Jews, including Arabs, would live as a protected minority within the Jewish national home.[13] Howard Grief, a specialist in the legal foundations of Israel, has written the following in this regard:

> If one of the purposes of the Mandate had been to detail Arab national rights then those would be evident in the provisions of the document but that was not the case as one will search in vain for those rights in the Mandate apart from the right to use Arabic.[14]

To the third anti-Mandate argument—that there is no legal basis for claiming that the Jewish people's historical connection to Israel gives them the right to reconstitute there—there is a simple response. The Palestine Mandate is itself the legal basis. The Mandate for Palestine is recognized under international law. When the League of Nations approved the Palestine Mandate in 1922, it gave legal recognition to the historical rights of the Jewish people in respect to the Holy Land.[15] To say that there is no legal *precedent* for basing a regional claim on historical connection is a different matter. True or not, it doesn't amount to a valid argument against Israel's claim. As we noted above, the Mandate for Palestine was designed to be unique, *sui generis*. In acknowledging in law the Jewish people's historical connection to Palestine and recognizing this connection as grounds for their sovereignty rights, the Mandate was one of a kind.

The British Perspective

During the Mandatory period, a number of British statesmen responded to the various Arab objections and complaints. Their responses are instructive. The general tone was one of indignation. In June 1922, Lord Balfour, speaking in the British House of Lords, said the following: "Of all the charges made against this country, I must say that the charge that we have been unjust to the Arab race seems to be the strangest."[16] Balfour felt that Arab liberation from Turkish rule had come at the cost of British lives and military efforts. He argued that Arab sovereignty in virtually all of the Middle East (Syria, Iraq, and the Arabian Peninsula) was owing to British efforts in World War I and that it was the British "who have done more than has been done for centuries past to put the Arab race in the position to which they have obtained."[17] Balfour added that the Arabs' charging the British with being their enemies "seems to me not only unjust to the policy of this country, but almost fantastic in its extravagance."[18]

During the spring of 1923, with Arab criticism mounting after the Palestine Mandate's confirmation, the British secretary of state for colonies, the Duke of Devonshire, asserted the following: "What we promised [in the McMahon-Hussein letters of 1915] was to promote Arab independence throughout a wide area. That promise we have substantially fulfilled."[19] Like Balfour, he was aware of all the Arabs had attained through British efforts during World War I and of the territorial concessions already granted them—including the creation of Transjordan through the 1922 partition of the original Mandate Palestine. The Duke of Devonshire thought that the Arabs, having gained so much from the British, ought to comply more readily with Britain's pledges to the Jews regarding what was left of Palestine (that is, the area west of the Jordan River), an area that "for historical and other reasons, stands on a wholly different footing from the rest of the Arab countries."[20]

David Lloyd George was also critical of the Arab response to the policies of Britain and the League of Nations. In *The Truth about the Peace Treaties*, he wrote the following:

> No race has done better out of the fidelity with which the Allies redeemed their promises to the oppressed races than the Arabs. Owing to the tremendous sacrifices of the Allied nations, and more particularly of Britain and her Empire, the Arabs have already won independence in Iraq, Arabia, Syria and Transjordania, although most of the Arab races fought throughout the War for their Turkish oppressors. Arabia was the only exception in that respect. The Palestinian Arabs fought for Turkish rule. The Balfour Declaration represented the convinced policy of all parties in our country and also in America.[21]

Conditions in Mandatory Palestine

The Growth of the Yishuv

Having assumed responsibility for Palestine, the British set about developing it. They had taken over a country that was economically crippled and under-populated, with little industry or trade and few known natural resources. The British did much to build the economy, especially in the area of agriculture. They also made wide-ranging improvements in communications and infrastructure. Arabs and Jews both benefited from these efforts. Jewish settlement in Palestine (the Yishuv) significantly increased during the decades of the 1920s and 30s. Arab immigrants, too, were flooding into the country as a result of the new economic opportunities and development.

The Jewish population of Palestine grew by leaps and bounds. Between 1919 and 1923, a total of 37,000 Jewish immigrants poured in from Eastern Europe. Most of them were fleeing revolutions, discriminatory laws, pogroms (organized massacres), and civil wars. This influx is known as the "Third Aliyah." In 1924, an unexpected mass of 70,000 Polish Jews, facing enforced unemployment in their native country, began to arrive in Palestine. This is called the "Fourth Aliyah." Between 1922 and 1929, the Jewish population of Palestine grew from 84,000 to 154,000.[22]

In the early 19th century, the Arab population of Palestine was 275,000. By 1914, this number had nearly doubled.[23] In 1922, the British recorded an Arab population of over 600,000. By 1931, under the British Mandate, the figure had grown even more dramatically, to roughly 840,000. This was 81 percent of the country's inhabitants. Most of them worked the land, and many were *fellahin*— tenant sharecroppers.[24]

The rise of the Yishuv created economic opportunities that stimulated the Arab population's growth. Several thousand Arabs worked as laborers on Jewish agricultural settlements, and the movement of the Arab population within Palestine was largely toward regions of Jewish concentration. From the Yishuv came Jewish tax revenues that funded Britain's spending in the region, which was a benefit to Arab and Jew alike. The economic growth opened new markets for Arab produce and created new opportunities for Arab labor. Many Arabs saw the advantages that Jewish settlement was bringing to Palestine.

The Arabs were on the rise in the region, and yet the Jews continued to outpace them, economically and otherwise. One factor in this economic disparity was that, after 1922, the Jewish immigrants to Palestine were arriving from the advanced societies of Germany and Central Europe. These people were highly educated and accomplished, equipped with the latest skills in business and industrial management. This know-how gave them a significant advantage over the Arab *fellahin* when it came to building an economic infrastructure. The Jewish newcomers were also more sophisticated than the Arabs in a political sense. This helped their nation-building aspirations. By the 1930s, the Jewish communities of the Yishuv had organized their own political, religious, educational, and social organizations, and had in fact—as Churchill remarked--developed "national characteristics."[25]

Arab–Jewish Relations

The Jewish presence brought material benefits to the Arabs of the region. But there were occasions for grievance as well. The Zionist goal of building an autonomous Jewish economy in Palestine sometimes cost the Arab workers their livelihoods. Many Jewish-owned plantations had been hiring Arabs instead of Jewish immigrants for years; the experienced Arab workers were cheaper and more productive than the urban Eastern European Jews, most of them new to manual labor. In response, the *Histradut* (Jewish Labor Federation) began to organize strikes against managers or owners of Jewish plantations who did not give priority to Jewish laborers over Arab ones. Jews arriving destitute from Eastern Europe and expecting employment in Jewish-owned orchards desperately needed this kind of affirmative action. But it did little to improve Arab–Jewish relations.[26]

Labor tensions were one source of Arab hostility toward Zionism in Palestine. The other important factors were the following:

- Fear on the part of the Palestinian Arab aristocracy that Zionist socialist ideas would influence the *fellahin* (Arab peasantry and tenant farmers) and destabilize the Arab social order.

- Fear of how Jewish immigration and land purchases would affect Palestinian Arabs' own aspirations to statehood.

- Resentment and envy at Jewish progress in the region, which surpassed that of the Arab community. The Westernized Jews arriving in Palestine, as well as being better educated than the Arabs, had the financial backing of Jewish philanthropists abroad and Jewish agencies such as the JNF.

Escalation of Anti-Jewish Violence

Violent altercations between Jews and Arabs in Palestine were relatively rare from 1921 to 1929, despite economic and political tensions. Things began to unravel in

1928. That year, on the Jewish holy day of Yom Kippur, the Jews set up a movable wall at the Western Wall of Jerusalem's Temple Mount, to separate the men from the women during prayer—in keeping with Orthodox Jewish tradition. There was a Mandate law against fixtures at holy sites. The movable wall was not a fixture, but the Arabs protested its presence there, and the British police removed it.

The Muslim leadership in Jerusalem—led by Haj Amin al-Husseini (1893–1974), Grand Mufti of Jerusalem and future Nazi collaborator—organized a demonstration against the Jewish "threat" to the Christian and Muslim Holy Places. A young Jewish boy was murdered after kicking a soccer ball into the house of an Arab neighbor. Following this incident, there was a Jewish demonstration at the Western Wall. Muslim agitators traveled across the country exhorting the Arab peasantry to protect the al-Aqsa (the mosque on the Temple Mount) against "Jewish attacks."

On the night of August 23, 1929, Arabs armed with weapons poured into Jerusalem. Incited by al-Husseini, the mob attacked the Orthodox Jewish Quarter, and violence spread rapidly to other areas of Palestine. By the time order was restored, 133 Jews had been killed and 399 wounded. The Arabs had suffered 87 deaths and 178 casualties.[27] At first, the British condemned the Arabs and levied heavy fines against them. Haj Amin al-Husseini vigorously protested these measures, and the High Commissioner responded with a second proclamation stating that an inquiry into the conduct of both sides would be held as soon as possible.

Britain as Mandatory: Shifting Policies

Many British statesman, as noted above, thought Arab grievances over Palestine unjustified. Nonetheless, the Arab outcry against Zionism eventually took its toll. Over time, in response to Arab complaints over Jewish immigration and land purchases, the British government began to reconsider its obligations as Mandatory.

Response to Arab Unrest

The political fall-out from the 1929 Arab–Jewish violence in Palestine was significant. The British colonial office dispatched a royal commission—the Shaw Commission—to Palestine to inquire into the immediate causes of the violence and to make recommendations on how to avoid a recurrence. The Shaw Commission sat as a public court of inquiry, hearing testimony from the Palestine government, the Jewish Agency, and the Arab executive.

The Shaw Commission issued its report on March 30, 1930. They found the Arabs responsible for the violence. At the same time, they blamed Jewish immigration and progress in Palestine for Arab hostility. Arab violence, according to the report, was owing to the disappointment of their political and national aspirations and to the thwarting of their economic future. The report urged the Mandatory administration to tighten its control of Jewish immigration, to tighten regulations on Jewish land purchases, and to ensure that the Jewish Agency—the public body created, under Article 4 of the Palestine Mandate, "for the purpose of advising and co-operating with the Administration of Palestine"—no longer shared in the region's governance.

On May 12, the British Colonial Office instructed the Mandatory to suspend Jewish immigration to Palestine. The League of Nations' Mandate body rejected the Shaw Report's findings—the notion that limiting Jewish immigration and land purchases was the best protection for Arab rights. But London continued to explore the recommendations outlined by the Shaw Report.

The month the Shaw Report was published, London dispatched Sir John Hope Simpson to Palestine, and he issued a report of his own on October 20, 1930. This report essentially echoed Arab grievances and recommended, with the Shaw Report, that Jewish immigration and land purchases be restricted.

The British reports, especially Simpson's suggestion that Jewish land purchases were stifling Arab growth, angered the Zionists. They pointed out that the entire Yishuv held only 6.3 percent of the arable land in Palestine. They pointed out that the dramatic rise in Arab living standards was owing in large part to Jewish settlement in Palestine. If Arab immigrants, no less than Jews, were now flooding into the country, it was largely because of the new economic opportunities created by the Zionist enterprise.

Before the Zionists could submit these arguments, London released an official policy statement, a White Paper issued by the Colonial Secretary, Lord Passfield. The Passfield White Paper claimed that no land remained for agricultural settlement by Jews and that Jewish immigration must be suspended. It also threatened Jews with an embargo on additional purchases of land. Not surprisingly, the Arabs favored the White Paper. Jews in Palestine, Britain, and America were outraged.

There was outrage in England, too. Winston Churchill condemned the document in the House of Commons, and David Lloyd George attacked Prime Minister Ramsay MacDonald for breaking England's promise to the Zionists. Under this intense attack, MacDonald reversed his policy, acknowledging that the British government remained responsible, as set out in Article 6 of the Palestine Mandate, for facilitating Jewish immigration and "close settlement" of the land.

The Arab executive in Palestine voiced their objections to MacDonald's reversal. In a letter to the High Commissioner on February 19, 1931, they stated that any understanding between the Jews and Arabs was now impossible.

The British were learning by now that the Palestine Mandate had set them a terribly difficult task. They were finding it all but impossible to meet the Mandate's legal obligations—to foster the growth of the Jewish national home while protecting Palestinian Arabs' civil and religious rights (and deflecting their nationalist aspirations).

Arab Growth and Continued Unrest

By 1935, in a budding economy stimulated by Jewish capital, the Palestinian Arab population had increased to 960,000. They were prospering in other ways as well. By 1935, no fewer than 700 Arab cooperatives were functioning, and new opportunities were opening for them in medicine, law, government employment, journalism, and teaching. The number of Arab children attending schools had grown from less than 2 percent in 1920 to about 13 percent in 1936.[28] Rising literacy, an expanding middle class, and growing numbers of white-collar workers and professionals—these were indications that Palestinian Arabs were moving in a positive direction.

Despite this progress, or possibly because of the confidence it inspired, Palestinian Arab unrest continued to increase. After April, 1936, they expressed this unrest through continual violence. Incited mainly by Haj Amin al-Husseini, the Grand Mufti of Jerusalem, Arab leaders requested an end to all Jewish immigration to Palestine and to Jewish land purchase in the region.

Worn down by Arab opposition, the British government began to abandon its international commitments to the creation of a Jewish state. Its first step was gradually to make Jewish immigration "illegal." In other words, Britain abandoned its legal obligation, under Article 6 of the Palestine Mandate, to "facilitate Jewish immigration" and to encourage "close settlement by Jews" in Palestine.

The obligation conferred on the British by Article 6 was supposed to be binding regardless of Arab opposition. It was not conditional on the Arab inhabitants' consent. From a legal perspective, Britain was required to fulfill the duties and obligations set out in its Mandate; they could not unilaterally modify the terms and conditions. But that is precisely what they did. And they did so just as the Jews worldwide, with Nazism on the rise in Germany and a growing threat to all of Europe, were most in need of a national home, a safe haven.

The Palestine Royal Commission

A Palestinian Arab rebellion began in the spring of 1936 and continued until the summer of 1937. The British government's response was to organize a commission of inquiry (the Palestine Royal Commission), headed by Lord William Robert W. Peel, to investigate the turmoil. During the inquiry, Arabs again demanded restrictions on Jewish immigration, a prohibition on sales of Arab properties to Jews, and the discontinuation of all plans or initiatives relating to a Jewish National Home in Palestine. The greatest challenge for the Peel Commission was finding a solution that met the Balfour Declaration and Palestine Mandate's dual obligation, namely,

1. the facilitation of the creation of the Jewish national home, and
2. the preservation of the rights of non-Jews.

The Peel Commission's preferred solution to the Arab–Jewish conflict was the partition of Palestine. This solution would allow, among other things, Britain to terminate its responsibilities as Mandatory. It would leave the two new "states" to stand on their own.

The 1937 Partition Plan

According to the Peel Report's "Partition Plan," signed on June 22nd, 1937, approximately 40 percent of the land west of the Jordan River would become the Jewish State. The rest of the territory would constitute a new Palestinian Arab State, with the exception of a carefully delineated area around Jerusalem that would not become part of either the Jewish or the Palestinian Arab State.

Jewish leaders were, despite certain reservations, generally supportive of the Partition Plan. Their major objection was that the land allocated to the Jewish state was considerably smaller than the territory previously requested.

The Arabs, however, were opposed to any solution in Palestine other than an independent state in "all of Palestine," ruled by them. On January 15th, 1938, King Abdul Aziz Al-Saud made a speech in Jeddah, in the presence of the British Ambassador, Sir Polard, which expressed the views of Arab leaders on Palestine. The Saudi King said the following: "The partition scheme of Palestine is in fact a catastrophe, a great catastrophe to Arabs and Muslims." [29]

Arab leaders had two main reasons for opposing the Partition Plan. One was their conviction that Palestinian Arabs' rights to all of Palestine "are derived from actual and long-standing possession, and rest upon the strongest human foundation. Their connection with Palestine goes back uninterruptedly to the earliest historic times."[30] Another was their belief that the 1915 McMahon–Husain correspondence had promised them the sole right to sovereignty over the entire territory of Palestine (see Chapter 10).

After the British House of Commons approved the recommendations of the Peel Royal Commission, it went to the Permanent Mandates Commission of the League of Nations on July 30th, 1937. Notwithstanding its discontent with Britain's attempt to end the Palestine Mandate prematurely and restrict Jewish immigration, the Commission accepted the concept of dividing Palestine into two independent states.

British Restrictions on Jewish Immigration and the Threat of Nazi Germany

During the evening of November 9th, 1938, on a night now remembered as *Kristallnacht*, Nazis in Germany and in Austria destroyed Jewish synagogues, shops, businesses, and homes, in accordance with government policies in these countries. These events marked the beginning of the Holocaust, which led to the murder of the majority of European Jews. Needless to say, these murdered millions were among those who, as one of the "sacred trusts of civilization" covered in Article 22 of the Covenant of the League of Nations and subsequently acknowledged in the Mandate for Palestine, had received the rights to settle in Palestine.

The MacDonald White Paper–May 1939

The conflict between the Arabs and Jews in Palestine continued to intensify through 1938. This led the British government to issue another White Paper (that is, a policy paper). It was prepared by Malcolm MacDonald, the British Colonial Secretary, and was released on May 17th, 1939.

The MacDonald White Paper was a shocking negation of earlier British promises regarding a Jewish homeland. The document declared that a Jewish National Home in Palestine had already been developed in accordance with the Balfour Declaration and Mandate for Palestine. Its grounds for saying this were that "the population of the National Home has risen to some 450,000 [Jews], approaching a third of the entire population of the country."[31] The revised British aims, as set out in the MacDonald White Paper, were to promote the establishment of an independent Palestine with an Arab majority and to ensure that the Jewish population of Palestine would not exceed 30 percent of the total population. The document also outlined a new immigration policy, setting a quota of 10,000 Jewish immigrants per year for five years, after which all Jewish immigration would be discontinued. Britain's new policy also introduced restrictions on further transfers of "Arab land" to Jews.

The policies set out in MacDonald's White Paper were radically different from those of previous British governments. These policies constituted a rejection of all previous plans, including partition. This meant, in other words, that no Jewish State would be established in Palestine.

Winston Churchill asked for the abolition of the paper, but after a long and heated debate, it was approved by the British House of Commons.

Jewish Response to the White Paper

The MacDonald White Paper was immediately declared unacceptable by the representatives of the Zionist Organization and was unanimously rejected at the twenty-first Zionist Congress, which was held in Geneva from August 16th to August 25th, 1939. In an official statement concerning the White Paper, the Jewish Agency described it as a "breach of faith" and "a surrender to Arab terrorism." The day after it was issued, Dr. Weizmann presented his objections. One of them was the following: "If a state is to be built up of two-thirds of Arabs and one-third and never more than one-third of Jews, then call it what you like, but it is an Arab State."[32]

For Weizmann, the new policy constituted a breach of Great Britain's pledges to the Jewish people. And it came at a time when millions of Jews were at risk in Europe, which made it even more objectionable. In reference to the terrible timing of the British measure, the Jewish Agency said the following: "It is in the darkest hour of Jewish history that the British government proposes to deprive the Jews of their last hope, and to close the road back to their homeland."[33] The MacDonald White Paper, by limiting Jewish immigration to Palestine for the long term, contravened both the spirit and the letter of the international obligations previously accepted by Great Britain.[34]

Despite these vigorous objections, the British government, frustrated by the situation in Palestine and concerned about its military forces there, decided to adopt the recommendations of the White Paper.

The Response of the League of Nations

The Permanent Mandates Commission of the League of Nations rejected MacDonald's White Paper, declaring that its policies were not in accordance with the Palestine Mandate. Despite this rejection, the British administration in Palestine continued to enforce the restrictions set out in the White Paper. Only 10,643 Jews were allowed to enter Palestine in 1940, 4,592 in 1941, and 4,206 in 1942.[35] These restrictions caused the deaths of hundreds of thousands of European Jews.

After the publication of MacDonald's White Paper, the Zionists realized that if they wanted their state, they would have to fight for it. They would have to fight the

British as well as the Arabs. This combative mindset became predominant among the leaders of the Yishuv—men such as Ben Gurion and Begin—during the Mandate era. And it was this mindset that forged the way to the founding of the state of Israel.

Endnotes

1   Howard Grief, *The Legal Foundation and Borders of Israel under International Law* (Jerusalem, Mazo, 2008), 11, 122.

2   Jacques Paul Gauthier, *Sovereignty Over the Old City of Jerusalem: A Study of the Historical, Religious, Political and Legal Aspects of the Question of the Old City*, Thèse No. 725 (Geneva: Université de Genève, 2007), 421.

3   Norman Bentwich, "Mandate Territories, Palestine and Mesopotamia (Iraq)," *British Yearbook of International Law* 2 (1921-1922): 53.

4   Gauthier, *Sovereignty Over the Old City*, 396-7.

5   Ibid, 394.

6   Khaled El Shalakany, "The Status of Jerusalem Under International Law," *Revue Egyptienne de Droit International* 47 (1991): 77-78.

7   Ibid.

8   Henry Cattan, *Palestine and International Law—The Legal Aspects of the Arab-Israeli Conflict.* (London: Longman, 1973), 8.

9   Gauthier, *Sovereignty Over the Old City*, 412.

10   Ibid, 420.

11   Ibid.

12   Ibid, 430.

13   Ibid, 394.

14   Grief, *Legal Foundation and Borders of Israel*, 123, 130.

15   Gauthier, *Sovereignty Over the Old City*, 429.

16   Blanche Dugdale, *Arthur James Balfour: A Biography* (London: Hutchinson & Co., 1936), 2: 220.

17   Ibid.

18   Ibid.

19   Gauthier, *Sovereignty Over the Old City*, 453.

20   Ibid.

21   David Lloyd George, *The Truth About the Peace Treaties* (London: Gollancz, 1938), 2:1119.

22   Howard Sachar, *A History of Israel: From the Rise of Zionism to Our Time*, 3rd ed. (New York: Alfred A. Knopf, 2010), 154.

23   Benny Morris, *Righteous Victims* (New York: Vintage Books, 2001), 4; Sachar, *History of Israel*, 167; Harry Charles Luke [assistant governor of Jerusalem] and Edward Keith Roach [assistant chief secretary to the governor of Palestine), eds., *Handbook of Palestine* (London: MacMillan and Co., 1922), 2.

24   Sachar, *History of Israel*, 167.

25   Secretary of State for the Colonies, British White Paper of June 1922, The Avalon Project, Yale Law School, http://avalon.law.yale.edu/20th_century/brwh1922.asp.

26   Sachar, *History of Israel*, 157.

27   Ibid, 174.

28   Ibid, 179.

29   King Abdul Aziz Al-Saud, *The Holy Quran & the Sword: Selected Addresses, Speeches, Memoranda and Interviews by: HM the Late King Abdul Aziz Al-Saud*, ed. Mohyiddin al-Qabesi (Riyadh: Saudi Desert House for Publishing, 1998), 156.

30   George Antonius, *The Arab Awakening* (Safety Harbor, Fl: Simon Publications, 2001), 390.

31   Gauthier, *Sovereignty Over the Old City,* 527.

32   Quoted in Gauthier, 529.

33   "The Statement of the Jewish Agency," *The New Judea* (May-June 1939), 173-174; John Moore, ed., *The Arab-Israeli Conflict*, vol. 3, documents, 223-4. See also, Appendix XXXI. in Gauthier 531-2.

34   Gauthier, *Sovereignty Over the Old City*, 531.

35   Martin Gilbert, *The Routledge Atlas of the Arab–Israeli Conflict*, 9th ed. (London: Routledge, 2008), 31.

Chapter 14

Israel and the Arabs: After the Mandate

Introduction

As the mid-point of the 20th century neared, the Jewish people's national home in Palestine was facing momentous developments. The Palestine Mandate was coming to an end. British restrictions on Jewish immigration to Palestine in the 1930s and 40s—policies that placated the Arabs at the cost of countless Jewish lives—had left the Zionists outraged, weary of British bungling and eager for Jewish statehood. They wanted the British out. The British, for their part, finding themselves unable to resolve the Arab–Jewish conflict, were keen to hand off their Mandate obligations to the fledgling United Nations (UN). The UN settled on partition as the solution to the tensions in Palestine. The Jews accepted this but the Arab states did not, and the latter promised war if partition were imposed.

The British Mandate ended and the State of Israel was officially established, publicly declared by David Ben Gurion, on 14 May, 1948. The Arab states attacked the following day, and the War of Independence had begun.

This chapter focuses on these events and on related developments and controversies, including the Arab rejection, in 1947, of the UN Partition Resolution, the alleged Israeli atrocities of the 1948 war, and the refugee problem that the war left in its wake. It also considers the international context after 1948 and the major developments of the next decades, such as the Knesset's passing of the Law of Return and the Suez Canal Conflict of 1956.

Backgrounds to the War of Independence

By 1947, despite decades of Arab violence and resistance, the Jewish population in Palestine had grown to over 500,000.[1] The Arab population in the region had also grown during this period, to over 1,000,000. To the leaders of the Yishuv, men such as Ben-Gurion and Menachem Begin, the assurance of free immigration for Jews was of prime importance.

The unhampered flow of Jewish refugees from Europe was a British obligation under Article 6 of the Palestine Mandate. Tragically for the Jews in Europe, the British government backed away from this obligation; it permitted the provisions of the MacDonald White Paper of 1939 to supplant the country's legal responsibilities under Article 6. The British policies prevented hundreds of thousands of Jews, desperate to escape persecution in Europe, from immigrating to Palestine.

According to historian Martin Gilbert, only 44,100 European Jews gained admittance to Palestine between 1939 and 1944. Some of this immigration was "illegal." Nearly six million Jews were left to their fate in a continent controlled by Nazi Germany.[2]

Menachem Begin, leader of the Irgun—a Jewish paramilitary group—decided that Britain's controversial policies called for violent resistance. He felt the Jewish people would be better off without the British in Palestine, and he took extreme measures, such as blowing up the King David Hotel in Jerusalem, to bring this about. Begin's approach was more radical than that of David Ben Gurion, the leader of the Haganah (another Jewish paramilitary group), who would become Israel's first prime minister. Their different approaches created factional strife among Israelis.

On February 14, 1948, British Foreign Secretary Ernest Bevin announced that His Majesty's Government had dealt long enough with the problem of Palestine and that he was referring the matter to the United Nations (UN). The fledgling UN now faced a problem that would be on its agenda for decades to come.

The United Nations, UNSCOP, and the Partitioning of Palestine

The UN was established on October 24, 1945, after the end of World War II. Fifty-one states signed the UN Charter. They thereby committed themselves to preserving peace through international cooperation and to promoting respect for human rights. Among the UN's first challenges was Palestine. Great Britain requested a special session of the UN General Assembly to discuss ending its involvement as Mandatory.

The special session resulted in the General Assembly's appointing the UN Special Committee on Palestine (UNSCOP) to make recommendations on the future of the territory. The eleven-nation UNSCOP committee subsequently invited Arab and Jewish representatives to attend public and private hearings held in June and July.[3] The Jewish Agency and several Arab groups made comprehensive submissions to the committee, but the Arab High Committee did not accept the invitation, and the Palestinian Arabs refused to participate.

International lawyer Jacques Gauthier believes that the British government, when it unilaterally decided to withdraw its administrative structure and armed forces from Palestine, was abandoning its obligations as Mandatory for the region. The Mandate territory of Palestine was "held on trust" by Great Britain. This obliged the British government to ensure that the rights of the beneficiaries of the trust—the Jewish people—were protected. This is not to say that the British withdrawal left the Jewish people entirely unprotected. As Gauthier points out, Article 80 of the new UN Charter also clearly preserved the rights of the Jewish people in this regard. It obligated the UN to uphold the rights granted by its predecessor, the League of Nations, which had approved the mandate system.[4]

The Partition Plan: Geography and Demographics

Members of UNSCOP visited Palestine in August, 1947. Their recommendations, favoring the partition of Palestine, were presented to the UN General Assembly on August 31, 1947. The Partition Plan proposed that

- a Jewish state be established, in a territory approximately one-eighth the size of the territory of Palestine prescribed by the Palestine Mandate; and
- an independent Arab State be established in most of the remaining territory.

UNSCOP viewed Jerusalem as a special case. It would be part of an international zone (*corpus separatum*, which is Latin for "separated body"), to be administered by the UN. The international zone would include the Old City and Bethlehem and the area around these two cities.[5]

Under the committee's recommendations, approximately 57 percent of Palestine west of the Jordan would be allotted to the Jews. This area would include most of the coastal plain, the Eastern Galilee, and most of the Negev desert, including the northeast, central, and southern portions. According to the plan, the population of the Jewish state would be composed of 498,000 Jews and 407,000 Arabs. The Arab state, largely in central Palestine, would comprise 725,000 Arabs and 10,000 Jews.[6] In other words, the population of the Jewish state was to be approximately 55 percent Jewish and 45 percent Arab, while the Arab state was to have a ratio of 99 percent Arab to 1 percent Jewish.

The international zone would have a Jewish population of 100,000 and an Arab population of 105,000.[7] UNSCOP included Bethlehem in the area of "Jerusalem" in order to reduce the significant Jewish majority that existed in the Old City at that time (that is, in 1947, prior to the 1948 war), when there were 100,000 Jews to 60,000 Arabs. Why did they wish to reduce the Jewish majority in the Old City? According to the Partition Plan, a referendum was to be held after 10 years; the residents of the Old City would vote regarding its sovereignty status. UNSCOP foresaw that a Jewish majority would likely have voted for Jerusalem to be under Jewish sovereignty.

The Partition Plan also provided that Jewish immigration would be limited to 150,000 persons during a two-year transition to an independent Jewish state. If, at the end of this two-year transition period, Jewish independence had not yet been achieved, 60,000 Jews would be allowed to immigrate yearly. If independence had been achieved, the Jewish state would become responsible for determining the number of people it felt it could absorb.[8]

The UNSCOP report's proposals were based on the assumption that Great Britain would remain in Palestine until September 1949, to implement the Partition Plan. However, in September of 1947, the United Kingdom gave notice to the UN that it would fully withdraw from Palestine on August 1, 1948. Then it pushed the date up to May 14, 1948.

UN Partition Resolution 181

After receiving the UNSCOP recommendations, the UN General Assembly approved Resolution 181 (the "Partition Resolution") on November 29, 1947. Thirty-three nations voted in favor of it. According to this resolution, Palestine was to be divided into two separate, independent nations—an Arab State and a Jewish State—on August 1, 1948.

Had the Partition Resolution been implemented, it would have been the second time in 30 years that Palestine was partitioned to the advantage of the Palestinian Arabs, with the Jews in the region conceding land. The Jewish national home was shrinking. As we saw in Chapter 12, Palestine was first partitioned in 1922, when Great Britain divided it to create what today is Jordan. The Partition Resolution also provided for the termination of the Mandate for Palestine.

Resolution 181 was a General Assembly motion. This meant that, unlike Security Council decisions, it was not binding in international law. It could *become* a legal agreement, but only if both Jewish and Arab representatives accepted it.

Zionist and Arab Responses

According to Gauthier, the Jewish Agency could have refused to accept the Partition Resolution on the grounds that it contravened the fundamental terms of the Mandate for Palestine regarding the establishment of a Jewish national home (or a Jewish State) in all of Palestine (that is, in Palestine west of the Jordan River).[9] But the Jewish Agency—which was recognized as the Jewish people's public representative in Palestine—accepted the resolution. The prospect of full statehood, even at the cost of territory, appealed to the Zionists. Ben-Gurion said the following of the UN resolution: "I know of no greater achievement by the Jewish people ... in its long history since it became a people."[10] Pressure on the Jewish leadership to accept partition also stemmed from the fact that hundreds of thousands of European Jews, displaced by World War II, were waiting in refugee camps to immigrate to Israel.

If both parties had accepted the Partition Resolution, it would have been legally binding on the State of Israel and on the Arab States, including the newly created Arab State in Palestine.[11] But the Council of the League of Arab States, during its Cairo session in October 1948, flatly rejected the UN resolution. And the Arabs made it clear that any attempt to implement it would lead to war.

The Arab rationale for rejecting the plan was demographic in basis. They thought it unfair that the resolution gave 55 percent of the land to 37 percent of the people, and that almost half of the Palestinian population was to be converted overnight into a minority, subject to alien rule. They thought it fair that the Jews be a minority population in a unitary Palestinian state. Though understandable, the Arab point of view reflects a startling disregard for all previous treaties and agreements concerning Palestine.

What response is there to the argument—a staple among Arab jurists—that the Partition Plan violated democratic principles by bestowing political rights on the minority (the Jewish population) at the expense of the majority (the Arab population)? The main response is that the Mandate for Palestine rendered that argument irrelevant. Jurist Ilan Dunsky has written the following in this regard:

> Although Jews constituted only about 15 percent of the population [of Palestine] at that time, the effect of the Mandate was to consider *all* Jews as entitled, or "virtual" citizens. The Mandate was to run for their benefit, and not for the benefit of [Palestine's] Arab majority.[12]

In other words, it was the roughly 14 million Jewish people worldwide who were the recipients of the rights of the Mandate, not just the Jews of Palestine. Dunsky's point is that the Mandate for Palestine had declared all Jews throughout the world entitled citizens of Palestine. In other words, the Jewish population of Palestine at the time of the Partition Plan, according to the terms of the Mandate document, was "potentially" or "virtually" 14,000,000.

But what about the fact that the Partition Resolution provided for the termination of the Mandate for Palestine? Here again, we may turn to basic legal principles. The legal rights conferred on the Jewish people by the Mandate document did not end when Britain's mandate expired at midnight of May 14-15, 1948. These rights were protected from the fickleness of international politics by virtue of the doctrine of *estoppel*. This is essentially a legal principle whereby a person is barred from denying what judicial decisions have established as the truth. In *The Legal Foundations and Borders of Israel Under International Law*, Howard Grief notes the following:

> If acquired legal rights belonging to the Jewish People over the territory comprising the Jewish National Home, could be so easily changed at will, by transferring them to Arabs (i.e. Palestinians), there would be no value at all to international law as a body of respected law.[13]

Independence and the 1948 War

The end of the British Mandate over Palestine and the complete withdrawal of the British armed forces were immediately followed by Israel's Declaration of Independence on May 14, 1948. The same day, the United States announced that it would recognize Israel as an independent state, and the next day, May 15, the U.S.S.R. and Poland did likewise.

Israel, however, was given little time to celebrate. The Arabs refused to recognize any Jewish state, and their threats of war over the Partition Resolution had not been idle. On the evening of May 14th, Arab legions from Transjordan, Syria, Lebanon, Iraq, and Egypt began to mass around Jerusalem, the Galilee, the Jordan Valley, and the southern border, respectively. On May 15, 1948, the Arab armies attacked. This initial assault followed upon a number of preliminary battles between Arabs and Jews in April and early May, 1948, primarily in Tiberias, Safed, and Haifa. The 1948 Arab invasion was simply the commencement of the "official war" after many months of fighting.[14]

The Arab League sent a cable to the UN on May 15th claiming that the invasion was necessary. Among the reasons they cited for its necessity was the need to establish security and order. The UN Security Council rejected the Arab rationale.

The Arab armies' invasion of Palestine violated international law, which prohibits the use of force in relations between states except where force is authorized by the UN Charter.[15] The non-Arab world was virtually unanimous in condemning the Arab use of military force in Palestine in 1948.

Critical Encounters in the 1948 War

For those inclined to find divine providence in historical events, Israel's War of Independence offers interesting possibilities. It involved some mysterious incidents. Divinely inspired or not, fortune seemed to favor the Israeli forces.

In the early days of the war, forty-five Syrian tanks moved toward Jewish settlements on the southern end of Lake Galilee. The Jewish forces had no artillery to resist their advance. The only heavy weapons they possessed were four ancient howitzers, the kind used by the French army in the Franco-Prussian War of 1870. Two of these archaic pieces were dismantled and rushed to Degania where the local commander, Moshe Dayan, had them reassembled just as the first Syrian tanks were advancing through the community's perimeter. The Israelis fired, and scored a direct hit on the lead tank. Howard Sachar has written the following about this incident:

> Had the Syrians known that these two obsolete weapons represented half the arsenal of Jewish field guns in Palestine, they might have pressed the attack. Instead, the armored vehicles swung around in their tracks and clattered back up the mountain road. They never returned.[16]

Critical battles were also being waged up the coast and in the south, as well as in the Judean Hills, where the Jordanians were laying siege to Jerusalem.

On the coast, the Egyptians moved to within sixteen miles of the outskirts of Tel Aviv. Yigael Yadin, a young Israeli commander, decided to risk a tactical offensive. On May 29, he ordered reinforcements from the Jerusalem corridor to circle the Egyptian positions at night, and then he attacked the Egyptians from the rear. Though the Israeli troop strength was barely half that of the invaders, their surprise attack threw the Egyptians into confusion. Yadin shrewdly exploited their disorganization; he called a press conference and announced that overwhelming concentrations of Israeli troops had cut the Egyptian supply lines. This "news" was immediately dispatched over the international wire services and eventually reached Cairo, where the Egyptian high command accepted the story at face value and radioed the Egyptian commander to halt the advance on Tel Aviv. This Egyptian setback proved to be a turning point. Tel Aviv was never again in jeopardy.

The Israeli defenders were less successful in protecting the Jewish community of Jerusalem's Old City. King Abdullah of Jordan, determined to capture Jerusalem in its entirety, shelled the city and cut off its Jewish residents from the coastal plain. The Arab Legion had massively garrisoned in Latrun to blockade Jerusalem and prevent supplies and medical aid from reaching the city's Jewish defenders. Meanwhile the

UN imposed a truce, to take effect on June 11. In the weeks prior to that date, the Israeli forces launched three unsuccessful assaults on Latrun in an effort to free the road to the city. On May 28, 1948, the Jewish Quarter of the Old City fell to the Arab Legion, which was under the leadership of a British general named John Bagot Glubb. The Jewish population was expelled, and the Israeli fighters were taken to Jordan as prisoners.

Harry Levin, a foreign correspondent in Jerusalem at that time who kept a record of his impressions and experience of the siege, spoke for many Jews when he said it was

> hard to think of the Old City without a single Jew. When last was there such a time? Nearly 800 years ago Maimonides found Jews there. The Old underground synagogue of Yohanan ben Zakkaai is reputed to have been standing nearly 2,000 years ago; now, like the neighboring Hurva [synagogue], it is in shambles. Jews were in the Old City when the Seljuks conquered it, and in the days of the Crusades, when the Turks took it over. Allenby found them when he conquered it from the Turks. But today not one is left.[17]

Truce and the Egyptian Defeat

On June 11th, the UN-brokered truce took effect. This lasted 28 days. During the month-long truce, the Israeli high command seized the opportunity to strengthen their military arsenal. Small armament factories moved into full production, and weapons were secretly smuggled into the country through coastal sites. Thousands of tons of ammunition, military equipment, and clothing arrived, much of it donated from Jewish sources throughout the world. The Czechoslovakian government also sold large quantities of military supplies to the Jews.

The truce also gave the Israeli military an opportunity for the intensive training of new recruits. With 60,000 men in service and a growing store of European and American equipment at its disposal, the fledgling army was systematically being transformed into a modern fighting force whose military power would become a solid fact of Middle Eastern geopolitics for decades to come.

On July 8, before the first UN truce had expired, the Egyptian forces renewed their attack in the south. Intense diplomatic efforts by the UN led to a second truce, to go into effect on July 18. Before the imposition of the second truce, Israel received UN approval to provision their settlements, and they dispatched an unarmed convoy across the Egyptian-controlled crossroads in the south. The lead vehicles were subsequently blown to bits. In fact, the Israelis had dynamited the trucks themselves, to make it appear the Arabs were attacking them in defiance of the UN. Armed with the pretext they needed, the Israeli forces went into action immediately. Yigal Allon launched his offensive against the Egyptians with such speed that they were unable to mount a strong response.

Fighting continued through the remainder of 1948, and in early January 1949, UN-mediated discussions opened between Israel and Egypt, followed by negotiations between Israel and the other Arab states.

The 1949 Israel–Jordan Armistice Agreement

On April 3, 1949, on the island of Rhodes, Israel and the Hashemite Kingdom of Trans-Jordan (renamed *Jordan* two months later) signed an armistice agreement. The territories under the control of Israel and the territories under the control of Jordan were separated by an armistice line referred to as the "Green Line."

The 1949 Armistice Line—the Green Line—has become one of the most significant dividing lines in Middle East history. It demarcates the territory now called the "West Bank," so named because it's on the west side/bank of the Jordan River. It is very important to note that, prior to the 1948 war, there was no distinct territory called the West Bank. Historically, the territory comprised the regions of Judea and Samaria. The territory only became known as the West Bank after Jordan *occupied* it in the wake of the 1948 War.

The UN has made the 1949 Armistice Line almost sacrosanct. They used it to broker a peace between Israel and the Palestinian Authority, and it has become the standard demarcation for the "two-state solution."

Gauthier vehemently disagrees with the UN view of the 1949 Armistice Line:

> Although the "Green Line" resulted from an understanding between the parties concerning which components of the disputed territories were under the control of Israel or Jordan, *it did not constitute an agreement pertaining to the establishment of boundaries.*[18] (emphasis added)

In other words, the 1949 Armistice line did not constitute a border and should not be used to determine territorial rights. That is precisely what is happening, however. Almost every Arab–Israeli peace plan has earmarked the West Bank as the territory of the future Palestinian state.

Another significant but little-known fact about the Armistice Line is that it divides Jerusalem into east and west portions, leaving the Old City on the east side. The Palestinian Authority is demanding all territory on the east side of the Green Line for their state. If this demand were met—if the Green Line became the border within a two-state solution—the Temple Mount in the Old City, the holiest site to the Jewish People, would not be included in the Jewish state.

History shows that the religious rights and holy sites of non-Muslims in the Old City have not fared well under Jordanian Arab control. Between 1948 and 1967, when the Jordanians governed the Old City, synagogues were destroyed—the Hurva Synagogue, for example—and Jewish cemeteries desecrated. Jews were prohibited from entering the Old City or from worshipping at the Western Wall, and they were not given access to the sacred Jewish burial grounds on the Mount of Olives. The Jordanians prevented Christians, too, from visiting their holy places except for special ceremonial events, such as Christmas. These restrictions contravened the provisions of the Armistice Agreement between Transjordan and Israel.[19] Given the Arab record in the Old City, one doubts whether Jews or Christians would enjoy freedom of worship there if it were under Arab sovereignty, as it would be if the Green Line were adopted as the border between the Jewish and Palestinian states.

The territory under the State of Israel's control after the signing of the Armistice Agreement was significantly larger than the territory allotted to the Jewish state under the Partition Resolution. But the Old City was not in that territory. And it is the Old City—the Temple Mount, in particular—that is the ultimate bone of contention in the current conflict between Israel and the Arabs.

Aftermath of the War: Controversies and First-Hand Accounts

There are still discussions and debates about what happened in 1948. According to the UN, the war resulted in over 700,000 Arabs becoming refugees. The UN and the international community hold Israel responsible. Even some Jewish/ Israeli academics have accused Israel of "ethnic cleansing" with respect to the Palestinian Arabs.

There is no doubt that hundreds of thousands of Arabs from the territories previously covered by the Mandate for Palestine suffered tremendously as a result of the 1948 war. But are allegations of "ethnic cleansing" warranted?

Deir Yassin

In a 2009 interview, Ilan Pappe, Israeli author of *The Ethnic Cleansing of Palestine*, said the following:

> Most Israeli Jews believe that the Palestinians left voluntarily in 1948. They are not aware or do not want to be aware, of the fact that an ethnic cleansing took place in 1948. ... We found out that there was a systematic expulsion of Palestinians and there was an entire ethnic cleansing operation taking place.[20]

Pappe claims that Israel had a plan called Plan Dalet, which he calls "the blueprint for ethnic cleansing."[21] Its purpose, he says, was to take as much territory in Palestine and to expel as many Palestinians as possible. Pappe charges that "the systematic nature of Plan Dalet was manifest in Deir Yassin."[22] Deir Yassin was a Palestinian Arab village on the outskirts of Jerusalem—now called Har Nof—and was outside the boundaries of the Jewish state as outlined in the Partition Plan. On the morning of April 9, 1948, a month before war was officially declared, paramilitaries from Menachem Begin's Irgun attacked the village. Palestinians were killed, although it is not clear how many. According to Pappe, "recent research has brought down the accepted number of people massacred at Deir Yassin from 170 to ninety-three."[23]

Pappe alleges that, in accordance with Plan Dalet, Jewish war crimes were committed in Deir Yassin with the intention of cleansing the territory of Arabs, and that these war crimes set off the flight of hundreds of thousands of Arab refugees.

Pappe's charge is echoed by Arabs, who have called the outcomes of the 1948 war the Nakba ("Catastrophe").

The village of Deir Yassin was situated on a hill about 2600 feet high, less than a mile from the suburbs of Jerusalem. Arab forces, which had engaged in sporadic and unorganized ambushes since December 1947, began to make an organized attempt to cut off the highway linking Tel Aviv with Jerusalem—the city's only supply route. The Arabs controlled several strategic vantage points overlooking the highway, and these enabled them to fire on the Jewish convoys trying to supply Jerusalem. One of these Arab vantage points was Deir Yassin. On April 6, the Jewish forces under Begin launched an operation to open the road to Jerusalem. The village of Deir Yassin was among the Arab villages to be occupied as part of this operation.[24]

Yehuda Avner emigrated to Israel from Manchester, England, shortly before independence in 1947. He entered the Israeli Foreign Service in the late 1950s and served as speech-writer and secretary to prime ministers Levi Eshkol and Golda Meir, and adviser to prime ministers Yitzhak Rabin, Menachem Begin, and Shimon Peres.

In *The Prime Ministers*, Yehuda Avner writes about Deir Yassin. Avner had lodgings in the suburb of Beit Hakerem, across the valley from Deir Yassin, during the siege of Jerusalem in 1948. On April 9 of that year, at five in the morning, an explosion from the direction of Deir Yassin roared across the valley with such force it practically knocked him out of bed. He was told that Irgun fighters were attacking the village.[25] Avner recorded the events of that day in his diary. Avner's diary noted that he crawled down the valley to investigate from behind a rock. He saw a crashed Jewish truck as well as Arab prisoners with their hands up. He said that there were rumours they were later shot. Walking home he saw captive Arab women and children sitting in a truck.

In 1980, Avner found himself working alongside the man who actually commanded the attack on Deir Yassin. His name was Yehuda Lapidot, a soft-spoken professor of biochemistry at the Hebrew University. One day over coffee, Avner shared with Lapidot his diary entry of Friday, April 9, 1948. Lapidot mulled over Avner's diary. The diary noted that, in Avner's experience, Deir Yassin had always been very quiet and quite friendly, though he had been told that Arab gangs had pushed into the village.

After reading Avner's diary, Lapidot spoke. His voice tinged with sadness, he said there had been no deliberate massacre at Deir Yassin but that things had not gone as planned. The Israeli soldiers fighting alongside Lapidot were being repeatedly hit, and the casualties were heavy. He had taken over command himself after the officer in charge went down.

Lapidot then elaborated, remembering how

our men were ordered to avoid bloodshed as much as possible. We had a loudspeaker mounted on an armored truck which was to drive ahead to warn the villagers, to give them a chance either to flee or surrender. The plan was to smash right into the center of the village with the truck and to blare a warning, but the vehicle plunged into a newly dug ditch at the very first row of houses, and that's when the calamity began. The overturned vehicle you'd seen on the crest of the hill was that loudspeaker truck. Though it had crashed we switched on the loudspeaker and made the announcement which said: "You are being attacked by superior forces. The exit of Deir Yassin leading to Ein Kerem is open! Run immediately! Don't hesitate! Our forces are advancing! Run to Ein Kerem. Run!" Heavy fire was directed at the truck and injuries were reported. When the other units mounted their assault they were met with the most fierce resistance. Every house was a fortress. We had many wounded. We thought the Arabs would surrender. But having been alerted by our truck announcement they opened up with everything they had. ...We were pinned down. They were better armed than we were. We were about eighty men, and between us we had about twenty rifles, three Bren Guns, thirty to forty Sten-guns—most of which were defective—and grenades. They fought from house to house. We had no experience in house-to-house fighting; we'd never been in such a battle before.[26]

Lapidot told Avner that each house had to be taken individually and that some of the buildings were dynamited—these were probably the explosions heard in the suburb of Beit-Hakerem. Instead of smashing through to the heart of the village as planned, it took two hours of horrific fighting to capture the mukhtar's house and raise the flag.

Lapidot concluded:

So I say to you again, no, ABSOLUTELY NO: there was no deliberate massacre at Deir Yassin. ...The dazed and shaken Arabs you saw being driven through Jerusalem on trucks that Friday afternoon were not being taken away to be shot. That was a pernicious lie spread by the anti-Irgunists. They were taken to the Arab side of town and released.[27]

The misrepresentation of what happened at Deir Yassin and of other events from 1948 continues. The actual intent of Plan Dalet is fiercely debated, with historians on one side claiming it was entirely defensive, and others asserting that its aim was maximum conquest and expulsion of the Palestinians.

Refugees: Casualties of the 1948 War

Benny Morris is a Jewish-Israeli academic and author of several histories, including *1948: A History of the First Arab-Israeli War*. He has tried to give a nuanced picture of the events of 1948. During a 2008 debate on the television program "Democracy Now!" Morris summarized his perspective on the events of 1948:

The traditional Zionist narrative about what had happened in 1948, especially relating to the refugee problem, was that the refugees had been ordered, instructed, advised by their leaders, by Palestinian leaders or Arab leaders outside the country, to flee, and that is why 700,000 left their homes. The documentation gives us a much, much broader and a more nuanced picture of what happened. Most of the people who were displaced fled their homes. A small number were expelled. Most fled their homes as a result of the war, the fear of battle, the fear of being attacked, the fear of dying. A small number also left because of the economic conditions. And a small number were advised or instructed by their leadership, as in Haifa in April 1948, to leave the country. But it's a mixed bag, with the war itself, the hostilities themselves and fear of being hurt being the main precipitant to flight. …

The fact is—and this is something most Arab commentators ignore or don't tell us—the Palestinians rejected the UN partition resolution; the Jews accepted it. They accepted the possibility of dividing the country into two states, with one Arab state and a Jewish state. And the Jewish state, which was to come into being in 1947-48, according to the United Nations, was to have had an Arab population of 400,000 to 500,000 and a Jewish population of slightly more than 500,000. That was what was supposed to come into being, and that is what the Zionist movement accepted. When the Arabs rejected it and went to war against the Jewish community, it left the Jewish community no choice. It could either lose the war and be pushed into the sea, or ultimately push out the Arab minority in their midst who wanted to kill them. It's an act of self-defense, and that's what happened. …

The Palestinian National Movement, led by Haj Amin al-Husseini in the 1920s, '30s and '40s, wanted to expel the Jews. The Jews felt they had a moral right to live in the country and to reestablish their sovereignty in the country, at least in part of it. And the Palestinians thought not. They didn't care about Jewish history. They cared nothing about Jewish tragedy or persecution over the 2,000 years and wanted to expel them from the country. They didn't get the chance, because they lost the war. So something like the reverse [of what the Arabs planned] had happened. … [O]ne has to look also at the context in which things happened, and this was the context: an expulsionist mentality, an expulsionist onslaught on the Jewish community in Palestine by Palestine's Arabs and by the invading Arab armies, and a Jewish self-defense, which involved also pushing out large numbers of Palestinians. …

My belief is the cause, the Zionist cause, was just, and they had good reasons to believe—to see themselves as good. But every war has its dark side, especially civil wars, which are notably vicious. And '48 also had a dark side, which involved the displacement of 700,000 people.[28]

Ralph Lowenstein, an American volunteer in the Israeli army in 1948 and now a professor of Journalism at the University of Florida, has provided a personal account that corroborates Morris's perspective and Lapidot's experiences:

I did see virtually every Arab village on a line between Safad and Kadesh on the Lebanese border during Operation Hiram, and the pattern was: villages occupied by Christian Arabs unharmed; Muslim villages deserted, long before any Israeli troops got there. There were rumors at the time that a massacre had occurred in one village [probably Deir Yassin], and a week after we had returned from combat a directive in English and Hebrew was distributed to each army post mentioning such rumors and warning of the dire consequences to any enlisted person or officer who could be convicted of engaging in such incidents. There were no rumors of rape or ethnic cleansing, only of one isolated massacre committed in the heat of battle.

The Jews of Palestine…drove out the occupants of Tireh, who had the bad habit of shooting up Jewish traffic on the Haifa–Tel Aviv highway, and they drove out the occupants of Kastel and other villages that bloodied the Jerusalem–Tel Aviv road. So as to open up the sea roads to the arms markets and refugee camps of Europe, they took the seaport of Haifa; to free Tel-Aviv from continual gunfire, they took Jaffa; to cut the Palestinians off from their Lebanese and Syrian armorers, they conducted operation Hiram and took the Galilee.[29]

The evidence suggests that in 1948 the Jewish paramilitary groups were pursuing a strategy of self-defense and of securing an independent Jewish state. There is no disputing the fact that the 1948 Arab–Israeli War displaced hundreds of thousands of Arabs. The UN General Assembly has adopted numerous resolutions relating to the Palestinian refugees of 1948, one of them being UN Resolution 194(III), which called for the return of refugees to their homes.

We should keep in mind that the Palestinian Arabs weren't the only people displaced by these events. In the wake of the 1948 war, there was a vicious backlash against Jewish people living in Arab countries. Iraq, for example, where Jewish communities had existed peaceably for 2,500 years, saw hundreds of Jews murdered, thousands imprisoned, and Jewish synagogues, shops, and homes burned and destroyed. Between 1948 and the mid-70s, over 800,000 Jews were stripped of all they owned and driven from Arab countries. (*The Forgotten Refugees* is a 2005 documentary describing these events.) What about these people? The UN has never approved a resolution concerning Jewish refugees—those expelled from Arab countries, or those displaced from the Jewish Quarter of the Old City, or those who suffered loss or damage to their properties as a consequence of Arab aggression.

Political Events after the War of Independence

Israel Joins the UN—May 1949

On May 11, 1949, Israel was admitted as a member of the UN. Since then, it has been the subject of numerous UN resolutions. In 2007, for example, Israel was the subject of 76 percent of the country-specific General Assembly resolutions and 36 percent of the Human Rights Council resolutions. The UN has never supported Israel's proclamation—made on December 13, 1949—that Jerusalem is its capital, and it has never supported the Knesset's subsequent move there. The Trusteeship Council opposed this proclamation following a vote at a special session held on December 20, 1949. The reason for this opposition, most likely, is that the Israeli proclamation runs contrary to the original UN plan to make Jerusalem an international zone.

The Law of Return

In 1950, on the anniversary of Herzl's death, only two years after Israel achieved statehood, the Knesset (the Israeli Parliament) enacted the twin laws: the Law of Return, granting every Jew the right to immigrate to Israel; and the Nationality Law, defining the rights of all Israelis, both Jews and non-Jews, living in Israel. These laws were adopted after spirited discussion.

The following are the key provisions of the Law of Return:

1. Every Jew has the right to come to this country as an *oleh* (a Jew immigrating to Israel).
   a. Aliyah (immigration of Jews) shall be by *oleh's* visa.
   b. An *oleh's* visa shall be granted to every Jew who has expressed his desire to settle in Israel, unless the Minister of Immigration is satisfied that the applicant:
      i. is engaged in an activity directed against the Jewish people; or
      ii. is likely to endanger public health or the security of the State.
2. Any Jew who has come to Israel and subsequent to his arrival has expressed his desire to settle in Israel may, while still in Israel, receive an *oleh's* certificate.
3. Every Jew who has immigrated into this country before the coming into force of this Law, and every Jew who was born in this country, whether before or after the coming into force of this Law, shall be deemed to be a person who has come to this country as an *oleh* under this Law.[30]

Remarkably, in the discussions that preceded the passing of the Law of Return, the Knesset paid no attention to the legal definition of "a Jew." The second amendment to the Law of Return did include a definition, which was as follows: "For the purposes of this Law, 'Jew' means a person who was born of a Jewish mother or has become converted to Judaism and who is not a member of another religion."[31]

Some people have maintained that the Law of Return and the Nationality Law discriminate against Arabs. According to this view, these laws unfairly offer citizenship to any potential Jewish immigrant to Israel while denying the same right to Arab refugees who want to return to Israel/Palestine. We need to keep in mind, in this regard, that one of the aims of Israel's Law of Return was to ease the absorption of Jewish refugees—including 600,000 of the 850,000 Jews driven from Arab states after 1948 (see above). And meanwhile the Arab states in the Middle East, with the exception of Jordan, have made no equivalent effort to absorb Palestinian Arab refugees; they have left them festering in the camps. And they have, needless to say, extended no "right of return" to the 850,000 Jewish refugees they expelled after 1948.

The International Context after 1948

The Cold War

The Middle East took on international strategic importance after World War II. The US and the Soviet Union were locked in a Cold War and sought influence in this area of the world, as in others. The two ascendant superpowers saw the value of having military bases in the Middle East, and they were aware of the area's valuable national resources, especially its oil.

The Soviet Union aligned itself with those of the Arab states—Syria, Iraq, and Egypt—that embraced a relatively revolutionary, socialist ideology, wooing them with economic aid, military training, and arms. The Soviet military presence in Syria and Egypt was significant by the late 1960s—the largest such presence outside the communist bloc. The client states of the United States were Jordan, Saudi Arabia, and—until 1958—Iraq. The US offered these countries military protection in return for access to cheap oil.

Where did Israel stand in this context? Interestingly, it was unclear during this period which of the two superpowers—if either—would prove a support to Israel. The Soviets offered backing between 1948 and 1951, in acknowledgement, perhaps, of political Zionism's socialist underpinnings. But they turned viciously against the Jewish people after 1951; Stalin returned to the anti-Semitic template of pre-Revolutionary Russia, only now, unlike the 19th century tsarist regimes, he prohibited Jews from leaving the country. The United States, for its part, kept Israel at arm's length, wanting to protect its profitable *entente* with the Arab oil states. In 1957, when the US announced the Eisenhower Doctrine—offering economic and military assistance to Middle Eastern countries that opposed communist infiltration—Israel asked to join the alliance, and was refused.

The Suez Canal Conflict—1956

Despite the 1949 Armistice Agreement, the Arab states were not reconciled to Israel's existence and remained bent on destroying the Jewish state. They organized various boycotts intended to cripple the Israeli economy—boycotts of Jewish products and manufactured goods; boycotts of Arab states that traded directly with Israel; boycotts of any company worldwide that did business with Israel. They went even further in this direction, blacklisting companies with ties to other companies that did business with Israel. Egypt sought to hurt the Israeli economy with a maritime boycott, prohibiting cargo ships from going to or from Israel via the Suez Canal. With Resolution 95 (September 1, 1951), the UN Security Council ordered Egypt to open the canal to Israeli shipping, but the Egyptians refused to comply.

In 1956, a more pointed dispute arose over the Suez Canal when the president of Egypt, Gamel Abdel Nasser, nationalized the Suez Canal Company out from under its main shareholders, England and France. These two countries, looking to resolve the dispute by force, brought in Israel as an ally. The three countries planned a military response to Nasser.

Israel, backed by Britain and France, attacked Egypt on October 29, 1956. When the war ended in November, Israel had conquered the entire Sinai all the way to the Suez Canal and had secured the Strait of Tiran. In March 1957, Israel withdrew from Gaza and the Sinai in exchange for UN "guarantees" of freedom of passage for Israeli ships through the Strait of Tiran to the Gulf of Aqaba.

After the events of 1956-57, the situation between the Arabs and Israel remained relatively unchanged until events in 1967 precipitated the Six Day War.

Endnotes

1   Jewish Virtual Library, "Demography of Palestine & Israel, the West Bank & Gaza 1553-2006," http://www.jewishvirtuallibrary.org/jsource/History/demograhics.html.

2   Martin Gilbert, *The Routledge Atlas of the Arab–Israeli Conflict*, 9th ed. (London: Routledge, 2008), 15.

3   Ibid, 571.

4   Jacques Paul Gauthier, *Sovereignty Over the Old City of Jerusalem: A Study of the Historical, Religious, Political and Legal Aspects of the Question of the Old City*, Thèse No. 725 (Geneva: Université de Genève, 2007), 570-571.

5   Ibid, 573.

6   UN General Assembly, UNSCOP Report A/364, September 3, 1947, http://unispal.un.org/unispal. nsf/0/07175de9fa2de563852568d3006e10f3.

7   Ibid.

8   Ibid.

9   Gauthier, *Sovereignty Over the Old City*, 579.

10   Yehoshu'a Freundlich, *From Destruction to Resurrection: Zionist Policy from the End of the Second World War to the Establishment of the State of Israel* (Israel: Mif'alim Universitaim, 1994), 199.

11   Julius Stone, *Israel and Palestine—Assault on the Law of Nations*, ed. Ian Lacey (Baltimore: Johns Hopkins University Press, 1981), 62-63; see extracts from this book at www.strateias.org/international_ law.pdf.

12   Ilan Dunsky, "Israel, the Arabs and International Law: Whose Palestine Is It, Anyway?" *Dalhousie Journal of Legal Studies* 2 (1993): 169.

13   Howard Grief, *The Legal Foundation and Borders of Israel under International Law* (Jerusalem, Mazo, 2008), 131.

14   Gauthier, *Sovereignty Over the Old City*, 617.

15   Ibid, 620.

16   Howard Sachar, *A History of Israel: From the Rise of Zionism to Our Time*, 3rd ed. (New York: Alfred A. Knopf, 2010), 319.

17   Harry Levin, *Jerusalem Embattled—A Diary of the City Under Siege March 25th, 1948 to July 18th, 1948* (London: Cassell, 1997), 209.

18   Gauthier, *Sovereignty Over the Old City*, 643.

19   Ibid, 623.

20   Ilan Pappe, *An Interview with Ilan Pappe*, accessed May 1, 2012, http://www.youtube.com/watch?v=vFsLattNYJQ.

21   Ilan Pappe, *The Ethnic Cleansing of Palestine* (Oxford: Oneworld Publications, 2006), 86.

22   Ibid, 90.

23   Ibid, 91, note 8 on 271–272. Pappe says that, though contemporary accounts put the number of victims of the Deir Yassin massacre at 254, this figure was likely inflated by the Zionist military in order to sow fear among the Palestinians and panic them into a mass exodus.

24   Mitchell Bard, "Deir Yassin," *Jewish Virtual Library,* accessed August 8, 2012, http://www.jewishvirtuallibrary.org/jsource/History/deir_yassin.html.

25   Yehuda Avner, *The Prime Ministers*, 4th ed. (New Milford CT: Toby Press, 2012), 89.

26   Ibid, 95-96.

27   Ibid, 96.

28   Benny Morris, "As Israelis Celebrate Independence and Palestinians Mark the 'Nakba,' a Debate with Benny Morris, Saree Makdisi, and Norman Finkelstein," Democracy Now!, 2008, accessed May 22, 2012, http://www.democracynow.org/2008/5/16/as_israelis_celebrate_independence_and_palestinians

29   David Gutmann, "The Arab Lie Whose Time Has Come," *FrontPageMagazine.com*, April 21, 2004, http://archive.frontpagemag.com/readArticle.aspx?ARTID=13508.

30   Law of Return 5710-1950, Israel Ministry of Foreign Affairs, accessed May 30, 2012, http://www.mfa.gov.il/MFA/MFAArchive/1950_1959/Law+of+Return.

31   Ibid.

Chapter 15

Israel and the Arabs 1967–1987

Introduction

Arab hostility toward Israel continued in the wake of the Suez Crisis of 1956 and through the 1960s. But it was the rivalries between the Arab states, sometimes referred to as the "Arab Cold War," that dominated the politics of the Middle East during these years. Israel figured in these inter-Arab tensions insofar as the Arab leaders sought to surpass one another in anti-Zionist rhetoric. Promising destruction of Israel was a surefire way to gain pan-Arab support. Arab leaders rattled their sabres in Israel's direction, but with their eyes on each other.

A series of confused provocations and pronouncements from the Arabs set the 1967 war in motion. The Israelis, by contrast, were clear in their aims. Feeling their very existence at stake, they made war on the aggressors with devastating results. One focus of this chapter is the Six-Day War and its direct consequences, as well as the major events of the two decades following the war: Israel's so-called occupation of the disputed territories and the economic impact of this occupation; the 1973 Yom Kippur War and the Arabs' deployment of the "oil weapon" against the West; and Israel's 1982 war on the PLO in Lebanon.

On the diplomatic front, the years 1967–1987 saw a shift in the international perspective on Israel. Feeling pinched by the 1973 oil embargo, some world powers began finding merit in the Arab point of view and in the grievances of the PLO, an organization increasingly invested with authority and legitimacy in the region. The UN's ever more censorious approach to Israel reflected this new international sympathy for the Arab cause. This chapter will also consider certain legal questions related to these developments, such as the meaning of *occupation* and the legitimacy of Israel's 1980 annexation of Jerusalem.

The Lead-Up to War

Arab provocation of Israel continued in the years leading up to 1967. In 1963, Israel announced the National Water Carrier system, a pipeline that would carry much-needed water from the Jordan River to other parts of Israel. The Arab nations objected, charging that Israel was taking more than its share, and they made plans to divert two-thirds of the new Israeli water supply. At the same time, they formed the United Arab Command (UAC), a joint force consisting of Egyptian, Jordanian, Lebanese, and Syrian forces, led by an Egyptian general. When Syria proceeded to put the water-diversion plan in place, Israel struck with artillery and air attacks.

As the Israelis responded forcefully to Arab aggression, the potential for war increased. Jordan and Syria sponsored raids into Israel, including *fedayeen* terrorist attacks on Israeli civilians, and Israel retaliated against military targets. Egypt and Syria formed an alliance—the Egyptian-Syrian Defence Agreement—pledging that an Israeli attack on either country would be met with a joint response.

Another Israeli response to Syrian terrorist attacks was to cultivate land in the demilitarized area between the countries. This marked the beginning of the settlements. Syria proceeded to bomb these farms and villages from the Golan heights, and Israel responded by destroying the Syrian artillery installations. The Syrians complained about the lack of Egyptian support in this conflict, invoking the terms of the Egyptian–Syrian treaty. Other Arab states joined Syria in condemning Nasser's inaction in the face of the Zionist threat.

Syrian-sponsored Palestinian raids and terrorist attacks on Israeli civilians intensified in the spring of 1967, occurring almost daily. Israel warned of a strong response, and Arabs throughout the region interpreted this as a threat of a large-scale Israeli campaign. The situation had become so serious by the late spring of 1967 that war correspondents from all over the world began to converge on Israel.

The Soviets played a curious but crucial role in the events immediately preceding the 1967 war. The Suez War of 1956 had spelled the end of British influence in the Middle East. Thereafter, as we noted in Chapter 14, it was the Soviets and the US vying for influence in the region. The Soviets increased their support for Syria, Iraq, and, especially, Egypt after 1958, while the US drew closer to Jordan and the Saudis.

On May 13, 1967, for reasons still unclear to historians, the Soviets informed the Egyptians that the Israelis were massing troops on the Syrian border. This was totally untrue, as the Egyptians soon determined. And yet Nasser, still smarting from the previous month's condemnation of his leadership, announced that the Soviet reports were true and that Egypt would side with Syria against Israeli aggression. Why did Nasser seize on this pretext for war? Historians are uncertain. He may have believed that Egypt's military strength, thanks to a decade-long influx of Soviet weaponry, was now greater than Israel's and that he could fulfill at last his long-held promise to wipe Israel off the map.

On May 15, 1967, Nasser moved two divisions of his armed forces into the Sinai Peninsula. The next day, he ordered the United Nations Emergency Force (UNEF) to relocate to camps in the Gaza Strip. UNEF had been positioned in the Sinai after the 1956 Suez Crisis as a condition of Israel's withdrawal, and it had successfully kept the peace there for the past decade. Egypt had no authority over UNEF, but UNEF acceded to Nasser's demands.

The following week, on May 22, Nasser announced a blockade against Israeli ships in the Strait of Tiran. The official declaration targeted Israel: "The Strait of Tiran is part of our territorial waters. No Israeli ship will ever navigate it again. We also forbid the shipment of strategic materials to Israel on non-Israeli vessels."[1] This amounted to an act of aggression under international law. Israel appealed to the UN to break the blockade and pointed out that, under Article 51 of the UN Charter, it had the right to defend itself against an act of aggression. The UN offered no solution. Nasser, noting the sluggish international reaction, decided Israel was isolated and vulnerable.

Three days later, on May 25, the governments of Syria, Iraq, Jordan, and Saudi Arabia, on the directives of Egypt, began mobilizing troops along Israel's borders. By May 31, Egypt had moved 100,000 troops, 1,000 tanks, and 500 heavy guns into the Sinai buffer zone—the area between Israel and Egypt that had been established as neutral under earlier armistice agreements.

Psychological Context of the 1967 War

Outbursts of anti-Israel statements from Arab leaders and their government-controlled radios accompanied the movement of troops. On May 27, just a few days before the war, Nasser summed up the Arab objectives:

Our basic objective will be the destruction of Israel. The Arab people want to fight. ... The mining of Sharm el Sheikh [the Strait of Tiran] is a confrontation with Israel. Adopting this measure obligates us to be ready to embark on a general war with Israel.[2]

Nasser's statements were followed by those of Iraqi President Aref, on May 31: "The existence of Israel is an error which must be rectified. This is our opportunity to wipe out the ignominy which has been with us since 1948. Our goal is clear—to wipe Israel off the map."[3]

A few days later, on June 1, the chairman of the PLO, Ahmed Shukairy, declared the following:

This is a fight for a homeland. It is either us or the Israelis. There is no middle road. The Jews of Palestine will have to leave. ... Any of the old Palestine Jewish population who survive may stay, but it is my impression that none of them will survive.[4]

The quietly sinister tone of the PLO chairman's words was consistent with the historical ambitions of the Palestinian Arab leadership. Clearly, the 1967 agenda still bore the imprint of an earlier authority, Haj Amin al-Husseini, a man whose varied credentials we have noted in previous chapters. His anti-Semitic exploits are not widely recognized in the West and are worth briefly detailing here. Doing so will help us understand the Israeli psychology in 1967 regarding their Palestinian Arab opponents, a perspective born of hard and sometimes deadly experience.

Husseini led the Palestinian Arabs for the better part of three decades. Still revered by radical Islamist sects throughout the Middle East, he exerted a tremendous influence on the Arab population of Palestine, and this influence has done much to poison Arab–Jewish relations in the region. His attainments include the following: Grand Mufti of Jerusalem; inciter of deadly anti-Jewish riots in the Old City in the 1920s, during which Jewish women and children were massacred; head of the Nazi's Arab Office in Berlin under Hitler in the 1930s (the two men agreed on the best solution to the "Jewish problem" in their respective regions); and, during World War II, organizer of a Muslim SS Division in Yugoslavia that committed many atrocities, including the slaughter of 200,000 Orthodox Christian Serbs, and that was subsequently indicted for war crimes. He was also a co-founder of the Arab League, in 1944.

By 1967, the world had noticed Haj Amin's dangerous character, and he was in exile in Lebanon. But his influence persisted in the strong Arab Muslim ambition, intensified rather than lessened by the events of 1948, to drive Israel—and all of Middle Eastern Jewry with it—into the sea. It is worth bearing in mind that none of the Arab states had, at this point, acknowledged Israel's right to exist. With respect to Arab anti-Semitism in general, the 800,000 Jewish refugees expelled from Arab states after the War of Independence were symptomatic of the basic Arab attitude. We should keep these refugees in mind, too, when we come across Arab claims, dear to uninformed liberals in the West, that they are not anti-Jewish, merely anti-Israel.

In Israel, in the days before the 1967 war, a sense of impending doom was everywhere, with memories of the Holocaust still fresh in many minds. A countrywide call went out for Moshe Dayan, the former Haganah commander, to become defense minister. People considered him the only one capable of leading the Israeli Defense Force (IDF) and preventing another Holocaust. On Sunday June 4, Prime Minister Levi Eshkol convened an emergency War Cabinet meeting and passed a resolution to launch a pre-emptive strike against the Arab States, which were now clearly poised for war. The Jewish state's 264,000 soldiers, 800 tanks, and 300 combat aircraft would attempt to defend Israel against the combined strength of the Arabs' 350,000 soldiers, 2,000 tanks, and 700 aircraft.[5]

The Six-Day War

Israel's many appeals to the UN failed to prevent a conflict. On June 5, 1967, Israel launched a pre-emptive aerial attack that destroyed almost all of the Egyptian air force.

Israeli Prime Minister Levi Eshkol sent word to King Hussein of Jordan, through the UN and the Americans, that if Jordan stayed out of the war, Israel would not attack them. Had Jordan complied, its occupation of the West Bank and the Old City of Jerusalem would have continued as it had since 1948. That did not happen, however. Hussein's response was to shell Israel.

Menachem Begin, now a newly appointed Cabinet minister after two decades of being ostracized by Ben-Gurion's governments, saw an advantage in the Jordanian aggression. He proposed to Eshkol that the Jewish people now had an historic opportunity to recapture the Old City of Jerusalem. Eshkol approved of this proposal.

Only three hours after the Cabinet had given the go-ahead to Moshe Dayan and the IDF to take the Old City, Motta Gur, the commander of the brigade that entered the Temple Mount/ Haram al-Sharif area, proclaimed to his superiors on a radio, "Har Habayit b'Yadenu" (the Temple Mount is in our hands). For the first time in 2,000 years, Jews were in control of all of Jerusalem. When Israeli soldiers prayed at the Western Wall on June 7, 1967, it marked the end of nearly 2,000 years of restricted Jewish access to the site.

The war lasted only six days and was a very one-sided affair. Israel, galvanized by the prospect of extinction and endowed with military skill far surpassing the Arabs', succeeded in destroying the air forces of Egypt, Syria, Jordan, and Iraq, as well as these nations' tanks and heavy artillery. More than 10,000 Arab soldiers were killed, compared with only 700 on the Israeli side.

At the end of it, Israel entered and "occupied" the West Bank, the Gaza Strip, the Sinai Peninsula, and the Golan Heights, which were territories of the defeated Arab nations.

When the Israelis entered the Old City in June 1967, they found that all but one of the thirty-five synagogues there had been destroyed. These synagogues were centuries old. Among them was the Hurva Synagogue, which had stood as a landmark since 1267. In the ancient graveyard on the Mount of Olives, the Jordanians had defaced or profaned 38,000 of the 50,000 Jewish graves.[6]

Shortly after capturing the Temple Mount/Haram al-Sharif, the government of Israel made a decision to return custody of it to Muslim administrators. This was a remarkable decision, considering that Jewish access to the area had been denied under Jordanian occupation and that the Temple Mount is Judaism's holiest site. On the other hand, within days of capturing the Old City, Israel destroyed many houses adjacent to the Western Wall, in the Mughrabi Arab Quarter, in order to create a large esplanade next to the Western Wall where Jews could pray.

The 1967 War: Self-Defense or Aggression?

Was Israel the aggressor in the Six-Day War, or were its actions justified on the basis of self-defense? Legal opinions differ on this, though the general view is that Israel was justified. The UN General Assembly put forward several resolutions attempting to condemn Israel as the aggressor, but these were defeated by a majority of the members. In other words, most members of the UN considered Israel's pre-emptive strike to be not an act of aggression but a legitimate response to the situation.

Article 51 of the Charter of the UN authorizes its members to use force in self-defense "if an attack occurs"; this authorization is based on "the inherent right of individual or collective self-defense." Jurists disagree, however, about the right of self-defense in international law in the event of a "*threat* of an imminent attack."[7]

Boundaries of Jerusalem and the Holy Places

On June 27, 1967, just a couple of weeks after the war, the Knesset enacted legislation to include the Old City and "east" Jerusalem under Israeli administration and Israeli law. The new legislation also included the Protection of Holy Places

Law 5727 (1967), which stipulated that holy places were to be protected from desecration and "anything likely to violate the freedom of access of the members of the different religions to the places sacred to them or their feelings with regard to those places."[8] Israel gave the Muslim Waqf—the governing body that oversees Muslim endowments—the authority to administer various Muslim holy sites, including the Temple Mount/Haram Al-Sharif, the Dome of the Rock, and the Al-Aqsa Mosque. Since 1967, Israel has continued to protect all faiths' freedom of access to and worship of their respective holy sites. This freedom of access did not exist during the Jordanian occupation from 1948 to 1967.

On July 4, just a week after Israel's reunification legislation, the UN General Assembly followed up with Resolution 2253, which was titled "Measures taken by Israel to change the status of the City of Jerusalem." With this resolution, the UN declared Israel's actions invalid and called upon Israelis to rescind their measures regarding Jerusalem.[9] The UN has repeatedly opposed Israel's attempts to reunify Jerusalem and maintain sovereign claims over it.

Security Council Resolution 242

Many members of the UN demanded the withdrawal of the Israeli forces from "newly occupied" territories in the West Bank. On November 22, 1967, the Security Council of the UN passed Resolution 242, which required Israel to withdraw from the West Bank, Gaza, the Sinai, and the Golan Heights on the condition that Arab belligerence came to an end.

Resolution 242, drafted by the British ambassador Lord Caradon, is a masterpiece of constructive ambiguity. The British diplomat's wording was deliberately vague, with language that permitted both Israelis and Arabs to interpret the resolution according to their own requirements. Notwithstanding its ambiguity, Resolution 242 ranks, along with the Partition Plan of 1947, as one of the most important of the UN resolutions regarding the Arab–Israeli conflict. To this day, it is a cornerstone of diplomatic efforts in the Middle East.

Resolution 242 said the following:

The Security Council,

Expressing its continuing concern with the grave situation in the Middle East,

Emphasizing the inadmissibility of the acquisition of territory by war and the need to work for a just and lasting peace in which every State in the area can live in security,

Emphasizing further that all Member States in their acceptance of the Charter of the United Nations have undertaken a commitment to act in accordance with Article 2 of the Charter,

1. *Affirms* that the fulfillment of Charter principles requires the establishment of a just and lasting peace in the Middle East which should include the application of both the following principles:

(i) Withdrawal of Israeli armed forces from territories occupied in the recent conflict;

(ii) Termination of all claims or states of belligerency and respect for and acknowledgement of the sovereignty, territorial integrity and political independence of every State in the area and their right to live in peace within secure and recognized boundaries free from threats or acts of force;

2. *Affirms* further the necessity

(a) For guaranteeing freedom of navigation through international waterways in the area;

(b) For achieving a just settlement of the refugee problem;

(c) For guaranteeing the territorial inviolability and political independence of every State in the area, through measures including the establishment of demilitarized zones.[10]

Not surprisingly, Israel and the Arabs have interpreted Resolution 242 differently. The Palestinians took the position that Israel had first to withdraw from *all* the territories occupied in 1967 before negotiations could begin. Many Arab jurists and lay people today blame Israel's "unwillingness" to comply with Resolution 242 for the fact that there is no peace in the Middle East.

Israel accepted Resolution 242 but maintained that it did not have to withdraw from *all* the territories occupied and that withdrawal would only take place after the completion of a direct negotiation process between the parties involved. As far as Israel was concerned, that negotiating process needed to include the determination of "secure and recognized boundaries" and the signing of a peace treaty. In other words, any settlement would have to include Arab recognition of Israel. Such recognition—an acknowledgment of Israel's right to exist—has been a key requirement by Israel in every peace initiative up to today.

Some jurists have maintained that Resolution 242 did not specify that Israel should withdraw from all territories occupied during the Six-Day War. The basis for their maintaining this is that the resolution did not actually say *all*.[11] And Golda Meir, the Israeli prime minister of the time (1969–1974), could not accept the Arab argument—an argument endorsed by many in the international community—that peace between the Arabs and Jews in the Middle East depended on the withdrawal of Israel from all the territories occupied in 1967. The following is from her autobiography *My Life*:

[I]n June 1967, the Sinai, the Gaza strip, the West Bank, the Golan Heights and East Jerusalem [including the Old City] all were in Arab possession, so that it is ludicrous to argue today that Israel's presence in those territories *since* 1967 is the cause of tension in the Middle East or was the cause of the Yom Kippur War [in 1973].[12]

Meir's point, a simple but compelling one, is that Arab possession of these territories did not prevent them from starting the Six-Day War. Why would the Arabs suddenly turn peaceable if these territories were returned to them?

A number of jurists and many in the international community support the Palestinian and Arab position that Israel must withdraw from all territories captured in 1967. Since 1967, the UN General Assembly has passed many resolutions objecting to Jewish settlements and to Israel's activities in east Jerusalem.

"Occupation" in International Law

Resolution 242, which has sparked so many debates, arguments, and disputes, marked the first time that a UN resolution had applied the term "occupation" to the case of Palestine. Since then, a number of UN resolutions have unequivocally declared Israel to be in belligerent occupation of east Jerusalem, including the Old City. When Jordan took control, in 1948, of the area that came to be known as the West Bank, the term "occupation" was not applied. What is *occupation*? Is Israel occupying the West Bank and Gaza?

Answering these questions is difficult. Since the end of the 19th century, many documents concerned with the law of war have defined the term "occupied territory." Most of these documents define "occupation" in terms of the presence and control of an enemy army in the territory in question. In recent years, the International Committee of the Red Cross (ICRC) has defined "occupation" as follows: "Under international law, *there is occupation when* a State exercises non-acquiesced effective *control over a territory on which it has no sovereign title* [emphasis added]."[13]

Is it true that Israel has "no sovereign title" to the territories they took control of in 1967? Or does Israel have sovereign title to these territories? Some international jurists have argued that Israel (as the agent of the Jewish people) has the strongest claim of any state to sovereign title over some of these territories (West Bank and Gaza). (We covered these arguments, which center on the San Remo Resolution and the Palestine Mandate, in some detail in Chapters 12 and 13.)

If Israel has sovereign title over the West Bank and Gaza, then its presence there cannot be classified as an "occupation" in the sense defined by the ICRC.

The International Court of Justice (ICJ) has defined another condition that must be present for an occupation to exist; the Court has determined that "*in order for a belligerent occupation to exist the occupying army must* actually exercise its authority in the territory, and thereby *supplant the authority of the sovereign government of that area* [emphasis added]."[14]

What "sovereign" government did Israel supplant in 1967? The only other state in history, apart from Israel, that could be considered a sovereign government over the West Bank is Turkey. But Turkey relinquished all claims to sovereignty when its government signed the Treaty of Lausanne on July 24, 1923. Israel, on the other hand, received rights and title to the territory known as the West Bank when the League of Nations approved the Mandate for Palestine in July 1922. The Mandate recognized the Jewish people's right to build their national home in Palestine, and the West Bank was within that territory. Other than Israel, there has been no sovereign government with legal title over the West Bank (which includes all of Jerusalem) since 1923.

In short, as the above suggests, it is debatable whether Israel's control of the West Bank and Gaza constituted an "occupation" under international law.

In regards to the Golan Heights and the Sinai, which were acquired by Israel in 1967, the conditions of occupation did apply. The question is whether Israel's occupation of those territories in 1967 was legal or illegal. According to international law, occupations can be legal or illegal.[15] A state can legally occupy a territory if it needs to do so in order to maintain the security of its own domain. In other words, it is allowed to continue an occupation if giving up control of the territory in question would present a threat to its security and peace.

Israel "occupied"—and is still occupying—the Golan Heights for security purposes. According to both international law and Resolution 242, Israel is perfectly within its rights in doing so; security needs justify it. The Golan Heights is a rocky plateau in the mountains that overlook Syria, Lebanon, and Israel. It is a place from which a hostile army could inflict significant damage on northern Israel. Control of this plateau provides a strategic military advantage to whoever possesses it.

It was likewise for security reasons that Israel held the Sinai territory, and over time Israeli settlements were built there. This state of affairs lasted until 1982, when Israel forcibly pulled its citizens out of the Sinai Peninsula and returned the territory to Egypt. The occupation ended then. Like the Sinai, Gaza's status also changed when Israel forcibly moved its citizens from there in 2005. (We will consider Gaza's change of status in Chapter 16.) In 1967, however, Israel's control over Gaza was on par with its control over the West Bank; the Gaza Strip was included in the territory allocated to the Jewish people in the Mandate for Palestine.

The Khartoum Conference and the PLO Charter

On June 19, 1967, Israel offered Egypt and Syria the Sinai Peninsula and the Golan Heights respectively in exchange for permanent peace treaties. The Arab states rejected the Israeli proposal outright. They did so by way of the Khartoum Resolution, which was issued on September 1, at the conclusion of an Arab League summit. This resolution, which formed the basis of Arab governments' policies toward Israel until the 1973 Yom Kippur War, called for continued belligerency towards Israel. It is famous for containing what became known as the "Three 'No's'": "No peace with Israel; no recognition of Israel; no negotiations with it."[16]

By the time of the Khartoum meetings, a number of "Palestinian" Arab nationalist groups had been established. The most influential of the groups was *Harakat al-Tahrir al-Watani al-Filastini* (The Palestinian National Liberation Movement), better known by its reverse acronym, *Fatah*, which means "conquest" in Arabic. Fatah became in the 1960s—and it remains today—the main Palestinian political party in the West Bank.

Yasser Arafat was one of the founders of Fatah, in 1958, and led it until his death in 2004. Under Arafat, Fatah would soon become the driving force behind the

Palestine Liberation Organization (PLO), which was formed in 1964 at the first Palestine National Council (PNC) meeting, under the instructions and approval of the Arab League. The intent in forming the PLO was to rein in the independent *fedayeen* groups and mobilize the Palestinian people, with the ultimate aim of liberating Palestine from the state of Israel and establishing Arab hegemony in the region.

Fatah took control of the PLO and revised the original charter document of 1964. The PLO's charter document, the Palestine National Covenant (Charter), was adopted in Cairo in July 1968. This document exhorted its leadership and the Palestinian people to armed struggle and violence. It set out provisions concerning the liberation of all of the territories of Palestine—including the area encompassing the State of Israel prior to the Six-Day War.

Article 2:

Palestine, with the boundaries it had during the British Mandate, is an indivisible territorial unit. ...

Article 9:

Armed struggle is the only way to liberate Palestine. This is the overall strategy, not merely a tactical phase. ...

Article 19:

The partition of Palestine in 1947 and the establishment of the state of Israel are entirely illegal, regardless of the passage of time, because they were contrary to the will of the Palestinian people and to their natural right in their homeland, and inconsistent with the principles embodied in the Charter of the United Nations; particularly the right to self-determination. ...

Article 20:

The Balfour Declaration, the Mandate for Palestine, and everything that has been based upon them, are deemed null and void. Claims of historical or religious ties of Jews with Palestine are incompatible with the facts of history and the true conception of what constitutes statehood. ...

Article 21:

The Arab Palestinian people, expressing themselves by the armed Palestinian revolution, reject all solutions which are substitutes for the total liberation of Palestine. ...[17]

Hamas, currently the governing Palestinian faction in Gaza, still vehemently holds to these provisions and to their premise that all of Palestine, including the territories held by Israel prior to 1967, must be liberated. In other words, Hamas does not acknowledge Israel's right to exist.

Consequences of the Six-Day War

The Six-Day War changed the nature of the conflict between Israel and the Arabs. This was especially true in areas previously under Jordanian control: the West Bank and Jerusalem. After June 1967, over 600,000 Arabs living in the West Bank were brought under Israeli military administration.[18]

The UN, along with the world media and various human rights organizations—Amnesty International, for example—often portrays Israeli administration over the West Bank as very detrimental to the millions of Arabs living in the region. In reality, Israeli administration has greatly benefited these people. In the years immediately following the 1967 war, the Israelis encouraged and financed economic development in the West Bank. By the end of 1970, Arab unemployment there had dropped from 12 percent to 3 percent. By 1972, 600,000 Arabs from the West Bank found their daily employment in Israel, and 44,000 Arabs who had fled from the West Bank in 1967 had returned.[19]

Palestinian Economic Growth

George Gilder, in *The Israel Test*, divides the economic history of the Palestinian Arabs into three eras, each roughly two decades long. The first era was 1947–67. During that period, the Jordanians controlled the West Bank and the Egyptians controlled Gaza. Gilder notes the following in regards to that first era:

- The economy in the West Bank showed modest growth, with per capita annual income around $800.
- In Gaza, the economy stagnated under Egyptian rule.
- Both Egypt and Jordan—the respective occupants of Gaza and the West Bank—received substantial foreign aid during that time.

The second era of Palestinian economic history began after the 1967 war, when Israel took control of the West Bank and Gaza and administered their economies until the intifada of 1987. Gilder reports the following of that second era:

- The economies of the West Bank and Gaza grew at a rate of 30 percent a year from 1969–1979.
- Annual investment soared from under $10 million in 1969 to some $600 million in 1991.
- The Arab population rose from roughly 1 million to almost 3 million in some 261 new towns, while the number of Jewish settlers in the territories rose to merely 250,000 (from zero in 1967).
- Despite the nearly triple growth in population, per capita income tripled in the West Bank; in Gaza, per capita income rose from $80 to $1,706.

■ The territories stopped depending on foreign aid, their economies boomed, and business activity and standard of living increased dramatically.[20]

Ephraim Karsh reports that at the beginning of Israel's takeover in 1967, conditions in the territories were quite dire. Life expectancy and the level of education were low, while rates of malnutrition, infectious diseases, and child mortality were high. Also, prior to the 1967 war, fewer than 60 percent of all male adults had been employed, with unemployment among refugees running as high as 83 percent. Israeli occupation after the war led directly to dramatic improvements in these regards.[21]

Karsh also notes the following about this postwar period:

■ During the 1970s, the West Bank and Gaza constituted the fourth fastest growing economy in the world.

■ The number of Palestinians working in Israel rose from none in 1967 to 109,000 by 1986, accounting for 35 percent of the employed population of the West Bank and 45 percent in Gaza.

■ Close to 2,000 industrial plants, employing almost half of the region's workforce, were established in the territories under Israeli rule.

■ By 1986, 92.8 percent of the populations of West Bank and Gaza had electricity 24 hours a day, as compared to 20.5 percent in 1967.

■ With respect to higher education, there were no universities in the West Bank and Gaza in 1967 but by the early 1990s, there were seven, hosting some 16,500 students.[22]

Gilder notes that equivalent advances occurred in the areas of hygiene, healthcare, child mortality, immunizations, and communications, all improving to levels equal to or exceeding other Middle Eastern countries.

Things began to go wrong in the territories following the 1973 Yom Kippur War, owing to events we will discuss below.

The Yom Kippur War

On Saturday October 6, 1973, while Israel was engaged in the holy day services of Yom Kippur and the Jewish Sabbath, Egypt and Syria launched a surprise attack on the country's southern front, near the Suez Canal, and on the northern front of the Golan Heights. Many Israeli soldiers on those fronts were not at their usual positions, due to the holy day. The first days of the war were dire for the Israelis, as Golda Meir, the Israeli prime minister at the time, has recalled in her autobiography.[23] The Arabs, heavily armed by the Russians, had significant military success at first. The Egyptians crossed the Suez Canal in the south and battered Israel's forces in the Sinai, while the Syrians penetrated the Israeli defences in the Golan Heights. By Wednesday, October 10, the fifth day of the war, Israel had managed to push the Syrians back in the north and to stop the Egyptian advance in the south. However, they were in desperate need of military aid. Meir recalls that the US Defense Department was initially reluctant to send military supplies to Israel, even though huge transports of Soviet aid were being brought by sea and air to Egypt and Syria, and Israel was losing aircraft at an alarming rate to Soviet missiles on both fronts.

On Sunday October 14, US President Richard Nixon ordered military aid—tanks, ammunition, air-to-air rockets, and fighter aircraft—to be sent to Israel. The next day, the tenth day of the war, the Israeli forces crossed to the Egyptian side of the Suez Canal and sandwiched the Egyptian army in the Sinai. By October 19, the thirteenth day of the war, although the fighting had not ended, the Russians began a full-scale campaign for a quick cease-fire. Their "clients" were now badly losing. The eighteen-day war ended with a cease-fire on October 24, 1973. But the end of this war marked the beginning of a new one—namely, the Arabs' non-military war on Israel.

The 1973 Oil Crisis

The Arab defeat in the 1973 conflict led to a change in their military strategy regarding Israel. In 1973, members of the Organization of Arab Petroleum Exporting Countries or the OAPEC (consisting of the Arab members of OPEC, plus Egypt, Syria and Tunisia), declared an oil embargo to protest the United States' supplying the Israeli military during the Yom Kippur war. The "oil weapon" targeted not just the US, but also the industrialized nations of Great Britain, Canada, Japan, and the Netherlands. The Arab hope was that the embargo would change these governments' foreign policies in regards to Israel. The resulting "oil crisis," which started in October 1973, lasted until March 1974.

The strategy was successful. Western Europe and Japan began switching from pro-Israel to pro-Arab policies. Japan, the country most heavily dependent on Middle East oil, issued a statement on November 22 that did the following:

1. asserted Israel should withdraw from all of the 1967 territories,
2. advocated Palestinian self-determination, and
3. threatened that Japan would reconsider its policy toward Israel if Israel refused to accept these preconditions.

By December 25, Japan was considered a friendly state by the Arab coalition. The new Arab strategy also affected Great Britain, which now refused to allow the United States to use British bases to airlift supplies to Israel.

Pan-Arab Endorsement of the PLO

Following the Arab oil embargo, there was a crucial meeting of the League of Arab States in Rabat, Morocco, in October 1974. The Rabat Summit brought together the representatives of the PLO and the leaders of twenty Arab states. The PLO leaders demanded that any Palestinian territory liberated by Arab forces be turned over to the "Palestinian people," as represented by the PLO. Jordan, recently embroiled in a "civil" war with the PLO and Arafat, protested, but without effect; the parties arrived at a solution that favored PLO interests over Jordan's. The declaration that emerged from this conference formally acknowledged the right of the Palestinian people to a separate homeland. Most important, the Rabat Summit marked the first time that all of the Arab states officially recognized the PLO as the "sole legitimate representative of the 'Palestinian' people."[24]

The Rabat Summit declaration granted the PLO a legitimacy it hadn't had before. It gave official Arab recognition to PLO territorial claims to the West Bank, and it unambiguously put the fate of the Palestinian people solely in the hands of the PLO. King Hussein of Jordan opposed the declaration, although he eventually signed it under intense Arab pressure, and after the Arab oil-producing states promised to provide Jordan with an annual subsidy of $300 million (US).[25]

The Rabat statement allowed Arafat to proceed against Israel without worrying about other Arab countries, such as Jordan, laying claim to territories acquired by the PLO.

On November 23, 1974, following the Rabat Summit, the UN General Assembly made the remarkable decision to grant the PLO "Permanent Observer" status. Why was this remarkable? Non-member *states* of the UN can apply for the status of Permanent Observer. Permanent Observers have free access to most meetings and relevant documentation. For a non-state actor to gain such international legitimacy was, as one Middle East specialist has said, unprecedented.[26]

Also during this period, the UN General Assembly established a new permanent committee under the name "Committee on the Exercise of the Inalienable Rights of the Palestinian People." The main task of this permanent committee was to provide recommendations for the realization of Palestinian political rights, now officially recognized by the UN.[27] From this point on, the number of the UN Resolutions targeting Israel increased dramatically, and their tone became more hostile.

Zionism Condemned by General Assembly: November 1975

On November 10, 1975, the UN General Assembly adopted Resolution 3379 (XXX), which declared Zionism to be a form of "racism and racial discrimination." Denouncing Israel as the "racist regime in occupied Palestine" whose policies were aimed "at repression of the dignity and integrity of the human being,"[28] Resolution 3379 associated Israel and Zionism with South African apartheid, colonialism, occupation, and imperialism.

There is an interesting similarity between the phrases in UN Res. 3379 and those used in the Palestinian Charter of 1968. The latter described Zionism as

> a national political movement organically associated with international imperialism. ... It is racist and fanatic in its nature, aggressive, expansionistic, and colonial, in its aims, and fascist in its methods. Israel is the instrument of the Zionist movement and a geographical base for world imperialism placed strategically.

It seems more than coincidence that these phrases began to appear in UN resolutions shortly after the PLO received international recognition and Arab states had begun exerting pressure on the West by means of the oil embargo.

Between 1948 and 1982, the UN "condemned," "deplored," or "censured" Israel 38 times; it didn't blame the Arabs even once. This statistic reflects how far the supposedly objective, unbiased UN had compromised its impartiality where the Arab–Israeli conflict was concerned. As Ilan Dunsky remarked in this regard, "Unless one believes that the Israeli–Arab dispute is essentially one between demons and angels, this figure is cause for some concern."[29]

The UN General Assembly nullified Resolution 3379 on December 18, 1991, with the approval of Resolution 48/86. Even today, however, more than twenty years after its nullification, we are still seeing the damage done by Resolution 3379. We are seeing this damage annually on college campuses across North America, as students engage in their official week of anti-Israel demonstrations and apply the apartheid label to Israel.

The Camp David Accords

Egyptian President Anwar Sadat's historic and unexpected visit to Jerusalem on November 19, 1977, struck an incongruously positive note amidst the ominous events that followed the 1973 war. Sadat's visit set off widespread protest and demonstrations among other Arab nations and met with strong objections from the PLO.

Less than a year after Sadat's visit to Jerusalem, meetings took place over a fifteen-day period at Camp David, in the state of Maryland, between US President Jimmy Carter, Egyptian President Anwar Sadat, and Israeli Prime Minister Menachem Begin. From those meetings emerged the "Framework for the Conclusion of a Peace Treaty Between Egypt and Israel," as well as guidelines for negotiations between Israel, Jordan, and Egypt called the "Framework for Peace in the Middle East."

The agreements concluded at Camp David eventually resulted in the signing of a peace treaty between Israel and Egypt in March 1979, in Washington. In return for the termination of hostilities, Israel agreed to gradually withdraw from the Sinai Peninsula. This set the stage for future land-for-peace strategies by Israel.

Several Arab states opposed the Camp David agreements. They pursued a joint strategy to prevent any further such arrangements for peace and to continue their violent struggle against the Jewish State.

UN Resolution 446—Illegality of Settlements

The international community, pressured by the Arab oil weapon, continued to discover legitimacy in the Palestinian cause, and the UN pumped out further resolutions supporting this cause and denouncing measures taken by Israel. On March 22, 1979, the UN Security Council adopted Resolution 446. This resolution addressed the issue of Israeli settlements in the territories it had occupied since 1967, including Jerusalem. Referring to the West Bank, East Jerusalem, and the Gaza Strip as Palestinian, and the Golan Heights as Syrian, the resolution determined that

the policy and practices of Israel in establishing settlements in the Palestinian and other Arab territories occupied since 1967 have no legal validity and constitute a serious obstruction to achieving a comprehensive, just and lasting peace in the Middle East.[30]

After this point, arguments against Israel's settlement in the so-called occupied territories became part of the international community's general attack on Israel's claims to sovereignty in the West Bank (Judea and Samaria) and in Gaza.

The Political Program of Fatah

With Palestinian political legitimacy firmly established, the Fourth Fatah Conference, held in May 1980, further defined the political program of the dominant faction of the PLO. The program's Preamble emphasized that "Fatah is a revolutionary patriotic movement that aims to liberate the whole of Palestine and establish a democratic Palestinian state on the whole of Palestinian soil." The program spoke of the need "to step up the armed struggle inside the occupied land and across all confrontation lines against the Zionist enemy."[31] Fatah's political position in regards to the territory of Palestine is clearly reflected in their coat of arms, which shows a map of the State of Palestine that includes all of the land currently belonging to the State of Israel. In other words, Fatah does not acknowledge Israel's statehood or right to exist.

Israel's Annexation of East Jerusalem and the Old City

On July 30, 1980, the Israeli Parliament officially declared its claim to sovereignty over the entire city of Jerusalem, and annexed the eastern areas which include the Old City. The Israeli legislation—"The Basic Law: Jerusalem, Capital of Israel"—was enacted despite the UN's adoption, a month earlier, of UN Resolution 476, which expressed the Security Council's strong objections to the Knesset's annexation bill.

Could Israel validly, under international law, annex the eastern areas of Jerusalem and the Old City and claim territorial sovereignty over them? Jurists agree that a state cannot unilaterally annex a territory acquired in a war and then justify its sovereignty over it. This prohibition is in keeping with the principle in international law according to which legal title can never be acquired by forcible means.[32] And this is inarguably how Israel acquired the Old City and eastern Jerusalem in the 1967 war. But what if the victor captures territory that it previously held title to?

Jurist Antonio Cassese has argued that Israel's annexation of Jerusalem was contrary both to conventional and to general law. In his view, only the previous holders of sovereignty over Jerusalem—that is, the League of Nations (or its successor as of 1946, the UN) and the United Kingdom (the former Mandatory of the region)—could grant Israel legal title to the Old City. And he points out that such a transfer of legal title had never been made, either formally or implicitly.[33]

Cassese's comments disregard the fact that the Jewish people's sovereignty rights to Palestine and Jerusalem were established by the decisions of the Principal Allied Powers in San Remo in April 1920 and then by the League of Nations, when it approved the Mandate for Palestine, in July 1922.[34] As of those agreements, the Jewish people were granted sovereignty rights and legal title to Jerusalem.

Israel's annexation of Jerusalem was, predictably enough, totally unacceptable to the Palestinians.

The Israel–Lebanon War

While the PLO was gaining political momentum, it was also expanding its paramilitary and terrorist campaign, with attacks in Israel, Lebanon, and Europe. It attempted to assassinate the Israeli ambassador to London, and it renewed its shelling of northern Israel from bases in Lebanon. In response, with a view to destroying these PLO bases, Israel invaded Lebanon on June 6, 1982.[35]

While successful militarily, the 1982 Lebanon war damaged Israel's international reputation and resulted in deep political problems domestically. Israel had initially planned on penetrating only 40 kilometers into Lebanon to create a security zone. But the goal of the invasion changed; the revised aim was to completely expel the PLO and to help the PLO's rival, the Maronites (Lebanese Christian Arabs), take control of the country so that Lebanon could sign a peace treaty with Israel.

On September 14, 1982, the newly elected Lebanese president, Bashir Gemayal, was assassinated in Beirut, after entering peace discussions with Israel. The following day, IDF forces commanded by Ariel Sharon surrounded the Palestinian refugee camps of Sabra and Shatila, controlling access to them. PLO fighters were believed to be hiding there.

Christian Phalange forces were a right-wing paramilitary organization in Lebanon, led by Gemayal until his death and supported by the country's Maronite Christians. On September 15, the day after Gemayal's assassination, these forces proceeded to enter the Sabra and Shatila camps, which Israel had sealed off. They did so under the pretense of hunting PLO fighters, but they proceeded to massacre hundreds of Palestinian and Lebanese civilians, including women and children. According to the Phalange forces, the massacre was retaliation for the assassination of Gemayel and for the PLO's killing of Maronite civilians during Lebanon's civil war.

In Israel and around the world, there was outrage over the killings. Sharon and Israeli Prime Minister Menachem Begin denied that the IDF was responsible. The Israeli government established the Kahan Commission to investigate the massacres. The commission found that Israeli military and government officials bore indirect responsibility, even though the killings had been carried out by Christian Phalange forces. Ariel Sharon was demoted to a junior Cabinet position.

Generally speaking, Israel's 1982 Lebanon War had long-term ramifications for the country. After the war, the IDF maintained a military presence in southern Lebanon. This occupation contributed to the creation of the Iranian-backed *Hizballah* ("Party of God") party. Israel's hostilities with the PLO in Lebanon ultimately gave way to ongoing conflict with Hizballah fighters in the region.

In addition, the PLO defeat in Lebanon led to this organization's adopting a new strategy for Palestinian autonomy in the disputed territories (West Bank and Gaza). The strategy was to piggyback on Jordan's negotiations with Israel. Yasser Arafat and King Hussein of Jordan signed an agreement in February of 1985 pledging a joint Palestinian and Jordanian peace initiative. However, the cooperation between the PLO and Jordan ultimately broke down, and Israel was left without a Jordanian option to solve the Palestinian Arab issue. Israel had hoped that the Palestinians' future could become part of its peace negotiations with the Jordanian state, Jordan being a more stable potential peace partner than the PLO.

In December of that year, the situation changed when the Palestinian people themselves initiated an uprising that came be known as the intifada.

Endnotes

1   Jacques Paul Gauthier, *Sovereignty Over the Old City of Jerusalem: A Study of the Historical, Religious, Political and Legal Aspects of the Question of the Old City,* Thèse No. 725 (Geneva: Université de Genève, 2007), 670.

2   Martin Gilbert, *The Routledge Atlas of the Arab-Israeli Conflict,* 9th ed. (London: Routledge, 2008), 66.

3   Ibid, 67.

4   Ibid, 67.

5   Yehuda Avner, *The Prime Ministers,* 4th ed. (Jerusalem: Toby, 2012), 152.

6   Gauthier, *Sovereignty Over the Old City,* 672

7   Ibid, 675.

8   Protection of Holy Places Law 5727, June 27, 1967, The State of Israel, http://www.knesset.gov.il/laws/special/eng/HolyPlaces.htm.

9   United Nations, Resolution 2253 (ES-V), "Measures taken by Israel to change the status of the City of Jerusalem," July 4, 1967, accessed June 4, 2012, http://unispal.un.org/UNISPAL.NSF/0/A39A906C89D3E98685256C29006D4014.

10   United Nations Security Council, Resolution 242, "The Situation in the Middle East," November 22, 1967, http://unispal.un.org/unispal.nsf/0/7D35E1F729DF491C85256EE700686136.

11   Gauthier, *Sovereignty Over the Old City,* 684.

12   Golda Meir, *My Life* (New York: Dell, 1975), 351.

13   International Committee of the Red Cross (ICRC), "Contemporary challenges to IHL—Occupation: overview," accessed October 8, 2012, http://www.icrc.org/eng/war-and-law/contemporary-challenges-for-ihl/occupation/overview-occupation.htm.

14   Alan Baker, ed., *Israel's Rights as a Nation-State in International Diplomacy* (Jerusalem: World Jewish Congress / Jerusalem Center for Public Affairs, 2011), http://jcpa.org/wp-content/uploads/2012/02/israels-rights-full-study.pdf.

15   Gauthier, *Sovereignty Over the Old City,* 699.

16   League of Arab States, "Khartoum Resolution," September 1, 1967, Council on Foreign Relations, accessed July 30, 2012, http://www.cfr.org/international-peace-and-security/khartoum-resolution/p14841.

17   Palestinian National Council, "The Palestinian National Charter: Resolutions of the Palestine National Council," July 1-17, 1968, Avalon Project, Yale Law School, accessed July 22, 2012, http://avalon.law.yale.edu/20th_century/plocov.asp.

18   Gilbert, *Atlas of the Arab-Israeli Conflict,* 74.

19   Ibid.

20   George Gilder, *The Israel Test* (USA: Richard Vigilante Books, 2009), 45-60.

21   Ephraim Karsh, "What Occupation?" *Commentary,* July/August 2002, accessed August 19, 2012, http://www.aish.com/jw/me/48898917.html.

22 Ibid.

23 Meir, *My Life*, 405-421.

24 Palestine Facts, "Rabat Arab Summit Conference," accessed June 8, 2012, http://www.palestinefacts. org/pf_1967to1991_rabat_1974.php.

25 Ibid.

26 Gauthier, *Sovereignty Over the Old City*, 709.

27 Ibid.

28 UN General Assembly, Resolution 3379, "Elimination of all forms of racial discrimination," November 10, 1975, http://daccess-dds-ny.un.org/doc/RESOLUTION/GEN/NR0/000/92/IMG/ NR000092.pdf?OpenElement.

29 Ilan Dunsky, "Israel, the Arabs and International Law: Whose Palestine Is It, Anyway?," *Dalhousie Journal of Legal Studies* 2 (1993): 65.

30 United Nations Security Council, Resolution 446, "Arab territories occupied by Israel since 1967, including Jerusalem," March 22, 1979, accessed July 30, 2012, http://unispal.un.org/UNISPAL. NSF/0/BA123CDED3EA84A5852560E50077C2DC.

31 Gauthier, *Sovereignty Over the Old City*, 716,

32 Ibid, 718.

33 Antonio Cassese, "Legal Considerations on the International Status of Jerusalem," *Palestine Yearbook of International Law* 3 (1986): 29.

34 Gauthier, *Sovereignty Over the Old City*, 719.

35 Gilbert, *Atlas of the Arab-Israeli Conflict*, 124.

Chapter 16

Israel and the Arabs 1987–2007

Introduction

The years 1987–2007 saw no official wars between the Arab states and Israel over territorial rights in Palestine. But an unofficial war on Israel began during this period. This new war took the form of mass uprisings and of terrorist violence launched from inside Israel's disputed borders and, increasingly, from outside them. It was a war condoned and supported by certain of the Arab states, but primarily waged by militants from the growing mass of desperate Palestinian refugees. Israel, disinclined to compromise the safety of its citizens, tried to quell this violence by various means—by force, by negotiation, and, in 2002, by the unpopular but effective security barrier.

There was also a propaganda war being waged. The Palestinians were effective in this sphere, managing to persuade the international community that their grievances against Israel were justified; the UN passed numerous resolutions condemning Israel.

The Palestinian leadership, represented by Yasser Arafat and the PLO, pushed the UN hard to recognize an independent Palestinian state, a homeland for the large numbers of Arab refugees. The stateless Palestinians, their population swelled by Jordan's strategic revocation of their citizenship, were a growing problem for Israel during this period, an ongoing source of civil unrest and a breeding-ground for extremist factions such as Hamas.

At the same time, the years 1987–2007 saw continual attempts, most of them sponsored by the US, to establish a lasting Arab–Israeli peace. Israel welcomed and encouraged these initiatives, but the Palestinian leadership, pressured by extremist factions still bent on Israel's liquidation, was more ambivalent. A few of the negotiations for peace bore fruit. Most were sabotaged by bad faith and mistrust. These and other developments are the focus of this chapter.

Intifada and Formation of Hamas

On December 9, 1987, a grassroots Palestinian uprising known as the *intifada* (the Arabic term for "shaking off" or "uprising") began in Gaza and spread throughout the Arab towns and villages of the West Bank (Judea and Samaria). It was intended to pressure Israel and to attract international support for an independent Palestinian state. During the next three years, Arab terrorist attacks killed dozens of Jewish soldiers and civilians and led, by way of Israeli retaliation, to hundreds of Arab deaths. Thousands more were injured on both sides.[1]

Among the factors in the intifada were the high rate of unemployment in the West Bank and Gaza, and the perception among Palestinian Arabs, especially its youth, that they couldn't count on either their own leadership or the Arab states to resolve their problems. Yitzhak Rabin, the Israeli minister of defence, tried to crush the rebellion with a harsh iron-fist policy. Israeli forces used rubber bullets and tear gas against demonstrators, imposed curfews, and imprisoned thousands of Palestinian Arabs, including leading activists.

Israel now faced international disapproval as well as domestic stress. By 1987, the world media's portrayal of Israel had radically changed from twenty years before. Israel was now seen as the harsh oppressor, the Palestinian Arabs as the oppressed. The Palestinians had secured international sympathy for their cause. The two major political parties in Israel had very different views on how to move forward in regards to Arab relations. The Labor Party was committed to a land-for-peace strategy, while the Likud Party was opposed to giving any more territory to the Arabs.

Hamas

The Palestinian Arabs were facing internal struggles of their own. As the intifada continued, Yasser Arafat's PLO began losing ground in Gaza to a growing political faction known as *Hamas* (Arabic for "enthusiasm" or "zeal"). Sometimes referred to as the Islamic Resistance Party, Hamas was formed at the beginning of the Palestinian uprising. It is the largest of the Egyptian-based Muslim Brotherhood movements in Gaza and its aim is to establish an Islamist Palestinian society. The ideology of Hamas, rooted in radical Islam, is much more extreme than the secular ideology of Fatah, the dominant faction within the PLO, and its public policies are comparatively harsh and uncompromising.

In mid-1988, Hamas set out its guiding principles in a Charter. The thirty-six articles in this document include the following:

Article 7: The Islamic Resistance Movement is one of the links in the chain of the *struggle against the Zionist invaders*. ...

Article 11: The Islamic Resistance Movement believes that *the land of Palestine is an Islamic Waqf* consecrated for future Moslem generations until Judgement Day. It, or any part of it, should not be squandered: it, or any part of it, should not be given up. ...

Article 13: Initiatives, and *so-called peaceful solutions and international conferences, are in contradiction to the principles of the Islamic Resistance Movement.*

Abusing any part of Palestine is abuse directed against part of religion. ... There is no solution for the Palestinian question except through Jihad. ... [emphasis added]

Article 14: The question of the liberation of Palestine is bound to three circles: the Palestinian circle, the Arab circle and the Islamic circle. Each of these circles has its role in the struggle against Zionism ... Since this is the case, *liberation of Palestine is then an individual duty for every Moslem* wherever he may be. [emphasis added]

Article 15: In face of the Jews' usurpation of Palestine, it is compulsory that the banner of Jihad be raised ... It is necessary to instill in the minds of the Moslem generations that *the Palestinian problem is a religious problem*, and should be dealt with on this basis. [emphasis added]

Subsequent articles in the Hamas Charter are crudely anti-Semitic, in the style of Nazi Germany and Haj Amin al-Husseini. It is suggested, for example, that the Jews "control the world media," have formed secret associations "for the purpose of sabotaging societies and achieving Zionist interests," and "were behind World War I and II." The Charter also says that the Jews "aim at undermining societies, destroying values, corrupting consciences, deteriorating character and annihilating Islam" and that this aim "is embodied in the 'Protocols of the Elders of Zion.'"[2]

In summary, Hamas's Charter

■ dismisses any initiatives that aim at peace or recognition of Israel,

■ ultimately aims to liberate all of Palestine and place it under Islamic control, and

■ denies that any Jewish state can legitimately exist.

Arafat, conscious of losing support to Hamas among the Palestinian people of Gaza, announced in June 1988 that he was prepared to make significant concessions to resolve the Israeli–Palestinian conflict. It was an announcement driven by political necessity. By initiating a peace process, Arafat aimed to recapture the spotlight he needed to recover his political authority.

PLO Announcement of Palestinian State

At an Arab League meeting in June 1988, Arafat's PLO unveiled a plan for a two-state solution to the Israeli–Palestinian conflict. A few months later, on November 15, at the Palestine National Council (PNC) meeting in Algiers, Arafat proclaimed the establishment of the State of Palestine. He included the West Bank and Gaza in his definition of the state. On December 14, the PNC Declaration of Independence was presented to the UN General Assembly.

In his speech to the UN, Arafat noted that the first and most decisive resolution of the PNC was the establishment of the State of Palestine, with the holy city of Jerusalem (*al-Quds ash-Sharif*) as its capital. Arafat claimed that the State of Palestine was established by virtue of the Palestinian Arab people's natural, historic, and legal right to their homeland, as well as by the sacrifices of generations of Palestinians in defense of the liberty and independence of that homeland.[3]

Arafat also asserted the following in his speech:

- UN resolutions 242 and 338 enshrine the international legitimacy of the Palestinian Arab territorial claims.
- Palestinian refugees have a right to return to their homeland according to UN Resolution 194.
- The Palestinian Arab people have a right to self-determination, political independence, and sovereignty "on their soil."

Arafat proclaimed Palestinian statehood even though certain elements required for statehood under international law were not present. A treaty entitled *The Montevideo Convention on the Rights and Duties of States*, signed on December 26, 1933, established the standard definition of a state under international law. It sets out four criteria:

- a permanent population;
- defined boundaries;
- a government; and
- a capacity to enter into relations with other states.

A number of jurists have contended that Palestinian statehood does not meet all of these criteria. For example, territorial boundaries for a Palestinian state have never been finalized. Arafat's contention that, under international law, the Palestinians were entitled to self-determination and sovereignty is also questionable. As we discussed in Chapter 13, it was not the Arabs but the Jewish people who, under the Palestine Mandate, received self-determination and sovereignty rights in Palestine. The Arabs received these rights in the territories of Syria, Lebanon, Iraq, and Transjordan. The Mandate for Palestine guaranteed the Arab inhabitants of Palestine their civil and religious rights, but not political rights of self-determination and sovereignty in that territory.[4]

Israelis were skeptical about Arafat's pronouncement of a two-state solution and his public renunciation of violence. They were skeptical because the PLO charter (and that of Hamas) still called for Israel's destruction.

Jordan Relinquishes Its Claim to the West Bank

Another significant consequence of the intifada was King Hussein's 1988 announcement that Jordan was relinquishing its claims to sovereignty over the West Bank and terminating its ties with the Palestinian Arabs living there. Hussein had struggled for years with Arafat and Palestinian militancy, as well as with the other Arab states, over Jordan's ambitions in Palestine. Now he was giving up that fight. This left Israel and the Palestinians as the sole stakeholders to the disputed West Bank territories of Judea and Samaria.

Increase in Stateless Palestinians

In severing Jordan's ties with the West Bank, King Hussein also took the step of revoking the Jordanian citizenship status of West Bank residents. With this measure, he was undoing a policy of nearly forty years standing. In December 1949, in the wake of the 1948 War of Independence, the government of Jordan had extended full Jordanian citizenship to all Palestinian Arabs who had taken refuge in Jordan or who had remained in western areas controlled by Jordan (West Bank). Palestinian Arabs had been given no say in the matter, but in general they welcomed this measure; it had spared them the hardship of living without citizenship. After Israel's capture of the territories in 1967, these residents of the West Bank had remained Jordanian citizens according to Jordanian law.

In the early 1980s, the Jordanian government had begun to change its citizenship policies regarding Palestinians. It had begun issuing citizenship cards of different colors, to differentiate between those living in the West Bank and those living in Jordan. Those who lived in the West Bank were issued green cards, while those who lived in Jordan but had material and/or family connections in the West Bank were issued yellow cards. The cards enabled Jordanian authorities at the Allenby Bridge—the only crossing point between Jordan and the West Bank—to monitor cardholders' movements and to ensure that Palestinian West Bankers who crossed into Jordan returned to their West Bank homes.

Why the change in policy in the mid-80s? Why the need to distinguish between Palestinians living in the West Bank and those living in Jordan proper? The likely reason is that, as Arafat and the PLO gained political momentum, Hussein's territorial designs on the West Bank (and Jerusalem) began to fade. With this hope gone, he foresaw no advantage to his country in having a large West Bank Palestinian population with claims to Jordanian citizenship.

July 31, 1988 was the date on which King Hussein relinquished all claims of sovereignty over the West Bank. The colored cards now became the criteria for determining each Palestinian's citizenship status. As of July 31, those who habitually lived in the West Bank—that is, holders of green cards—were deemed "Palestinian citizens," while those who were living in Jordan or abroad were Jordanian. One Arab observer has remarked that "more than 1.5 million Palestinians went to bed on 31 July 1988 as Jordanian citizens, and woke up on 1 August 1988 as stateless persons."[5]

The holders of yellow cards—Palestinians who retained their Jordanian citizenship after Jordan's 1988 disengagement from the West Bank—have also had their Jordanian citizenship revoked in recent years. To this day, Jordan continues to try to offload its Palestinian population on to Israel and the Palestinian Authority. The "stateless" Palestinians created by these measures have become part of the region's refugee problem.

The intifada not only intensified the Palestinian refugee problem; it also had a dismal effect on the economies and the standard of living in the disputed territories. The forms of Palestinian civil disobedience included strikes and refusal to pay taxes to the Israeli government. Israel responded with harsh countermeasures, such as the levying of heavy fines on local stores and factories in Gaza and the West Bank.

The Impact of the Soviet Union's Collapse

The beginning of the 1990s saw more significant changes in the region. With the collapse of the Soviet Union, hundreds of thousands of Russian Jews found the old obstacles to their emigration removed, and they sought a better life elsewhere. From January 1990 to June 1991, over 330,000 Russians immigrated to Israel. The PLO fiercely protested the influx of Jews into Israel even though only 1,947 (less than 0.8 percent) of them went to settlements in the West Bank.[6]

While trying to absorb the massive immigration of Russian Jews, Israel also had to contend with the Gulf War and the 30 Scud missiles from Iraq that hit Tel Aviv and Haifa during January and February of 1991.[7] Yasser Arafat publicly supported Saddam Hussein during the Gulf War.

Arab–Israeli Negotiations for Peace

The Madrid Conference

The end of the Gulf War found the United States the most influential superpower in the Middle East. The US used this influence to try to bring peace to the region. It organized a conference in Madrid that brought together representatives from Israel, Syria, Lebanon, and Jordan, as well as Palestinian Arabs from the West Bank and Gaza. The Madrid peace process, which began on October 30, 1991, broke down without any real progress being made. However, the framework it involved—the implementation of Security Council Resolutions 242 and 338—set the agenda for negotiations two years later.

Following the breakdown of the Madrid talks, Prime Minister Yitzhak Shamir refused to contemplate the land-for-peace strategy any further—that is, the strategy whereby Israel, in return for the termination of Palestinian hostilities, would withdraw (as prescribed by UN Resolution 242) from territories it had acquired in 1967. When new Israeli elections were held in June 1992, Shamir's Likud Party lost to Yitzhak Rabin. The country had decided a new approach was required.

The Oslo Accords

In September 1993, shortly after Rabin's Labor coalition-led government came to power, secret negotiations began in Oslo, Norway, between Israeli and PLO representatives. The Israelis now deployed the land-for-peace strategy that had successfully produced the 1982 peace treaty with Egypt.

Another productive factor in the Oslo negotiation was the Israeli Cabinet's approval, in February of 1993, of a plan for three large Palestinian enclaves in the West Bank. This was an updated version of a 1991 plan proposed by Clinton Bailey, an Israeli expert on Palestinian affairs. The aim was to create areas of contiguous Arab settlement which would take in a maximum number of Arabs and a minimum number of Jews. This would make security in the territory easier for the Israeli military administration and create opportunities for Palestinian autonomy.

The West Bank has an area of approximately 5,600 square kilometres (2,100 square miles). This area comprises 21.2 percent of the territory that remained as Palestine after the larger area of Mandate Palestine was partitioned in 1920 to form Jordan (see Chapter 13). Bailey found that almost 90 percent of the West Bank Arab population (1,076,000) lived in or near major Arab cities and towns such as Nablus, Jenin, Ramallah, Jericho, Tulkarm, Bethlehem, and Hebron. Bailey proposed that these population centers become Palestinian enclaves; this would allow most Arabs to be released from Israeli control. Following the same principle, 90 percent of the Jews in the West Bank would reside in other enclaves, such as the town of Maale Adumim. These Israeli enclaves, while still in the West Bank, would become Israeli territory contiguous with the state of Israel. According to Bailey's blueprint, only 10 percent (12,470) of the Jewish population in the West Bank would remain inside Arab enclaves. Jerusalem and the Old City would be under Israeli sovereignty, while Gaza in its entirety would become another Palestinian enclave.[8]

The Cabinet's approval of this plan was the catalyst for an eight-month period of secret negotiations that resulted in the Oslo Peace Accords. The actual signing of the accords, which were also called the "Declaration of Principles on Interim Self-Government Arrangements" (DOP), took place at the White House in Washington on September 13, 1993. The signatories were Arafat, Rabin, and Peres, overseen by U.S. President Bill Clinton.

Four days prior to the signing of the DOP, PLO Chairman Yasser Arafat sent a letter to Prime Minister Rabin, in which he stated unequivocally that the PLO

- recognizes the right of Israel to exist in peace and security;
- accepts UN Security Council Resolutions 242 and 338;
- commits itself to a peaceful resolution of the conflict;
- renounces the use of terrorism and other acts of violence;
- assumes responsibility over all PLO elements to ensure their compliance, to prevent violations, and to discipline violators;
- affirms that those articles of the PLO Covenant which deny Israel's right to exist are now inoperative and no longer valid; and
- undertakes to submit to the Palestinian National Council for formal approval the necessary changes to the Covenant.[9]

In response, Israel agreed to recognize the PLO as the Palestinians' representative in the peace negotiations.

The DOP provided for immediate Palestinian self-rule in Gaza and Jericho and an agreement on self-government after the election of a Palestinian council. The Preamble stated the following:

> The Government of the State of Israel and the PLO team (in the Jordanian-Palestinian delegation to the Middle East Peace Conference) (the "Palestinian Delegation"), representing the Palestinian people, agree that it is time to put an end to decades of confrontation and conflict, recognize their mutual legitimate and political rights, and strive to live in peaceful

coexistence and mutual dignity and security and achieve a just, lasting and comprehensive peace settlement and historic reconciliation through the agreed political process.[10]

By this agreement, Israel and the PLO recognized each other for the first time and committed themselves to a peaceful solution to the conflict. Prior to Oslo, Israel had viewed the PLO as a terrorist organization.

The aims of the DOP were set out in Article 1 and stated the following:

The aim of the Israeli–Palestinian negotiations within the current Middle East peace process is, among other things, to establish a Palestinian Interim Self-Government Authority, the elected Council (the "Council"), for the Palestinian people in the West Bank and the Gaza Strip, for a transitional period not exceeding five years, *leading to a permanent settlement based on Security Council Resolutions 242 and 338.*[11] (emphasis added)

The DOP was essentially an agenda for negotiations, with a five-year plan to transfer authority from Israel to a Palestinian government. During this interim period, further negotiations were to take place that would lead to a "final status" agreement on the remaining issues in the conflict, including the most difficult ones—for example, Jerusalem, refugees, settlements, security arrangements, borders, and relations with other states in the region.

The DOP also provided for an Israeli–Palestinian Committee that would focus on cooperation in regard to practical matters: water, electricity, energy, finance, transportation, communications, trade, industry, labor, environment, and any other programs of mutual interest.

Gaza–Jericho Agreement

Following Oslo, Rabin and Arafat met in Cairo. On May 4, 1994, they signed a further agreement, the Gaza–Jericho Agreement, setting the terms of the Israeli forces' withdrawal from Jericho and from parts of the Gaza strip. Under this agreement, the Palestinian Authority (PA) would have legislative, executive, and judicial powers and responsibilities in these regions, including its own armed police force, and it would have control over internal security, education, health, and welfare.

In addition to Israel's withdrawal, the Gaza–Jericho Agreement required commitments from both sides in regards to fostering a relationship of mutual tolerance. Article 12—"Relations between Israel and the Palestinian Authority"— said the following:

Israel and the Palestinian Authority shall seek to foster mutual understanding and tolerance and shall accordingly abstain from incitement, including hostile propaganda, against each other and, without derogating from the principle of freedom of expression, shall take legal measures to prevent such incitement by any organizations, groups or individuals within their jurisdiction.[12]

As per the agreement, Israeli troops left Jericho on May 13. Four days later they withdrew from Gaza, and the first phase of the agreement had been fulfilled.

For their efforts in support of the Oslo Agreements, the Nobel Prize was awarded to Prime Minister Yitzhak Rabin, PLO Chairman Yasser Arafat, and Israeli Foreign Minister Shimon Peres on October 14, 1994.

Israel–Jordan Peace Treaty

The talks with the PA created momentum for negotiations between Israel and Jordan. The talks between the two countries that had begun in Madrid in 1991 were followed by preliminary agreements in September 1993, and culminated in a peace treaty on October 26, 1994. The peace treaty, the second between an Arab state and Israel, ended forty-six years of hostility between the two nations and was signed near Akaba in the presence of US President Bill Clinton and the international media.

The treaty provided that Israel and Jordan would recognize and respect each other's sovereignty, territorial integrity, and political independence. The peace treaty also addressed a host of diverse issues: boundaries, water, police cooperation, the environment, border crossings, refugees, infrastructure, tourism, agriculture, and economic development, among others.

To supplement the treaty, the US committed substantial financial and military support to Jordan as it had to Egypt in 1982.

Israeli and Palestinian Responses to the Peace Process

Most Israelis supported the various efforts to make peace with the Arabs. Others, however, did not believe that the Palestinian leadership would ever accept a Jewish state. They felt that attempts to make peace with the Palestinians were naïve on the part of the government, that Arafat could never be trusted, and that giving away land to make peace only weakened Israel. The Israeli ambivalence about surrendering some or all of the disputed territories took a deadly turn when Yigal Amir, an Israeli religious extremist, assassinated Yitzhak Rabin on November 4, 1995.

Many Palestinians also responded unfavorably, in some cases violently, to the Oslo agreements. Hamas embarked on a campaign of violence and terror. Arafat himself began to send out worrying signals. Observers began to notice that his Arabic statements about the peace process often contradicted his reassuring English ones. Doubts arose about his real intentions and about the value of his official pledges. Israelis were understandably dismayed when, for example, speaking publicly to Arabs, Arafat dismissed the peace process as a temporary sacrifice that would ultimately lead to Israel's destruction and to the creation of a Palestinian state in the entire territory. An article in *Time* magazine noted how Arafat's duplicity undermined the peace process:

On the day the Oslo agreement was signed, Arafat could be heard on Jordanian radio pledging to take back all of Palestine. Soon after, during a speech at a South African Mosque [made May 10 in Johannesburg], he vowed to carry the Jihad to Jerusalem. And so the pattern continued, with one message broadcast to western media, a very different one to the Arab World. By repeatedly reinforcing the notion that compromise was not an option, the groundwork for peace was never established.[13]

Arafat's speech in South Africa basically restated the 1974 PLO strategy of "stages." According to this strategy, the war against Israel would be won not all at once but in phases. One stage would be the acquisition, through "peace" negotiations, of territory from which a military war could then be waged.

The Oslo II Accord

Despite Arafat's double dealing, the peace process went forward. Following the initial agreements, a further "Interim Agreement" of September 28, 1995, often referred to as the Oslo II Accord, subdivided the West Bank and the Gaza Strip into three areas (A, B, and C). The goal was to continue the process begun two years earlier with the Oslo Accords and the Gaza–Jericho Agreement.

Israel's obligations during this interim period included withdrawing in phases from major Arab areas in the West Bank and the Gaza Strip. To ease the transition of these areas from Israeli to Palestinian administration, the territory was divided up along the lines of Bailey's map:

- Area "A" transferred full civil and security control to the Palestinian Authority (PA). This area included Palestinian cities and their surrounding areas, with no Israeli settlements. Entry into this area was strictly forbidden to all Israeli citizens and is currently enforced by Israeli checkpoints and identified by a red sign. The IDF and Israeli police maintain no presence in these areas.
- Area "B" came under Palestinian civil control with joint Israeli–Palestinian security control. This area included Palestinian towns and villages, and areas with no Israeli settlements.
- Area "C" remained under full Israeli security control, but with Palestinians coming under Palestinian civil control and Israelis answering to Israeli civil authority. These areas included all Israeli settlements (cities, towns, and villages), the land in the vicinity of these settlements, most of the roadways connecting the settlements, as well as strategic areas described as security zones. Jerusalem and the Old City were part of Area C.

The agreement gave the Palestinians self-rule in Bethlehem, Hebron, Jenin, Nablus, Qalqilya, Ramallah, Tulkarm, and some 450 villages.

The division of the West Bank into Areas A, B, and C was supposed to expire in 1999, at the end of the interim period. It did not move forward, however. Israel felt that the Palestinians had not fulfilled certain of their obligations, including the following crucial ones: recognizing Israel's right to exist; amending the Palestinian National Charter accordingly; and promoting peace through changes to the education of their youth. The continuing existence of the West Bank's territorial divisions remains a source of contention with respect to land development for both

Israelis and Palestinians; Israel still maintains military control of the majority of the territory and determines the particulars of land development.[14]

The Peace Process 1996–1999

In January of 1996, the Palestinians held their first elections. Yasser Arafat was elected President of the PA. In April, just three months later, the PA voted on whether to remove from the PNC's 1968 Charter all provisions calling for Israel's destruction. This was a specific requirement of Oslo II. The vote passed, but the Charter was not amended. Why not? The likely reason, given Arafat's mixed messages in the wake of the earlier agreement, is that he and the Palestinian leadership never really intended to recognize Israel in writing. Recognition of Israel would have put Arafat in direct conflict with Hamas, the rival Palestinian party. Hamas has never acknowledged Israel's legitimacy and has vowed to fight until Israel is destroyed. Political necessity aside, there is no strong evidence that Arafat's ultimate ambitions concerning Israel ever differed much from those of Hamas.

In March 1996, Israelis again found themselves under attack when the Iranian- and Syrian-backed Hizbullah forces began firing Katyusha rockets from Lebanon into Israeli towns in the Galilee (northern Israel).

When Israelis went to the polls in May of that year, their choice for prime minister was Benjamin Netanyahu, who campaigned on a platform of offering no more concessions until the PA fulfilled its Oslo commitments. Israel thus rejected the more compromising stance of Shimon Peres's Labor party. Netanyahu went even further in the non-concessional direction by lifting the ban on settlement building that Rabin had imposed.

Between the renewal of Israeli settlement construction and Hamas's bomb attacks, there was little support on either side for renewing the peace process. After nearly two years of unsuccessful US attempts to restart negotiations, Netanyahu finally bowed to intense pressure from the Clinton administration to transfer more territory in Area "A" to the PA.

The Wye River Memorandum

In an effort to implement the 1995 "Interim Agreement," President Clinton organized a summit at the Wye River Plantation in Chesapeake Bay in October, 1998. It was attended by Prime Minister Netanyahu and Chairman Arafat. Clinton's key negotiators, Secretary of State Madeleine Albright and Dennis Ross, set out a new schedule for further withdrawal of the Israeli military presence from the West Bank. The Palestinians, for their part, were to amend their Charter, which they still had not done.

Making the concessions required for this agreement hurt Netanyahu politically. His government subsequently received a vote of no confidence in Israel. On the Palestinian side, Hamas stepped up its terrorist attacks in an effort to stall the peace process, and these efforts were successful. The PA took advantage of the stalled peace process to heighten their propaganda attack on Israel, thus violating Article

12 of the Oslo Accord—the pledge to foster mutual understanding and tolerance between Israelis and Palestinians.

The PA ignored other elements of the Oslo Accord that were intended to promote good will. They never got around to removing the PLO Charter provision calling for Israel's destruction. The agreement had also called on them to revise the anti-Semitic textbooks used by Palestinian youth, with a view to ending the cycle of sectarian hatred. But where Israel revised its history curriculum in an effort to incorporate the Palestinian point of view, the books issued by the PA contained the same old invectives against Israel and the Jewish people. Palestinian maps of the Middle East made no mention of Israel, which was labeled only as Palestine.

The Camp David Summit

Bill Clinton was eager to negotiate a final peace agreement between Israel and the Palestinians before the end of his presidency. He invited Prime Minister Ehud Barak and Palestinian Chairman Yasser Arafat to Camp David in July of 2000. Meetings in the president's Maryland retreat were held between July 11 and July 24.

At this summit, it was decided to address some of the final status issues, such as Jerusalem and final borders. Despite its official position that Jerusalem was to remain united and under Israeli sovereignty, the Israeli delegation indicated it might be willing to exclude certain sectors of eastern Jerusalem from Israeli sovereignty. President Clinton hoped this concession would lay the ground for negotiations over a new Palestinian state.

During the summit, President Clinton presented a proposal to Arafat and his delegation that would have given the Palestinians control of a continuous territory encompassing 91 percent of the West Bank and 100 percent of the Gaza Strip.[15] (The Palestinian numbers were different; according to their interpretation, the final proposal offered them only 83 percent of the West Bank.[16])

Arafat rejected the offer presented to him at Camp David and submitted no counterproposals. His rejection frustrated many people, including Arabs. Prince Bandar, the Saudi ambassador to the United States, was quoted as saying the following to Arafat: "I hope you remember, sir, what I told you. If we lose this opportunity, it is not going to be a tragedy. This is going to be a crime."[17]

The Al-Aqsa Intifada—2000-2004

Amid the tensions arising from the failed talks at Camp David, Ariel Sharon, then leader of the opposition in Israel, visited the Temple Mount on September 28, 2000, with a small group of Israelis and a large contingent of Israeli police. This visit triggered severe violence and riots throughout the West Bank, Gaza Strip, and within the Arab communities inside Israel. The Palestinians blamed the uprising, which is often referred to as the "Al-Aqsa Intifada," on Sharon's visit to the Temple Mount. The Israelis in turn blamed Arafat, saying that the intifada was planned long before the Temple Mount visit—a way of deflecting the negative attention he'd received on account of his performance at Camp David.

The Peace Process—2001-2004

Despite the escalating violence of the second intifada, peace initiatives continued for the next four years. Meetings and peace negotiations were held in January 2001, on the eve of the Israeli elections, in Taba on the Sinai Peninsula. The meetings between representatives of the Ehud Barak's Israeli government and key Palestinian negotiators ended without a final agreement. The two sides agreed, however, that the basis for the borders between Israel and the future state of Palestine would be UN Security Council Resolution 242. Resolution 242 required Israel to withdraw from the territories it had controlled since the 1967 war, leaving the Palestinians all of the West Bank and Gaza. As it turned out, this agreement concerning borders had no practical significance. After the Israeli elections, the new government, led by Ariel Sharon, declared that it would not support the concessions offered by Barak at the Taba meetings. And so Clinton's presidency ended without a final peace agreement.

The Taba negotiations were followed, in October 2002, by another attempt to solve the Israeli–Palestinian conflict—namely, the "Road Map" or Performance-Based Proposal. This came about through the initiatives of the United States, the European Union, Russia, and the UN (collectively referred to as the "Quartet"). It entailed a peace plan involving several phases and echoed the language of previous initiatives insofar as

- it was based on the principle of land for peace;
- territorial boundaries would be based on UN resolutions 242 and 338;
- it required of the PA full recognition of Israel;
- it granted Israelis the right to live in peace and security; and
- it required Israel to freeze settlement building in the West Bank.

Two years of unofficial negotiations followed the Quartets' efforts. Led by former Israeli minister Yossi Beilin and by a former minister of the PA, Yasser Abed Rabbo, both of whom were veterans of the 1993 Oslo negotiations , these talks resulted in a non-binding agreement called the Geneva Accord, on December 1, 2003.

This agreement stipulated that, in return for peace, Israel would withdraw from almost all of the West Bank and the Gaza Strip. Jerusalem would become a shared capital of Israel and the new Palestinian State, and the Old City would be partitioned, with Israel retaining sovereignty rights only over the Jewish Quarter and the Western Wall. To the government of Israel and to most Israelis, this was giving up too much for peace. They rejected the Geneva Accord.

Natan Sharansky, then the Israeli Minister for Jerusalem and Diaspora Affairs, published the following statement in *Haaretz* regarding the terms of the Geneva Accord:

It should be noted that if we totally relinquish every value for the sake of peace, we won't have peace either. Just as in the past, this time, too, the Palestinians will interpret such a relinquishing of what constitutes our very identity as a tremendous weakness that calls for war.

The values symbolized by Jerusalem are not only religious in nature. One doesn't have to be religious to understand that without our historical connection to Jerusalem, without the link to the past, without the feeling of continuity with the ancient kingdoms of Israel for whom the Temple Mount was the center of existence, we really are foreign invaders and colonialists in this country.

One doesn't have to be religious in order to understand that relinquishing the Temple Mount is a justification of the Palestinian argument: You have no right to exist in this country, you have no connection to it, get out of here. One doesn't have to be religious in order to understand that relinquishing the Temple Mount is not only relinquishing the past, it is primarily relinquishing the future. The future of all of us, here. ...

Without Jerusalem, Israel will become just another Jewish community, one of many in the world, like that of New York, London or Toronto—except more dangerous, less wealthy and less comfortable. It will not be the center of the Jewish world, not the focus of its existence—just one more community. And if that's the case, why continue to live in it? For what? In the name of what? [18]

The Security Barrier

The peace efforts continued, but so did the violence. The number of suicide bombings in Israel increased from four in 2000 to thirty-four in 2001, to a peak of fifty-five in 2002.[19] The attacks by militant wings of Fatah and Hamas claimed the lives of 305 men, women, and children, and left hundreds of others maimed or injured. In 2002, the Israeli government decided to build a security barrier to protect their citizens from the suicide bombings. The barrier became the focus of much negative international attention, though its success in preventing attacks was undeniable. As the construction of the security barrier progressed, the number of attacks and casualties dropped by approximately 50 percent each year until, in 2007, there was only one attack.

Because the barrier was successful in its practical aims, the majority of Israelis supported its construction. On the other hand, Israeli settlers and Palestinians living on the east side of the barrier were vehemently opposed to it; the barrier interfered with their freedom of movement and their access to services and land. The UN did not view the barrier as justified and asked the International Court of Justice (ICJ) to rule on its legality.

ICJ Verdict on the Wall

On December 8, 2003, the General Assembly of the UN passed Resolution ES-10/14. It described the UN members as

Gravely concerned at the commencement and continuation of construction by Israel, the occupying Power, of a wall in the Occupied Palestinian Territory, including in and around East Jerusalem, which is in departure from the Armistice Line of 1949 (Green Line).[20]

The resolution went on to request that the International Court of Justice (ICJ) render an urgent legal opinion on Israel's constructing the wall in "Occupied Palestinian Territory."

On July 9, 2004, the ICJ issued the following statement: "The Court finds that the construction by Israel of a wall in the Occupied Palestinian Territory and its associated régime are contrary to international law."[21] The ICJ held that the construction of the wall in occupied territories violated the rules and principles of the Law of Nations. The Court referred to Israel's illegal measures in Jerusalem, and it pointed out that the wall prevented the Palestinians from exercising their rights of self-determination, thus contravening Israel's obligations with regard to these rights.

The ICJ's opinion completely contradicts the earlier international decisions regarding rights to self-determination in Palestine. As we noted in Chapters 12, 13, and 15, there is no legal basis for referring to east Jerusalem and the Old City as "occupied territory." This phrase implies that these places fundamentally belong to the Palestinians.[22] The ICJ analysis contained no reference whatsoever to San Remo, to the Mandate for Palestine, or to the policies of the Balfour Declaration enshrined in the Mandate, which basically gave the political rights to the Jewish people. According to international lawyer Jacques Gauthier, the ICJ opinion, by failing to consider the earlier documents, "takes away the rights and entitlements acquired by the Jewish people over the last century."[23] Since the Mandate for Palestine essentially made Israel sovereign over the territory west of the Jordan river, the Israeli government would have the right to take measures—for example, the construction of a security barrier—to protect its civilian population, which included over 1 million Arabs as well as Jews.

Legal implications aside, the construction of the wall did not help an already ailing Palestinian economy.

The Palestinian Economy in the Early 21st Century

According to the World Bank, the economy of the disputed territories shrank by some 40 percent in the first five years of the new century. By 2004, the economy in Gaza was much worse off than that of the West Bank. This shrinkage occurred despite a massive influx of foreign aid—to the tune of $4 billion annually—to the PA.[24]

What went wrong? Measures taken by Yasser Arafat were largely responsible. According to Gilder, author of *The Israel Test*, when Arafat returned from his exile in Tunisia in July of 1994, he shifted the Palestinian economy from a growth dynamic, driven by entrepreneurs, to a model whereby foreign aid was delivered to the PLO. The Palestinian economy clearly suffered from these policies. Arafat himself, on the other hand, was making out nicely during these years. While per capita income among Palestinians in the disputed territories plummeted, Arafat's personal portfolio was reported to be close to $1 billion.[25] He died on November 11, 2004. Most Palestinians hail him as a hero, and he unquestionably put Palestinian identity and nationalism on the map. At the same time, he left behind a legacy of violence, corruption, and missed opportunities for peace. Mahmoud Abbas succeeded him as head of the PLO and president of the PA.

Gaza Disengagement 2005

With no end in sight to the problems posed by the Gaza Strip and Hamas, Prime Minister Sharon and Deputy Prime Minister Ehud Ohlmert publicly floated the idea of a withdrawal from Gaza. The plan called for the dismantling of all 21 Jewish settlements in Gaza and the removal of their 8,000 plus settlers, and the dismantling of four small settlements in the West Bank.

Sharon's disengagement plan shocked many in Israel and was met with fierce opposition from settlers and from government officials, including some from Sharon's own party. Nonetheless, on February 20, 2005, the Israeli cabinet voted in favor of the withdrawal from Gaza and from the four West Bank settlements.

At midnight on August 14, Gaza was sealed off, and the settlers who had not already left were given 48 hours to leave voluntarily, after which they would be forcibly removed. There were some minor incidents, but the withdrawal was carried out peacefully, and the last of the settlements was evacuated on Monday, August 22, 2005.

The majority of Israelis had supported the Gaza withdrawal, hoping that this concession would be a major stepping-stone to both peace and a two-state solution. Instead, Israeli cities and towns have endured a bombardment of rocket attacks since this event. Hamas and Iranian-backed terrorist groups in Gaza have fired nearly 12,000 rockets towards Israel in the past decade, the majority of them launched since Israel's withdrawal from Gaza.

The 2006 Lebanon War

While absorbing these attacks from Gaza in the west, Israel also had to address hostilities on its northern border. On July 12, 2006, Hizbullah terrorists crossed the border from Lebanon into Israel and attacked a group of Israeli soldiers patrolling the border, killing eight and kidnapping two others. After Israel responded with air strikes aimed at Hizbullah positions inside Lebanon, Hizbullah unleashed a barrage of Katyusha rockets, targeting civilian population centers in certain of Israel's northern cities, including Kiryat Shmona, Haifa, and Safed. They fired more than 100 rockets daily—nearly 4,000 rockets in total—at Israel during this conflict, which lasted close to five weeks.

In retaliation, Israel sought to disable the infrastructure through which Iran and Syria supplied weapons to Hizbullah—for example, by bombing Beirut's airport and certain roads and bridges. Israel also launched a ground offensive aimed at expelling as many Hizbullah terrorists as possible from southern Lebanon. Hizbullah had occupied southern Lebanon since Israel's withdrawal in 2000 and had attacked Israel more than 20 times with cross-border raids and rockets. These terrorists were elusive targets, and unscrupulous in their methods. They dwelt among civilians, held meetings and stored their weapons in civilian houses, and—in direct violation of international humanitarian law—fired rockets into Israel from civilian neighborhoods.

Sacrificing the element of surprise in order to spare innocent lives, Israel, in advance of strikes in civilian areas, dropped fliers and sent radio messages warning civilians to leave. Despite these efforts, the strikes against Hizbullah terrorists led to the temporary displacement of 800,000 Lebanese civilians and to the deaths of an estimated 1,000 non-Israeli combatants and non-combatants.

The conflict subsided with the adoption of UN Security Council Resolution 1701 on August 11, 2006. It called for a full cessation of the hostilities, for the withdrawal of Israeli forces from Lebanon, and for the "unconditional release of the abducted Israeli soldiers, that have given rise to the current crisis." Hizbullah released the corpses of the two kidnapped soldiers—Ehud Goldwasser and Eldad Regev—to Israel in July 2008, two years after their abduction, as part of a prisoner exchange. Until that time, Hizbullah had refused to provide information as to their fate.

The years 1987–2007 saw peace initiatives between Israel and the Palestinians begin with optimism but conclude with pessimism. Most observers were left wondering where Israel and the Palestinians could go from there.

Endnotes

1   For statistics concerning deaths and injuries caused by the intifada, see Martin Gilbert, *The Routledge Atlas of the Arab-Israeli Conflict*, 9th ed. (London: Routledge, 2008), 130.

2   Hamas Covenant 1988, The Avalon Project, Yale Law School, http://avalon.law.yale.edu/20th_century/hamas.asp.

3   Yasser Arafat, "Speech to the UN General Assembly," (Geneva, December 13, 1988), MidEast Web, accessed June 26, 2012, http://www.mideastweb.org/arafat1988.htm.

4   Jacques Paul Gauthier, *Sovereignty Over the Old City of Jerusalem: A Study of the Historical, Religious, Political and Legal Aspects of the Question of the Old City*, Thèse No. 725 (Geneva: Université de Genève, 2007), 731.

5   Hazem Jamjoum, "Interview: Jordan revoking citizenship from Palestinian refugees," The Electronic Intifada, February 27, 2011, accessed June 28, 2012, http://electronicintifada.net/content/interview-jordan-revoking-citizenship-palestinian-refugees/9241.

6   Gilbert, *Atlas of the Arab-Israeli Conflict*, 133-134.

7   Ibid, 132.

8   Ibid, 145.

9   Israel Ministry of Foreign Affairs, "Israel-Palestinian Negotiations," 2012, accessed June 28, 2012, http://www.mfa.gov.il/MFA/Peace+Process/Guide+to+the+Peace+Process/Israel-Palestinian+Negotiations.htm?DisplayMode=print,.

10   Israel Ministry of Foreign Affairs, "Declaration of Principles on Interim Self-Government Arrangements, 13 September 1993," accessed June 28, 2012, http://www.mfa.gov.il/MFA/Peace+Process/Guide+to+the+Peace+Process/Declaration+of+Principles.htm?DisplayMode=print.

11   Ibid.

12   Israel Ministry of Foreign Affairs, "Agreement on Gaza Strip and Jericho Area, 4 May 1994," http://www.mfa.gov.il/MFA/Peace+Process/Guide+to+the+Peace+Process/Agreement+on+Gaza+Strip+and+Jericho+Area.htm?DisplayMode=print.

13   Robert Isler, "Arafat's Strategy of Hate," *Time*, March 20, 2001, http://www.time.com/time/world/article/0,8599,103236,00.html.

14   Amira Hass, "UN: Much of West Bank closed to Palestinian building," *Haartez.com*, Dec. 16, 2009 http://www.haaretz.com/misc/article-print-page/un-much-of-west-bank-closed-to-palestinian-building-1.2053?trailingPath=2.169%2C2.225%2C2.226%2C.

15   Dennis Ross, "Map Reflecting Actual Proposal at Camp David," *The Missing Peace* (New York: Farrar, Strauss and Giroux, 2004), xvii.

16   Ibid.

17   Elsa Walsh, "The Prince," *The New Yorker*, March 24, 2003, 58.

18   Natan Sharansky, "Temple Mount is more important than peace," *Haaretz.com*, October 16, 2003, accessed July 1, 2012, http://www.haaretz.com/misc/article-print-page/temple-mount-is-more-important-than-peace-1.102869?trailingPath=2.169%2C2.225%2C2.227%2C.

19   Israel Ministry of Foreign Affairs, "Suicide and Other Bombing Attacks in Israel Since the Declaration of Principles (Sept 1993)," accessed July 1, 2012, http://www.mfa.gov.il/MFA/Terrorism-+Obstacle+to+Peace/Palestinian+terror+since+2000/Suicide+and+Other+Bombing+Attacks+in+Israel+Since.htm?DisplayMode=print.

20   UN General Assembly, Resolution ES-10/14, "Illegal Israeli actions in Occupied East Jerusalem and the rest of the Occupied Palestinian Territory," December 12, 2003, http://domino.un.org/UNISPAL.NSF/a06f2943c226015c85256c40005d359c/f953b744269b9b7485256e1500776dca.

21   International Court of Justice, "Legal Consequences of the Construction of a Wall in the Occupied Palestinian Territory," Press Release 2004/28, July 9, 2004, http://www.icj-cij.org/docket/index.php ?pr=71&code=mwp&p1=3&p2=4&p3=6&ca.

22   Ibid, 782.

23   Gauthier, *Sovereignty Over the Old City*, 781.

24   George Gilder, *The Israel Test* (USA: Richard Vigilante Books, 2009), 54.

25   Tricia McDermott, "Arafat's Billions," 60 Minutes, February 11, 2009, accessed July 1, 2012, http://www.cbsnews.com/2100-18560_162-582487.html.

Chapter 17

Contemporary Challenges Facing Israel—Security

Introduction

This chapter looks at security-related problems that Israel has faced during the last decade, and at some of the larger ethical questions these problems raise. The first of these problems is a domestic one, related to military conscription. The next relates to the construction of the barrier wall and to the use of checkpoints. This issue raises a larger philosophical question about how to balance collective and individual rights. Another problem concerns Israel's recent wars against non-state actors—in Lebanon, in 2006; and in Gaza, in 2008. These conflicts have raised questions about when war is justified and how to conduct it, and how the principles of "just war" apply to asymmetrical conflicts. Another security issue for Israel relates to the US and its efforts to bring peace to the Middle East. These efforts have increasingly called on Israel to make concessions that would, as we shall see, render the country's borders indefensible and compromise its basic security.

Military Service

Few Israelis want to go to war. But all young Jewish men and women, at the age of 16 and a half, receive their first army call-up notice. Then comes an 18-month process that culminates in their being drafted into the IDF at age 18, men for three years and women for two. Men also do reserve duty into their 40s.

The ultra-Orthodox youth from the religious (*haredi*) sector also receive a call-up notice at this point. Historically, however, instead of being inducted into Israel's defence forces, these youths have brought a letter from the seminary where they study, and on the strength of this have been given an automatic exemption until the age of 22. During that five-year period, they have not been allowed to work, but have had to study full-time. By the time they reach the age of 22, the army has usually chosen not to enlist them. A total of 54,000 ultra-Orthodox youth received army exemptions this year alone.[1]

As of August 1, 2012, however, there are no longer legal exemptions for the haredi youth. The Tal law, which governed the exemption process, officially expired this year, and the Israeli Supreme Court ordered last February that this law not be renewed. Barring the introduction of new laws, the military service law of 1986 is in effect, so anyone turning 18 is drafted into the army. Defence Minister Ehud Barak ordered the army to prepare to draft the ultra-Orthodox. Most Israeli experts say they do not expect to see this order enforced.

The ultra-Orthodox represent 10 to 12 percent of the Israeli population and (because of very high birth rates) more than 20 percent of the children in primary school.

The ultra-Orthodox have stayed away from the army for several reasons:

■ the strict separation of men and women is one of their beliefs;
■ they believe the army fails to meet their very strict standards of Jewish dietary laws; and
■ they believe that the best way to serve G-d is through their full-time study.[2]

Drafting the ultra-Orthodox has become a significant issue among Israelis. Many ultra-Orthodox say that they would rather go to jail than serve in the army. Rabbis in the haredi community are threatening to tell their followers to ignore the call-up orders. Many Israelis have come to resent the reluctance of most of the religious community to serve. The view of the ultra-Orthodox Jews is in stark contrast to the Druze—an Islamic religious sect living primarily in northern Israel—whose religion requires that they serve in the military to defend the country in which they live.

One of the duties that Israeli soldiers perform is to patrol the security barriers and checkpoints that separate Israel from the disputed territories.

Security Barrier and Checkpoints

One measure for which the international community has roundly condemned Israel is the construction of a security barrier. Started in 2002, it separates the population in the West Bank—Jewish and Arab communities—from the rest of Israel. In order to move from one side of the barrier to the other, and to move between regions on the west side of it—that is, within the West Bank—Israelis and Palestinians must cross through inspection points known as *checkpoints*. A checkpoint is a barrier or manned entrance where travelers are subject to security checks. In the West Bank, these are manned by the Israeli Military Police, the Israel Border Police, or other soldiers whose aim is the security of Israeli settlements and Israeli citizens (Arab/Muslim, Christian, and Jew). Human rights organizations and the world media have condemned these checkpoints for the hardship they have caused the Palestinian population. Do the checkpoints place too much emphasis on Israel's collective rights and too little on the individual rights of the Palestinians?

Human Rights

Relative or Universal?

The UN Universal Declaration of Human Rights is among the world's most important human rights documents. Many people acknowledge the rationale behind a *universal* declaration of human rights, but there are differences of opinion in this regard. These differences often lead to spirited debate.

One of the debates concerns whether human rights are a relative or a universal concept. We touched on this issue in Chapter 5 when we discussed the world view of ethical monotheism in relation to that of secular humanism. The former would argue that basic human rights are universal, applicable to all people. The relativists charge that the UN notion of human rights is an imposed Western one and that civilizations, societies, peoples, and groups have different conceptions of human rights, all equally valid.

Which side do you come down on? Imagine, for example, that you were a governor in the British Imperial Government in India in the 19th century, with complete control over your jurisdiction. One of your aides informs you that the Hindus in your area are about to engage in suttee—the practice of burning a widow with her husband's corpse. This is a conventional Indian practice, consistent with the local conception of human rights.

Would you stop it?

Your answer will depend on whether you think human rights are universal or relative. In other words, is there an objective code of morality and human rights that supersedes that of the individual or culture?

Collective versus Individual Rights

A second human-rights debate concerns whether priority should be given to the rights of the individual or to the rights of collective society. Consider, for example, the following true story. When a murderer escaped from a North American prison in September of 2007, officials refused to release his photograph, citing departmental privacy policy. The 39-year-old inmate was serving a life sentence for second-degree murder and was considered violent. But prison officials maintained that, under the institution's privacy rules, they could not release a photo of the convict unless he gave permission and signed a release form. Even though he broke out of jail, he still had a right to privacy as an inmate.[3]

Most people believe that when someone commits a criminal act or is a threat to society, the rights of society should take priority over the rights of the individual. Israel's policies in regards to collective and individual rights have come under the scrutiny of human rights organizations and the world media over the years.

Checkpoints and Human Rights

Israel maintains that checkpoints are a necessary and effective measure for protecting Israeli citizens' basic right to life, liberty, and security of person as described in Article 3 of the UN Universal Declaration of Human Rights. The Palestinian position is that the checkpoints humiliate and oppress them and therefore violate their basic right not to be subjected to "cruel, inhuman or degrading treatment" or be inhibited in their "right to freedom of movement" within the borders of the country where they live—as set out in Articles 5 and 13 of the UN document.

Checkpoints in the Mass Media

Filmmaker Yoav Shamir produced a documentary movie in 2003 called *Checkpoint*.[4] It shows the day-to-day tribulations that Palestinians face as a result of the checkpoints, and it portrays numerous troubling situations, including the following:

- a school bus filled with children trying to get to school,
- an ambulance filled with patients trying to get to a hospital (including a two-year-old in need of cancer treatment),
- a family trying to visit relatives who have been recently bereaved,
- a young woman trying to get to university,
- a man trying to deliver a package to his bride for their wedding the next day,
- a truck driver who is trying to return home after making a delivery.

Shamir described his movie as "my part in the struggle against the injustices of occupation."[5] The harsh reality shown in Shamir's film is unquestionably part of day-to-day life for many Palestinians. But is his presentation biased?

Media bias is the bias of journalists, news producers, or others in the mass media in their selection of events and stories and in how they are reported or covered. It implies a prejudice in favor of or against a particular person or group.

To determine whether Shamir's portrayal is biased, one must ask whether checkpoints are, as the film suggests, simply an unjust Israeli initiative to oppress and harass the Palestinians. Or is there information missing from Shamir's presentation? One way to test the perspective of Shamir's film is to consider what soldiers at checkpoints actually have to face.

Checkpoint Realities

Consider the following scenario[6]:

A young woman who lives in the West Bank arrives at an Israeli army checkpoint terminal where thousands of Palestinians pass into Israel each day. As she passes through the magnetic gate, the alarm goes off. The soldiers at the gate have instructions to do one of two things:

1. Not allow her to go through the gate, or
2. Take any precautionary measures necessary (including the use of firearms) in the event that they suspect this person is a suicide bomber.

The woman at the magnetic gate starts crying, saying that she needs to get to the hospital urgently for treatment. She explains that the metal-detector alarm went off because she has metal plates in her leg.

In the past months, a number of women have attempted suicide bombings. If you were the one who had to make a decision, what action would you take?

Here are your options:

1. Send her away—and prevent her from receiving the treatment she claims she needs—and, by doing so, eliminate the possibility that she can activate a bomb in Israel.
2. Accept her explanation, and ask her to accompany a female soldier to a special room where it can be determined that she isn't carrying explosives.

Consider also that, as the person in charge, you are under instructions to make life easier for the Palestinians who need to pass through the checkpoint. This especially applies to a person who needs urgent medical attention.

You decide to let her through. A female soldier accompanies her to a private room to be searched. The Palestinian woman then falls over and, as people rush to help her up, she activates explosives on her body, murdering those in her immediate vicinity and wounding several others.

How would this event affect your policy at the checkpoint the next morning? Would you deny entry to the thousands of Palestinians going to work in Israel to provide for their families? Would you deny entry to any Palestinian claiming that he or she needs medical attention? Or would you simply put this incident behind you and carry on risking your life?

Shamir's film, with its emphasis on Palestinian hardship, never touches on the terror attacks that created the need for checkpoints in the first place. Shamir never mentions the intelligence-based warnings that have led to checkpoint closures, and he never reveals the effectiveness of the checkpoints in preventing terror attacks. The film never explains that checkpoints are intended to prevent those who wish to do harm from crossing into vulnerable areas. Now let's consider two real-life situations.

Case 1–Hussam Abdo

In March 2004, major news stations broadcast an unforgettable image. Fifteen year-old Hussam Abdo was standing alone at a checkpoint, explosives strapped to his chest, confused, trying to follow Israeli instructions on how to dismantle his bomb. A few months later, James Reynolds, a BBC Jerusalem correspondent, interviewed Abdo from an Israeli prison.

Reynolds asked Abdo why he chose to become a suicide bomber. "Some teenagers want to be footballers, others want to be singers. You wanted to be a suicide bomber. Why?" Abdo said, "It's not suicide—it's martyrdom. I would become a martyr and go to my God. It's better than being a singer or a footballer. It's better than everything."[7]

Reynolds said, "When you put on that belt, did you really know as a 15-year-old that you were going to go and murder people, that you were going to go and cause great suffering to mothers and fathers, that you were going to be a mass murderer? Did you really know that?"

Abdo replied, "Yes. Just like they came and caused our parents sadness and suffering they too should feel this. Just like we feel this—they should also feel it."[8]

How did Abdo become a suicide bomber? He provided the following account:

> I was sitting with a friend of mine and he comes to me and says can you find me a martyr bomber? Then I told him I'll do it. My friend says—really? And I answer—yes, I'll do it. So he agreed and he took me to see another guy. The guy's name was Wael. He was from Al Aqsa Martyrs' Brigades. He was 21.[9]

In the interview, Abdo came across as a regular teenager. He also seemed to harbor no real animosity toward the Israelis who, he said, had caused his people's suffering and thereby made him decide to become a suicide bomber. He said that the soldiers who took him into custody "were nice to me—they treated me well."[10]

Case 2—Wafa al-Biss

On June 20, 2005, twenty-one-year-old Wafa al-Biss, who had a permit to enter Israel for medical treatment, attempted to smuggle an explosives belt through the Erez crossing (Gaza—Israel border). She had a permit to enter Israel for medical treatment. She was intending to carry out a suicide bombing.

The previous year, in 2004, al-Biss had suffered severe and life-threatening burns in a kitchen fire accident in her parents' home. Afterwards she was admitted to the Soroka Medical Center in Beersheva (Israel), where she underwent a series of successful treatments for her massive burns. The doctors at the Soroka hospital saved her life, and she developed a good relationship with the whole medical team.

During an interview in 2007, while in prison for the bombing attempt, she said that the Israelis at Soroka, where she had spent three months undergoing treatment for her burns, treated her with "respect and dignity. ... They had been very kind."[11] Her family was so appreciative that they wrote a letter of thanks and commendation to the doctors saying "the care was wonderful and warm."[12]

In between treatments, she returned to Gaza with a medical pass, so she could return to Soroka hospital for any necessary follow-up treatments. The pass allowed her to enter Israel via the Erez crossing point.

Her homecoming might have meant a return to normal life for Wafa, but her fiancé rejected her because of her scars. She went into a severe depression and told her parents she was contemplating suicide. Word of her emotional state reached the Fatah recruiters of suicide bombers in the Gaza Strip. Later, under interrogation after her arrest, al-Biss gave an account of the tactics used by her terrorist recruiter, a man called Abul Khair, from the Al-Aqsa Martyrs Brigade. "Abul Khair kept calling," she said. "He told me a guy they were counting on had backed out of an operation; they needed me. 'Look at your future,' they told me. 'No one will ever marry you.'"[13]

They urged her to become a suicide bomber so that she could die with honor, as opposed to merely committing suicide and thus dying with shame. Since she wanted to commit suicide, they argued, she might as well do it in a way that would bring glory to herself and her whole family.

On June 20, 2005, al-Biss entered the Erez crossing, ostensibly on her way to Soroka hospital for further treatment. But this time she hid an explosives belt in her underclothes. Her aim was to carry out a suicide bombing at the hospital. Her heavy clothing aroused suspicion at the crossing, however, and she was stopped and searched. When the explosive belt was revealed, she attempted to detonate it. The detonator failed to function. An NBC video clip captured the incident.[14]

Under questioning, al-Biss revealed the details of the suicide bombing plan and its ultimate target—a crowded portion of the Soroka hospital. Had it succeeded, al-Biss would likely have killed the doctors and nurses who saved her life, other Gazan Arab patients, and the Israeli Arab Muslims working at the hospital who had made her stay there so comfortable.

Her story doesn't end there. Wafa al-Biss was one of the 1,027 Arab prisoners released in October 2011 in exchange for Gilad Shalit, the kidnapped Israeli soldier. After six years of imprisonment, she returned home to Gaza, where she now hosts grade school children at her home, and urges them to "walk the same path we took and God willing, we will see some of you as martyrs." The children respond with cheers and, waving Palestinian flags, they chant the following: "We will give our souls and our blood to redeem the prisoners. We will give our souls and our blood for you, oh Palestine."[15]

In other words, al-Biss is now a recruiter for the Palestinian terrorists, enticing impressionable young children into the ranks of suicide bombers.

The mass media and human rights organizations often condemn Israel for the conditions imposed on the Palestinians, citing the checkpoints and the barrier wall as glaring examples of oppression. As the above case studies show, these security measures need to be seen in context. Only then can we address the relevant ethical questions concerning collective and individual rights.

War—Is It Just?

In addition to patrolling checkpoints and security barriers, IDF soldiers—many of whom are teenagers—also have to go to war. As we have discussed, Israel has been involved in several wars with its Arab neighbors since its declaration of independence in 1948. Is war ever justified? Some people hold that war can never be a morally acceptable response to a situation. Others hold that, under certain conditions, going to war is morally justifiable, but only if it is entered into for the right reasons and conducted in the right way.

Armed conflicts are not unique to Israel, of course. In recent decades, the United States has been in armed conflicts in Somalia, Iraq, and Afghanistan. The Russians have gone to war in Chechnya, the Georgians in South Ossetia.

Israel's most recent conflicts have been in Lebanon, in 2006, and in Gaza, in 2008–2009. These conflicts differed from traditional wars insofar as they were not between two states; Israel was fighting non-state actors and so the Geneva Conventions, which establish the standards for the protection of civilians in and around a war zone, did not automatically apply to them.

What happens when a state is embattled with a non-state actor—a terrorist organization, a militia, or an organized armed band—that embeds itself within the civilian population? What happens when the non-state fighters dress as civilians, hide their weapons and equipment in civilian houses and places of worship, launch rockets from school areas, and deliberately fight from within the civilian population? What is the state to do when the other side's fighters, every time they are attacked, seek protection by surrounding themselves with civilians (who voluntarily or under duress participate in these actions)?[16] This is what Israel has been facing.

Just-war doctrine holds that war is justifiable under certain conditions and if carried out according to certain protocols. How does this doctrine apply to modern armed conflicts between state and non-state actors—conflicts sometimes called *asymmetrical wars*—such as Israel's war in Gaza in 2008-2009?

Just-War Doctrine

Advocates of just-war doctrine hold that war is justifiable under certain conditions but that there are or should be limits on the violence used to fight a war. The doctrine is concerned with two kinds of justice related to war:

- *jus ad bellum* (the justness of engaging in a war), and
- *jus in bello* (the justness of the manner in which a war is fought).

Jus ad bellum involves a set of criteria for determining when it is lawful and moral to enter a war. In everyday society, we take action to prevent aggression; internationally as well, states act to stop or prevent aggression from other states. Some argue that only wars fought in self-defence, against aggression, are just. From this basic principle come criteria by which advocates of just-war doctrine measure the justness of a war. A just war must

- be a war of last resort, with all other means of resolution explored;
- be authorized by a legitimate authority, either the state or an international organization;
- be waged for a just cause, not for aggression or a desire for vengeance;
- have a good chance of successfully achieving a desirable outcome (wars fought for good causes that are ultimately hopeless are not justifiable); and
- end in a peace that is preferable to the situation that existed before the outbreak of war.[17]

The other set of criteria involved in just-war doctrine concern the manner in which a war is fought—in other words, how it is conducted. The notion of *jus in bello* comprises two principles:

1. A just war must be fought in a manner consistent with the principle of *proportionality*. This means that the positive effects of a military action (of an airstrike, for example) must outweigh its negative consequences (destruction

and death). The method and level of violence deployed to fulfill the aims of the mission must pose the lowest possible risk to the civilian population and must take into account the military value of the target.

2. A just war must *discriminate* between combatants and noncombatants; the two must be treated differently. Civilians cannot be the intentional targets of military operations, and civilian casualties, often called *collateral damage*, must be minimized so far as possible.

In short, just-war theory argues that rules of behavior should and generally do govern the conduct of a war. Few wars ever follow all of the rules, and so debates about the justness of a particular war generally revolve around the degree to which certain principles have been adhered to or violated.

The Gaza War—Just or Unjust?

The Gaza War, also known as Operation Cast Lead, was a three-week armed conflict in the Gaza Strip between Israeli forces and Hamas fighters. Hamas is the Palestinian Islamic fundamentalist movement that became the governing political party of Gaza in 2007. The war began with Israeli air strikes on December 27, 2008. The Israeli ground invasion began on January 3. The war ended on January 18. Israel declared a unilateral ceasefire and Hamas did the same twelve hours later. Israel completed the withdrawal of its armed forces on January 21.

The media and various human rights organizations scrutinized Israel and the pro-Palestinian factions. Each side accused the other of violating international humanitarian law.

Was the Gaza War a just one? Let's consider it in light of the criteria set out above.

1. *Last resort.* In the eight years before the war, Israel's civilian population was the target of thousands of rocket and mortar attacks by Hamas. Israel repeatedly dispatched letters to the Secretary General of the UN and the president of the Security Council, drawing attention to Hamas's attacks. The country also made numerous attempts to work through third parties to stop the attacks, exhausting diplomatic channels. Israel also joined members of the international community in instituting economic sanctions against Hamas. None of these measures worked. Hamas continued to bomb.

2. *Legitimate authority.* All states have the inherent right, as well as the obligation, to defend themselves against armed attacks. Israel, as a recognized state, is legally justified and obliged to use force against Hamas to defend its civilians. Gaza is not a recognized state and had no official international sanction for its aggression.

3. *Just cause.* For eight years before the war, Hamas had been using the Gaza Strip to launch terrorist attacks on Israeli civilians, and these attacks had been increasing in intensity and geographical range. Tens of thousands of civilians in Israeli towns and villages within rocket range of Gaza were living in terror of rocket fire. They had suffered casualties, destruction, and emotional trauma. Hamas's military build-up made it urgent that Israel stop the attacks and impair its enemy's military ability. Hamas argued that Israel's blockade was causing

a humanitarian crisis by restricting basic supplies and humanitarian aid from entering Gaza. The parties had the following objectives in their respective acts of aggression:

Israel's objectives were as follows:

a. To stop the bombardment of Israeli civilians by destroying Hamas's mortar and rocket-launching apparatus and infrastructure.

b. To reduce the ability of Hamas and other terrorist organizations in Gaza to perpetrate future attacks against the civilian population in Israel.

Hamas's objectives were as follows:

a. To end Israel's naval and military blockade of Gaza.

b. To frustrate all attempts at peace and to liberate *all* of Palestine (including land under the sovereignty of the State of Israel) through jihad. (See the Hamas Covenant Articles 6 and 13.)

4. *Desirable outcome.* Prior to the conflict, the IDF had the reasonable assumption it could stop or reduce Hamas's rocket attacks. Hamas's aggression, on the other hand, was less justifiable in this regard. It had no reason to believe that its rocket attacks would end an Israeli blockade that was, in the first place, a response to the rocket attacks.

5. *Greater peace.* According to the Israel Security Agency's annual report, Palestinians launched 150 rocket and 215 mortar attacks on Israel in 2010—a significant decrease from 2009, when there were 569 rocket and 289 mortar attacks.[18] Over the course of 2011, 680 rockets, mortars and Grad missiles were fired from the Gaza Strip into Israel.[19] Clearly the war effort, though effective in the short term, did not bring long-term benefits.

6. *Proportionate.* After the conflict, the IDF formally released figures detailing Palestinian casualties incurred during Operation Cast Lead. It was addressing allegations concerning civilian deaths, leveled against Israel in the international community. Of the 1,166 Palestinians who died, Israel identified 709 as Hamas terror operatives. According to the IDF, 162 Palestinian men killed during the operation did not belong to any organization. Israel also reported that a total of 295 Palestinian non-combatants died during the operation. Of these people, 89 of them were under the age of 16, and 49 of them were women.[20] Hamas's Interior Minister Fathi Hamad later confirmed significant personnel losses in Hamas' military wings. He said, "On the first day of the war, Israel targeted police stations and 250 martyrs who were part of Hamas and the various factions fell." He added that "about 200 to 300 were killed from the Qassam Brigades, as well as 150 security personnel." Hamad's figures were in line with the IDF's numbers.[21]

7. *Discriminate.* During and after the war, Hamas accused Israel of intentionally targeting and killing civilians. Numerous media outlets and human rights organizations supported this accusation, charging Israel with "indiscriminate" use of force. They claimed the IDF had attacked densely populated civilian areas, schools, and non-military buildings. After the war, the UN produced the

Goldstone Report. This was a scathing document, based on testimony from Palestinians in Gaza, that supported Hamas's claims. The IDF criticized the report for bias and insisted that its armed forces took "extensive measures" to avoid striking noncombatants. These measures included the following:

a. issuing warnings via leaflets,

b. broadcasting warnings in Palestinian media outlets, and

c. placing phone calls to homes in the conflict zone, warning the occupants to leave the area.

Given the above information, would you say that Israel's war in Gaza meets the criteria of a just war?

Judge Richard Goldstone, who was commissioned by the UN to issue a report, did not think so. Goldstone charged Israel with numerous human rights abuses in his 500-plus page report, and his conclusions led to allegations of war crimes.

In the wake of the Goldstone Report, Colonel Richard Kemp, a highly respected British soldier and writer, carefully examined the evidence concerning Gaza and then delivered the following testimony to the United Nations:

I am the former commander of the British forces in Afghanistan. I served with NATO and the United Nations; commanded troops in Northern Ireland, Bosnia and Macedonia; and participated in the Gulf War. I spent considerable time in Iraq since the 2003 invasion, and worked on international terrorism for the UK Government's Joint Intelligence Committee.

Mr. President, based on my knowledge and experience, I can say this: During Operation Cast Lead, the Israeli Defence Forces did more to safeguard the rights of civilians in a combat zone than any other army in the history of warfare.

Israel did so while facing an enemy that deliberately positioned its military capability behind the human shield of the civilian population.

Hamas, like Hizbullah, are expert at driving the media agenda. Both will always have people ready to give interviews condemning Israeli forces for war crimes. They are adept at staging and distorting incidents.

The IDF faces a challenge that we British do not have to face to the same extent. It is the automatic, Pavlovian presumption by many in the international media, and international human rights groups, that the IDF are in the wrong, that they are abusing human rights.

The truth is that the IDF took extraordinary measures to give Gaza civilians notice of targeted areas, dropping over 2 million leaflets, and making over 100,000 phone calls. Many missions that could have taken out Hamas military capability were aborted to prevent civilian casualties. During the conflict, the IDF allowed huge amounts of humanitarian aid into Gaza. To deliver aid virtually into your enemy's hands is, to the military tactician, normally quite unthinkable. But the IDF took on those risks.

Despite all of this, of course innocent civilians were killed. War is chaos and full of mistakes. There have been mistakes by the British, American and other forces in Afghanistan and in Iraq, many of which can be put down to human error. But mistakes are not war crimes.

More than anything, the civilian casualties were a consequence of Hamas' way of fighting. Hamas deliberately tried to sacrifice their own civilians.

Mr. President, Israel had no choice apart from defending its people, to stop Hamas from attacking them with rockets.

And I say this again: the IDF did more to safeguard the rights of civilians in a combat zone than any other army in the history of warfare.[22]

In January 2010, the Israeli government released a response criticizing the Goldstone Report and disputing its findings. In 2011, Judge Goldstone recanted his earlier judgment. He wrote that he no longer believed that Israel intentionally targeted civilians in Gaza.

United States Foreign Policy and Israel's Security

Israel has forged a strong relationship with the United States over the past six decades. The US supported Israel as its only democratic partner in the Middle East during the Cold War years, and Israel has received significant US support—financial, military, and political. But the US has also pressured Israel intensely to make peace with its Arab neighbors through concessions. The Obama presidency has been the most aggressive to date in this regard. A few months after being elected, Obama traveled to Cairo, Egypt, where, in a 2009 speech, he outlined his administration's Middle East foreign policy. Obama made the following observations:

- The Palestinians endure daily humiliations under Israeli occupation.
- The only resolution is a two-state solution.
- The United States does not accept the legitimacy of continued Israeli settlements.

Two years later, on May 19, 2011, President Obama delivered a major address at the State Department. In that speech, President Obama shocked Israelis with the following assertion, which publicly asked more of Israel, in the way of concessions, than any president ever had before:

The United States believes that negotiations should result in two states, with permanent Palestinian borders with Israel, Jordan, and Egypt, and permanent Israeli borders with Palestine. The *borders of Israel and Palestine should be based on the 1967 lines* with mutually agreed swaps, so that secure and recognized borders are established for both states. The Palestinian people must have the right to govern themselves, and reach their potential, in a sovereign and contiguous state.[23] (emphasis added)

Obama's speech concluded by suggesting that Israel's only option for peace with the Palestinians was a two-state solution established along the pre-1967 lines (that is, according to the 1949 Armistice Agreement between Israel and Jordan—the "Green Line").

Obama was the first US president to explicitly refer to 1967 as the determiner of borders for a Palestinian state and to connect that to Resolution 242, which had required Israel to withdraw from territories it gained from the 1967 war.

Prior US administrations had emphasized that territorial concessions would be conditional on the second provision of Resolution 242, which acknowledged Israel's right to "secure boundaries," meaning defensible borders.

Obama's speech also stated the following: that Israel's "occupation" was an obstacle to its being considered a democracy, that the status of Jerusalem and the Palestinian refugees must be resolved, and that peace depended on Israel's aligning itself with US demands.

Is Obama's vision viable? Is the way to peace really a two-state solution along the lines of the pre-1967 borders, with Jerusalem as a shared capital, and with Palestinian refugees having a right of return? Is Israel's presence in the disputed territories inconsistent with democracy?

On May 24, 2011, Prime Minister Netanyahu was invited to speak to the US Congress. In his speech Netanyahu directly addressed Obama's statements about occupation, Israeli democracy, the two-state solution, the borders of a future Palestinian state, dividing Jerusalem, settlements, and the future status of Palestinian refugees. The following are some excerpts from the speech:

> In Judea and Samaria, the Jewish people are not foreign occupiers. We are not the British in India. We are not the Belgians in the Congo. This is the land of our forefathers, the Land of Israel, to which Abraham brought the idea of one God, where David set out to confront Goliath, and where Isaiah saw a vision of eternal peace. No distortion of history can deny the four thousand year old bond, between the Jewish people and the Jewish land. ...
>
> In a region where women are stoned, gays are hanged, Christians are persecuted, Israel stands out. ... We have a free press, independent courts, an open economy, and rambunctious parliamentary debates. Courageous Arab protesters are now struggling to secure these very same rights for their peoples, for their societies. We're proud that over one million Arab citizens of Israel have been enjoying these rights for decades. Of the 300 million Arabs in the Middle East and North Africa, only Israel's Arab citizens enjoy real democratic rights. I want you to stop for a second and think about that. Of those 300 million Arabs, less than one-half of one-percent are truly free, and they're all citizens of Israel. This startling fact reveals a basic truth: Israel is not what is wrong about the Middle East. Israel is what is right about the Middle East. ...
>
> We must also find a way to forge a lasting peace with the Palestinians. Two years ago, I publicly committed to a solution of two states for two peoples:

A Palestinian state alongside the Jewish state. …I am willing to make painful compromises to achieve this historic peace. As the leader of Israel, it is my responsibility to lead my people to peace. This is not easy for me. I recognize that in a genuine peace, we will be required to give up parts of the Jewish homeland. So now here is the question. You have to ask it. If the benefits of peace with the Palestinians are so clear, why has peace eluded us? Because all six Israeli Prime Ministers since the signing of Oslo accords agreed to establish a Palestinian state. Myself included. So why has peace not been achieved? Because so far, the Palestinians have been unwilling to accept a Palestinian state, if it meant accepting a Jewish state alongside it. You see, our conflict has never been about the establishment of a Palestinian state. It has always been about the existence of the Jewish state. This is what this conflict is about. In 1947, the United Nations voted to partition the land into a Jewish state and an Arab state. The Jews said yes. The Palestinians said no. In recent years, the Palestinians twice refused generous offers by Israeli Prime Ministers, to establish a Palestinian state on virtually all the territory won by Israel in the Six Day War. They were simply unwilling to end the conflict. And I regret to say this: They continue to educate their children to hate. They continue to name public squares after terrorists. And worst of all, they continue to perpetuate the fantasy that Israel will one day be flooded by the descendants of Palestinian refugees. My friends, this must come to an end. President Abbas must do what I have done. I stood before my people, and I told you it wasn't easy for me, and I said—"I will accept a Palestinian state." It is time for President Abbas to stand before his people and say—"I will accept a Jewish state". … With such a partner, the people of Israel will be prepared to make a far reaching compromise. I will be prepared to make a far reaching compromise.

This compromise must reflect the dramatic demographic changes that have occurred since 1967. The vast majority of the 650,000 Israelis who live beyond the 1967 lines [commonly referred to as the settlements] reside in neighborhoods and suburbs of Jerusalem and Greater Tel Aviv. These areas are densely populated but geographically quite small. Under any realistic peace agreement, these areas [settlements], as well as other places of critical strategic and national importance, will be incorporated into the final borders of Israel.

The status of the settlements will be decided only in negotiations. But we must also be honest. So I am saying today something that should be said publicly by anyone serious about peace. In any peace agreement that ends the conflict, some settlements will end up beyond Israel's borders. The precise delineation of those borders must be negotiated. We will be very generous on the size of a future Palestinian state. But as President Obama said, the border will be different than the one that existed on June 4, 1967. Israel will not return to the indefensible lines of 1967.

We recognize that a Palestinian state must be big enough to be viable, independent and prosperous. President Obama rightly referred to Israel as the homeland of the Jewish people, just as he referred to the future Palestinian state as the homeland of the Palestinian people. Jews from around the world have a right to immigrate to the Jewish state. Palestinians from around the world should have a right to immigrate, if they so choose, to a Palestinian state. This means that the Palestinian refugee problem will be resolved outside the borders of Israel.

As for Jerusalem, only a democratic Israel has protected freedom of worship for all faiths in the city. Jerusalem must never again be divided. Jerusalem must remain the united capital of Israel. I know that this is a difficult issue for Palestinians. But I believe with creativity and goodwill a solution can be found.

This is the peace I plan to forge with a Palestinian partner committed to peace. But you know very well, that in the Middle East, the only peace that will hold is a peace you can defend. So peace must be anchored in security. In recent years, Israel withdrew from South Lebanon and Gaza. But we didn't get peace. Instead, we got 12,000 thousand rockets fired from those areas on our cities, on our children, by Hezbollah and Hamas. The UN peacekeepers in Lebanon failed to prevent the smuggling of this weaponry. The European observers in Gaza evaporated overnight. So if Israel simply walked out of the territories, the flow of weapons into a future Palestinian state would be unchecked. Missiles fired from it could reach virtually every home in Israel in less than a minute. I want you to think about that too. Imagine that right now we all had less than 60 seconds to find shelter from an incoming rocket. Would you live that way? Would anyone live that way? Well, we aren't going to live that way either. The truth is that Israel needs unique security arrangements because of its unique size. Israel is one of the smallest countries in the world. ... Israel on the 1967 lines would be only nine miles wide. So much for strategic depth.

So it is therefore absolutely vital for Israel's security that a Palestinian state be fully demilitarized. And it is vital that Israel maintain a long-term military presence along the Jordan River. Solid security arrangements on the ground are necessary not only to protect the peace, they are necessary to protect Israel in case the peace unravels. For in our unstable region, no one can guarantee that our peace partners today will be there tomorrow. And when I say tomorrow, I don't mean some distant time in the future. I mean tomorrow. Peace can be achieved only around the negotiating table. The Palestinian attempt to impose a settlement through the United Nations will not bring peace. It should be forcefully opposed by all those who want to see this conflict end. I appreciate the President's clear position on this issue. Peace cannot be imposed. It must be negotiated. But it can only be negotiated with partners committed to peace.[24]

Netanyahu's speech showed a return to a pre-Camp David "Security-first" policy based on defensible borders. Wasn't that always Israel's policy?

The West Bank: Brief History of Israeli Policy

Israeli policy, from after the Six-Day War in 1967 until the Oslo Accords in 1993, has centered on finding a formula that would enable Israel to avoid two things:

1. exercising authority over the Palestinians,
2. returning to the insecure pre-war 1967 lines.

With these aims in mind, Israel neither annexed Judea and Samaria (West Bank) and Gaza in 1967 nor spoke of a Palestinian state within those territories. Israel had no intention, ever, of establishing a Palestinian state within the pre-war 1967 lines. This was the case at the 1978 Camp David Accord meetings between Begin and Sadat, which called for "autonomy for the Palestinian people." And it was no less the case later, in 1993, when Prime Minister Yitzhak Rabin entered into the Oslo Accords. Those Israeli leaders knew that these lines were indefensible.

Rabin's vision for Judea and Samaria was something along the lines of the "Allon Plan," originally drafted by Yigal Allon, a former foreign minister under Rabin. The Allon Plan was drafted shortly after the Six-Day War. It called for Israel to retain sovereignty in some of the territories it now controlled in Judea and Samaria, but not to settle in areas with large Arab populations. This was also a premise behind the Bailey Plan, discussed in Chapter 15.

Allon's plan also mapped out a secure border. It gave Israel control of the Jordan Valley and the steep eastern slopes of the Judea–Samaria mountain ridge. It also gave Israel sovereignty over an undivided Jerusalem: Israel's capital. The Allon Plan served as the basis of the security policy for Israeli governments from 1967 until far into the 1990s. Rabin was very clear on the need to maintain defensible borders for Israel while providing Palestinian autonomy.

The basic goal of defensible borders began to be compromised in 2000, when Israeli Prime Minister Ehud Barak went to the Camp David summit to negotiate, with PA Chairman Yasser Arafat and US President Bill Clinton, an end to the Palestinian–Israeli conflict. Barak wanted to expose Arafat's true intentions, so he abandoned the particulars of the Allon Plan and offered him and the PA virtually all of Judea and Samaria (including the Jordan Valley) as well as eastern Jerusalem. Barak's ploy worked. Arafat rejected the offer, thus revealing that he wanted not just the territory he claimed to want but all of sovereign Israel, too. In other words, he was not yet ready to acknowledge Israel's right to exist.

Arafat was induced to reveal his real intentions, but Israel paid a heavy price for that revelation—one that it continues to pay today. Barak's strategem set out a new land-for-peace paradigm that the Palestinians and the international community did not forget. From that point on, the borders that Barak had proposed were assumed to be acceptable to Israel. Western policymakers, urged on by the Palestinian leadership, took it that the "1967 lines"—that is, the 1949 armistice lines—should be the basis for all future negotiations, as opposed to the "secure and recognized boundaries" unanimously approved by the UN Security Council after the Six-Day War.

In light of what Israel underwent after Barak's offer to Arafat—intifadas, Hamas and Hizbullah rockets, Iran-sponsored terror—the Netanyahu government has readopted the notion that meeting Israel's vital security requirements is the only viable path to a durable peace with the Palestinians. Netanyahu's policy reflects a broad Israeli consensus.

Borders and Israel's Security

Why is a two-state solution based on the pre-1967 borders and a divided Jerusalem such a danger to Israel's security?

Israel is a small state surrounded by Arab countries 650 times its size. The combined width of Israel and the West Bank averages about 40 miles from the Mediterranean to the Jordan River. The regimes in a number of the neighboring Arab states are friendly to organizations that carry out global terror sponsored by Iran and committed to Israel's destruction.

After the Six-Day War in 1967, the UN passed Security Resolution 242—which we discussed in Chapter 15—stating that Israel has a "right to live in peace within *secure* and recognized boundaries[emphasis added]." Prior to 1967, the eastern boundary of Israel was the 1949 Armistice Line—the Green Line. For Israel, the 1949 boundary is not secure. In other words, it is not defensible given today's advanced weaponry. Israel's claim is that *secure* borders are borders other than the 1949 lines.

The debate over defensible borders is primarily a debate about Judea and Samaria (the West Bank) and the calamities that could befall Israel should this territory fall under the control of radical Fatah factions or, as has happened in Gaza, of Hamas.

What are defensible borders for Israel? What are its essential security needs?

The Jordan Rift Valley

The Jordan Rift Valley on Israel's eastern frontier forms a natural barrier between Israel and the Arab countries of Jordan, Iraq, and Iran. The valley rises from an area 1,200 feet below sea level to a hilly ridge of up to 3,000 feet above sea level. This creates a steep, 4,200-foot barrier against any force attacking from the east.

The Jordan Valley is also strategically vital because the border with Jordan lies within it. That border could become similar to the border between Gaza and Egypt, where weapons, terrorists, and other forms of support are easily smuggled to Hamas. When Israel withdrew from Gaza in 2005, it left the Philadelphi Corridor unpatrolled for the first time since 1979. This is a narrow strip of land, 14 km in length, situated along the border between Gaza Strip and Egypt. Israel had patrolled it since 1979. Israel's withdrawal from this zone resulted in the terrorist infiltration of Gaza and the influx of hundreds of tons of ammunition and weaponry (rockets and mortars) from all over the Arab world, subsequently launched at Israeli civilians.

Think of the Jordan Valley as the West Bank equivalent of Gaza's Philadelphi corridor.[25]

The Mountain Ridge

Israel's Mountain Ridge—the spine of which runs north-south and parallel to Israel's coast for seventy kilometers—rises up to 3,000 feet and overlooks Israel's major coastal cities. More than 70 percent of Israel's population, 80 percent of its industry, and all of its airports and seaports are located here. If Judea and Samaria (West Bank) were to become a Palestinian state, much of the Mountain Ridge would be under Palestinian control. What danger would this pose?

One threat is rockets. Today, Hamas possesses rockets with a range of more than 50 kilometers. If Israel were forced back to the 1949 armistice lines (that is, the Green Line), its width would be reduced to a mere nine miles. From the mountain ridge, which overlooks Israel's coastal plane, a hostile force deploying more advanced weaponry would be able to hit virtually any point in Israel—Ben-Gurion Airport; the Trans-Israel Highway (Route 6), which runs north–south only meters from the West Bank; Israel's National Water Carrier; the country's power plant and power lines. Most of its population and infrastructure would be in easy range of rockets and even mortars. Ben-Gurion Airport—Israel's only international airport—would be especially vulnerable. It would be in range of even primitive rockets or shoulder-launched anti-aircraft missiles, so all planes taking off and landing would be under constant threat. In short, it would be impossible to defend the State of Israel.[26]

United Jerusalem

Making Eastern Jerusalem the capital of a Palestinian state would require dividing the city. East Jerusalem for the Arabs, West Jerusalem for the Jews—it sounds like a simple solution. Is it? What are the implications of a divided Jerusalem?

Historically, there has been no division of Jerusalem into east and west. The only time Jerusalem has been divided in its 3000-plus-year history was during a 19-year period after the 1948 War, owing to the Jordanian occupation. That division, however, is no longer possible. Why not? Dramatic growth and changes have occurred since 1967, when Israel took control of the city after the Six Day War. In the mosaic of neighborhoods called "East Jerusalem," 270,000 Arabs and well over 200,000 Jews now live. Arab and Jewish neighborhoods are often intermingled, with their urban infrastructures fused. Jewish and Arab neighborhoods share water systems, sewage pipelines, electricity networks, and roads that serve as vital arteries of transportation. Tens of thousands of Arabs work in Jewish neighborhood. Dividing Jerusalem is not technically feasible due to the intermingling of populations, neighborhoods, and vital infrastructures.

Today, citizens of Jerusalem as well as visitors move freely throughout the city. The situation was very different under Jordanian rule. Arab snipers on the east side of the barbed-wire barrier dividing the city were continually shooting at Israeli residents on the other side. The security threat created by the division of the city in 1948 also resulted in the mass immigration of 25,000 Jews from the areas which fell to Jordan, a quarter of the city's Jewish population at the time.

Any division of Israel's capital city will invite sniper attacks and mortar and rocket fire from the surrounding high ground. Were the Palestinians to obtain full sovereignty in Judea and Samaria, those areas—like Gaza before them—would become vulnerable staging grounds for attacks on Israel and a magnet for regional terrorist groups seeking to infiltrate the West Bank. Such a situation could be disastrous, with so many non-state Islamic jihadist and terrorist organizations, including Hamas and Hizbullah, sitting on Israel's borders and in Palestinian controlled areas.

Jerusalem is surrounded by hills that overlook the city's major access routes and the major Jewish and Christian holy sites in and around the Old City. For example, the West Bank village of Beit Iksa, an Arab village located on a hill, is only a few hundred yards from the main Jerusalem–Tel Aviv highway, the main transportation artery connecting the country's two largest cities. In 1967, the Jordanian Army exploited the terrain around Jerusalem to launch some 9,000 artillery shells into the city's Jewish neighborhoods.

With a divided Jerusalem, anybody in west Jerusalem, resident or tourist, would be under constant threat. During 2000 and 2001, before the security fence was built, there were hundreds of attacks by gunfire and mortar on the Gilo neighborhood in southern Jerusalem. These attacks came from Beit Jalla, a Palestinian town 1,000 feet away. Jewish neighborhoods and holy sites that are only metres away from Arab neighborhoods in eastern Jerusalem would be at even greater risk.

Proof of this? Holy sites and their surrounding areas that have come under Palestinian security control since the Oslo Accords have become dangerous for Jews and Christians to visit. Apart from the basic physical threat, then, a divided Jerusalem would compromise the freedom of worship in the city for Christians as well as Jews. The following fact seems telling: the only time in history that all residents of Jerusalem—Christians, Muslims, and Jews—have enjoyed freedom of religion has been under Israeli sovereignty.

Owing to technological advances, the security risk posed by a divided Jerusalem today is much greater than it was in 1948, when Jordan took control of east Jerusalem. With modern artillery, Arab-controlled neighborhoods would present a mortal threat not only to Jewish neighborhoods in Jerusalem but also to the State of Israel. The IDF would be unable to defend the Western areas of the city or most of the Jewish State from Palestinian attacks carried out from the hilltops of east Jerusalem. Such attacks would be lethal and impossible to defend against because of their proximity to major population centers and to Israel's coastal plain. And, as we mentioned earlier, Israel is a tiny country, only 40 miles wide. One only has to look at what has happened in the Gaza Strip to recognize the threat that a militarized area controlled by Palestinians poses to Israel. Gaza—though its threat increases as Iran and other enemy states supply Hamas with ever more advanced rockets and mortars—is comparatively remote; it sits at sea level and is a defensible distance from Israel's major population centers.

A divided Jerusalem poses other problems, apart from security ones. The Arab and Jewish residents of the city share medical and welfare facilities, academic institutions, shopping centers, and recreation sites. Many Jerusalem Arabs would prefer to remain under Israeli rule. When Israel began to construct the security fence between 2000 and 2003, some 70,000 Arab residents left their homes to ensure they would remain under Israeli sovereignty.

Other Security Needs: A Culture of Tolerance

Perhaps the most important factor in maintaining secure and defensible borders is a cultural one. Peace will become possible when Palestinians at all levels of society begin to inculcate in their people a culture of tolerance. Leaders and teachers will need to stop indoctrinating their young with hatred and inciting them to violence and terror. They will need to accept the Jewish people's 3,300-year connection to the Land of Israel and their right to live there peacefully and securely, in a Jewish nation-state.

Unfortunately, Palestinians have continued to cultivate a national narrative of armed struggle that denies Israel's right to exist as a Jewish nation-state. Their textbooks continue to teach the young that a future Palestinian State will encompass all of Israel as well as the West Bank and Gaza. Israel may make any number of concessions, agreements, or unilateral withdrawals. But until Palestinians start teaching their children—through television, radio, and the internet—not to idolize suicide bombers, the peace process will remain an illusion and Israel will not be secure.

Endnotes

1   Linda Gradstein, "Tal Law Expires: Israel's Religious Young Men, Women to Be Drafted," *Jewish Tribune*, August 7, 2012, http://www.jewishtribune.ca/news/2012/08/07/tal-law-expires-israels-religious-young-men-women-to-be-drafted.

2   Ibid.

3   Untitled and unauthored short report at the top of the page of the *National Post*, Saturday September 8, 2007, A14.

4   Yoav Shamir, *Checkpoint - every day life in Israel - Documentary*, 2003, YouTube, accessed August 13, 2012, http://www.youtube.com/watch?v=e7lLluBf0xs.

5   Ibid. The quotation is from the jacket of the DVD.

6   Adapted from "So why shouldn't we REALLY treat the Palestinians in a more humane way?," Concept Wizard Website: Visual Information About the Middle East Conflict, accessed March 2011, http://www.conceptwizard.com/art-humane.html.

7   James Reynolds, "Nobody is going to live forever," BBC News, July, 16, 2004, http://news.bbc.co.uk/2/hi/middle_east/3899015.stm. See also *Israeli TV - 14 year old Suicide Bomber*, YouTube, 2006, accessed August 14, 2012, http://www.youtube.com/watch?v=PPU4UN03t7E (Accessed Aug 14, 2012)

8   Ibid.

9   Ibid.

10   Ibid.

11   David Meir-Levi, "The Depravity of the Homicide Bomber's Recruiters," *frontpagemag.com*, November 10, 2011, http://frontpagemag.com/2011/david-meir-levi/the-depravity-of-the-homi-cide-bomber%E2%80%99s-recruiters/.

12   Ibid.

13   Ibid.

14   *Female Homicide Bomber (suicide)*, YouTube, 2006, accessed August 14, 2012, http://www.youtube.com/watch?v=22XEkJY62VA&feature=watch_response.

15   Meir-Levi, "The Depravity of the Homicide Bomber's Recruiters."

16   Amichai Cohen, *Proportionality in Modern Asymmetrical Wars* (Jerusalem: Jerusalem Center for Public Affairs, 2010), 5.

17   Allen Sens and Peter Stoett, *Global Politics* 3rd ed. (Toronto: Thomson Nelson, 2005), 341.

18   Israel Security Agency, *2010 Annual Summary—Data And Trends in Terrorism*, December 25, 2010, http://www.shabak.gov.il/English/EnTerrorData/Reviews/Pages/2010summary-en.aspx .

19   Israel Defense Forces, "680 missiles, rockets and mortars fired at southern Israel in 2011," May 1, 2012, http://www.idf.il/1283-14436-en/Dover.aspx.

20   Yaakov Lappin, "IDF releases Cast Lead casualty numbers", *Jerusalem Post,* March 26, 2009, http://www.jpost.com/Israel/Article.aspx?id=137286.

21   Backspin Editor, "Hamas Concedes on Gaza War Casualties," *Backspin: Daily Blog from HonestReporting*, November 1, 2010, http://honestreporting.com/hamas-concedes-on-gaza-war-casualties/.

22   Colonel Richard Kemp, *UN Human Rights Council Debate on Goldstone Report*, 12th Special Session, October 16, 2009. See *Goldstone Gaza Report: Col. Richard Kemp Testifies* at U.N. Emergency Session, YouTube, http://www.youtube.com/watch?v=NX6vyT8RzMo

23   Barak Obama, "Remarks by the President on the Middle East and North Africa," (speech, Washington, DC, May 19, 2011), http://www.whitehouse.gov/the-press-office/2011/05/19/remarks-president-middle-east-and-north-africa.

24   "Benjamin Netanyahu's epic speech before Congress," *The Right Scoop,* May 24, 2011, http://www.therightscoop.com/benjamin-netanyahus-epic-speech-before-congress/.

25   Two videos demonstrating the critical issues regarding dividing Jerusalem and explaining Israel's essential security needs can be found at the following sites: http://www.jcpa.org and http://jcpa.org/video/israels-critical-security-needs-for-a-viable-peace-abridged-2/.

26   See pictures and illustrations under "Strategic Value of Samaria," Shomron Central, accessed October 10, 2012, http://shomroncentral.blogspot.ca/p/1-strategic-value-of-samaria.html.

Chapter 18

Israel in the 21st Century

Introduction

In the 21st century, various representatives of the international community—the United Nations, Amnesty International, Human Rights Watch, and the media worldwide—have portrayed Israel as a habitual abuser of human rights and international law. In the court of world opinion, Israel's guilt often goes unchallenged. Most of this opinion concerns Israel's alleged mistreatment of the Palestinians in Gaza and the West Bank. Having explored the Israeli–Palestinian relationship in several chapters of this work, we're now prepared to consider whether the world opinion is just in this respect. Do most people take a fair view of Israel's difficult relationships with the Palestinians and its other Arab/Muslim neighbors? This question is the focus of our chapter.

The BDS and IAW Movements

No-one attacks Israel's reputation more vigorously than the Boycott-Divestment-Sanctions (BDS) and Israel Apartheid Week (IAW) movements. The BDS movement aims to punish Israel for its alleged mistreatment of the Palestinians by

- calling on people to refuse to buy Israeli made goods and services;
- pressuring corporations, organizations, and institutional funds to stop engaging or investing in Israeli commerce;
- lobbying the international community to impose harsh penalties—for example, restrictions on trade—on the State of Israel.

The "Israel Apartheid Week" (IAW) movement supports BDS. IAW is an annual anti-Israel spring event on college campuses. The term *apartheid* refers to state-sponsored segregation or discrimination on grounds of race. It is normally applied to the policies of the South African government during the period of 1948 to 1991. Does it really apply to Israel?

Anyone who has ever been to Israel knows that, in its biggest cities, Arabs and Jews live in close proximity, shop at the same malls and markets, and work at the same places. There are Arabs that serve in the Israeli army, in the government, and on the Supreme Court. Reverend Kenneth Meshoe, a South African MP—a black man who suffered the injustices of apartheid firsthand—recently said, after a visit to Israel, that finding similarities between Israeli policies and the apartheid policies of twentieth-century South Africa is "nonsense": "There is nothing to it. When people see Israel themselves, they understand." Meshoe noted the following:

> I have seen Israelis and Palestinians living together. They use the same public transportation and go to the same stores, schools and beaches. It was not like that in apartheid South Africa—stores had separate doors for blacks and whites.[1]

The South African MP's view is that people who call Israel's policies apartheid "just want to raise emotions, because everyone hates apartheid. The word 'apartheid' gets attention." Meshoe objects to such easy, inflammatory tactics, because they minimize the pain of those who actually suffered under the racially segregated South African regime. "If Israel is an apartheid state like South Africa was, then apartheid would not have been so painful," he added.

Usually, people who label Israel an apartheid state are referring to its policies in the West Bank and Gaza and not necessarily in Israel proper. But those policies are not based on "race." As we saw in the previous chapter, they are based on security requirements and are a response to terrorism.

Israel in Education

The politics of the BDS and IAW movements have made their way into the classrooms of universities in the West. Some professors take advantage of their positions of authority to disseminate their own fashionable biases. This is unfortunate, for university professors wield a great deal of influence and should use it responsibly. Where the Middle East is concerned, educators in their professional roles

- write books and articles that influence the way the region and in particular Israel are seen;
- set the tone for how the Middle East is regarded on campuses across North America;
- shape the views of students who go on to occupy influential positions, such as business leaders and politicians;
- influence the public debate via lectures, panels, teach-ins, newspaper articles, quotations in media outlets, and appearances on radio and television;
- influence government by helping politicians formulate positions, by advising intelligence agencies, and by providing help to congressional staffers writing briefs.

The topic of Israel poses difficulties for educators. Some teachers complain that their *academic freedom* is restricted when it comes to discussing Israel and the Middle East.

Academic Freedom and Middle East Education

In April, 2009, William I. Robinson, a USCB sociology professor, sent an email to students on Martin Luther King Day under the heading "Parallel Images of Nazis and Israelis." It included more than two dozen side-by-side photos of Nazis and Israelis. His email included the following passage:

> I am forwarding some horrific, parallel images of Nazi atrocities against the Jews and Israeli atrocities against the Palestinians. Perhaps the most frightening are not those providing a graphic depiction of the carnage but that which shows Israeli children writing "with love" on a bomb that will tear apart Palestinian children. Gaza is Israel's Warsaw—a vast concentration camp that confined and blockaded Palestinians, subjecting them to the slow death of malnutrition, disease and despair, nearly two years before their subjection to the quick death of Israeli bombs. We are witness to a slow-motion process of genocide (Websters: "the systematic killing of, or a program of action intended to destroy, a whole national or ethnic group"), a process whose objective is not so much to physically eliminate each and every Palestinian than to eliminate the Palestinians as a people in any meaningful sense of the notion of people-hood.[2]

The email made Robinson the focus of an academic investigation that he claimed was an attack on his academic freedom.

The next installment in this episode was the following posting, on the website of controversial writer Norman Finkelstein:

> This is an obvious attack on Professor Robinson's academic freedom, one that ominously recalls similar campaigns against other critics of Israel across the nation. This is part of a broader campaign to automatically vilify and attack any and all critiques of Israel's policies and practices through unfounded use of the term "anti-Semitic." A critique of the Israeli state, its policies, and the leaders responsible is not and should not be considered an affront to Jewish people as a collective, the Jewish religion, or Jewish heritage.[3]

Finkelstein's argument here is that critics of Israel are automatically and unfairly smeared as anti-Semitic. He posits an organized "campaign" against Israel's detractors.

Finkelstein and Robinson's arguments raise the following questions:

- Is there really a concerted effort to restrict the academic freedom of educators in discussing the Middle East on high school and college campuses?

■ Is it true that this effort to restrict academic freedom is applied only to educators who criticize Israel and/or Jews?

■ Should academic freedom give educators free license to discuss anything in any manner they choose in their classrooms?

Campus Watch's Findings

Campus Watch is an organization that was formed to critique the way the Middle East is studied in North America. Its members agree that there are problems on university campuses when it comes to bias about the Middle East. But their conclusions are different from those of Robinson and Finkelstein. Campus Watch concluded that scholars enjoy significant academic freedom in this area so long as their views are critical of Israel. There is less tolerance for views that are uncomplimentary to Islam or the Palestinians. Campus Watch cited a case at the University of Chicago. There, a student who wanted to write a doctoral dissertation on militant Islamist ideologies was discouraged from doing so on the grounds that the media had sensationalized the topic in order to further Zionist interests.[4]

In another example of anti-Israel bias, students in a "global studies" course at a prestigious North American university were given a paper to review that focused on understanding Palestinian suicide bombers. Among the claims in the paper were the following:

1. the Israeli government uses Palestinian suicide bombers (PSBs) as an excuse to transform [Palestinian] cities into rubble; and

2. the Israeli government shares the suicide bombers' lack of concern about the people they murder.[5]

Campus Watch found that educators and scholars tend to evade, ignore, or apologize for topics that do not fit their politicized agenda on the Middle East. The organization cited examples of topics that are typically excluded from academic discourse:

■ internal repression by governments in Libya, Sudan, Syria, Iraq, Iran, and by the Palestinian Authority (PA);

■ PA support for suicide bombing against Israeli civilians;

■ the long-term goals of Islamist movements, Islamic fundamentalism, and militant Islam;

■ the Syrian occupation of Lebanon.

■ the anti–American, anti–Christian, and anti–Semitic statements that pervade state-run media through most of the Middle East.[6]

Campus Watch questioned complaints by Finkelstein and Robinson that professors face serious reprisals whenever they criticize Israel. To support its skepticism, the organization asked the following simple question: "What examples of professors being punished or publicly reprimanded, suspended or fined are there?"

The Anti-Israel/Pro-Palestinian Movement on Campus

The reality on campuses across North America is that Israel is freely and heavily criticized in and out of the classroom. During IAW anti-Israel protests or pro-Palestinian rallies, it is not uncommon to see the Israeli flag or Star of David twinned with Nazi swastikas in an attempt to equate Israel/Jews with Nazis—just as Professor Robinson did. The latitude given to IAW demonstrations or anti-Israel positions is shown by the following firsthand accounts:

> I was rushing to my last class of the day, yet I could not help but notice an anti-Israel display and demonstrators. … They had a long cardboard wall with photos pasted along it that seemed to imply that the Israeli Defense Forces (IDF) are exploitive militaristic aggressors. The main point of their argument seemed to be that the purpose of the security wall that Israel erected is to segregate and ghettoize the Palestinians, similar to Jews' experience in the Holocaust.[7]

> It was my last semester of College at Hofstra University. … One day, one of my professors came into class and began talking about the flotilla incident. … My professor began telling the class Israel stopped a ship that was transporting food and other essential aid to the people of Gaza. He then added that Israel attacked the ship and beat and killed many on the ship, including a young American man. … At that point I saw anti-Semitism spreading in front of my eyes.[8]

To the professor's credit, the student quoted in the second passage was granted an opportunity to present Israel's side. However, such academic freedom is not always upheld. For example, in September 2002, anti-Israel protestors at Montreal's Concordia University held a violent rally that forced the cancellation of a speech by former Israeli Prime Minister Benjamin Netanyahu.

Are there times when academic freedom should be limited and is Netanyahu's talk an example of that?

The Limits of Academic Freedom

On February 8, 2010, members of the Muslim Student Union at the University of California, Irvine tried to silence Israel's US Ambassador Michael Oren. They interrupted Oren repeatedly during his speech. The outburst and subsequent arrest of the protesters sparked controversy over whether the protesters were exercising free speech, as they claimed they were, or whether, as university officials claimed, they were actually suppressing free speech (that is, of Oren's right to have a free exchange of ideas with his audience).

On September 23, 2011, a jury convicted 10 Muslim students at UC Irvine for disrupting Oren's February 2010 speech. They were sentenced to community service hours and three years of informal probation.

Would the students who fought for Ambassador Oren's right to speak also have fought for UCSB Professor Robinson? Would the students who fought against Ambassador Oren's right to speak also have protested against Professor Robinson's right to email twinned images of Nazis and Jews? Lastly, are the two cases analogous in terms of academic freedom? If not, what's the difference?

Just as Jewish and pro-Israel students raise concerns about anti-Israelism and anti-Semitism in Middle East studies, so do Muslim and pro-Palestinian students raise concerns about "Islamophobia" and "Palestinian marginalization."

When students and educators allege that there is a war on their academic freedom, are they justified, or are they using a form of "lawfare"? The term *lawfare*, a recent coinage, refers to "the use of the law as a weapon of war" or, more specifically, the manipulation of Western laws and judicial systems to achieve political ends. By means of lawfare, human rights laws are used to accomplish purposes other than, or even contrary to, those for which they were originally enacted. Lawfare is also evident in the manipulation of domestic legal systems (by state and non-state parties) to implement laws inconsistent with general principles of liberal democracy.[9]

Are educators using lawfare strategies when they accuse the system of making "war" on their academic freedom? Do the professors and teachers who protest in this way also protest the silencing of those who oppose them? Are the Jewish students who, on the grounds of anti-Semitism, call for restrictions on speech also engaging in lawfare?

Human rights laws are in place to protect certain rights and freedoms, such as academic freedom and free speech. But clearly there are times when people abuse these freedoms. So how do we distinguish between the appropriate and the inappropriate use of our protected freedoms?

What Should Academic Freedom Protect?

It's difficult to determine what practices should be protected and which should not. But Campus Watch and Natan Sharansky—a former Soviet *refusenik* (term for Soviet Jews who were denied permission to emigrate) and prisoner, Israeli politician, human rights activist, and author—have provided some good starting points.

Campus Watch calls on educators and educational institutions to do the following:

- Provide studies on relevant topics.
- Deliver an honest appraisal of sensitive issues.
- Foster a healthy debate in the classroom.
- Alert university stakeholders (administrators, alumni, trustees, regents, parents of students, state/provincial and federal legislators) to problems in Middle East studies and encourage these stakeholders to address these problems.
- Not passively accept error, extremism, intolerance, misplaced apologetics, and abuse when they occur.
- Recognize their correlative obligations as described in the American Association of University Professors 1915 Declaration of Principles, which affirms that

the freedom of the academic teacher entail[s] certain correlative obligations. The university teacher should, if he is fit for his position, be a person of a *fair and judicial* mind; he should, in dealing with such subjects, set forth *justly*, without suppression or innuendo, the divergent opinions of other investigators and he should, above all, *remember that his business is not to provide his students with ready-made conclusions, but to train them to think for themselves.*[10] (emphasis added)

The New Anti-Semitism and the 3D Test

Sharansky suggests certain criteria for distinguishing between anti-Semitism and legitimate criticism of Israel, and these criteria could equally be used to distinguish legitimate criticism of the Palestinians (or of militant Islamic regimes) from illegitimate criticism of them. These criteria are part of what Sharansky calls the "3D test":

[T]he so-called "new anti-Semitism" poses a unique challenge. Whereas classical anti-Semitism is aimed at the Jewish people or the Jewish religion, "new anti-Semitism" is aimed at the Jewish state. Since this anti-Semitism can hide behind the veneer of legitimate criticism of Israel, it is more difficult to expose. Making the task even harder is that this hatred is advanced in the name of values most of us would consider unimpeachable, such as human rights.

Nevertheless, we must be clear and outspoken in exposing the new anti-Semitism. I believe that we can apply a simple test—I call it the "3D" test—to help us distinguish legitimate criticism of Israel from anti-Semitism.

The first "D" is the test of *demonization.* When the Jewish state is being demonized; when Israel's actions are blown out of all sensible proportion; when comparisons are made between Israelis and Nazis and between Palestinian refugee camps and Auschwitz—this is anti-Semitism, not legitimate criticism of Israel.

The second "D" is the test of *double standards.* When criticism of Israel is applied selectively; when Israel is singled out by the United Nations for human rights abuses while the behavior of known and major abusers, such as China, Iran, Cuba, and Syria, is ignored; when Israel's Magen David Adom, alone among the world's ambulance services, is denied admission to the International Red Cross—this is anti-Semitism.

The third "D" is the test of *delegitimization:* when Israel's fundamental right to exist [or defend itself] is denied—alone among all peoples in the world—this too is anti-Semitism.[11]

Sharansky's 3D test can also be applied to cases where Israel has been the focus of intense media scrutiny and international condemnation. The 2010 Gaza flotilla was one such case.

Applying the 3Ds: the Gaza Flotilla

On January 3, 2009, Israel established a naval blockade off the coast of the Gaza Strip as part of its armed conflict with Hamas. A number of so-called humanitarian organizations set out to protest Israel's naval blockade by mobilizing a flotilla to deliver aid. In late May 2010, six vessels, with approximately 700 persons on board, left Turkey for the coastline of Israel. The largest of the ships in the flotilla, the Mavi Marmara, had approximately 590 passengers and a crew on board.

In the early hours of May 31, the Israeli navy's special forces launched a military operation to enforce the blockade and take control of the ships. In the takeover of some of the vessels, IDF soldiers used force and passengers suffered casualties. The international media and human rights organizations almost unanimously condemned Israel for its actions in this episode. They were even accused of war crimes and piracy.

Was the criticism legitimate? Would it pass Sharansky's 3D test? The early reports in the media painted the following picture of the incident:

■ The main purpose of the flotilla was to deliver humanitarian aid by sea (medical supplies, construction materials, school supplies, toys) to the Palestinians in Gaza.

■ The convoy was organized by humanitarian and peaceful organizations and the passengers on the flotilla were hundreds of non-violent protestors.

■ When the convoy was still in international waters, Israeli speed boats carrying heavily armed soldiers circled the flotilla and opened fire at the biggest of the vessels, the Turkish ship, the Mavi Marmara.

■ At the same time, IDF helicopters flew overhead and commandos descended on ropes and, as they prepared to board, shot at the passengers on deck of the Mavi Marmara.

■ As a result of the Israeli special forces' violence, nine of the ships' passengers were killed and over fifty were wounded.

Later reports, supported by the IDF's video footage of what happened, painted a far different picture of the flotilla incident. The following are some key points that were missing from the early headlines in the world media:

■ In response to thousands of mortars and rockets being fired from the Gaza Strip at towns in Israel, the Israeli military launched operation "Cast Lead" in 2008–2009 (see Chapter 17). During this period, Israel imposed a naval blockade to prevent masses of arms being delivered by sea to Hamas.

■ This was not the first flotilla attempting to breach Israel's naval blockade on Gaza. Prior to the May 2010 incident, several ships tried to reach the Gaza Strip but either turned back or were intercepted by the Israeli navy, which used no force in these operations and brought the ships to a port in Israel. Israel proceeded to transport any humanitarian supplies on board these ships to the Gaza Strip via the land crossings.

■ The May 2010 flotilla was larger than previous ones. A coalition of various organizations organized the flotilla. The leading participant was the IHH, a Turkish humanitarian organization that also assists terrorist groups with a radical-Islamic and anti-Western orientation. The IHH supports Hamas and does not conceal its ties to that organization.

■ The State of Israel took various diplomatic and other peaceful measures, both openly and covertly, to prevent the departure of these flotillas.

■ The largest group of passengers on board the Mavi Marmara were peace activists. But there was also a second group that included approximately 40 activists in the IHH organization as well as activists in other organizations and additional flotilla participants who had decided, for various reasons, to affiliate themselves with the IHH. This second group, IHH activists and their affiliates, was the one that was involved in the violence on board the Mavi Marmara.

■ Before the flotilla reached the coast of Israel, the ships were warned several times that they were approaching the area of a naval blockade, and they were requested to turn back. These warnings also stated that if the ships did not comply, the Israeli navy would adopt all of the measures at its disposal to enforce the naval blockade. These warnings also stated that, after a security inspection, the humanitarian cargo on board the ships could be sent to the Gaza Strip via the land crossings.

■ All but one of the flotilla vessels responded to the radio communications, but the vessels did not change course. The captain of the Mavi Marmara announced over the radio that he would not stop.

■ When the ships were approximately 70 nautical miles from the coast and still had not responded to the warnings, the Israeli navy started a military operation to take control of them. They descended from helicopters and boarded the ships from the navy's speedboats.

■ The takeover of the Mavi Marmara began with an attempt by the Israeli navy to board from the speedboats. This attempt failed because the IHH activists violently resisted. They threw objects at the Israeli boats, shot water at them with hoses, cut the ladders on which the IDF soldiers were climbing, and used lights to blind them. At this stage, the IDF decided to have fifteen soldiers descend to the ship's roof from the first helicopter and either take it over directly or clear the side so that the soldiers from the speedboats could board.

■ The video records, as well as testimony from the IDF soldiers who descended from the first helicopter, indicate that a number of activists violently attacked the soldiers as soon as they landed on the roof, striking them with metal rods and pushing, punching, and kicking them. The first three soldiers were attacked and beaten, their gear and weapons taken away from them, and then they were thrown onto the lower deck. They were taken below deck, where they were beaten and refused proper medical care.

- ■ The IDF forces switched back and forth between less-lethal and lethal weapons depending on what kind of violence was directed at them.
- ■ Once the IDF had secured the vessel, they checked the flotilla participants for weapons. Several passengers had knives as well as scarves and flags of the Hamas movement and its military arm. No humanitarian supplies were found on board the Mavi Marmara.

Blockading an enemy's coast is an established military tactic and is legal under international law. It is often enforced in international waters. There are specific rules about how to implement a blockade. It must be publicly declared and notification sent to all states whose vessels are likely to be nearby. A maritime blockade must be for security purposes only, and must allow humanitarian assistance to the civilian population of the area deprived by the blockade. The rules state that since the ships sailing for Gaza were on a declared humanitarian mission, those on board had the right to expect that any humanitarian goods would ultimately find their way to their intended recipients. On the other hand, the rules also give the blockading party the right to take incoming ships to a nearby port and search them. Israel had no obligation to take the ships' crew at their word as to the nature of the cargo. The rules state that a neutral party should supervise this inspection, to prevent both the unwarranted seizure of humanitarian supplies and the blockaded party's abuse of the humanitarian-assistance loophole.

Finally, the rule of proportionate force, applicable to all armed conflict, applies equally to a naval blockade. Blockading navies are obliged to arrest a ship rather than simply fire on it, and the boarding soldiers' actions must be proportionate to the threat they meet.

How did the early reports and assessments from the international media and human rights measure up in terms of Sharanksy's 3Ds, discussed above? Did the media demonize and blow out of proportion the IDF's actions by labeling them war crimes and piracy? Did the initial reports pass the double-standards test? Or was criticism of Israel harsher than it would have been for another state? Lastly, was Israel's fundamental right to defend itself acknowledged?

Tikkun Olam

Israel, like most states, is far from perfect. However, there is a vast difference between states that habitually concern themselves with the welfare of others and those that habitually cause harm. Which kind of state is Israel?

There is a concept in Judaism called *tikkun olam*, which literally means "repair the world." It is considered a biblical obligation. There are numerous ways in which *tikkun olam* can be achieved. ISRAEL21c, an organization offering news and information about 21st-century Israel, is an apolitical nonprofit organization that has turned its focus away from the Middle East conflict; it publishes articles on how Israelis from all walks of life and religion innovate, improve, and add value to the world. Among the areas to which Israeli endeavors have contributed worldwide are humanitarian efforts, bio-medical technology, and environmental technology.

Humanitarianism

Save a Child's Heart (SACH) is an Israeli-based international humanitarian project. Its mission is to improve the quality of pediatric cardiac care for children from developing countries who suffer from heart disease. It brings medical personnel from such countries to Israel and trains them. SACH is totally dedicated to the idea that all children deserve the best medical treatment available, regardless of their nationality, religion, color, gender, or financial situation. SACH states explicitly that it is motivated by the age-old Jewish tradition of *tikkun olam*—repairing the world by mending the hearts of children, regardless of their origin.

SACH has been featured by KLM Airlines and by *Al Jazeera*, an Arab news channel with a global audience. Since 1995, it has saved the lives of 2,880 children of all nationalities, religions, and races, from 37 countries around the world. Almost half of those sent to Israel for life-saving heart procedures are from Gaza and the Palestinian territories. While SACH's staff and volunteers are almost entirely Jewish, about 90 percent of the children treated are Muslim. Young patients also come from other Middle Eastern countries, as well as from Africa and Asia. The children, predominantly babies, are operated on at the Wolfson Medical Centre in Holon, Israel.

This "humanitarian" image of Israel is in stark contrast to the now fashionable image of it as a human rights abuser, a violator of international law and an "apartheid" state.

According to the doctrine of *humanitarianism*, people's duty is to promote human welfare. By contrast, an *abuser* (as in human rights abuser) is someone who damages or harms people. These terms are obviously contradictory.

IsraAid is another example of an organization that shows how important the concept of *tikkun olam* is to the Israeli psyche. Since its creation in 2001, IsraAID has coordinated and facilitated aid programs all over the world, including the following:

- relief to cyclone victims in Myanmar,
- long term aid programs for starving communities in Malawi,
- rehabilitation and relief in South East Asia following the devastating tsunami,
- psycho-social programs for Darfur refugees on the Chad-Sudan border, and
- aid to Somali war refugees in Kenya.

Recently, IsraAid's response to two major catastrophes made headlines. The first was in January 2010, in Haiti. Following the earthquake that killed over 300,000 people, injured hundreds of thousands more, and left millions homeless, IsraAID organized one of the biggest Israeli civilian relief missions ever. Seven of its aid agencies and partners offered a wide range of programs, from relief to reconstruction. They offered medical aid, search-and-rescue assistance, and many other services. Within forty-eight hours of the earthquake, Israel had sent the best field medicine available to Haiti. A CNN news team reported that the Israeli field hospital's level of assistance and sophisticated equipment were unsurpassed. The CNN team found this remarkable, considering that the Israelis had come from half way around the world.

IsraAID also distinguished itself after the Japan tsunami/earthquake, in March 2011. With its member agency FIRST, it sent a 50-member medical team as well as a cargo plane carrying tons of equipment, blankets, coats, and other necessities to assist the victims. It distributed over 20 tons of relief items and medicines. It opened a field hospital in Japan's quake-ravaged Miyagi district.

Inventions and Innovations

Inventions and innovations are another expression of *tikkun olam*. Few countries have contributed as much in this regard as Israel has. Even if you don't live in Israel, the chances are you have something that was invented there. These inventions are helping to connect the world, preserve the planet, and save lives.[12] With a population of only 7 million people, Israel has the third largest group of companies represented on the NASDAQ stock exchange in New York, with only the United States and China ranking higher. Israel's products are solving some of the most important issues facing the planet today.

Water Technologies

In the Middle East, fresh water is a very scarce resource and a more valuable commodity than oil. Water technologies, including desalination, drip-irrigation technology, and wastewater management, are among those in which Israel has become a world leader. Desalination is a process for creating fresh water. It involves removing salt and other minerals from sea water so that it is suitable for human consumption or irrigation. While the process sounds simple, it is extremely difficult and expensive. Israel supplies the Palestinians and Jordanians, as well as its own population, with fresh water produced by this method.

Drip irrigation is a method for producing the best possible crops by means of the least amount of water. It is an invaluable technology for farmers in hot, dry climates and is widely used across Israel. Israeli companies producing this kind of technology include Plastro, Netafim, and NaanDan Jain. Unlike much of the innovation in Israel that starts in the lab or research institute, modern drip irrigation was pioneered in the field by farmers. Israeli drip-irrigation techniques are constantly shared with other countries through the Foreign Ministry's MASHAV Center for International Cooperation.

Wastewater technology enables a society to recycle its used water. Israel's achievements in this area are unsurpassed. A whopping 50 percent of Israel's irrigated water comes from recycled wastewater. The country that comes closest to Israel's level of water reuse is Spain, which only reuses about 20 percent of its liquid resource.

Biomedical Technologies

Israeli companies are making major breakthroughs in the areas of human health and disease. Israeli innovations include the following:

- *The PillCam.* This is a miniature camera enclosed in a pill, and it allows physicians to observe the person's gastrointestinal tract as the pill passes through his or her body, removing the need for an invasive procedure or surgery.

■ *Dental lasers*. This is a technology that does the work formerly done by the dentist drill, reducing the need for anesthetics.

■ *ExAblate*. This is a scanning machine that destroys tumors without surgery.

■ *ReWalk*. This is an alternative to the wheelchair for individuals with severe walking impairments, enabling them to stand, walk, and ascend and descend stairs.

■ *BabySense*. This is a device for monitoring an infant's breathing, and can help prevent sudden infant death syndrome.

■ *ViaDerm*. This is a chair that enables people to take medication without a needle. The medicine is absorbed through the skin when the patient sits in the chair.

Hi-Tech

It is a little-known fact that some of the hi-tech devices we use on a daily basis were invented in Israel. Outside of Silicon Valley in California, no other place has more technology start-ups than Israel. Intel, Microsoft, Google, and most of the other giants of the technology industry have major operations in Israel. Consider, for example, the following:

■ Israeli engineers working at Motorola developed the original cell-phone technology.

■ The USB drive was developed by three Israelis.

■ Windows NT and XP operating systems were developed primarily in Israel.

■ Mobileye, a device that sits on the dashboard of a car, warns the driver of an impending collision and even stops the car.

■ Powermat, an Israeli product, lets you do away with cables. All you have to do is put your electronic devices anywhere on it.

■ Xbox's Kinect games were developed in Israel.

Israel has made significant humanitarian and technological contributions to the world—the same world where it is portrayed in the international media, more often than not, as a pariah state. Those who censure Israel rarely seem to give it credit, and it's not easy to understand why.

Endnotes

1   Lahav Harkov, "MP Touts Defeat of SA settlement product labeling," *JPost.com*, accessed October 10, 2012, http://www.jpost.com/DiplomacyAndPolitics/Article.aspx?id=286395.

2   Duke Helfand, "Professor's Comparison of Israelis to Nazis Stirs Furor," *Los Angeles Times*, April 30, 2009, http://articles.latimes.com/2009/apr/30/local/me-professor30; Brad A. Greenberg, "Santa Barbara Professor Compared Israelis to Nazis," JewishJournal.com, April 27, 2009, http://www.jewishjournal.com/thegodblog/item/santa_barbara_professor_compared_israelis_to_nazis_20090427/.

3   Norman Finkelstein's Facebook page, "Another day, Another Zionist witch-hunt – what we can do," April 23, 2009, www.normanfinkelstein.com.

4   "About Campus Watch," Campus Watch: Monitoring Middle East Studies on Campus, accessed September 27, 2012, http://www.campus-watch.org/about.php.

5   Ghassan Hage, "'Comes a Time We Are All Enthusiasm': Understanding Palestinian Suicide Bombers in Times of Exighophobia," *Political Culture* 15(1): 65-89.

6   "The Problems in Middle East Studies," Campus Watch: Monitoring Middle East Studies on Campus, accessed September 27, 2012, http://www.campus-watch.org/about.php.

7   Andrew Aziz. "Civilized Discrimination," *The Official Newsletter of the Israel and Zionist Committee of UMJCA*, November, 2011, http://www.kanissanews.com/mashadisforisrael2.pdf.

8   Carol Hadjibay, "Ryan Akhavan's Experience with Anti-Zionism on Campus," *The Official Newsletter of the Israel and Zionist Committee of UMJCA*, November, 2011, http://www.kanissanews.com/mashadisforisrael2.pdf.

9   "What Is Lawfare?" The Lawfare Project, accessed September 27, 2012, http://www.thelawfareproject.org/what-is-lawfare.html.

10   "Our Ideal of the University," Campus Watch: Monitoring Middle East Studies on Campus, accessed September 27, 2012, http://www.campus-watch.org/about.php. http://www.campus-watch.org/about.php.

11   Natan Sharansky, "3D Test of Anti-Semitism: Demonization, Double Standards, Delegitimization," *Jewish Political Studies Review* 16 (Fall 2004): 3–4, http://www.jcpa.org/phas/phas-sharansky-f04.htm.

12   Raphael Shore, *Israel Inside*, DVD (Jerusalem Online University, 2011), 55 min.

Maps and Photographs

Arch of Titus

Engravings on the Arch of Titus showing artifacts, including a menorah, being carried from the Jewish Temple after the Roman victory in the Great Revolt of 66 CE. (Photos Shutterstock.com)

Key Figures in the Founding of the Modern State of Israel

Arthur Balfour

Chaim Weizmann

Leaders of the Supreme Council on the steps of the Villa DeVachan during the 1920 San Remo Conference which led to the creation of the modern Jewish State.
(Photos Courtesy of Dr. Jacques Gauthier)

Husain's Territorial Demand: A United Arab Kingdom

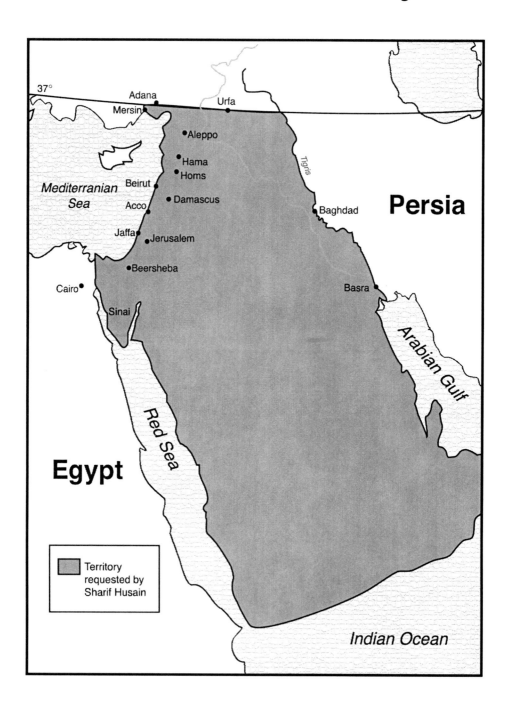

McMahon's Delimitation of the Proposed Arab Kingdom

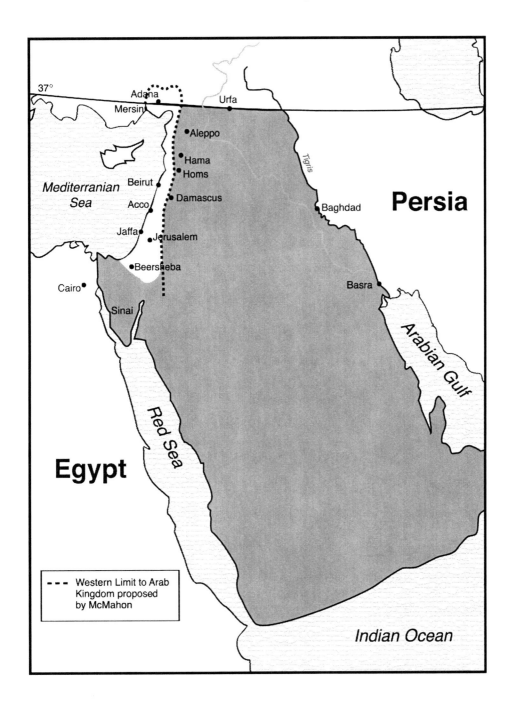

Legend:
- - - Western Limit to Arab Kingdom proposed by McMahon

Sykes-Picot Agreement (1916)

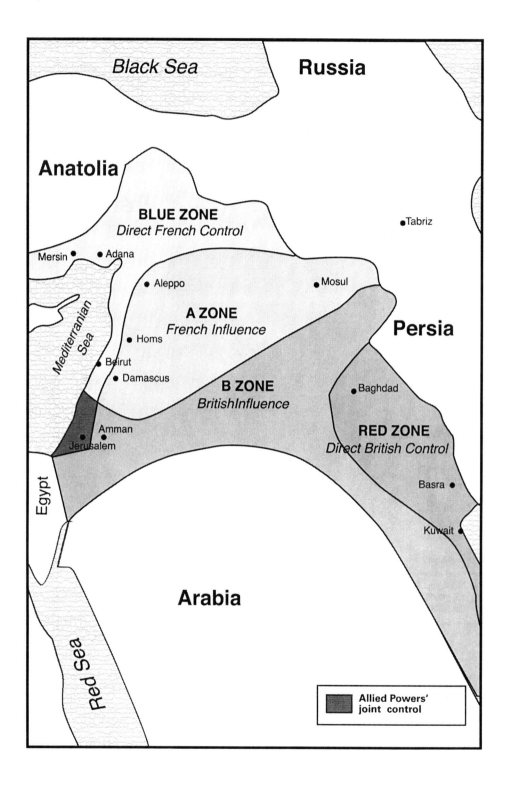

Territory Claimed by the Zionist Organization: Paris Peace Conference (1919)

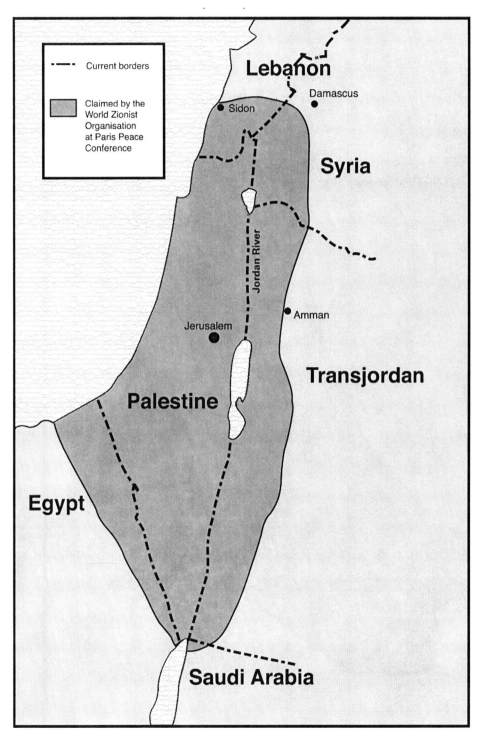

Land Allotted to the Twelve Tribes: The Book of Joshua

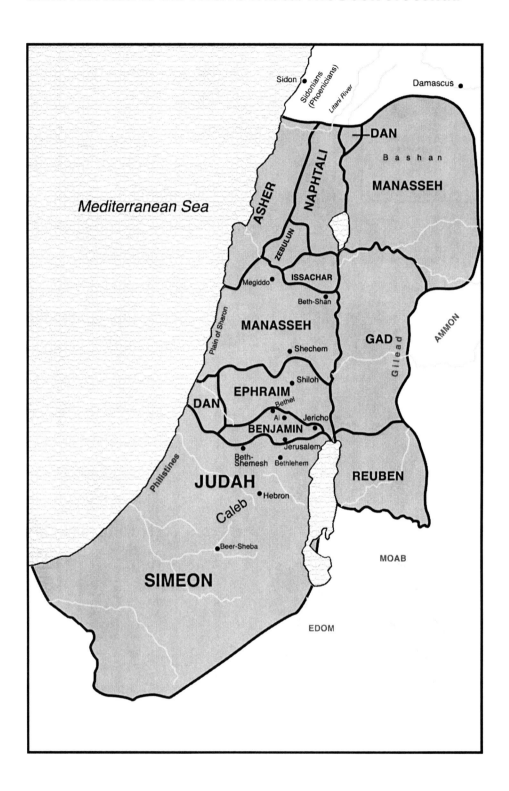

Lloyd George's "Dan to Beersheba" Formula for the Jewish National Home

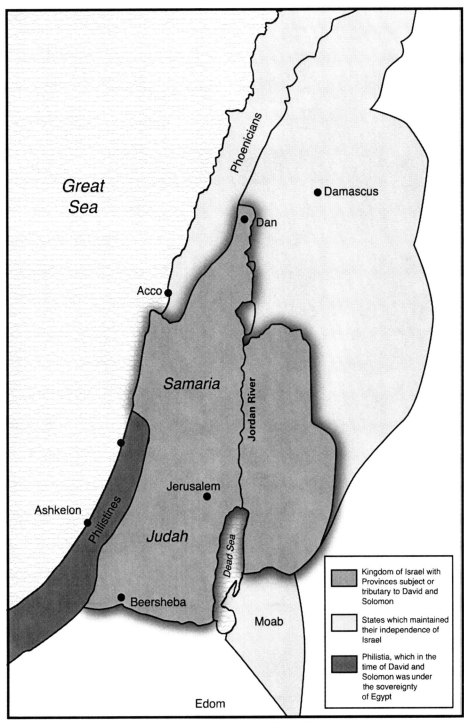

Based on George Adam Smith Map: *Palestine under David and Solomon*

Mandate Palestine (1920) Under Great Britain

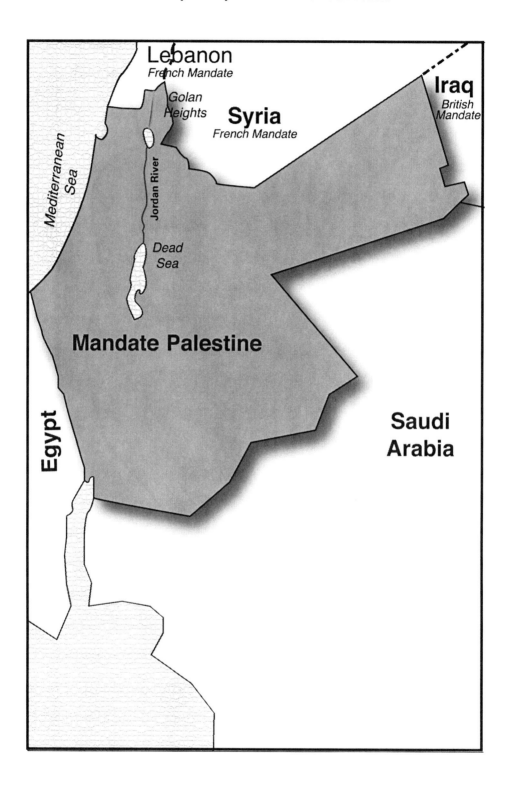

Great Britain's Partition of Mandate Palestine (1921)

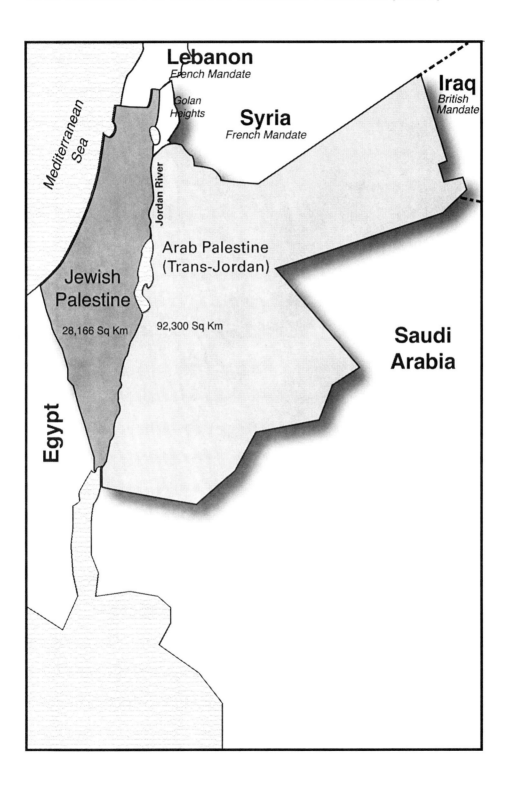

Peel Partition Plan (1937)

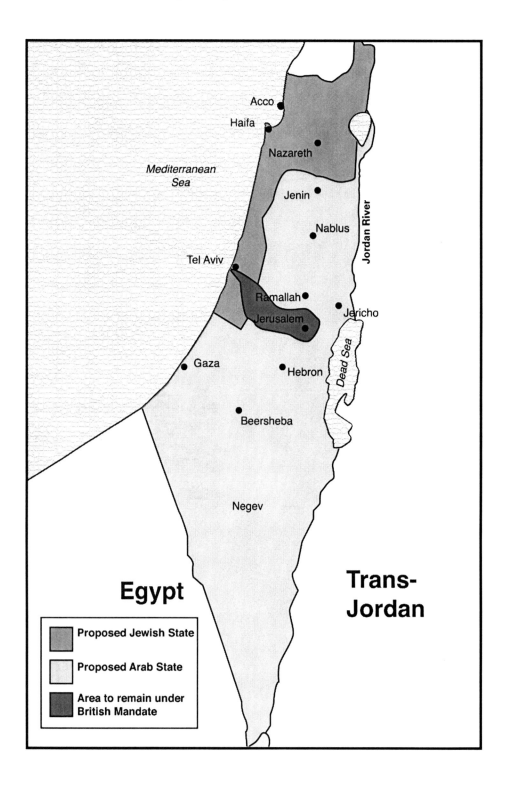

Acco

Haifa

Nazareth

*Mediterranean
Sea*

Jenin

Nablus

Jordan River

Tel Aviv

Ramallah

Jerusalem

Jericho

Dead Sea

Gaza

Hebron

Beersheba

Negev

Egypt

**Trans-
Jordan**

Proposed Jewish State

Proposed Arab State

Area to remain under
British Mandate

United Nations Partition Plan (1947)

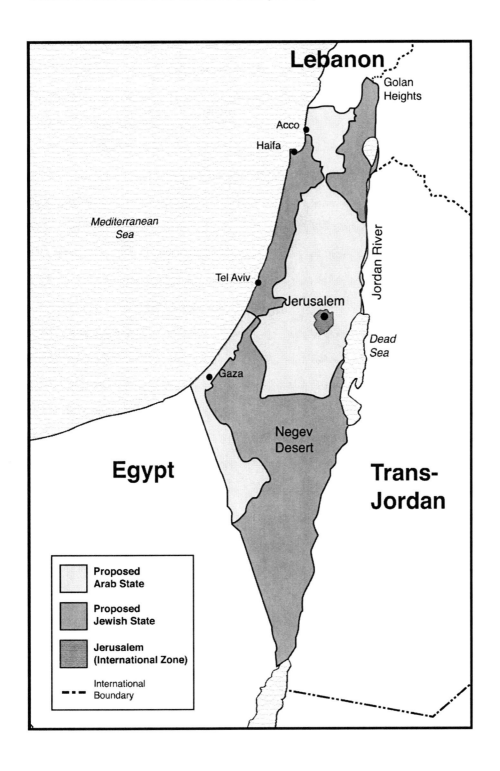

Lebanon

Golan
Heights

Acco

Haifa

Mediterranean
Sea

Jordan River

Tel Aviv

Jerusalem

Dead
Sea

Gaza

Negev
Desert

Egypt

Trans-
Jordan

Proposed
Arab State

Proposed
Jewish State

Jerusalem
(International Zone)

International
Boundary

Arab Invasion (1948)

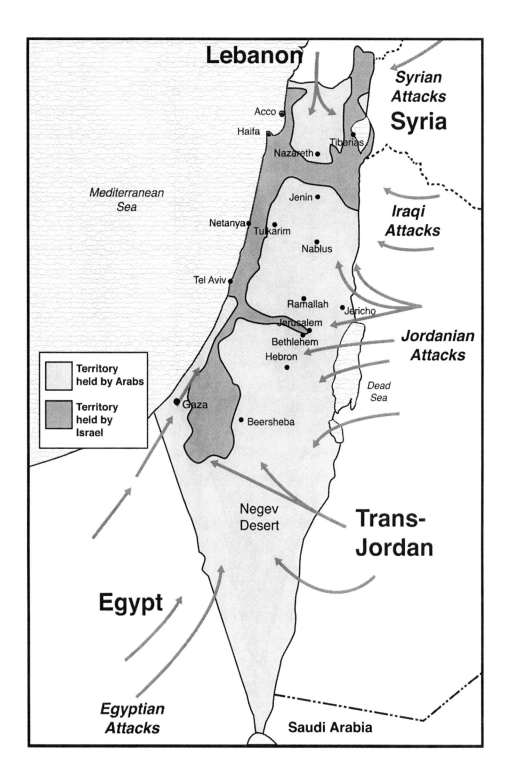

Israel's Territory After the 1948 War

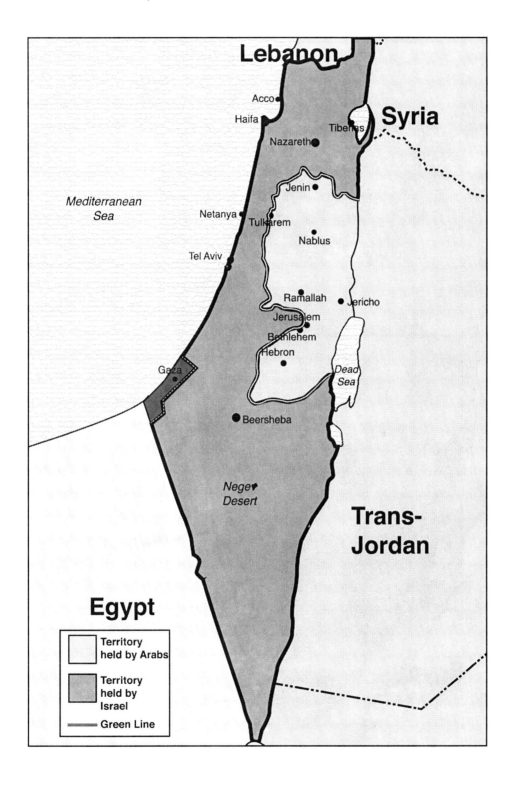

Israel's Territory After the 1967 War

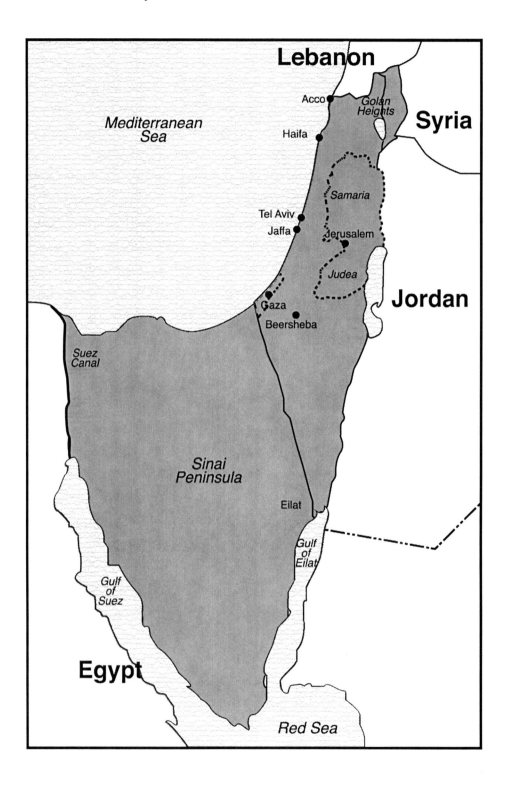

West Bank Subdivisions

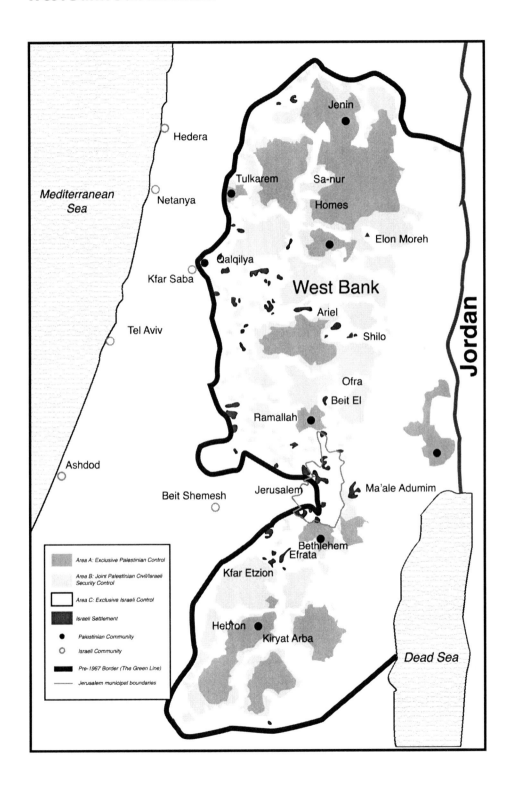

Israel and the Coastal Plain: Area and Topography

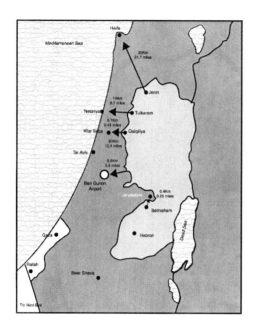
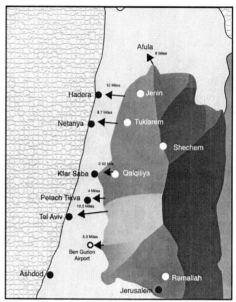

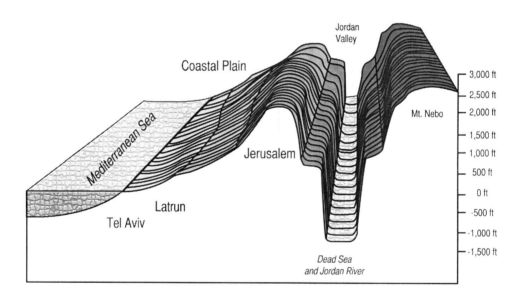

The Area and Population of States in the Middle East Region

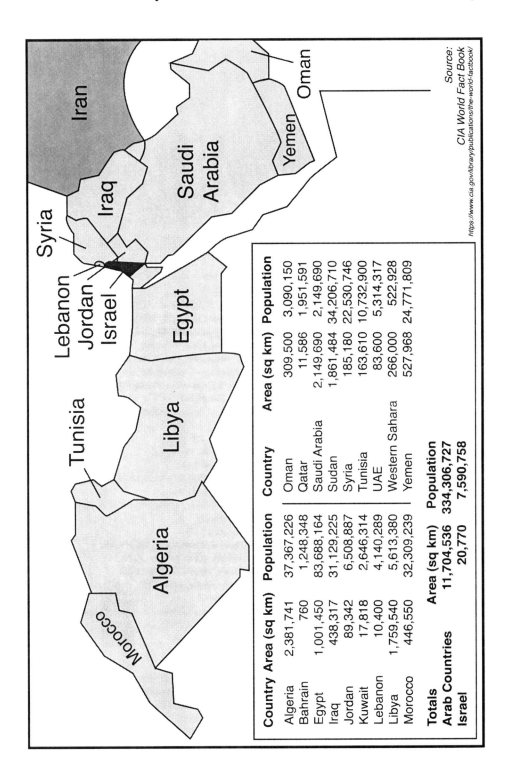

Source:
CIA World Fact Book
https://www.cia.gov/library/publications/the-world-factbook/

Country	Area (sq km)	Population		Country	Area (sq km)	Population
Algeria	2,381,741	37,367,226		Oman	309,500	3,090,150
Bahrain	760	1,248,348		Qatar	11,586	1,951,591
Egypt	1,001,450	83,688,164		Saudi Arabia	2,149,690	2,149,690
Iraq	438,317	31,129,225		Sudan	1,861,484	34,206,710
Jordan	89,342	6,508,887		Syria	185,180	22,530,746
Kuwait	17,818	2,646,314		Tunisia	163,610	10,732,900
Lebanon	10,400	4,140,289		UAE	83,600	5,314,317
Libya	1,759,540	5,613,380		Western Sahara	266,000	522,928
Morocco	446,550	32,309,239		Yemen	527,968	24,771,809

Totals	Area (sq km)	Population
Arab Countries	11,704,536	334,306,727
Israel	20,770	7,590,758

Index

CPSIA information can be obtained at www.ICGtesting.com
Printed in the USA
BVOW022223140513

320741BV00007B/144/P